Cognitive-Behavioral Therapy
for Deaf and Hearing
Persons With Language
and Learning Challenges

COUNSELING AND PSYCHOTHERAPY: INVESTIGATING PRACTICE FROM SCIENTIFIC, HISTORICAL, AND CULTURAL PERSPECTIVES

A Routledge Book Series

Editor, Bruce E. Wampold, University of Wisconsin

This innovative new series is devoted to grasping the vast complexities of the practice of counseling and psychotherapy. As a set of healing practices delivered in a context shaped by health delivery systems and the attitudes and values of consumers, practitioners, and researchers; counseling and psychotherapy must be examined critically. By understanding the historical and cultural context of counseling and psychotherapy and by examining the extant research, these critical inquiries seek a deeper, richer understanding of what is a remarkably effective endeavor.

Published

Counseling and Therapy with Clients Who Abuse Alcohol or Other Drugs
Cynthia E. Glidden-Tracy

The Great Psychothearpy Debate
Bruce Wampold

The Psychology of Working: Implications for Career Development, Counseling, and Public Policy
David Blustein

Neuropsychotherapy: How the Neurosciences Inform Effective Psychotherapy
Klaus Grawe

Principles of Multicultural Counseling
Uwe P. Gielen, Juris G. Draguns, Jefferson M. Fish

Forthcoming

The Pharmacology and Treatment of Substance Abuse: Evidence and Outcomes Based Perspective
Lee Cohen, Frank Collins, Alice Young, Dennis McChargue

Making Treatment Count: Using Outcomes to Inform and Manage Therapy
Michael Lambert, Jeb Brown, Scott Miller, Bruce Wampold

The Handbook of Therapeutic Assessment
Stephen E. Finn

IDM Supervision: An Integrated Developmental Model for Supervising Counselors and Therapists, Third Edition
Cal Stoltenberg and Brian McNeill

The Great Psychotherapy Debate, Revised Edition
Bruce Wampold

Casebook for Multicultural Counseling
Miguel E. Gallardo and Brian W. McNeill

Culture and the Therapeutic Process: A Guide for Mental Health Professionals
Mark M. Leach and Jamie Aten

Beyond Evidence-Based Psychotherapy: Fostering the Eight Sources of Change in Child and Adolescent Treatment
George Rosenfeld

Cognitive-Behavioral Therapy for Deaf and Hearing Persons With Language and Learning Challenges

Neil Glickman

Illustrated by Michael Krajnak

Routledge
Taylor & Francis Group
New York   London

Routledge
Taylor & Francis Group
711 Third Avenue
New York, NY 10017

Routledge
Taylor & Francis Group
2 Park Square
Milton Park, Abingdon
Oxon OX14 4RN

© 2009 by Taylor & Francis Group, LLC
Routledge is an imprint of Taylor & Francis Group, an Informa business

International Standard Book Number-13: 978-0-8058-6399-4 (Softcover) 978-0-8058-6398-7 (Hardcover)

Library of Congress Cataloging-in-Publication Data

Glickman, Neil S.
 Cognitive-behavioral therapy for deaf and hearing persons with language and learning challenges / Neil Glickman.
   p. ; cm. -- (Counseling and psychotherapy)
 Includes bibliographical references and index.
 ISBN 978-0-8058-6398-7 (hardbound : alk. paper) -- ISBN 978-0-8058-6399-4 (pbk. : alk. paper)
   1. Deaf--Mental health. 2. Hearing impaired--Mental health. 3. Language disorders--Treatment. 4. Learning disabilities--Treatment. 5. Cognitive therapy. I. Title. II. Series.
 [DNLM: 1. Cognitive Therapy--methods. 2. Hearing Impaired Persons. 3. Deafness--psychology. 4. Language Disorders--psychology. 5. Mental Disorders--diagnosis. 6. Mental Disorders--therapy. WM 425.5.C6 G559c 2008]

 RC451.4.D4G55 2008
 616.89'1425--dc22
                            2008015130

Visit the Taylor & Francis Web site at
http://www.taylorandfrancis.com

and the Routledge Web site at
http://www.routledge.com

Contents

Series Preface

This innovative new series is devoted to grasping the vast complexities of the practice of counseling and psychotherapy. As a set of healing practices delivered in a context shaped by health delivery systems and the attitudes and values of consumers, practitioners, and researchers, counseling and psychotherapy must be examined critically. By understanding the historical and cultural context of counseling and psychotherapy, and by examining the extant research, these critical inquiries seek a deeper, richer understanding of what is a remarkably effective endeavor.

When the field considers psychotherapy for various racial, ethnic, and cultural groups, we typically think of adapting existing treatments in a manner that will be acceptable and effective with the particular groups—that is, the focus is on the treatment rather than on the people who seek treatment. Neil Glickman, in *Cognitive-Behavioral Therapy for Deaf and Hearing Persons with Language and Learning Challenges,* focuses on people who are deaf and who have psychological problems related to language deprivation, with the progressive notion that understanding people first informs how effective services can be designed and delivered. Understanding this population in the context of the culture is critical to providing psychotherapy that does not incorporate some destructive assumptions that often are made about deaf people. The challenges to providing effective services to this population are formidable, yet Glickman provides an optimistic, but realistic, perspective. This optimism is based on fostering progress built on the person's strengths and resources within the context of Deaf culture. This approach conveys a profound respect for the person and a recognition of the importance of the context.

Bruce E. Wampold, Ph.D., ABPP
Series Editor
University of Wisconsin–Madison

Acknowledgments and Dedication

The treatment approach presented in this book is an adaptation of best practices in the field of cognitive behavior therapy. I have borrowed most heavily from the work of Donald Meichenbaum, which lends itself, I have found, very easily to adaptation for this population of language and learning challenged clients. I am especially grateful to Dr. Meichenbaum for giving me a critical read of the manuscript. I am also indebted to McCay Vernon, not only for his own pioneering work in education and mental health care of deaf people, but also for his own critical review of the manuscript. Individual chapters were reviewed by Michael Harvey, Sherry Zitter, Robert Pollard, Amanda O'Hearn, Marc Marschark, Philip Candilis, Joel Skolnick, Dan Lambert, and Susan Jones, all of whom gave helpful feedback. I have also been fortunate to work closely for many years with a talented communication department consisting of Wendy Petrarca, Susan Jones, and Michael Krajnak and, more recently, Gabrielle Weiler. Besides developing the skill cards presented on the CD and throughout the text, Michael Krajnak performed the communication assessments on our deaf clientele that formed the basis for our judgments about their language skills. Working with Wendy Petrarca and Susan Jones, these assessments often involved videotaping of patients and then carefully studying their sign language abilities. It was through these studies that we became aware of the widespread problem of sign language dysfluency in our clientele. Patricia Black, doing her dissertation research on the Deaf Unit, then drew the connections between this language dysfluency and other variables of psychosocial functioning as described in Chapter 1.

The Westborough State Hospital Deaf Unit has been in existence since 1987, and I have been director or codirector of that program for 15 years (as of 2008). During that time, I have worked with dozens of talented Deaf and hearing staff, all of whom made contributions to our developing program. At the time of publication of this book, unit staff are: Susan Salinas, Diane Trikakis, William Olivier, James Gilmour, Kathy Torrey, Kathy Lopez, Greg Shuler, Phil Wrightson, Andrea Galeski, Donna Peacott, Jean Granger, Sam Appiah, Tom Waugaman-Bransfield, Charley Thorne, Lynn Lulu, Deborah Abelha, Roland Demers, Kwame Amoah, Justine Santos, Tony Stratton, Dean Waugaman-Bransfield, Susan Jones, Gabrielle Weiler, and Michael Krajnak.

The Deaf Unit has also been fortunate to receive an enormous amount of administrative support locally at Westborough State Hospital (principally through Dan Lambert and Joel Skolnick), in the MetroSuburban Catchment Area (principally through Barbara Fenby and Ted Kirousis), and from

Commissioners of the Massachusetts Department of Mental Health, especially Elizabeth Childs and Barbara Leadholm.

I have also been privileged to have had a large number of terrific teachers over the years, the influence of all of whom is found in this book. Between 1980 and 1983, I was a staff member and then a graduate student at Gallaudet College, and classes I took with Betty Colonomos and M.J. Bienvenue opened my eyes to the Deaf Community and Culture and challenged me to begin considering what it means to be Hearing. I cannot imagine having been able to make any connections between the world of mental health and the world of the Deaf Community, or to have drawn upon a multicultural frame of reference in this work, without their influence. Also while at Gallaudet, I had the good fortune to have Bill McCrone as my faculty advisor and teacher. Dr. McCrone modeled for me the ability to teach the essentials of counseling, to get to the heart of a matter, and to always strive for greater clarity and relevance. In my experiences teaching since, I have tried to live up to his example.

Later, as a doctoral student in psychology at the University of Massachusetts, I had the additional great fortune to study closely with Allen Ivey. Dr. Ivey supported my interest in drawing connections between Deaf culture and mental health. He also developed a model of counselor education in which he broke down counseling into what he calls "microskills." He went on to develop an approach to counseling in which he matched counselor interventions to the cognitive developmental abilities of clients. When I later found myself and my team working mainly with deaf persons with language and learning challenges, I remembered the wisdom of Ivey's skill-based, culturally affirmative, and developmental approach. We could do this work provided we found counseling interventions that matched both cultural frames of reference and cognitive developmental abilities of our clients.

In the Deafness mental health world, clinicians such as Hilde Schlesinger, Kay Meadow, Eugene Mindel, McCay Vernon, Edna Levine, Larry Stewart, Franz Kallman, John Rainer, Kenneth Altschuler, Luther Robinson, Glenn Anderson, John Denmark, Allen Sussman, and Barbara Brauer pioneered this work. Clinicians, teachers, and administrators I have had the pleasure and good fortune to work closely and personally with include McCay Vernon, Sanjay Gulati, Robert Pollard, Irene Leigh, Michael Harvey, Gail Isenberg, Philip Candilis, Susan Salinas, Diane Trikakis, Steve Hammerdinger, and Theresa Johnson.

At Routledge, the production of this book was competently led by Dana Bliss, Christopher Tominich, and Linda Leggio, with whom it has been a pleasure to collaborate.

Since 1980, I have been blessed by having the loving support of my life partner, now husband, Steven Riel. For me, this marriage makes everything possible.

Finally, I have been taught by hundreds of deaf clients, each demanding in his or her own way that I rethink everything I thought I knew about counseling. Ultimately, it is your clients who tell you whether or not your theories and interventions work. To all my teachers, but especially to these clients, my best teachers, I dedicate this book.

Introduction

Developing Psychosocial Skills and Life-Affirming Stories

A Really Good Story

I start by reminding you of a story that, chances are, you already know.

At the end of the movie version of *The Wizard of Oz* (Leroy & Fleming, 1939), Dorothy, the scarecrow, cowardly lion, and tin man stand before the wizard and make their petitions. Dorothy, of course, wants to go home. The scarecrow wants a brain, the tin man a heart, and the cowardly lion wants courage. The wizard talks to each in turn, telling them that they already have the skills and qualities that they seek.

First, the wizard addresses the scarecrow. He tells him that brains are "a very mediocre commodity," and that back where he comes from, there are great thinkers in seats of great learning "who have no more brains than you have." However, what these thinkers have that the scarecrow lacks is a diploma. Digging into his bag, he pulls one out for the scarecrow and confers upon him the honorary degree of "Doctor of Thinkology."

The scarecrow's response is striking. He immediately recites the Pythagorean theorem as if he knew it all along. He exclaims, "Oh joy! Rapture! I've got a brain!"

The wizard turns next to the cowardly lion. He tells him that he is "a victim of disorganized thinking," and that he has been "confusing courage with wisdom." He points out that the people back home called "heroes … have no more courage than you have." What they do have are medals. Digging again into his bag, he pulls out a medal. He pins on the cowardly lion "the triple cross … for meritorious conduct, extraordinary valor, and conspicuous bravely against wicked witches." The loquacious cowardly lion finds himself uncharacteristically speechless. A few minutes later, reading the word "courage" on his medal, he exclaims, "Aint it the truth! Aint it the truth!"

Turning then to the tin man, the wizard offers the poignant comment that "a heart is not judged by how much you love but by how much you are loved by others." He then offers him the metaphorical equivalent of a heart, a ticking clock. The tin man beams, "Oh, it ticks! Look, it ticks!" By giving him this testimonial, the tin man discovers the heart he really has.

The only person the wizard cannot satisfy immediately is Dorothy, so he offers to take her home himself. Unfortunately, he proves incapable of following through. Dorothy's only hope of getting home then appears to lie with the good witch Glenda who, as we will see, uses a "treatment" strategy remarkably similar to that of the wizard.

On first take, the scarecrow would appear to be a poor candidate for a brain. After all, he is made of straw. The tin man is presumably hollow and therefore a poor candidate for a heart. The cowardly lion defines himself as, well, cowardly, and would therefore appear to be a poor candidate for courage.

This is a book about psychotherapy with people who, by most psychotherapists' reckoning, are poor candidates for psychotherapy. These clients are people who do not appear to have the motivation, understanding, or capabilities to make effective use of psychotherapy. So perhaps it is quite ironic that one of the key motivational strategies, discussed in this book as a *pretreatment* strategy, is to demonstrate to these clients that they already have many of the skills they need. As with Dorothy, the scarecrow, tin man, and cowardly lion, the first task of those who seek to provide them with skills and *a way home* (that is, a way to achieve their goals) is to show them, or invite them to discover, the abilities they already have. This can pull them into the process of developing these skills further. Much of this book is devoted to demonstrating how this is done.

You have already discovered another one of our main strategies. We work through stories. One of our key themes is that these "low functioning" persons already have, at least in embryonic form, many of the skills they need. We need a treatment approach that helps them notice these skills and motivates them to develop these skills further. We can do this by helping them construct new stories.

Who Are the Clients This Book Addresses?

I just used the term *low functioning*. In the deafness mental health world in which I work principally, the term *low functioning* has long been applied to a certain group of deaf clients, but many people have commented on how the term is pejorative and inappropriate. The term is especially offensive because for so many years the assumption of educators and mental health providers working with deaf people was that deaf people as a group were low functioning. As Lane (1992) demonstrated in his devastating critique of the *audist* hearing establishment, the "experts" who for decades educated and treated deaf people promoted policies and approaches that fostered disability. They then discovered in deaf people a host of problems and pathologies, labeled deaf people as sick, morally depraved, primitive, and certainly low functioning, and intervened in ways that created even greater suffering. When the Deaf Community finally rose up to affirm its own language and culture, it rejected these paternalistic efforts to fix all of its members' alleged pathologies beginning with hearing loss itself. The new emphasis has been on appreciating American Sign Language (ASL) as a language, recognizing the history, sociology, and culture of the Deaf Community, and generally validating the skills that culturally Deaf people demonstrate.*

This is not a book that describes deaf people as low functioning, but it is a book about mental health and rehabilitative care of that subset of deaf people who are frequently referred to as such. In Chapter 1, psychologist Patricia Black and I review the diagnoses and characteristics of the deaf clientele served on the specialty Deaf psychiatric inpatient unit I administer. We also review the research on deaf psychiatric inpatients, and we relate that research to the literature on the group that is now most often referred to as "traditionally underserved deaf" (Dew, 1999; Long, Long, & Ouellette, 1993; Long, 1993). This group of persons has been given other labels as well. Because, as we will see, the chief characteristic of this group of persons is severe language dysfluency related to language deprivation, the label I choose to use in this book is *language and learning challenged* (LLC). This may not be the best descriptor either, but it has the advantage of also being applicable to some hearing persons. Although the language problems faced by many deaf persons who have been raised without adequate sign language exposure are uniquely serious, deaf people are not alone in having significant language and learning problems.

My principal source of experience in mental health work with deaf people has been as psychologist and director of a specialty psychiatric inpatient unit for deaf people in a state psychiatric hospital in Massachusetts. This program, which I describe elsewhere, has always tried to operate from the cultural model of deafness.† This is the model put forward by the Deaf Community and its advocates in which deafness is understood as a cultural difference, not a disability.

As of this writing (June, 2008), the unit has been in existence for more than 20 years, and has treated hundreds of deaf persons with very severe psychiatric and behavioral problems. From the beginning it became apparent to us that most of the clientele we served were not the highly successful and articu-

---

* I follow a now well-established convention of using a capital D whenever I am clearly referring to the Deaf Community, Deaf Culture, or a culturally Deaf person. Whenever this is not clearly the case, as when I am referring to deaf people in general, I use the lowercase "d."

† My two previous books took the cultural model of deafness as a starting point for reconsidering mental health treatment of Deaf people. *Culturally Affirmative Psychotherapy With Deaf Persons* (Glickman & Harvey, 1996), co-edited with Michael Harvey in 1996, drew on the literature on cross-cultural and minority group psychotherapy, rather than the disability literature, to reconceptualize what *culturally affirmative* psychotherapy with Deaf people looks like. My second book, *Mental Health Care of Deaf People: A Culturally Affirmative Approach* (Glickman & Gulati, 2003), co-edited with Sanjay Gulati in 2003, presented numerous examples of mental health programs and treatment approaches that are embedded in a respectful attitude toward Deaf culture. The Westborough Deaf Unit is described in this second book.

late ASL users championed by proponents of the cultural model of deafness. Some of these *high functioning* Deaf people became our staff, but many of our clientele have had characteristics like these:

- They have levels of measured intelligence in the borderline to mildly mentally retarded range (appropriately assessed).
- Signing is their preferred communication modality, but they are not fluent users of ASL. Many have severe language dysfluency in ASL, a problem we relate to language deprivation associated with growing up deaf in a nonsigning or inadequately signing environment.
- They are either nonliterate or semiliterate. This means that we cannot draw upon most treatment materials using written English. It also means that materials that are captioned have limited utility.
- Most do not have major psychotic disorders such as schizophrenia. One of the most striking findings presented in Chapter 1 is that a much smaller percentage of our clientele is diagnosed with major mental illness such as schizophrenia and bipolar disorder than is true of the hearing clients in the hospital. While we observe much less of these major mental illnesses, we observe much more of what could be considered *developmental* problems: poorly developed social, academic, vocational, and psychological skills. These skill deficits accompany the lower levels of intelligence and lack of language fluency. Our initial assumption that our program would treat deaf people with major mental illnesses was gradually replaced by awareness that our clientele actually have some different problems than their hearing peers. They have psychosocial problems associated with inadequate language development.
- Behavior problems. By far, the major reason people are referred to our psychiatric unit is severe behavioral problems. It is fairly routine for our clients to get into trouble because they have assaulted peers, staff, or family members, damaged property, or hurt themselves. This forced upon us a central concern with treating persons who are sometimes violent. More than any other challenge, the threat and occurrence of violence are what make our work difficult and have led to "burnout" from many competent staff, deaf and hearing.
- Difficult to treat. Very few of our clients come to us with any correct understanding of, or inclination to use, mental health services. They have deficits in their fund of information about the world. This includes deficits in knowledge of what mental health treatment is and how to use it. As discussed in Chapter 4, they are often not culturally prepared to work with mental health clinicians; and neither are mental health clinicians culturally prepared to work with them. Whether we like it or not, we find ourselves face to face with the reality that the

majority of the persons we work with are, whatever you wish to call them, severely handicapped. They are handicapped in most aspects of psychological and social functioning in both the Deaf and the hearing worlds. Therefore, while intending no disrespect to the Deaf Community, we find that we must draw upon medical, disability, and rehabilitation perspectives, as well as cultural perspectives, in our work. All these perspectives have ideas and treatment strategies to offer. We often wish we just were working with a group of persons fluent in ASL, and that the only special treatment issues were translation into ASL. If this were true, our work would be so much easier.

As our program at Westborough State Hospital developed, we found that hearing units in the hospital were also drawn to it, and that much of our approach was easily applicable to hearing, difficult-to-engage persons. They were drawn in particular to our efforts to simplify mental health treatment and to the wonderful pictorial aids developed by our Deaf communication specialist Michael Krajnak. The language dysfluency problems we discuss in this book are pretty unique to our deaf clientele, but other kinds of language, learning, and cognitive problems are not. We have worked particularly closely with a program for hearing adolescent persons with severe behavioral and emotional problems. Chapter 3 presents a discussion of the language and learning challenges of this clientele.

Through our discussions with staff and work with clients in this hearing program, we eventually came to understand that we had culled from the world of psychotherapies an approach that seemed particularly well suited to "lower functioning" hearing persons, a group we will also refer to as "language and learning challenged." Therefore, although the emphasis in this book is unquestionably on the care of LLC deaf clients, I have intentionally broadened the discussion to include hearing LLC clients. This is done by adding a chapter specifically on this group, and by drawing on deaf and hearing case examples throughout the text. My hope is that the inclusion of hearing persons prevents readers from misconstruing my intentions as being that of treating all deaf persons as if they had these kinds of limitations. Perhaps that should not have to be said, but given the history of hearing persons misconstruing Deaf people (Lane, 1992) one cannot be too careful.

The treatment model presented here has limitations. In practice we have found that it becomes less successful with clients who have lower than mild levels of mental retardation or who have virtually no language skills at all. Although the model excels at addressing the kinds of behavioral problems common in the deaf LLC population, it is most useful with persons whose behavioral aggression is due to lack of skills. A distinction is made often in the literature between hostile or reactive aggression and instrumental aggression (Crick & Dodge, 1994; Meichenbaum, 2001; Vitiello & Stoff, 1997). Hostile or reactive aggression reflects a defensive reaction to perceived threats and is accompanied by visible displays of anger. Premeditated, instrumental, or predatory aggression is related to the attempt to obtain some goal or express dominance. This form of aggression is considered nonimpulsive, predatory, and intentional. Adults who display instrumental aggression often carry a diagnosis of antisocial personality disorder. We have not been successful in implementing this approach with the tiny minority of our clients who display this kind of aggression. This is because the underlying reason for the aggression is not lack of skills but lack of intention.

Theoretical Orientation

My clinical experience has included work in other inpatient, partial hospital, community mental health clinic, HMO, and private practice settings where I worked with hearing and deaf clients. I have also taught courses in counseling and psychotherapy to graduate students at Assumption College in Worcester, Massachusetts, and to staff at Westborough State Hospital. While preparing to teach these courses, I reviewed a wide range of psychotherapy theories, always with an eye toward gleaning approaches that were best suited for LLC deaf and hearing clients. I spend some time in these chapters summarizing key ideas from the most relevant psychotherapy approaches because I want to show how we have adapted these approaches and how psychotherapy is possible if one knows how to simplify. Also, I want to give credit where it is due. Some readers may find the theoretical sections of the book less compelling than the clinical stories, and they may wish to skip ahead to the more practical sections.

As a doctoral student in psychology at the University of Massachusetts, I was heavily influenced by counseling psychologist Allen Ivey (Ivey, 1971, 1986, 1991; Ivey, D'Andrea, Ivey, & Simek-Morgan, 2002; Ivey & Ivey, 2003) who was my advisor and dissertation chair. Ivey's work is noteworthy for three main contributions:

1. He broke the components of counseling and psychotherapy into what he calls "microskills," and developed a counseling education approach called "microskills training."
2. He was an early and persistent advocate for the development of multicultural counseling competencies. He championed the idea that psychotherapies must match with cultural orientations.
3. He developed an approach that he called developmental counseling and therapy (DCT), which provides a schema for matching the counseling approach to the "cognitive-developmental orientation" of clients.

All three of these ideas are reflected in this work.

Microskills are communication skill units representing the component parts of counseling and interviewing. For instance, some counseling microskills are nonverbal attending, open and closed questions, client observation, encouraging, paraphrasing, summarizing feelings and meaning, focusing, and confrontation. Ivey taught graduate school mental health counselors one microskill at a time. Overall counseling abilities are developed as more complex microskills are mastered and integrated into clinicians' own counseling style. Ivey had a clear understanding of how advanced skills develop out of simpler ones. That understanding is applied here.

The treatment approach I describe is oriented toward helping clients discover their own microskills. We break down coping, conflict resolution, and relapse-prevention skills into smaller microskills and then help clients discover that they already have many of these skills. The trick in discovering client abilities is to breakdown the skills into small enough microskills that one can locate them in people who are not functioning well overall. It is also to think developmentally, to understand how complex skills develop out of simpler ones. For instance, even our least skilled communicators have moments in which they listen and interact appropriately. We may discover in those moments various nonverbal attending skills (for example, eye contact, leaning forward, waiting before responding, asking questions, showing interest) that we can honestly label as instances of skill use.

I was initially drawn to Ivey's work because of his heightened sensitivity to cross-cultural issues, and he encouraged me to draw out the connections between mental health care of Deaf people and other cultural and linguistic minorities (Glickman & Gulati, 2003; Glickman & Harvey, 1996). Ivey understood that helping always occurs in a sociohistorical and cultural context, and that styles of helping must match with the dominant themes, beliefs, and thinking styles of a culture. For example, psychoanalysis as a means of helping is as culture bound as consulting a spiritual healer or engaging in certain kinds of meditation (Glickman, 1996). The assumption that the source of one's problems is found in such internal experiences as feelings, thoughts, and fantasies is as culture bound as the idea that the source is one's relationship to God or one's ancestors or the kind of karma one has accumulated. This idea of the culture-bound nature of helping encouraged my thinking about the match between Deaf Culture and mental health care that were explored in my previous two books. It is continued here even though the focus is not on Deaf people per se but deaf (and hearing) persons with language and learning challenges.

Ivey's later work focused on the creation of a model for understanding all psychotherapies and selecting those that best match clients. As noted earlier, he calls this approach DCT (Ivey, 1986, 1991). DCT is based on an extension of the work of Jean Piaget, who studied how thinking develops as children grow. Piaget proposed a model of cognitive developmental stages. He named these stages sensorimotor, preoperational, concrete operational, and formal operational. Ivey's model has four of what he calls cognitive–emotional orientations. The four orientations represent models of thinking and experiencing the world that vary in complexity and quality. Ivey says that many people have what he calls a predominant cognitive–emotional–developmental orientation. That is, they tend to think and feel typically in ways that are consistent with one of these orientations. This is a useful way of approaching psychotherapy for our deaf LLC clients. Their language and learning challenges imply the need for counseling approaches that work on either a sensorimotor or concrete-operational level. Thus, in Chapter 5, we discuss sensory modulation strategies that have sometimes been the only psychotherapy we could use with very language dysfluent persons. Our use of concrete, pictorially represented skills for coping, conflict resolution, and relapse prevention, as well as our reliance on stories, work because they match the thinking and language abilities of so many of our clients as well as their cultural orientations. By contrast, highly verbal psychotherapies, in which there is a search for insight into connections and patterns, tend to fail miserably.

The main ideas I take from Ivey's work are these: All helping interventions are culture bound. There is no one objective way of helping that works for all people. Counseling interventions must match the cultural context and must suit the individual cognitive–emotional developmental orientation. In addition, advanced skills develop out of simpler skills. Thus, rather than lament that so many of these clients are poor candidates for psychotherapy, we must select and adapt psychotherapeutic techniques that are a good match culturally and cognitively. When clients are unable to display sophisticated skills, they may well be able to display the developmental precursors of those skills. Counselors need to be able to adapt our treatment interventions to the cultural context and the individual needs of our clients. When counselors get stuck and do not feel effective with clients, it is often because they have a rigid understanding of counseling and a narrow set of skills. In fact, there are many kinds of psychotherapy interventions well suited for clients with language and learning challenges or clients who are culturally different.

Readers of this book will encounter brief discussions of a broad range of contemporary counseling theories with regard to their suitability for treatment of LLC clients. These approaches include psychodynamic therapy, rational emotive behavior therapy (Ellis, 1962), cognitive therapy (A. Beck, 1976; J. Beck, 1995), client-centered therapy (Rogers, 1951), reality therapy (Glasser, 2000; Wubbolding, 2000), relapse prevention (Marlatt & Gordon, 1985), motivational interviewing (Miller & Rollnick, 2002), dialectical behavior therapy (Linehan, 1993a), narrative therapy (White, 1995, 2007; White & Epston, 1990), and collaborative problem solving (Greene & Ablon, 2006). The three approaches I draw from most often are dialectical behavior therapy (DBT), collaborative problem solving (CPS), and the constructive narrative cognitive behavioral therapy of Donald Meichenbaum (Meichenbaum, 1977a, 1977b, 1985, 1994, 1996, 2001). Meichenbaum's work in particular provides the overall framework of cognitive-behavioral therapy (CBT) most suited to this population.

Meichenbaum, Professor Emeritus at the University of Waterloo, Canada, and current Research Director of the Melissa Institute for Violence Prevention and Treatment of Victims of Violence in Miami, Florida, is one of the founders of CBT. He was the first cognitive-behavioral theorist to shift attention from reinforcement theory to the teaching of coping skills. The emphasis on skill training is probably the heart of contemporary CBT and it is the core treatment strategy presented here. It was Meichenbaum who first created treatment paradigms for teaching psychosocial skills. Linehan, Greene, and others followed his lead.

In Meichenbaum's later work, he adopted what he calls a *constructivist narrative perspective* (Meichenbaum, 1994), tapping into themes also developed by Michael White (White, 1995, 2007; White & Epston, 1990). This approach offers many new techniques to help people change their thinking and behavior without expecting them to rationally analyze thinking errors. "A constructive narrative perspective focuses upon the 'accounts,' or 'stories' that individuals offer themselves and others about the important events in their lives" (Meichenbaum, 1994, p. 103). Psychological problems are related to stories about weakness, deficits, illness, and problems. Attending to client accounts of their lives (their stories), Meichenbaum contributed many more strategies to help people change their thinking.

Some of these strategies have to do with the nature of the questions we ask clients. We can ask them questions that lead them to discover abilities. Some of the strategies have to do with very careful attention to how clients use language. When they use metaphors or terms that suggest resiliency and skill, counselors "pluck" these metaphors, say them back, and embellish them. Some of the strategies have to do with putting clients in roles where they must demonstrate skills. In this book, we describe putting clients in helper or teacher roles. This strategy simultaneously builds skills and changes the clients' stories about their abilities.

The treatment approach presented here is anchored in the two themes of developing psychosocial skills and constructing life-affirming stories. Meichenbaum's work is noteworthy for the interweaving of psychosocial skill training with this newer narrative perspective. Certainly, psychosocial skill training does not require a narrative perspective, and narrative psychotherapy can be done without reference to skills, but the two approaches enhance each other. Skills and stories are the two key themes of this book. They are the two hooks on which we, metaphorically, hang our hat.

For our clients, skill development and story construction are easily wed. We find that the acquisition of new skills is fostered by the construction of new stories. Indeed, one of the key stories we construct with clients has to do with their developing mastery of various kinds of skills. "Getting better," we say, "amounts to learning skills." We will help clients come to think of themselves as "people with skills." We do this by noting the skills they already have, engaging them in the task of developing these skills further, and finally turning them into helpers, coaches, and teachers of these skills. Here we are working simultaneously on new stories and new skills. More than any other contemporary clinician/theorist, Meichenbaum has demonstrated this powerful connection.

I hesitate to provide a name for the approach presented in this book because I see it as a simplification and adaptation of Meichenbaum's work with a smattering of other best practices, especially from DBT and CPS, thrown in. Because the approach presented here is designed to be used by both professional and paraprofessional staff, I also hesitate to add more technical terms to the field. Linguistic clarity is very important, and I greatly favor the use of everyday language over technical jargon like "dialectic," "projective identification," or "constructivism." Consequently, where I must, for the sake of clarity, have a name for this approach, I will simply call it *skills and stories*.

Plan of the Book

Chapter 1 presents a detailed discussion of the question "who are the deaf severely mentally ill?" Based on the research of psychologist Patricia Black, the chapter describes the characteristics of deaf patients served on our specialty psychiatric inpatient unit for deaf people in Massachusetts over a 7-year period. Her striking findings help answer some basic questions that have long plagued our field. Specifically, are deaf psychiatric clients *different from* hearing psychiatric clients in clinical presentation? If there are differences, what implications do they have for assessment and treatment of this group? Is it more appropriate to look at deaf people through a cultural or medical-pathological framework?

Black's research finds that the key variable distinguishing among deaf clientele is not hearing loss, as the medical model would suggest, or language preference, as the cultural model would suggest, but rather language skill. She identifies language dysfluency related to language deprivation as the key factor influencing psychosocial functioning, and she posits that deaf persons with severe language dysfluency are legitimately considered disabled. Their disability is not deafness. It is this language dysfluency. The rest of the book is an attempt to draw out the implications for the mental health care of these persons. How do we assess them? How do we treat them? How do we develop treatment programs for them?

Chapter 2 looks more closely at this language dysfluency related to language deprivation in deaf persons and discusses the implications of such language dysfluency for psychological assessment. Language skills are such a key variable in assessment of mental status that persons unfamiliar with the language abilities and problems that people born deaf commonly have are very likely to make diagnostic errors. Clinicians unfamiliar with deaf people are likely to confuse language dysfluency related to language deprivation with language dysfluency related to severe mental illness. In this chapter, I discuss the differences.

Chapter 3, written by Jeffrey Gaines, Bruce Meltzer, and myself, presents an overview of language and learning challenges in hearing psychiatric adolescent patients. The Deaf Unit at Westborough State Hospital is right next door to a program for hearing adolescents with severe psychiatric and behavioral problems. Over the years, as staff in the two programs talked, we discovered many similarities in the patient populations. Chapter 3 discusses language and learning problems that are not related to severe language deprivation. Our deaf LLC clients have these problems also, but language deprivation is often such an overriding factor for them that it can be hard to parse out these other problems. For instance, it is all too easy to conclude that a deaf child with attention and behavioral problems has attention deficit hyperactivity disorder without considering the impact of inadequate language exposure.

Chapter 4 addresses what may be, apart from severe behavioral disorders, the most difficult challenge in mental health work with LLC persons, be they deaf or hearing. This is the problem of eliciting informed engagement in relevant treatment. *Pretreatment*, as described here, refers to strategies for educating and motivating clients to participate meaningfully in mental health care. Our models of mental health care are only as useful as our ability to solicit informed participation, and the long-held lament that such clients "are not suitable candidates" for psychotherapy testifies to how poorly equipped mental health clinicians have been to eliciting engagement from people not seeking out our services. This chapter reviews the many reasons these people can appear "resistant" to mental health care and then describes nine strategies that facilitate the kind of treatment participation clinicians look for.

Chapter 5 presents our approach to developing coping skills in these clients. Coping skills are defined here as skills for handling one's inner life; emotions, impulses, physiological experiences, thoughts, and behaviors. The chapter presents an overview of coping skills with an emphasis on simpler, less language dependent skills.

Chapter 6 presents interventions for developing nonviolent conflict resolution skills with clients with language and learning challenges. These skills are also broken down into component microskills and then taught through innovative games, stories, and other activities. As with the other kinds of skill training, clinicians are helped to discover how clients are already using some of these microskills and then engage them in activities designed to develop these skills further. In this chapter, I describe the importance of creating therapeutic environments oriented around skill development and story construction.

Chapter 7 presents work that is more advanced in the area of relapse prevention. As much relapse prevention requires better language skills and the ability to identify patterns and think abstractly, fewer of our LLC clients will be able to carry out a full relapse prevention plan. Relapse prevention also requires clients to be self-directed agents in their own recovery, fully in the treatment phase of this work. As described in this chapter, the principles of relapse prevention can be used to help staff develop crisis intervention plans in instances where they have responsibility to help people who are not able or willing to take full responsibility for themselves.

Chapter 8 addresses the issue of staff and program development. In most programs that serve clients with language and learning challenges, the majority of the staff members providing day to day supervision and assistance have the least amount of clinical training. These paraprofessional staff members often work at a bachelor's degree level or less yet they have enormous influence over the daily lives of their clients. One of the key benefits of the skills and stories model presented here is that it is fairly easily understood and implemented by staff. For instance, staff members also benefit from learning coping, conflict resolution, and even relapse prevention skills. The skills framework helps them with clients but they often also find it personally relevant. They also benefit when supervisors expand their skills by helping them notice and develop the skills *they* already have. They also learn well when engaged through stories. Chapter 8 also presents cross-cultural Deaf/hearing conflicts in the context of this therapeutic focus on skills and stories.

The book closes with a final chapter summarizing the main ideas and drawing out some of the implications. I return here to the question, discussed in Chapter 1, of whether or not some of these deaf persons with language and learning challenges have a unique clinical syndrome. If so, what are the diagnostic criteria for this syndrome, and what should we call it? This chapter also includes a discussion of how mental health treatment approaches are adapted for higher functioning deaf persons who are fluent ASL users so that these approaches become "Deaf friendly."

Accompanying this text is a CD-ROM with approximately 2,000 of the amazing pictorial aids developed by Michael Krajnak. Readers of my second book (Glickman & Gulati, 2003) will recognize many of the pictures from the CD-ROM that came with that book. This CD-ROM, version 2, contains nearly three times the number of pictures, many redone for even better quality. Pictures from the CD-ROM are used throughout the text. A discussion of how to use this resource is presented in Appendix I.

A word should be said about confidentiality. The stories presented in this book reflect incidents that actually happened, but in almost every case I have changed significant details to protect client confidentiality. The names used are never correct, and in some cases I have embellished or changed stories to further protect client privacy. The Deaf Unit has also served many ASL or English fluent clients, some with college and even graduate degrees. It is not my intention to imply that everyone served there is "low functioning" but rather to focus a prolonged discussion of mental health care on this underserved and difficult to serve group. Because the Deaf Community is small, some readers may think they recognize certain persons. I would encourage them to doubt themselves. Rather, what I hope people will recognize is the kind of client problems we work with often. When I present our work to professionals in the deafness mental health and rehabilitation fields, I usually begin by describing the characteristics of a few of the people we have served. I then ask the group, "Do you know these people?" Inevitably, a chorus of heads nod "yes." If the stories sound familiar to persons in this field, this reflects how common it is for our clients to have these kinds of clinical presentations. In other words, any similarities noted to real persons just means that you know persons *like* those described and perhaps that you can "relate" to the difficulties serving them.

The Wisdom of the Good Witch

At the end of *The Wizard of Oz*, Dorothy turns to the good witch Glenda to help her get home. Glenda's comments to Dorothy echo those of the wizard to her three compatriots: she already has what she needs. She has "always had the power to go back to Kansas." Glenda could not tell her this because Dorothy had to find out for herself. She had to discover for herself that "if I ever go looking for my heart's desire again, I won't go looking any further than my own back yard. Because if it isn't there, I never really lost it to begin with."

Dorothy was looking for something she already had. The scarecrow, cowardly lion, and tin man already had the skills and qualities for which they searched. When the timing was right, their "therapist" just had to help them discover that which they already had.

So here is our challenge: to engage in mental health care for these "difficult to treat" language and learning challenged clients by helping them discover and expand on skills they already have. It will not take a wizard or a good witch to make this happen, but it will require a stubborn determination to discover abilities where others do not see them and to weave these abilities into a new narrative about competence.

1

Language and Learning Challenges in the Deaf Psychiatric Population*

PATRICIA BLACK AND NEIL GLICKMAN

We might start with some naïve questions. How is mental health care with deaf persons different from mental health care with hearing people? Are not deaf psychiatric clients similar to hearing psychiatric clients, except they cannot hear?

There are some obvious answers. Some deaf people use sign language. Some use hearing aids or have cochlear implants. There is special technology that deaf people use. Beyond these obvious matters, why would anything else be different?

At the time of this writing, in the fall of 2007, the idea that mental health care of deaf people is in any significant way different than mental health care of hearing people is controversial. The mainstream assumption is that deaf people suffer the same psychiatric problems as hearing people, manifest them in the same way, and require no more special expertise to serve than the assistance of a sign language interpreter. Most deaf people treated in psychiatric settings are placed in hearing psychiatric units that have no particular expertise in working with deaf persons (Trybus, 1983). They may receive accommodations consisting of limited hours of interpreting services. Perhaps someone orders a hearing evaluation and adaptive equipment like hearing aids. Maybe the captioning on the television is turned on. Someone may produce the old tty (text telephone) from the storage room not realizing how far telecommunication for deaf people has advanced beyond it. One may fairly ask why anything more is required to serve deaf clients than this.

In the second half of the 20th century, a growing number of mental health clinicians came to understand that much more *is* required. There is far more to working with deaf people than audiological remediation and bringing in sign

* Earlier versions of this chapter were published as follows: Black, P., & Glickman, N. (2006). Demographics, psychiatric diagnosis, and other characteristics of North American deaf and hard of hearing inpatients. *Journal of Deaf Studies and Deaf Education.* 11(3), 303–321. This chapter revision is printed with permission of Oxford University Press. Black, P., & Glickman, N. (2005). Language dysfluency in the deaf inpatient population. *JADARA, 39*(1), 1–28. Reprinted with permission from the JADARA.

language interpreters. There is a large body of special knowledge to acquire, and the knowledge domains are not merely medical and audiological but also social, historical, psychological, rehabilitative, linguistic, and cultural. There are complex new skills to acquire. Skill in American Sign Language (ASL) is the most obvious, but other skills include nonverbal communication, linguistically informed work with interpreters, skills in adapting one's clinical role, skill in collaboration with Deaf Community helpers and leaders, and skills in adapting assessment and treatment interventions (Glickman, 1996; Zitter, 1996).

There is yet a third dimension of specialization in clinical work with deaf people. This is the dimension of self-awareness. Hearing people, *as hearing people*, have certain attitudes toward deaf people that can interfere with the establishment of a therapeutic alliance. An unexamined paternalistic and *audist* (Lane, 1992, 1996) attitude can be an even more formidable barrier to effective mental health care of deaf people than lack of signing skills. This problem leads Hoffmeister and Harvey to explore, somewhat tongue in cheek, the issue of whether there is a Psychology of the Hearing (Hoffmeister & Harvey, 1996).

In the latter half of the 20th century, mental health care of deaf persons emerged as a clinical discipline (Pollard, 1996). Besides a growing body of research and clinical literature, there are graduate programs that train students to work with deaf people, practica and internships in specialty programs, professional journals, and national and international conferences on various aspects of mental health care of deaf people. Indeed, as American Sign Language gained recognition as a real language and the Deaf Community gained recognition as a cultural community, an array of new ethical standards emerged for working with deaf people (Gutman, 2002). For instance, it is increasingly recognized that clinicians without specialized training who work with deaf persons are violating ethical standards of their discipline. Standard 2.01, Boundaries of Competence, of the 2002 American Psychological Association Ethical Principles of Psychologists and Code of Conduct states:

> (a) Psychologists provide services, teach, and conduct research with populations and in areas only within the boundaries of their competence, based on their education, training, supervised experience, consultation, study, or professional experience.
>
> (b) Where scientific or professional knowledge in the discipline of psychology establishes that an understanding of factors associated with age, gender, gender identity, race, ethnicity, culture, national origin, religion, sexual orientation, disability, language, or socioeconomic status is essential for effective implementation of their services or research, psychologists have or obtain the training, experience, consultation, or supervision necessary to ensure the competence of their services, or they

make appropriate referrals, except as provided in Standard 2.02, Providing Services in Emergencies. (American Psychological Association, 2002).

Are there significant differences between the characteristics of deaf and hearing psychiatric patients, beyond the issue of hearing loss, that warrant this special training?

The purpose of the first two chapters of this book is to address this question. Some of the controversy has focused on the question of whether there is such a thing as a *psychology of deafness*. At least four books have been published with this idea in the title (Levine, 1960; Myklebust, 1964; Paul & Jackson, 1993; Vernon & Andrews, 1990). We address it here by looking at characteristics of deaf psychiatric inpatients. As we review the literature, we will certainly find that deaf people have been diagnosed with all the same kinds of psychopathology as hearing people. However, the qualifications of the clinicians who performed these assessments and the validity of their assessments are open to challenge. Another issue, as we will see, is whether the population of deaf persons served in mental health facilities is in some significant ways different from their hearing peers. We will demonstrate that some differences are so pronounced that clinicians without specialized training are wholly unprepared for the task.

Both issues come together when we consider the subpopulation of deaf persons sometimes referred to as low functioning deaf (LFD). In this chapter we review some of the literature on LFD, followed by a review of the literature on deaf psychiatric inpatients. We then turn to an analysis of the characteristics of deaf patients on a specialty psychiatric Deaf Unit over a seven-year period. Our goal is to answer the naïve questions posed at the beginning of this chapter. How is mental health care with deaf persons different from mental health care with hearing people?

Traditionally Underserved Deaf People

The subgroup *of low functioning deaf persons* is well known in the Deaf Community and by service providers who work with deaf people. The name *low functioning deaf* is problematic because the group is heterogeneous, people may be skilled in some domains while unskilled in others, and because it is pejorative. Other labels that have been used include "severely disabled," "underachieving," "minimal language skilled," "multiply handicapped," and "traditionally underserved" (Dew, 1999). The last term is often favored because it is the least pejorative. I (Neil Glickman) offered the term *psychologically unsophisticated* (Glickman, 2003) but it has not caught on, even with me.

The use of the term *low functioning deaf* does not seem appropriate in this book because one of the key pretreatment strategies, discussed in Chapter 4, is to notice and reinforce the skills and strengths these persons do have. We are presenting a strength-based model, and that should be reflected in our language. In Chapter 2, we refer often to deaf persons who are *language dysfluent due to language deprivation*. For the purposes of this current chapter, we stay with *traditionally underserved* when not quoting directly because this is the term most accepted in the literature we review. In Chapters 3 through 9, we use the phrase *language and learning challenged* (LLC) for both the deaf and hearing clients who are the focus of our attention.

According to the comprehensive report of the Institute on Rehabilitation Issues Prime Study Group on Serving Individuals Who Are Low Functioning Deaf (Dew, 1999), Rehabilitation Services Administration (RSA) research between 1963 and 1998 produced consensus on six characteristics that seem to describe persons who are LFD.

1. **Inadequate communication skills due to inadequate education and limited family support.** Presenting poor skills in interpersonal and social communication interactions, many of these individuals experience difficulty expressing themselves and understanding others, whether through sign language, speech and speech reading, or reading and writing.

2. **Vocational deficiencies due to inadequate educational training experiences during the developmental years and changes in personal and work situations during adulthood.** Presenting an underdeveloped image of self as a worker, many exhibit a lack of basic work attitudes and work habits as well as a lack of job skills and/or work skills.

3. **Deficiencies in behavioral, emotional, and social adjustment.** Presenting a poorly developed sense of autonomy, many exhibit low self-esteem, have a low frustration tolerance, and have problems of impulse control that may lead to mistrust of others and pose a danger to self and others.

4. **Independent living skills deficiencies.** Many of these individuals experience difficulty living independently, lack basic money management skills, lack personal hygiene skills, cannot manage use of free time, do not know how to access health care or maintain proper nutrition, and have poor parenting skills.

5. **Educational and transitional deficiencies.** Most read at or below a fourth-grade level and have been poorly served by the educational system, are frequently misdiagnosed and misplaced, lack a supportive home environment, are often discouraged in school and drop out, and are not prepared for postschool life and work. Approximately 60% of the high school leavers who are deaf cannot read at the fourth-grade level.

6. **Health, mental, and physical limitations.** Many have no secondary physical disabilities, but a large number have two, three, and

sometimes more disabilities in addition to that of deafness. In fact, 30% of high school leavers who are deaf had an educationally signifi-cant additional disability. These secondary disabilities range from organic brain dysfunction to visual deficits. These problems are fur-ther compounded in many instances by a lack of knowledge on how to access health and/or self care. (Dew, 1999)

Long, Long, and Ouellette (1993) provide a useful definition based on responses to a survey conducted by the Northern Illinois University Research and Training Center on Traditionally Underserved Persons Who Are Deaf (NIU-TRC):

A traditionally underserved person who is deaf is a person who possesses **limited communication abilities** (i.e., cannot communicate effectively via speech, speech reading, sign language and whose English language skills are at or below the third grade level) **and** who possesses any or all of the following characteristics:

- Cannot maintain employment without transitional assistance or support;
- Demonstrates poor social/emotional skills (i.e., poor problem solving skills, difficulty establishing social support, poor emotional control, impulsivity, low frustration tolerance, inappropriately aggressive);
- Cannot live independently without transitional assistance or support [emphasis maintained from original]. (p. 109)

The most important distinguishing characteristic of this group is the poorly developed language skills. These language deficits are most easily measured in English or other spoken languages, but perhaps more important are the language deficits in what is usually their best language: ASL. These persons generally are not fluent in ASL and may have difficulty expressing themselves even among deaf people. The language deficits are significant because they create or contribute to most other problems these individuals face. To live in a predominantly English-speaking country without fluency in English is cer-tainly a major disadvantage, but to have no native language in which one is truly fluent is a handicap with far more serious ramifications.

Among hearing people, outside of those with extreme brain pathology or environmental deprivation, the kinds of language dysfluency we find in tra-ditionally underserved deaf people is extremely rare. This means that most teachers, physicians, rehabilitation workers, and mental health providers will not have come across this problem unless they have had very specialized clinical training or exposure to large numbers of deaf people. They will be unprepared for these clients, and they will make unintentional errors when assessing and treating them that can result in serious and sometimes life-long damage (Glickman & Gulati, 2003).

Population estimates for this group of persons are 125,000 to 165,000 (Bowe, 2004; Dew, 1999). Hard numbers are not available in part because the federal government has not funded specialized programming for them long enough to establish consistent, clear criteria for identifying them or to complete program evaluations and establish best practices (Harmon, Carr, & Johnson, 1998).

The primary social organizations responsible for helping traditionally underserved deaf persons have been schools and vocational rehabilitation programs. As noted above, many of these people drop out of school and have a lifetime of marginal functioning. The first federally funded vocational rehabilitation program providing specialized services to this group was the Crossroads Rehabilitation Center in 1966. Prior to the 1973 Rehabilitation Act, which placed greater emphasis on serving severely disabled persons, LFD were often denied vocational rehabilitation services because they were judged too severely handicapped to benefit from them. Vocational rehabilitation agencies also lacked staff that could communicate effectively with them, much less engage them in the process of vocational rehabilitation. Between 1963 and 1979, 16 programs received special funding to address the rehabilitation needs of LFD. In the 1980s, a research and training Center on Deafness was established at the University of Arkansas to address rehabilitation needs of deaf people. The U.S. Department of Education (DOE) funded another research and training center specifically to focus on LFD at Northern Illinois University. The DOE also funded two service centers, Project Vida in Seattle and the Lexington Center in New York, to serve LFD (Long, 1993).

In the 1990s, the Lexington Center continued to receive funding for its program, and two new programs, the Community Outreach Program for the Deaf in Tucson, Arizona, and the Southwest Center for the Hearing Impaired, in San Antonio, Texas, were also funded (Harmon et al., 1998). Support for these or other specialized rehabilitation centers for LFD was not continued under the George W. Bush administration in spite of evidence demonstrating their cost-effectiveness (Bowe, 2004).

It is perhaps a truism to say that severe language deficits contribute strongly to behavioral problems. This is easy to understand. Language is the chief ability that distinguishes humans from other animals. With language, we can communicate and act on ideas. We do not need to grab or push or threaten nonverbally to get what we want. Language is the major ability that makes psychological and social development possible. Children born deaf into environments where sign language is unavailable or partially available, and who grow up without the ability to receive the spoken language of their society, rarely acquire fluency in it. The result is people without a native language or with language skills only partially developed. This language dysfluency has dire effects on psychological, social, educational, and vocational development. Behavioral problems emerge early in childhood and may continue and intensify throughout adulthood. These behavioral problems are often what bring these persons into prisons, rehabilitation facilities, or mental health settings. Paul and Jackson (1993) comment:

> Deaf students with severe behavioral problems are disenrolled from schools and reported to penal agencies. Some of these students may be treated in inpatient mental facilities. Because of the lack of trained professionals and adequate facilities, the inpatient facilities tend to provide custodial care rather than mental health rehabilitative intervention. (p. 207)

Mathay and LaFayette (1990) conducted an interview survey of 40 professional service providers working in agencies that serve deaf people in the Northwest United States. The agencies represented state vocational rehabilitation departments, vocational training and evaluation programs, independent living skills training programs, mental health services, educational institutions, advocacy and support services, and deaf/blind services. The providers interviewed were the persons in the agencies who had the most contact with deaf clients. Mathay and LaFayette note:

> The topic of low achieving deaf persons brought very strong and eager responses from almost every respondent. Interviews were lengthy and each respondent expressed sincere concern, and often frustration, regarding this population. Several respondents commented that they spent more effort working with this population than other client groups, even though the success rate was very low. (p. 31)

The respondents in this research calculated that 25% to 100% of their deaf clients were low achieving. They described 57 obstacles facing low achieving deaf persons. The most commonly identified obstacle was the need for independent living skills. The respondents cited the difficulties in providing the comprehensive array of specialized services that this group of deaf persons needs to succeed in society.

Most of the federal vocational rehabilitation dollars devoted to the deaf population have gone toward funding services for higher functioning deaf (Long, 1993) Among these are community and four-year colleges. The usual means of accessing services is via sign language interpreters. The assumption is that deaf people just need communication access via interpreters to succeed in the same programs as their hearing peers. There is general consensus in the literature that traditionally underserved deaf persons need specialized services designed for them (Bowe, 2004; Dew, 1999; Harmon et al., 1998; Long, 1993). Chiefly because of their limited language skills, they cannot make good use of interpreters, especially when the interpreters are signing in a more English-like modality.

Traditionally underserved individuals who are deaf need staff with superb sign language skills who have been trained specifically in how to work with them. They also need an array of support services. In vocational rehabilitation, for instance, it has been long understood that the challenge of helping traditionally underserved deaf persons develop work skills is dwarfed by the far more difficult challenge of helping them develop work attitudes and behaviors. It is much easier to teach someone how to perform an unskilled or semiskilled job than it is to teach them how to get along with co-workers and supervisors and learn appropriate work habits. More often than not, it is these latter issues that cause their failure on the job.

Duffy (1999) described a strategy for clinical case management with traditionally underserved deaf adults. She noted that these persons are frequently isolated, ostracized from both their families and the Deaf Community, and that they can lack the ability to advocate for themselves. The most important reason they are referred for psychological services, she said, "is poor social skills. The client may be aggressive, have low frustration tolerance, have difficulty establishing social support, poor emotional control and/or poor problem-solving skills" (p. 334). Clinical case managers may become the treatment providers of choice because this population is not amenable to traditional psychotherapy.

> Good communication skills and capacity for insight are considered requisites for psychodynamic therapy. In clinical case management we generally address the mental health needs of individuals who have often been perceived as poor candidates for more traditional models of psychotherapy or who have been excluded from mainstream services due to prejudice or service delivery models that do not meet the needs of the client. What happens when clients are able to experience many of the dynamics of the therapeutic experience and yet lack the language to speak directly of their experiences? (Duffy, 1999)

Duffy's response is that the clinically trained case manager, using the self-psychology approach of Kohut (1984) can help.

> Mirroring clients' affect and validating their experiences allows them to more fully own their experiences.... To have someone bear witness to our struggles in a compassionate, nonjudgmental manner is beneficial, often healing, and unfortunately, for some, a rare experience. (p. 340)

Duffy cautions counselors to not overlook the strengths and skills these persons do possess. Empathic understanding as advocated by Kohut must be helpful, but for either clinicians or case managers to really help these traditionally underserved persons, we need to venture outside the psychodynamic world for just the reasons Duffy offered. Most of this book addresses how to do this.

We reviewed some of the literature on traditionally underserved deaf people before turning to the literature on deaf psychiatric patients because many deaf psychiatric patients actually come from this traditionally underserved group. Placed in mental health settings such as psychiatric hospitals, they then become mental patients and are vulnerable to receiving inappropriate diagnoses and treatment. As we reviewed this literature, we looked for references to difficulties clinicians had with diagnostic assessment, particularly due to language impairments, and to persons who do not seem to match the usual profile of psychiatric patients. We also examine the extent to which these traditionally underserved deaf persons showed up at Westborough State Hospital's Deaf Unit over a 7-year period.

Research on Deaf Psychiatric Inpatients

Prior to this research, only six published studies have been found that focus on psychiatric diagnosis of the adult deaf inpatient population in the United States (Daigle, 1994; Grinker et al., 1969; Pollard, 1994; Rainer & Altshuler, 1996; Rainer, Altshuler, & Kallman, 1963; Robinson, 1978; Trybus, 1983). Additional important research conducted in a specialty deaf psychiatric unit in Great Britain (Denmark, 1994) is also reviewed.

New York Psychiatric Institute, 1960s

The first major research on mental health and deafness in the United States was conducted in the late 1950s and early 1960s by a group of New York psychoanalytically trained psychiatrists (Altshuler & Rainer, 1968; Rainer & Altshuler, 1996; Rainer et al., 1963) Their studies were considered landmark research in the field of mental health and deafness at the time. Their work led to the development of the first inpatient deaf unit in the United States in 1963 at Rockland State Hospital and outpatient services at the New York Psychiatric Institute.

The research in these studies included a three-year survey of deaf patients in New York State mental institutions, evaluation and treatment of neurotic and psychotic individuals in the outpatient clinic for the deaf, and comprehensive interviews of families of deaf patients. The inpatient study included 230 psychotic deaf patients at 20 hospitals. This group consisted of all the deaf patients hospitalized in New York State psychiatric hospitals in 1958. The researchers stated that specially trained staff interviewed the deaf patients to verify diagnoses. They also state that staff learned sign language on the job.

Throughout this pioneering and important work, the researchers grappled with the difficulty of diagnosing and treating deaf patients with whom they could not communicate easily. One can infer from their writing that the sign communication skills of the staff were limited and that the only deaf people assisting were volunteers from the local community. This would not be surprising given the state of knowledge about sign language and the Deaf Community during this period. Descriptions of the communication abilities of deaf patients are very gross: whether they signed or spoke or did both.

The researchers note that "not all of the patients were proficient in using or understanding manual language. Often a final diagnosis had to be kept in abeyance until the patient had been taught effective means of communication" (Rainer & Altshuler, 1996, p. 29). The willingness of the staff to defer diagnosis in recognition that they could not communicate well with these patients is unusually judicious.

Rainer and Altshuler grappled with the dilemma that significant numbers of deaf patients did not appear to fit established diagnostic categories and were certainly not psychotic. They called one group of such patients "primitive personalities." Vernon and Andrews (1990) later summarized this term as referring to "deaf persons with extreme educational deprivation, almost no understanding of language, little socialization, and a generally psychologically barren life. The result is gross cognitive and social immaturity." They went on to conclude that "primitive personalities represent a significant percentage of deaf people needing mental health services" (p. 137).

Rainer and Altshuler also describe another group of deaf persons as having an "impulsive disorder." Their description is worth quoting in detail:

> Last to be presented are the case histories of a particular group of deaf patients among whom the problems of diagnosis, treatment, and outcome were especially puzzling. It has been noted elsewhere that the majority of deaf inpatients are admitted because of unruly, impulsive, sometimes bizarre behavior, regardless of the type of underlying illness. The patients in this group are no exception in this regard, yet examinations in depth often fail to reveal pathology of psychotic extent. Their behavior continues to be erratic, sometimes antisocial, short-sighted, and without perseverance. In some ways such patients appear to be like the hearing psychopath, a conscienceless character, antisocial and impulsive, a swindler, petty thief, or the like. Yet the deaf patients are generally without guile or malice, and have at times a clear awareness of right and wrong. When crossed, they may quickly give way to violent temper tantrums, but otherwise they are openly friendly and eager to please. They differ from the more primitive group previously discussed in possessing many functions (including the ability to communicate) that the others lack. These functions are developed unevenly, with special weaknesses in the area of control. This type of case is common in the deaf, representing 12% of the inpatients treated on the special unit. (Rainer & Altshuler, 1996, pp. 47–48)

Rainer et al. (1963, Chapter 14) found the diagnosis of schizophrenia present in 52.2% of the deaf inpatients and 56.5% of hearing inpatients. These figures represented 1.16% of the total New York State deaf population but only 0.43% of the hearing population at that time. The deaf patients diagnosed with schizophrenia remained in the hospital longer than hearing patients diagnosed with this disorder. The researchers believed that the number of deaf patients with schizophrenia was even higher than this but many were misdiagnosed as having "psychosis with mental deficiency."

This latter diagnostic category is especially interesting. One-fourth of all deaf patients and just 3.7% of hearing patients received this diagnosis. The researchers concluded that this category "represented a waste-basket classification for deaf persons with poor communication skills who at some time showed signs of emotional disturbance" (p. 199).

Another 17% of deaf individuals were diagnosed with various types of psychoses, such as senility and involutional psychosis. The authors point out that major communication problems existed in deaf patients who were psychotic.

> Often, physicians and patient are unable to understand each other not only because of obstructions in the physical means of exchanging ideas, but because of limitations in abstract thinking imposed on the psychotic deaf by their perceptual defect, and their illness. (Rainer et al., 1963, p. 199)

It is striking how the communication problems are attributed to the patients' "perceptual deficit" and not to the lack of sign communication skills of the clinician, and how these communication problems resulted in patients being given diagnoses like "psychosis with mental deficiency." Perhaps some of these deaf patients really were fluent ASL users. However, even with their presumably *primitive* knowledge of ASL, Altshuler, Rainier, and Kallman probably were correct in noting that many of their patients did not appear to be effective communicators in sign. In retrospect, we can now speculate that the communication difficulties they encountered were because many of these deaf patients were indeed language dysfluent as a result of their experience of language deprivation. Perhaps they were also language dysfluent related to mental illness. Altshuler, Rainier, and Kallman, as pioneers in the field of deafness mental health, were just not equipped to make this kind of distinction.

As someone who has administered a Deaf psychiatric inpatient unit for 15 years, it is very interesting to me (Neil Glickman) to read Rainer et al.'s early works. I have not only the benefit of their work and that of those who followed but also the benefit of much more information about ASL and the Deaf Community. Although Altshuler in particular has been criticized for contributing to a pathological view of deafness (Lane, 1992), I recognize in this early work many of the same diagnostic and treatment dilemmas we struggle with half a century later. Rainer, Altshuler, and Kallman were not sophisticated about sign language but they saw that many of their deaf patients could not communicate well and that this had hugely important implications for their psychosocial functioning. Rainer, Altshuler, and Kallman were able to recognize that many of their deaf patients were different from their hearing peers. The patients did not seem to fit the established diagnostic categories. They had terrible behavioral problems but they were not psychotic. Rainer, Altshuler, and Kallman struggled with how to diagnose and treat these persons, and they had no role models or reference points to draw on.

It is important to note that Rainer and Altshuler excluded deaf patients with known mental retardation from their study (Rainer & Altshuler, 1966, p. 27). One can speculate that the number of deaf patients diagnosed with these so called "primitive personalizes" and "impulsive disorders" would have been even greater had they included patients diagnosed with mental retardation. Given the state of knowledge about deaf people in the 1950s and early 1960s, the major fault I have with their work is not that they almost certainly misconstrued language dysfluency related to language deprivation as due to a thought disorder. It is their tendency to generalize from a very skewed, pathological sample to deaf people as a whole.* Their descriptions of their clientele ring very true and familiar but, of course, deaf people treated in psychiatric hospitals are no more representative of deaf people than hearing people treated in psychiatric hospitals are of hearing people. Presumably, they should have appreciated that it is inappropriate to draw conclusions about a population based on a sample of its most troubled and dysfunctional people.

Michael Reese Hospital in Chicago, 1969

Following the New York studies, Psychiatrist Roy S. Grinker of Michael Reese Hospital and colleagues (Grinker et al., 1969) received a grant to study the mental health needs of deaf individuals in the Chicago area. They studied a total of 159 patients, 38 inpatients, and 121 outpatients. Inpatients were placed on one of five wards at an 80-bed teaching and treatment hospital. Patients were placed in different wards based on the severity of their symptoms so deaf patients were grouped together only if they had similar behavior and management problems.

The project staff consisted of two half-time consulting psychiatrists, two psychologists, a social worker, and a teacher-interpreter of the deaf.† The researchers report that all *project* staff had previous work experience with

---

* For example, they make these wildly inappropriate generalizations about deaf people: "As a result of his hearing loss, the deaf child suffers both in the cognitive aspects of learning and thinking and the emotional correlates of communication with his parents in his early years. It was observed in the course of the project that certain unique personality features were present among deaf persons. They often showed a poorly developed ability to understand and care about the feelings of others; and they had inadequate insight into the impact on others of their own behavior and its consequences. With a generally egocentric view of the world and with demands unfettered by excessive control machinery (conscience), their adaptive approach may be characterized as gross coercive dependence" (Rainer & Altshuler, 1966, p. 141).

† Note the lack of reference to nursing and ward staff who constitute most of the people in daily contact with patients. These persons were not considered project staff and were not expected to be able to sign.

the deaf, an understanding of deaf subculture, and "knew the sign language" (p. 39). The teacher-interpreter taught sign to other staff members, functioned as "an auxiliary therapist," and "also served to teach basic skills in arithmetic, manual language, and other practical matters to those patients with gross educational deficiencies" (p. 39). These kinds of multiple roles for interpreters would be avoided in sophisticated programs for deaf persons today. They are an indication of how dependent the staff members were on the interpreter-teacher for the full array of clinical and rehabilitative services.

No distinction was made between inpatients and outpatients in the breakdown of the diagnoses. Of the deaf patients, 43 were diagnosed with schizophrenia, 25 with paranoid type; 9 patients (5.7%) had some form of severe depression as their primary diagnosis. Many other patients had depression as a secondary symptom. The personality disorders seen most often involved passivity, dependency, and impulse-control problems.

As with Rainer and Altshuler, assessments of patient communication skills are limited to whether or not the patients use "manual" or oral communication. The project staff also noted the prevalence of patients without functional communication skills in any language or modality:

> … One-fourth of the deaf patients seen had no adequate means of communication at all. They could not speak intelligibly. They did not know sign language. They had severely limited capacity to express themselves in writing and were unable to read more than simple nouns and rudimentary phrases.

> Many of these were bright adolescents or young adults for whom learning speech and speech reading had proven unsatisfactory, yet who had been forbidden by the schools to learn manual communication. They were not only unnaturally isolated and frustrated as a consequence, but they were also grossly undereducated. [Many of them] will probably go through life as nonverbal creatures with latent human qualities suppressed by an unnecessary isolation superimposed upon them by an insensitive "habilitation and education program." (p. 21)

The researchers stated that they did not provide specific diagnostic categories for the deaf inpatient sample because they believed that the presence of deafness could make such labeling misleading. However, they did note that two thirds of the patient displayed patterns of "inadequate and marginal functioning" (p. 42). They describe patients as having developmental delays and note that treatment consisted more in developing basic psychosocial competencies than in treating psychiatric disorders (p. 27). They note that "over seven percent of the patients bore the diagnosis of 'inadequate personality' and many others could have been so classified had not other pathology been more dominant" (p. 28). Most patients were never employed or worked for only short periods of time. They were felt to have a limited capacity for warm interpersonal relationships. They tended to shun close contact and preferred isolation. At other times, the patients tended to be passive and dependent with fragile impulse control. The researchers comment:

> Although some of our patients displayed fairly obvious and persistent psychotic-like behavior, we did not feel that the majority of patients belonged to the classical psychotic or schizophrenic picture. If any classification is to be used as a descriptive indicator, it would be the borderline syndrome. (p. 42)

The researchers do not define "borderline syndrome," a category whose meaning has changed over the years. We interpret their comments to indicate that, like Rainer and Altshuler, they found many deaf patients who showed serious emotional and behavioral problems but who did not appear to fit established diagnostic categories. Their problems appeared to resemble developmental deficits secondary to impaired communication. The Grinker team provides many poignant stories of deaf patients who could not communicate with their family members at all. Although they could not find a correlation between deafness and psychopathology, they did draw the tentative conclusion that when deafness is present, *"the degree of psychopathology is in proportion to the lack of communication between the child and significant family members"* (p. 51).

St. Elizabeth Hospital, 1978

The Mental Health Program for the Deaf at St. Elizabeth's Hospital in Washington, D.C., was developed in 1963 by psychiatrist Luther Robinson (1978) who was superintendent of that facility. After studying sign language and fingerspelling, Robinson began a treatment group of deaf patients. By 1973, he expanded services to a full-scale program and unit for deaf people. Robinson's program consisted of a multidisciplinary team of deaf and hearing professionals and paraprofessionals who had achieved "at least a minimal level of competence" before working with deaf patients. Training in sign language was conducted with support from Gallaudet College. By the end of 1975, approximately 400 staff members had enrolled in training in manual communication at the hospital.

The research on deaf patients was conducted from late 1963 through the fiscal year 1975 and included 173 admissions (150 patients). Admissions were voluntary, and consisted only of signing persons who had "deafness as a lifestyle." Persons with serious behavior problems were screened out. Robinson notes that over 50% of the patients with known educational histories had completed high school (p. 92). Most of these were graduates of a residential school for the deaf. Most were also residents of inner city Washington.

Robinson noted that well over 50% of all patients admitted to St. Elizabeth were diagnosed as psychotic, but only about 30% of patients admitted to the Deaf program were so diagnosed. Among hearing patients, situational disturbances accounted for only 2% of all admissions to the hospital. Among deaf patients, they accounted for 35% of the first admissions. The lower percentage of deaf persons diagnosed with a psychotic disorder and higher percentage of deaf persons diagnosed with a situational disorder (that is, an adjustment reaction) is the most striking finding from this study. The low rates of mental retardation and severe behavioral disturbance appear to be due to admission criteria that screened persons with these problems out.

At the time that Robinson wrote his research, deaf and hearing students from Gallaudet College and other schools were receiving training at the facility. Robinson pointed out:

> Any doubts that one might have regarding the efficacy of using sign language as the most important means of communicating with deaf patients would be dispelled by an exposure to the Mental Health Program for the Deaf at St. Elizabeth's Hospital. The comparison between deaf patients here and those unlucky enough to find themselves in a usual state hospital is dramatic testimony that without communication, there can be no treatment. (p. 119)

U.S. Public Psychiatric Hospitals Survey, 1983

The National Institute of Mental Health in conjunction with Gallaudet Research Institute conducted a study to determine the number and characteristics of deaf patients in public psychiatric hospitals (Trybus, 1983). The study did not include deaf individuals in private facilities or those in outpatient service programs. The timeframe of the study was not listed. This study is important for what it reveals about the plight of deaf persons hospitalized in nondeaf specialty programs.

The study located a total of 13,401 individuals (94 per 1,000 or 9.4%) in public psychiatric facilities. The breakdown included 13.5 deaf persons per 1,000 and 79.5 hard-of-hearing persons per 1,000. Of hospital units, 77% reported having one or more deaf patients, with the number varying from 1 to 155 per hospital, with a median of 15. Of all wards, 50% reported have one or more deaf patients, with a range from 1 to 49, and with a median of 2. This dispersion of deaf patients indicates that three quarters of all hospitals and half of the wards were treating deaf patients. However, the study also reported that in most of the hospitals, the only service offered was a hearing aid check and repair service. Communication equipment such as ttys was only available at 6% of the hospitals.

The study had four major findings: First, the greatest number of hearing impaired patients were either hard of hearing or persons who lost their hearing in adulthood. They were not signing deaf persons or members of the Deaf Community. Second, both deaf and hard of hearing persons were more likely than their hearing peers to have additional disabilities. Legal blindness was present in 13% of the deaf patients, as compared to 6% in hard of hearing patients and 0.5% in the general hospital population. Minimal brain injury was equivalent in both the hearing and hard of hearing groups (5% each) with a 0.4% rate in the general group. Emotional/behavioral problems were slightly higher in deaf patients (57%) than in the hard of hearing patients (54%). Both of these numbers were higher than the general population (3.6%). Learning disabilities were equal in the hard of hearing and deaf groups (3%) as compared to 0.5% in the other group. The communication problems and their additional disabilities created a need for staff with additional skills.

Third, and very striking in this study, was the greater prevalence of deaf clients evaluated as mentally retarded. Only 52% of the deaf patients fell within the average range of intelligence, whereas 69% of hard of hearing patients and 63% of hearing patients fell in this category. Only 5% of both hard of hearing and deaf patients fell into the above average range of intelligence as opposed to 7% of the hearing group. Although less than 2% of the entire hospital population is diagnosed with mental retardation, 30% of the deaf population and 20% of the hard of hearing are given this diagnosis. The researchers stated, "with respect to the likelihood of being moderately or profoundly retarded, the percentages are higher by a good bit for the deaf patients, 43% of whom are regarded as significantly below average in intelligence whether or not formally diagnosed as retarded in hospital records" (p. 5). The researchers believe these persons were being inappropriately evaluated.

Finally, hearing impaired patients had much greater lengths of stay than their hearing peers. One-third of the general population had a length of stay of less than 6 months. Only 12% of the deaf and hard of hearing had a similarly brief stay. More than one-third of deaf and hearing patients had hospital stays greater than 10 years.

The communication abilities and deficits of deaf patients are evaluated only in the most gross, rudimentary ways (that is, whether they sign), if at all. Patients and staff communicated primarily through gesture and pantomime and through written communication. In therapy settings, sign language was used in only one-third of the cases. In approximately two-thirds of the situations, "sign language is reported as being used in either direction for communication. At the same time, only in 1/3 of the cases is sign language used in providing therapeutic services to the deaf patients" (p. 6). Given that deaf patients are dispersed throughout various hospitals and wards with limited programming for deaf individuals, the claims about staff having any sign language capabilities need to be received with great skepticism.

Springfield Maryland Hospital Unit for the Deaf, 1994

Beth Daigle (1994) conducted a study of 146 deaf adult inpatients at Springfield Hospital Center Unit for the Deaf in Sykesville, Maryland. She compared this population with 146 randomly selected hearing inpatients from representative units at the hospital. Daigle studied the records of patients admitted to the deaf unit for a 10-year period between 1985 and 1994 and interviewed available patients and staff during the 1993 to 1994 year (Vernon & Daigle-King, 1999).

Of a total deaf sample, 129 patients received formal education: 46 patients did not complete high school; 46 others were high school graduates; 37 patients had gained some college experience. Approximately 42% attended residential school while 25% attended combined residential and public schools. The remainder appeared to receive primarily public school training.

Of the patients, 84% were considered to be "fluent" or "good" signers, compared to 16% who were "poor" or "nonsigners." The level of signing ability appeared to be related to the amount of time in residential or combined residential/mainstreamed educational experiences. Of the nonsigners, Daigle notes: "23 patients are unable to communicate in sign language. The majority of these patients are borderline mentally retarded (mean IQ = 78)." Patients identified with low IQs and no signing were most often diagnosed with pervasive personality disorders and avoidant/dependent disorders (71%).

On admission, many patients had at least two symptoms: 36% of the deaf patients showed delusions or hallucinations, 13% had drug abuse, and 7% presented with paranoia. Approximately half of the deaf group presented with violent and self-destructive symptoms.

In terms of diagnostic criteria, the study shows a higher percentage of schizophrenia in the hearing group (18%) as opposed to the deaf group (7%). Daigle noted that as staff became familiar with the deaf patients, many were rediagnosed as having either an organic problem or an adjustment disorder; 12% had nonclassified psychoses. Organic disorders accounted for 9% of the diagnosis of deaf patients but only 4% for the hearing patients. Adjustment disorder was more prevalent in the deaf sample (19%) than the hearing sample (12%).

Daigle's study showed a higher percentage of deaf patients diagnosed with depression than earlier studies. In the study, 13% of the deaf patients were diagnosed with depression, the identical percentage as with the hearing patients. However, bipolar disorder was diagnosed less often in deaf patients. Anxiety disorders were diagnosed infrequently in both deaf patients (4%) and hearing patients (1%).

Daigle noted that 47% of all hospitalized patients, with the deaf excluded, had more than one psychiatric diagnosis. The most common secondary diagnoses for deaf patients were: depression (24 cases), drug abuse (31), anxiety disorder (7), and organic mental disorders (16). For the hearing sample secondary diagnoses included adjustment disorder (1), depression (2), drug abuse (22), delusional paranoia (1).

The deaf sample included 19.8% who were diagnosed with antisocial, borderline, or narcissistic personality disorders as opposed to 6.16% of the hearing group; 11.6% of the deaf and 5.4% of the hearing patients were diagnosed with avoidant or dependent personality disorder; 10.9% of the deaf sample was diagnosed as mentally retarded, and none of the hearing patients was so diagnosed.

Daigle found that there were "more undiagnosed and diagnosis-deferred cases than in the hearing hospital population. Most of these were non-signing or low-functioning individuals" (p. 59).

Upon admission, most deaf patients displayed violent and self-destructive behaviors. Daigle felt that this was primarily because of the "frustrations caused by deaf patients' communication difficulties with non-signing parents, employers, and caretakers, an opinion also based on hospital records and interviews with parents" (p. 59). Vernon and Daigle-King (1999) comment that ASL is as sophisticated a language as English, French, or German,

> Yet, the psychiatrists and psychologists who have labeled the English language of deaf people "pathologically deficient" never describe their own incompetence in sign language as a pathology, nor do they note the competence of deaf people in sign language. (p. 60)

Rochester, New York

Robert Pollard (1994) conducted a study evaluating public mental health access, service utilization, and diagnostic trends pertaining to deaf and hard-of-hearing individuals (DHH) in the Rochester, New York area. Pollard's study was conducted between 1986 and 1991 and consisted of obtaining database records from six regional medical centers, inpatient facilities, and residential and supportive living services. A computer sort identified 84,437 records. A total of 343 records pertained to DHH (Pollard, 1994). The study compared the 343 DHH individuals with 68,329 hearing people on Axis I and 64,019 hearing individuals on Axis II. Results of the study did not break down inpatient and outpatient data.

Pollard found that "the Deaf and hard of hearing sample was overrepresented in small, supportive and miscellaneous programs that employed sign-fluent staff, volunteers, and interpreters and underrepresented in five out of the six community mental health centers (CMHCs)." The implication is that deaf persons are referred to places that offer specialized Deaf services regardless of whether those facilities offer the range or kind of services that particular deaf clients need. He adds,

> In the author's experience, many referrals of deaf patients to specialized programs are predicated on the communication access that exists in

those programs, rather than on a thorough evaluation of the quality of the match between the program's services and the patient's psychiatric needs. Unfortunately, this "either or" choice, which pits linguistic access against service breadth and, quite possibly, clinical appropriateness, is the norm in cities that have specialized programs for deaf individuals.

Pollard found that there was a more narrow range of diagnoses given to the DHH sample than to the hearing population. Diagnoses of mental retardation were found with greater frequency in the DHH group while substance abuse and antisocial personality disorder were diagnosed less frequently. He also found a significantly higher percentage of diagnoses were listed as deferred, missing, or no diagnosis was given. This strongly suggests that the clinicians lacked the same confidence to diagnose DHH clients as they felt with hearing clients. They avoided diagnosing to a greater degree, and when they did make diagnoses relied on a narrower range of most common conditions. Pollard concludes,

Clinicians who are overwhelmed with the task of communicating with or even relating to a deaf patient, especially if there is no interpreter present, are not likely to conduct an in-depth diagnostic examination. Their diagnostic conclusions may then be restricted to only the most common disorders, or they may fail to identify secondary conditions (such as substance abuse) beyond the primary diagnosis, or their diagnosis may be deferred or be missing altogether. All of these diagnostic events were taking place with DHH sample patients, judging from the data presented in this study. (p. 158)

Pollard speculates that the higher percentage of DHH persons diagnosed with mental retardation is either because some etiologies of deafness increase risk for mental retardation or because of misuse of psychological tests. Based on the research from the Deaf Unit at Westborough State Hospital, and the literature on low functioning deaf persons, we would add a third possible reason. This is that the cohort of deaf persons referred to mental health programs includes a significant number of low functioning deaf persons, many of whom have lower levels of tested or functional retardation. In other words, the cohort of low functioning deaf persons, many of whom are at least functionally retarded, *is* overrepresented in samples of DHH persons receiving mental health services.

Whittingham Hospital, Great Britain

John Denmark, a leading psychiatrist specializing in evaluation and treatment of deaf persons in Great Britain, reported on 250 referrals to the Department of Psychiatry for the Deaf at Whittingham Hospital (Denmark, 1994). Of these referrals, 124 (50%) were actually admitted to the hospital. Demark divided the 250 patients into three main diagnostic groups: "those with mental disorders, those with problems related to deafness and those with developmental disorders of communication" (p. 95).

Of the 104 patients diagnosed with a mental illness, the most common diagnosis was schizophrenia. A further 58 patients had what Denmark calls *problems related to their deafness.* Four such problems are listed: depression due to acquired deafness (3 persons), alcoholism due to acquired deafness (1 person), tinnitus (1 person), and by far the biggest group, behavioral and adjustment problems (53 persons). Denmark writes:

> The majority (with problems related to their deafness) presented with behavioral and adjustment problems which in the majority of instances were due to maturational delay. It is often difficult to know whether preverbally deaf people who present with problems of behavior and adjustment have a personality disorder per se or whether those problems are the result of immaturity consequent upon deprivation of language and experience. (p. 53)

Finally, the last category of patients includes persons with *developmental disorders of communication.* Here 48 persons are diagnosed with communication disorders. Denmark describes these persons as having "*no effective means of communication.*"

Key Points From Previous Studies

From the pioneering work of Rainer, Altshuler, and Kallman to the present day, clinicians have struggled with the issue of their competence to perform diagnostic assessments of deaf people. The language barriers are the most obvious challenge. It is relatively easy for hearing clinicians to notice that the spoken and written language skills of many of their deaf patients were very impaired. It is also relatively easy to notice that many used some kind of sign communication, and that clinicians without these language skills were at a disadvantage. It takes a much higher level of sign language competence to make assessments of the person's language skills in sign, and a rare level of competence indeed (discussed in the next chapter) to make clinical sense of the language problems that are observed. Because assessment of mental status is so dependent on understanding the clients' language, one sees throughout the literature some hesitancy in drawing conclusions about serious mental conditions like schizophrenia. Even Rainer, Altshuler, and Kallman, who found a higher prevalence of schizophrenia among their deaf patients, were concerned about misdiagnosis stemming from the poor communication abilities of the patients (and, to a lesser degree, the lack of sign competency in staff).

The prevalence rates for schizophrenia and other psychotic disorders in the deaf inpatient population have been a source of debate. Are they higher, as Rainer and Altshuler's research suggests, lower as Daigle's and Robinson's research suggests, or comparable? When higher rates of psychotic disorders are found, is that due to the lack of specialized assessment skills as suggested by Altshuler and Rainer (1968), Lane (1968), Pollard (1994), and Vernon and Daigle-King (1999). Is the lack of such specialized assessment competence also the reason that higher rates of mental retardation are sometimes found? (Pollard, 1994; Trybus, 1983).

In most of this literature, clinicians have been puzzled by high rates of behavioral problems and relatively low rates of psychotic disorders, and they have wondered whether they were seeing a unique psychiatric syndrome. One sees this in the creation of new diagnoses such as *surdophrenia* (Basilier, 1964) and *primitive personality disorder* (Rainer & Altshuler, 1996). One also sees it in diagnoses or categories like *psychosis with mental deficits* (Rainer and Altshuler, 1996), *borderline syndrome* and *inadequate personality* (Grinker et al., 1969) *minimal brain injury, nonclassified psychoses, problems related to deafness* (Denmark, 1994), diagnoses given with the tag *"atypical"* or *"not otherwise specified,"* or just large numbers of patients that clinicians could not diagnose (Daigle, 1994; Pollard, 1994).

The literature does suggest that the population of deaf persons served in psychiatric hospitals appears to be different in significant ways from that of their hearing peers. However, are these differences due to lack of specialized assessment skill in the clinical team? Clinicians were clearly grappling with how to assess and treat these persons, and many appeared very worried about the possibility of making mistakes. Certainly, the literature on deaf persons treated by nondeafness specialists gives one great cause to worry. Trybus's research demonstrated that administrators and clinicians were often not even aware they had patients who were hearing impaired, much less how to assess and treat them. Pollard's research shows that when specialized mental health programs for deaf people exist, deaf clients will go there even when they have to travel farther and even when that program does not offer treatment to fit their particular clinical needs. Among clinicians who specialize in work with deaf patients in inpatient settings, it is striking how often they comment that that most of their deaf patients did not appear to be psychotic or even mentally ill, yet they had very low levels of psychosocial functioning and very severe behavioral problems. All the deafness mental health specialists grappled with how to understand this large group of "low functioning deaf people." The most common reason these persons were hospitalized is severe behavioral problems, yet *frequently these problems do not appear to be secondary to mental illness per se. Rather they appear related to developmental deficits, especially in language, and they occur frequently enough to justify hypothesizing that some new syndrome is at play.*

Finally, one sees in this psychology literature until recently a relative inattention to diagnoses of mood, anxiety, and substance abuse disorders as well as an inattention to assessment of trauma. This reflects not so much problems in the deafness mental health world but general trends in the mental health community. It is only relatively recently that attention has been paid to dual diagnosis for substance abuse and to psychological trauma. These problems are diagnosed more reliably as the general mental health Zeitgeist has shifted. Mood disorders, substance abuse, and trauma are now very much a focus of psychiatric attention. Yet Pollard's research found that nondeafness specialists, perhaps because they were stymied by the diagnostic challenges, used a much more limited number of diagnostic labels when working with deaf clients.

With this as our background, we turn our attention to a new study of deaf psychiatric inpatients, also occurring in a specialized treatment facility. What can this new study add to our understanding of the question raised at the beginning of this chapter? Who are the people we are serving? Does this new study support the conclusion that many deaf patients treated in specialty Deaf mental health programs have significant language problems in their best communication modality, do not appear to fit established diagnostic categories, have developmental deficits in psychosocial skills and functioning and significant behavioral problems *not associated with severe mental illness*? If so, how do we understand these problems?

Method

Participants and Procedures

This study utilized archival data obtained from all 94 discharged adult patients at the Deaf Unit of Westborough State Hospital in Westborough, Massachusetts between 1999 and 2006. The first author of this chapter did her doctoral dissertation research on the Deaf Unit, studying the records of 64 deaf patients discharged between 1999 and 2004 (Black, 2005; Black & Glickman, 2006). Since this original work, 2 more years of Deaf Unit data (30 new deaf patients) became available and was factored into the same statistical analyses done in the original research.

The diagnostic assessments of deaf patients were all performed by psychiatrists assigned to the Deaf Unit. These psychiatrists all had established or developing expertise in clinical treatment of deaf people. They all worked with interpreters and were part of a clinical team specializing in psychiatric care of deaf people. Participants placed on this unit were either deaf or severely hard of hearing individuals, most of whom communicated in some variant of ASL or visual-gestural communication.

There was a hearing comparison group. This sample was used for comparisons of psychiatric diagnoses and of psychosocial risk and functioning scores, as measured by an instrument called the Clinical Evaluation of Risk and Functioning-Revised (CERF-R), described below. This sample consisted of all 180 hearing patients served at the hospital on one day in March 2006. The diagnoses of these patients were given by their treating psychiatrists and their CERF-R ratings by their respective clinical teams.

Table 1.1 General Demographic Variables for Deaf ($n = 94$) and
Hearing ($n = 180$) Patients

Variable	Deaf Patients		Hearing Patients	
	n	%	n	%
Gender				
Male	55	58.5	122	67.8
Female	39	41.5	58	32.2
Ethnicity				
African American	7	7.4	8	4.4
Asian	2	2.1	3	1.7
Caucasian	70	74.5	157	87.3
Hispanic	15	16	4	2.2
Others	0	0	8	4.4
Relationship Status				
Single	81	86.1	146	81.1
Married	6	6.4	3	1.7
Divorced	4	4.3	25	13.8
Widowed	2	2.1	2	1.1
Separated	1	1.1	1	.6
Unknown	0	0	3	1.7
Education				
Some Elementary	4	4.3	3	1.7
Graduated Elementary	6	6.4	2	1.1
Some HS	27	28.7	41	23
Graduated HS	27	28.7	38	21.1
GED	2	2.1	0	0
Some College	13	13.7	17	9.4
College Graduate	1	1.1	12	6.6
Masters Degree	4	4.3	2	1.1
Some Grad School	1	1.1	0	0
Special School	2	2.1	0	0
Technical School Grad.	1	1.1	0	0
Other	0	0	5	2.7
Unknown	6	6.4	60	33.3

Demographic information for both samples is presented in Table 1.1. The Deaf Unit is a statewide program and admits some patients from outside Massachusetts. It serves deaf persons with both acute and chronic psychiatric problems. The hospital as a whole serves people only from the Metro-suburban area of Massachusetts, roughly speaking the suburbs to the west and south of Boston. As a state psychiatric hospital, it serves primarily persons with severe and chronic forms of mental illness. The higher percentage of Hispanic and African Americans served on the Deaf Unit compared to the hearing units in the hospital is probably due to its drawing patients from urban areas throughout the state and not just from the relatively affluent suburbs surrounding the hospital. Particularly striking is the much higher percentages of Hispanic patients served on the Deaf Unit (16% compared with 2.2% in the hospital as a whole). The Deaf Unit also serves a more balanced mix of male and female patients whereas patients in the hospital as a whole are much more likely to be male. Both deaf and hearing patients were not likely to have been married, in roughly similar proportions.

Comparing educational achievement is trickier because many deaf patients attended residential schools where grade levels are not necessarily equivalent to hearing public schools. There is certainly a higher percentage of hearing patients with some postsecondary education (17.1% hearing vs. 4.8% deaf) though all of the patients tend to have lower levels of educational achievement.

Table 1.2 presents a comparison of diagnosis of deaf and hearing patients at Westborough. By using this archival data, the following analyses were made:

1. Demographic breakdown of deaf and hearing patients
2. Diagnostic breakdown of deaf and hearing patients
3. Frequency of trauma-related events in deaf and hearing patients
4. Cognitive functioning of deaf and hearing patients as measured by the Allen Cognitive Scale (ACL), described below
5. Communication abilities of deaf patients as rated by the unit's communication specialist using a communication scale
6. Psychosocial functioning of deaf and hearing patients as measured by the CERF-R scores from their respective teams

Frequency distributions were conducted to examine demographic variables, including the level of communication for deaf patients. Means and standard deviations were obtained for CERF-R scores, ACL scores, and DSM-IV diagnoses. *T*-tests were conducted to obtain mean differences on CERF-R scores and ACL scores for hearing and deaf patients upon admission.

Assessment Tools

American Psychiatric Association. (2000). Diagnostic and Statistical Manual of Mental Disorders (DSM-IV-TR, 2000) The DSM-IV-TR (American Psychiatric Association, 2000) is the standard classification system of mental health disorders used by professionals in the United States. Axis I contains clinical syndromes and Axis II consists developmental and personality disorders. For this study, Axis I and Axis II discharge diagnoses were obtained on deaf and hearing patients. For the analysis of Axis I diagnostic patterns, diagnoses were grouped under the major DSM-IV-TR disorder categories (that is, psychotic

Table 1.2 Frequency of DSM-IV Diagnosis for Deaf and Hearing Patients

Diagnosis	Deaf Patients n = 94		Hearing Patients n = 180	
	n	%	n	%
Axis I				
Mood Disorders				
Bipolar Disorder	8	8.5	17	9.4
Depression NOS	1	1.1	0	0
Depression (Secondary to Substance Abuse)	1	1.1	0	0
Major Depressive Disorder	17	18.1	15	8.3
Major Depression With Psychosis	3	3.2	0	0
Mood Disorder NOS	0	0	6	3.3
Total Mood Disorders	30	32.0	38	21.0
Anxiety Disorders				
Anxiety Disorder	2	2.1	3	1.7
Obsessive-Compulsive Disorder	6	6.4	1	0.6
Posttraumatic Stress Disorder	20	21.3	12	6.6
Total Anxiety Disorders	28	29.8	16	8.9
Somatoform Disorder				
Somatization Disorder	2	2.1	0	0
Psychotic Disorders				
Delusional Disorder	3	3.2	3	1.7
Psychotic Disorder	8	8.5	3	1.7
Schizoaffective	14	14.9	68	37.8
Schizophrenia	6	6.4	86	47.7
Total Psychotic Disorders	31	33.0	160	88.9
Dementia and Executive Functioning Disorders				
Dementia	0	0	14	7.7
Frontal Lobe Syndrome	0	0	1	0.6
Total Dementia and Executive Functioning Disorders	0	0	15	8.3
Impulse Control Disorders				
ADHD	1	1.1	2	1.1
Conduct Disorder	1	1.1	0	0
Hyperkinetic Syndrome NOS	0	0	1	0.6
Impulse Control Disorder	2	2.1	2	1.1
Intermittent Explosive Disorder	3	3.2	0	0
Total Impulse Control Disorders	7	7.5	5	2.8

(continued on next page)

Table 1.2 (continued) Frequency of DSM-IV Diagnosis for Deaf and Hearing Patients

	Deaf Patients n = 94		Hearing Patients n = 180	
Diagnosis	n	%	n	%
Eating Disorders				
Anorexia Nervosa	0	0	3	1.7
Eating Disorder NOS	0	0	2	1.1
Total Eating Disorders	**0**	**0**	**5**	**2.8**
Adjustment Disorder				
Adjustment Disorder	**5**	**5.3**	**0**	**0**
Sexual and Gender Identity Disorders				
Exhibitionism	0	0	1	0.6
Pedophilia	1	1.1	4	2.2
Total Sexual and Gender Identity Disorders	**1**	**1.1**	**5**	**2.8**
Substance Use Disorders				
Alcohol Abuse	8	8.5	13	7.2
Alcohol Dependence	2	2.1	30	16.7
Cocaine Abuse	0	0	3	1.7
Cocaine Dependence	0	0	3	1.7
Drug Abuse (unspecified)	0	0	8	4.4
Drug Dependence NOS	0	0	2	1.1
Marijuana Abuse	2	2.1	5	2.8
Marijuana Dependence	1	1.1	1	0.6
Polysubstance Abuse	7	7.4	8	4.4
Polysubstance Dependence	4	4.3	2	1.1
Total Substance Abuse Disorders	**24**	**25.5**	**75**	**41.7**

Axis II

	Deaf Patients		Hearing Patients	
Disorders First Diagnosed in Infancy, Childhood or Adolescence				
Aspergers	1	1.1	0	0
Borderline Intellection Functioning	7	7.4	0	0
Mental Retardation	18	19.1	8	4.4
Pervasive Developmental Disorder	6	6.4	4	2.2
Total Developmental Disorders	**32**	**34.0**	**12**	**6.6**
Personality Disorders				
Antisocial Personality Disorder	3	3.2	5	2.8
Antisocial Traits	3	3.2	0	0
Borderline Personality Disorder	11	11.7	12	6.6
Borderline Traits	4	4.3	0	0

Table 1.2 (continued) Frequency of DSM-IV Diagnosis for Deaf and Hearing Patients

Diagnosis	Deaf Patients n = 94		Hearing Patients n = 180	
	n	%	n	%
Dependent Personality Disorder	1	1.1	1	0.6
Dependent Personality Traits	2	2.1	0	0
Histrionic Personality Disorder	1	1.1	1	0.6
Narcissistic Personality Disorder	1	1.1	0	0
Narcissistic Personality Traits	1	1.1	0	0
Obsessive-Compulsive Traits	1	1.1	0	0
Paranoid Traits	1	1.1	0	0
Personality Disorder NOS	4	4.3	19	10.5
Schizoid Personality Disorder	1	1.1	1	0.6
Total Personality Disorders	34	36.5	39	21.7
No Diagnosis	2	2.1	0	0

Note: As some participants have multiple diagnoses, total *n* and percentage equal
more than 100.

disorders, mood disorders, and so on). Axis II data were analyzed in a similar fashion.

The Clinical Evaluation of Risk and Functioning Scale—Revised (CERF-R) The Clinical Evaluation of Risk and Functioning Scale-Revised (CERF-R) (Barry, Lambert, Vinter, & Fenby, 2007; Lambert et al., 1996, 1999) is an assessment tool designed by the clinician administrators of the Metro Suburban Area of the Massachusetts Department of Mental Health (DMH). It has been routinely used in the ongoing assessment of all hospitalized and community-based DMH hearing and deaf patients in east central Massachusetts since October 1999. Statewide release of the CERF-R began in January 2000.

The CERF-R provides a consistent, clear, valid, and reliable measure for recording assessment of patients' current risk levels, functional abilities, and intensity of services provided (Barry et al., 2007). The instrument is administered by a multidisciplinary team consisting of direct care staff, a nurse, a mental health clinician, the occupational therapist, a psychologist, the primary care physician, and the psychiatrist. On the Deaf Unit, the communication specialist is also a member of the team.

The CERF-R assesses nine functional abilities and seven risk factors, each of which is rated on a 6-point anchored Likert scale (see Appendices A and B at the end of this chapter for the rating scale and the full list of CERF-R items). A rating of "1" indicates no current problem behaviors in the area and a rating of "6" indicates a need for total supervision in this area by staff in order to prevent harmful behaviors. Thus lower scores reflect higher abilities and lower risk profiles. As the CERF-R is used for this study, a mean summary score of combined risk and functioning factors is given as well as a mean function items summary score and a mean risk items summary score. This breakdown indicates that the CERF-R functioning and risk scales can be examined independently as well as collectively.

Barry (2002) conducted reliability and validity testing on the CERF-R. He obtained interrater (interteam) reliability, high test–retest reliability, and high interitem reliability. A factor analysis yielded two factors: a functional ability factor and a risk factor. In addition, two clusters within the Risk Scale were identified: a risk of harm to others index and risk of harm to self index. Barry concluded that the factor analysis of the CERF-R, yielding factors relevant to the psychiatric commitment of persons, strengthened the instrument's construct validity.

The Allen Cognitive Levels Scale (ACL)   The ACL is an instrument commonly used by occupational therapists (Allen, Earhart, & Blue, 1992). The test yields information regarding a person's ability to learn, recognize and correct errors, and problem solve. The ACL provides a measure of cognitive ability that correlates with intelligence. It is used as a standard tool with patients upon admission to the Deaf Unit and on all hearing units at Westborough State Hospital. A strong point of the ACL is that it is a nonverbal test. It consists of a leather-lacing task in which the person is asked to replicate three stitch patterns of increasing complexity. Individuals' performances are rated on a 6-point scale from 0 to 6. The average range for this task falls between 5.4 and 5.8.

The ACL is found to have interrater reliability between .90 and .99 (Allen, Earhart, & Blue, 1992). In terms of validity, the ACL has been correlated with cognitive measures such as the Wechsler Adult Intelligence Scale (WAIS). Within the WAIS, Allen found the strongest correlations were between the ACL and Block Design and Object Assembly. Performance IQ also showed a high correlation with the ACL, a helpful finding because intelligence testing of deaf individuals with nonfluent English is most validly done using only the performance scales of the Wechsler or similar measures. Allen also reported that the ACL correlates significantly with functional abilities such as activities of daily living (ADLs), ability to live alone, social skills, and occupational functioning. These psychosocial functioning skills are also measured by the CERF-R.

Language Rating Scale   This study also included a measure of language abilities in the deaf patients. Deaf patients were interviewed by the Unit communication specialist, a Deaf near-native ASL user with linguistic training, and he classified patient communication skills into seven broad categories. In many cases, deaf patients were videotaped signing, and their sign language sample was evaluated by the communication specialist and lead interpreter working together. Because no validated ASL assessment tool was available for this research, these language assessments cannot be considered definitive. Nonetheless, the categories are broad enough and the language deficiencies usually obvious enough that we believe these conclusions have overall validity and utility. The seven categories of language skill are as follows:

1. Relies mainly on gesture, drawing, or other nonlinguistic means of communication.
2. Grossly limited or impaired language abilities. Very limited vocabulary, which is likely to include home signs. Signs using isolated signs or short sign phrases. Signs may be used incorrectly. Almost no grammatical structure.
3. Functional communication skills in a language but nonfluent. Has vocabulary sufficient for everyday conversation but misunderstandings are frequent. Consistent grammatical mistakes. Among these signers, some common errors are lack of topic/comment sentence structure and resulting confusion as to subject and object, poor use of time indicators and poor temporal sequencing, limited vocabulary with signs used incorrectly, unnecessary sign repetition instead of inflection, tendency to use short sign phrases rather than full sentences, inability to "code-switch" or modify signing to fit different receivers.
4. Fluent user of other spoken language such as Spanish or French.
5. Fluent user of spoken, written, or signed English. Command of English sufficient to affect signing. Signs generally in English word order. Generally lacks ASL grammatical features such as use of space, directionality, locatives, and sign inflection. May use some initialized signs.
6. Fluent user of ASL. Follows grammatical rules for ASL. Clear use of space, directionality, locatives, modifiers, and sign production.
7. Bilingual in ASL and spoken/written/signed English.

Deaf persons can be "language dysfluent" because of severe social and educational language deprivation, mental illness, or neurological problems (Pollard, 1998a). The communication specialist focused on gaps in language structure and function typically associated with language deprivation. This issue is discussed more fully in Pollard (1998a), Gulati (2003), and Black (2005), as well as in Chapter 2.

Results

DSM-IV-TR Diagnostic Results

A breakdown of DSM-IV-TR diagnoses is presented in Table 1.2. The most common diagnosis given for deaf patients was posttraumatic stress disorder

(PTSD) (n = 20; 21% of patients) followed by major depressive disorder (n = 17; 18% of patients). Overall, 32% (n = 30) of patients were diagnosed with at least one mood disorder, and 31 (33%) patients were diagnosed with a psychotic disorder. About a quarter of the patients were diagnosed with at least one substance abuse disorder and a third with a developmental disorder first evident in infancy, childhood, or adolescence, including mental retardation. Some individuals were diagnosed with personality traits that were close to meeting the criteria for personality disorders. If these were added along with full personality disorders, 37% (n = 34) of the deaf patients were diagnosed as personality disordered. If we only consider patients with full personality disorders, 22% (n = 21) meet criteria. In examining the diagnosis table, it is important to remember that most patients have more than one diagnosis.

Comparing the diagnoses of the 94 deaf patients treated over 7 years with the 180 hearing patients treated at one point in time produces some striking findings. *Psychotic disorders were diagnosed in 89% of the hearing patients but only 33% of the deaf patients.* Hearing patients also had a higher percentage of substance abuse disorders (41.7% hearing vs. 25.5% deaf). Deaf patients were much more likely to be diagnosed with a mood disorder (32% deaf vs. 21% hearing), an anxiety disorder (29.8% deaf vs. 8.8% hearing), a developmental disorder (34% deaf vs. 6.6% hearing), or a personality disorder/personality disorder trait (36.5% deaf vs. 21.6% hearing).

Of the deaf patients, 52% have a known history of abuse, as can be observed in Table 1.3a. An additional 11% of deaf patients had suspected abuse and 19% more could not be determined. One of the difficulties of working with deaf psychiatric patients is how often clear clinical histories are not available. Many deaf patients lack the language and cognitive abilities to provide a clear account of their lives, and reliable information from other sources is sometimes lacking. Case reports that accompany a patient may contain vague or unproven allegations of abuse. In the absence of reliable information, such vague reports tend to get passed along from one new assessment to another so that clients do not so much have a known history as they do a commonly accepted story. Our suspicion is that the incidence of trauma is much higher. Besides having known traumatic experiences, 21.3% of deaf patients were

Table 1.3a Frequency in Trauma-Related Events in Deaf Patients (n = 94)

Trauma in Deaf Patients	Abuse		Suspected		Unknown		PTSD	
	n	%	n	%	n	%	n	%
Physical Abuse Only	14	14.9	1	1.1	7	7.4	2	2.1
Sexual Abuse Only	20	21.3	8	8.5	5	5.3	9	9.6
Combined Physical and Sexual	15	15.9	1	1.1	6	6.4	9	9.6
Total	**49**	**52.1**	**10**	**10.7**	**18**	**19.1**	**20**	**21.3**

Table 1.3b Frequency in Trauma-Related Events
in Hearing Patients

Trauma in Hearing Patients	n	%
Any Trauma History	88	48.8
History of Emotional Trauma	49	27.2
Exposure to Acute Trauma	23	12.7
History of Physical Abuse	48	26.6
History of Rape	24	13.3
History of Sexual Abuse	34	18.8
History of Sexual Assault	25	13.8
Patients Diagnosed with PTSD	12	6.66

diagnosed with current PTSD. Data on trauma in hearing patients are presented in Table 1.3b.

Unfortunately, the way the hospital obtained and organized data changed between the time the data on the deaf and hearing patients were obtained. This means that the deaf and hearing data are not completely comparable. The categories overlap in ways that make direct comparisons difficult. However, a higher percentage of deaf patients (21.3%) were diagnosed with PTSD than the hearing patients (6.6%). In both deaf and hearing groups, there is a significantly higher number of patients with known trauma histories than were diagnosed with PTSD. This is to be expected as traumatic experiences do not always lead to PTSD. In the deaf group, 52.1% had a known history of trauma yet only 21.3% had a PTSD diagnosis. In the hearing sample, 48.8% had a history of trauma and 6.7% had this diagnosis. Because the data on hearing patients were collected in 2006, at a time when trauma information was a formal part of assessment, these data should actually be more reliable than the data on deaf patients collected between 1999 and 2006. For most of this period, an assessment tool was used that placed less emphasis on inquiry into trauma history and symptoms.

Cognitive Functioning

ACL scores were obtained on 89 of the 94 deaf patients. Table 1.4 presents the frequency of the occurrences of these scores. ACL scores ranged from 3.2 to 5.8 with a mean of 4.78 and a standard deviation of 1.27. Allen (1992) classifies levels 5.4 to 5.8 as within the average range of functioning. As can be seen, 63% of the deaf participants fell within the average range whereas 32% of individuals fell below this range (5% were unknown).

Means and standard deviations for ACL scores were obtained on 89 of the deaf patients and on 93 hearing patients. The 93 hearing patients are from the sample of 180 served during March 2006, but there were no ACL scores reported on the other 87 patients. The mean score for deaf patients was 4.6,

Table 1.4 Frequency of ACL Scores (Cognitive Functioning) in Deaf and Hearing Patients

ACL Score	Deaf n = 94		Hearing n v93	
	n	%	n	%
2.5	0	0	3	3.2
2.7	0	0	2	2.2
3.0	0	0	1	1.1
3.1	0	0	1	1.1
3.2	1	1.1	4	4.3
3.3	1	1.1	4	4.3
3.4	0	0	7	7.5
3.5	0	0	3	3.2
3.6	3	3.2	6	6.5
3.7	1	1.1	2	2.2
3.8	2	2.1	4	4.3
4.0	2	2.1	6	6.5
4.1	3	3.2	4	4.3
4.2	6	6.4	9	9.4
4.3	1	1.1	0	0
4.4	10	10.6	7	7.5
4.5	1	1.1	3	3.2
4.6	7	7.4	5	5.4
4.7	1	1.1	2	2.2
4.8	5	5.3	3	3.2
5.0	6	6.4	6	6.5
5.2	9	9.6	5	5.4
5.3	0	0	1	1.1
5.4	18	19	3	3.2
5.6	1	1.1	0	0
5.7	0	0	1	1.1
5.8	11	11.7	1	1.1
Unknown	5	5.3	0	0

with a standard deviation of 1.19. The mean score for hearing patients was 4.1 with a standard deviation of 0.76. A t-test indicated a significant difference between the deaf and hearing patients, $t(155) = -5.6$, $p < .001$) Scores for both the hearing and deaf groups scored indicate a below average level of cognitive functioning.

Hearing patients received a significantly lower score than deaf patients on the ACL. Why might this be so? The hearing patients are almost all persons with severe and chronic mental illness whereas the deaf patients include persons with both acute and chronic psychiatric problems. The ACL is also a very visual task. Its use is demonstrated to both deaf and hearing patients with spoken or signed explanations given as needed. No ACL data were available on 87 of the 180 hearing patients sampled, and the Unit occupational therapist reports that many hearing patients find the task unpleasant and refuse it. In contrast, not one Deaf Unit patient in 9 years has refused this task (though it could not be administered to visually impaired clients), and most seem to find it interesting and challenging. It is quite possible that the ACL comparison findings would be quite different if we had data on the nearly half of hearing patients who refused the task.

The mean ACL score of the deaf patients was 4.6. According to Allen (Allen, Blue, & Earhart, 1995), at this level, the person functions as follows:

a. Needs assistance with transportation
b. Requires supervision with medication administration
c. Requires assistance with balanced meal planning, shopping, and cooking
d. Needs assistance recognizing hazards in the environment
e. May need reminders to wash and dress regularly and appropriately and assistance with laundry
f. May require total or close supervision on money management
g. Requires cues to assist with staying focused on a task

Among the deaf patients, only 32% achieve the minimum ACL level needed to drive (5.4). About 63% of deaf patients are at or below 5.2, a level at which a coach is needed for the patient to succeed in supportive employment. According to the ACL interpretative guidelines, these patients cannot live alone without, at a minimum, someone checking in on them regularly. (Table 1.4 contains the ACL frequency scores for deaf and hearing patients.)

Communication Scores of Deaf Patients

Communication scores were examined and are presented in Table 1.5. Scores ranged from 2 to 7 with a mean score of 3.60 and a standard deviation of 1.46.

Table 1.5 Frequency of Degree of Communication Scores ($n = 94$)

Degree of Communication Score	n	Percent
1. Visual/Gestural	0	0
2. Grossly Impaired/Limited Vocabulary	22	23.4
3. Functional but Nonfluent	40	42.5
4. Fluent Foreign Language	1	1.1
5. Fluent English (sign, speech, writing)	22	23.4
6. ASL Fluent	3	3.2
7. ASL and English Fluent	6	6.4

Table 1.6 Psychosocial Functioning Scores (CERF-R Admission Scores) of Deaf and Hearing Patients: Mean and Standard Deviation

Variable	Deaf		Hearing	
	Mean	SD	Mean	SD
Summary Score on Admission	49.41	10.34	53.11	19.99
Functioning Items Summary on Admission	29.56	7.33	33.08	10.67
Risk Items Summary on Admission	18.00	4.92	20.03	9.32
a. Hygiene	2.10	1.22	2.31	1.28
b. Nutrition	3.02	1.1	2.78	1.25
c. Personal Finances	3.64	1.40	3.67	1.56
d. Holding a Job	4.20	1.35	5.19	1.11
e. Negotiating a Social Situation	3.90	.98	3.44	1.10
f. Pursuing Appropriate Independence	3.96	1.10	4.36	1.03
g. Using Services that Promote Recovery	3.74	.99	3.77	1.29
h. Appropriate Use of Psychiatric Medication	4.30	1.32	4.95	0.68
i. Recognizing and Avoiding Common Hazards	2.94	1.25	2.61	1.36
j. Physical Violence Toward Others	3.49	1.39	3.16	1.28
k. Committing Sexual Offenses	1.90	1.53	1.31	0.83
l. Deliberate Self-Harm	3.11	1.56	2.06	1.33
m. Significance Consequences Others Behaviors	3.13	1.68	3.36	1.38
n. Substance Use	2.39	1.67	3.34	1.74
o. Leaving Services Prematurely	3.01	1.29	3.17	1.58
p. Poor Impulse Control	3.85	1.05	3.63	1.18

The most significant finding here is that, according to the classifications of the Deaf Unit communication specialist, *66% of Deaf Unit patients could be classified as language deprived or language dysfluent.* The largest category had "functional" sign language skills and the second largest had "grossly impaired" sign communication abilities. Only 9.6% of the patients were judged as either fluent in ASL or bilingual in ASL and English, though 23.4% were judged to be fluent English users.

Data from the CERF-R on psychosocial risk and functioning of deaf and hearing patients are presented in Table 1.6. Level of communication scores was correlated with the functioning and risk scores of clients as measured on the CERF-R. We hypothesized that the communication scores would correlate significantly with both the risk and functioning scales independently. Results found a significant correlation between communication scores and average scores for the functioning scales and scores on individual functioning scales.

Table 1.7 Intercorrelations Between Level of Communication and CERF-R Functioning Items Summary on Admission and CERF Risk Items Summary on Admission ($n = 94$)

Variable	1	2	3
1. Degree of Communication		−.50**	.07
2. CERF Functioning Items Summary on Admission			.36
3. CERF Risk Items Summary on Admission	.		

Note: **$p < .01$ (one-tailed).

Table 1.8 Intercorrelations Between Degree Of Communication and Individual CERF-R Functioning and Risk Items on Admission ($n = 94$)

Variable	Degree of Communication
A. Hygiene on Admission	−.232**
B. Nutrition on Admission	−.314**
C. Personal Finances on Admission	−.474**
D. Holding a Job on Admission	−.396**
E. Negotiating a Social Situation on Admission	-.377**
F. Pursuing Appropriate Independence on Admission	−.442**
G. Using Services that Promote Recovery on Admission	−.184*
H. Appropriate Use of Psychiatric Med. on Admission	−.183*
I. Recognizing and Avoiding Common Hazards on Admission	−.216**
J. Physical Violence Toward Others on Admission	−.194*
K. Committing Sexual Offenses on Admission	−.087
L. Deliberate Self-Harm on Admission	.204*
M. Significance Consequences Others Behavior on Admission	−.119
N. Substance Use on Admission	.163*
O. Leaving Services Prematurely on Admission	−.057
P. Poor Impulse Control on Admission	−.148

Note: *p < .05, **p < .01. Items A through I are on the functioning scale. Items J through P are on the risk scale.

As expected, poor communication and poor psychosocial functioning appear correlated. This validates the definitions of traditionally underserved deaf that have been offered. This is presented in Table 1.7.

Communication scores did *not*, however, correlate with average scores on the risk subscales. As can be seen on Table 1.8, communication scores did correlate significantly with the scores on three risk subscales: deliberate self-harm ($r = .204$, $p < .05$), substance use ($r = .163$, $p < .05$), and risk of harm to others ($r = -.194$, $p < .05$). The correlations show that those with a higher level of communication skill had a higher risk of self-harm and substance use. Those with a lower level of communication had a higher risk of harm to others. There was no correlation between language skills and other kinds of risk such as the risk of committing sexual offenses, poor impulse control, and leaving services prematurely.

Discussion and Conclusions

Since the earliest studies of deaf persons in psychiatric hospitals, clinicians have noticed that at least some of the patients seemed different from their hearing peers. The most obvious and expected difference is communication abilities. In an era before public recognition of ASL, the Deaf Community, and Deaf culture, and before clinicians could be expected to have any skill in sign communication, it was an all too easy and common mistake to draw conclusions about language skills (and worse, mental status) based on samples of written English. Deaf people were, and in most of the world still are, hospitalized in settings where neither peers nor staff can communicate with them in their language or best communication modality, and where staff has no special expertise or sensitivity to deaf people. Conclusions continue to be drawn about deaf psychiatric patients, and from there, about deaf people, without appreciation for the effects of this oppressive context, and without appreciation that deaf psychiatric patients are no more representative of deaf people than hearing psychiatric patients are of hearing people.

Conclusions drawn about deaf psychiatric patients must always be taken with some caution even when they come from staff in established Deaf treatment centers because, even there, there is no standard way to guarantee clinical and communication expertise of particular clinicians. We are not yet at the point as a field that we have some credentialing process for deafness mental health professionals that would allow us to be confident of at least minimal levels of specialized knowledge and skills. Even established deafness mental health programs can have difficulty hiring appropriately qualified staff. Labor contracts, civil service guidelines, and other employment practices may prevent qualified persons from being hired when they are available. The assignment of psychiatrists to a Deaf Unit, for instance, may have much more to do with internal personnel matters than with demonstrated expertise in working with deaf people.

There is also a tendency in this field for clinicians doing this work to be considered expert much too quickly. One sees this in the ways that people turn to beginning signers to interpret for them. The second author of this chapter recalls with embarrassment a time, very early in his deafness career, when he was asked to interpret at a National Association of the Deaf convention. Ignorant about sign language and filled with grandiose notions about his own abilities, he agreed to do so, and he still has images of deaf people walking out of the room in the meeting he was "interpreting." Sadly, this kind of mistake is repeated by new hearing signers all the time. New hearing clinicians, by virtue of working with small numbers of deaf people, may suddenly find themselves touted as the local mental health deafness resource. All too quickly they may assume this role. The result is that there is very little quality control in this field, and the quality of service provision is notoriously uneven.

Nonetheless, the research conducted here, viewed in light of previous research, does answer many questions. We see, in particular, how much can be explained by noting the presence of the traditionally underserved deaf subgroup in our population sample. This group is heavily represented at the Westborough Deaf Unit, and there is every reason to believe it is heavily represented wherever there are specialized deafness mental health, rehabilitation, or educational services. These persons will be mental health patients in one setting, rehabilitation clients in another, difficult to serve students in another; and in all these settings staff will exert great effort to adapt assessment and intervention approaches. Inevitably, these are the clients that we spend most of our time struggling to find means to help.

Returning to the data from the Westborough Deaf Unit, noteworthy findings are the relatively broad range of psychopathology as well as the relatively low frequency of psychotic disorders. This finding is consistent with Daigle's (1994) and Robinson's (1978) study of deaf patients on other deaf inpatient units. It is also consistent with Pollard's (1994) finding that clinicians in non-deaf treatment settings gave a more narrow range of diagnoses to deaf and hard of hearing clients than to hearing clients. These findings support the conclusion that when clinicians without specialized training in work with deaf people encounter deaf clients, they are likely to think about their client problems through narrow, restrictive lenses. They are less able to bring their full range of diagnostic skills to this task. By contrast, deafness mental health specialists are less likely to find psychosis and more likely to find a range of less severe psychiatric problems in their deaf clients.

Probably the most striking and important finding from the Deaf Unit study is the huge contrast between the percentages of deaf clients diagnosed with a major psychotic disorder (33%) and the percentages of hearing clients in the hospital with these diagnoses (89%). Westborough State Hospital, it should be recalled, is a state psychiatric facility and would be assumed to treat more persons with severe and chronic mental illnesses than private, acute care psychiatric settings. This finding should not be interpreted to mean that deaf people are any more or less inclined to major mental illnesses because the Deaf Unit, as the only inpatient psychiatric program for deaf persons in New England, serves clients who, if they were hearing, would be in private, acute care settings. The finding does suggest that most of the deaf persons referred to psychiatric hospitals are not suffering from major mental illnesses. In a nonspecialized setting, they are easily misdiagnosed and presumed to have disorders like schizophrenia. In Chapter 2, we explore how language dysfluency related to language deprivation makes them especially vulnerable to such misdiagnosis.

If most are not suffering from major mental illnesses, what kinds of psychiatric problems do they have? The diagnostic data are also striking for the contrast between the percentage of deaf patients diagnosed with a developmental disorder such as mental retardation (34%) and the percentage for hearing patients in the hospital (7%). Trybus (1983) also found a higher percentage of mental retardation diagnosed in deaf patients (30%) than hearing patients (2%). At Springfield Hospital, Daigle found that 10% of the deaf patients were diagnosed as mentally retarded whereas none of the hearing patients received this diagnosis.

The assumption is often made that higher incidences of diagnoses of psychotic disorders and mental retardation in deaf patients are due to unqualified examiners doing inappropriate assessments. This research suggests that, while improper assessment may play a role, higher incidence of developmental problems such as mental retardation in the deaf inpatient population is more likely to be accurate. By contrast, higher rates of psychotic disorders in deaf clients, such as that reported by Altshuler and Rainer (1968), are likely to be inaccurate.

Evidence of generally low cognitive functioning in the deaf inpatient population is provided by testing using the ACL, where the mean score of 4.6 points to people needing a great deal of assistance in daily functioning. The incidence of deaf persons with mental retardation on the unit is influenced more by admission policies than by the accuracy of cognitive assessments. In Massachusetts, persons with mental retardation are served by the Department of Mental Retardation, not the Department of Mental Health (DMH). Under what circumstances persons with mental retardation can be admitted to a DMH state psychiatric hospital is a policy matter. The local answer at Westborough State Hospital has been that deaf persons with mental retardation could be admitted *for treatment of a mental illness*. This seems reasonable, but the referrals of deaf persons with mental retardation are almost always due to severe behavioral problems. The assessment question is whether such behavioral problems in a person with mental retardation are themselves evidence of mental illness or, as it is sometimes said, whether they are "just behavioral." In practice, we could screen these clients in or out based on whether we conclude their behavioral problems are evidence of mental illness. Strictly speaking, they are usually not evidence of mental illness, but this does not mean these clients cannot benefit from the services of a specialty inpatient unit designed around the needs of people just like them.

Because case managers at the Department of Mental Retardation have no other inpatient resource to draw on for their deaf clients with severe behavioral problems, they advocate for these clients to be admitted to the only state program with the resources to assess and treat them. Indeed, it would not be hard to get the numbers of deaf persons with mental retardation served on the unit to be even higher simply by screening in more of these referrals. *These data support the conclusion that deaf persons served in psychiatric hospitals are far more likely than hearing patients to have mental retardation, and that this may not be a result of inappropriate assessment. Rather, it is a result of there being a cohort of deaf persons with severe language and learning problems, some of whom are mentally retarded, showing severe behavioral problems and the local psychiatric hospital being regarded as the best resource for their care.*

Even if deaf clients do not have diagnosed developmental disorders such as mental retardation, they are far more likely than hearing clients to be suffering from other developmental problems. The most striking developmental problem is language impairment due to inadequate exposure to natural sign languages. Although the assessment criteria used on the Deaf Unit are crude, it is nonetheless striking that two thirds (66%) of the deaf patients were judged by the communication specialist to be nonfluent users of any language. Examples of what this looks like are presented in Chapter 2. Language problems are the most important criteria in defining the group of traditionally underserved deaf persons. The developmental problems we see include poor academic, vocational, social, and independent living functioning. The presenting problem and reason for referral is usually a longstanding behavioral disorder with a recent, severe behavioral outburst. *Thus, most of the patients we see are not suffering from a recent psychotic break or other forms of severe mental illness. Rather, they have developmentally based behavioral problems usually associated with significant language deprivation.* This is why so many deaf mental health programs have struggled with how to diagnose this population and why they have come up with new diagnostic categories like "primitive personalities" (Rainer & Altshuler, 1966). *The problems they are working with are primarily developmental in nature as opposed to being acute psychiatric disorders, although of course the latter also occur.*

Relative to hearing patients at Westborough State Hospital, the deaf patients were also more likely to be diagnosed with a mood disorder (32% deaf vs. 21% hearing), anxiety disorder (29.8% deaf vs. 8.9% hearing), impulse control disorder (7.5% deaf vs. 2.8% hearing), or personality disorder (36.5% deaf vs. 21.7% hearing). They were less likely than hearing patients to be diagnosed with a substance abuse disorder (25.5% deaf vs. 41.7% hearing). It is also striking that there were no deaf patients diagnosed with any eating disorder during this period. The second author cannot recall, in the 15 years of his tenure, even one deaf patient who had problems with anorexia.*

Attention to trauma in both deaf and hearing populations are relatively recent phenomena and the data are not as solid as we would like. In the deaf

---

* This raises the question of whether the incidence of eating disorders, especially anorexia, is lower in people who are deaf from birth or early life. Might deafness and the fund of information gaps that accompany language deprivation serve, ironically, to protect deaf adolescents from cultural messages that promote such eating disorders?

population, there were known incidences of physical or sexual abuse in 52.1% of deaf patients, suspected abuse in another 10.7%, and another 19.1% where no information was available (and the patient was not a reliable reporter). We have found the challenge of getting reliable, accurate information about trauma in our deaf patients to be formidable but our suspicion is that the incidence is higher than reported here. Actual PTSD was diagnosed in 21.3% of deaf patients and 6.7% of hearing patients. Both numbers are thought to be gross underestimates.

Although there are clear criteria for PTSD, the willingness of a psychiatrist to diagnose PTSD often goes beyond whether a patient demonstrates what are often viewed as narrow diagnostic criteria. Herman (1992), among others, considered the effects of trauma more broadly; and given that so many of the problems that deaf patients present are developmental, trauma is often presumed to be a causal factor. Thus, to make sense of diagnostic conclusions regarding trauma, one needs to know not only how solid the historical information is, but also what criteria the clinician is using to make the diagnosis. Our sense is that there is still enough ambiguity in assessments made at the hospital with regard to what information is available, what is considered trauma, and how PTSD is defined, that conclusions about trauma should be considered very tentative. Clear comparisons between trauma in deaf and hearing patients is probably premature except insofar as one considers the impact of abuse on a child without adequate language skills. Without the resource of language with which to make sense of trauma, the psychological damage inflicted by physical and sexual abuse would presumably be much greater. The expectations would be that the damage would take the form, at least, of attachment problems and behavioral disorders. In adulthood, these attachment problems are often diagnosed as personality disorders.

Both deaf and hearing inpatients had low levels of psychosocial and cognitive functioning but the cause appears to be different. The cognitive functioning of the hearing patients appeared to be compromised primarily by psychotic disorders whereas that of deaf patients appeared to be compromised primarily by language and other developmental problems. This is a very important difference.

The correlations between language scores and functioning in areas like hygiene, nutrition, personal finances, holding a job, and independent living provide further evidence of how central language fluency is to adequate psychosocial functioning. The correlational data also showed that persons with language fluency were more likely to exhibit self-harming behaviors while persons with language dysfluency were more likely to exhibit problems in aggression with others.* Why should poor language skills predispose one more to aggression toward others than oneself? Perhaps it takes a certain amount of

---

* Self-harming behaviors also had a significant correlation with PTSD, major depression, borderline personality disorder, and higher education levels.

language skills to engage in an internal dialogue in which one blames oneself. Perhaps with language dysfluency, it is more natural for persons to blame others and to have difficulty seeing their own role in their problems. We do see that many traditionally underserved deaf persons are difficult to engage in mental health treatment partially because they do not readily own responsibility for their problems. The challenge of engaging these clients, given this attribution style of blaming others, is explored further in Chapter 4.

In summary, deaf psychiatric inpatients are not just like hearing psychiatric inpatients except that they cannot hear and may use sign. Serving them requires more than the provision of sign interpreters. As a whole, the deaf adult inpatients have a different set of assets and problems, more akin to those of severely troubled adolescents (see Chapter 3). Some will be fluent users of ASL and will have language skills their hearing nonsigning staff cannot appreciate. They may also have cultural values, such as the appreciation of signed over spoken communication, or the belief that deafness represents a cultural difference, that their hearing staff may be unlikely to validate. Most, however, are likely to be language dysfluent related to experiences of language deprivation, a phenomenon with which clinicians outside of the deafness field will almost certainly be unfamiliar. These language issues make these clients particularly vulnerable to being mischaracterized as psychotic. The language dysfluency issues make meaningful communication, the heart of mental health treatment, problematic, even with the provision of sign language interpreters.

Although the Westborough Deaf Unit occasionally admits deaf individuals with a college or even graduate degree, these deaf persons often prefer to be admitted elsewhere. Even with the communication access that a Deaf Unit provides, higher functioning deaf persons often have concerns about being grouped with lower functioning peers and with the issue of confidentiality. They may know the staff on the unit, and in some cases they may have even worked as counselors with patients who are then on the unit. Higher functioning deaf persons may also have a relatively easier time in hearing settings with interpreters provided; although this may also be a myth (see DeVinney, 2003). The lower functioning persons are much harder for nondeaf programs to serve, tend not to stabilize quickly or easily, and so are more likely to get referred to specialized Deaf treatment programs.

We hypothesize that it is this group of lower functioning or traditionally underserved deaf people that have provided the most assessment and treatment challenges in mental health, rehabilitation, and educational settings. While hearing persons can also have severe language and learning challenges, there is no equivalent group among the hearing, and it is their presence, more than any other matter, that makes mental health care of deaf people unique. Nonspecialized settings are completely unprepared for such clients and will not have an appropriate framework with which to understand or treat them. Clinicians in nonspecialized mental health settings, for instance, will likely view them through the lens of severe mental illness when really their problems are much more developmental, language, and probably trauma based. They will also put them in treatment groups with, at best, a sign language interpreter without understanding that the interpreter cannot bridge the huge chasm in language and conceptual worlds.*

In Chapter 2, we look more closely at the nature of the language dysfluency we see and discuss how it confounds diagnostic assessment. In Chapter 3, we examine the kinds of language and learning challenges that hearing adolescent psychiatric inpatients have. Our deaf patients have these challenges also but they have them in addition to language dysfluency related to language deprivation. The effects of this language deprivation are usually so pronounced that it can be difficult to tease out more subtle problems such as attention and learning disabilities. However, there are enough similarities between deaf and hearing patients with language and learning challenges to help us appreciate the need to adapt significantly the nature of mental health interventions we attempt with both groups. Adapting best practices in mental health care for traditionally underserved deaf persons is very similar to adapting treatment for severely disturbed hearing children except that hearing children usually have better language skills. We mean, of course, nothing disparaging by this comment. Chapters 4 through 7 present a model of how to adapt cognitive-behavioral therapy for this groups which we prefer to call *language and learning challenged.*

Appendix A

CERF-R Rating Scale

Functional Abilities

    A. Currently able to maintain adequate hygiene (cleanliness of body, clothing, and living space)

    B. Currently able to maintain appropriate nutrition (eating a balanced diet, food shopping, and cooking)

    C. Currently able to manage personal finances

    D. Currently able to hold a job

    E. Currently able to negotiate social situations

    F. Currently able to pursue appropriate independence (including accepting changes)

    G. Currently able to use services that promote recovery (such as housing, employment, substance abuse and mental health services)

---

* See LaVigne and Vernon (2003), Vernon and Miller (2001), Vernon and Raifman (1997) for a discussion about how interpreters are also an insufficient way to provide access to legal proceedings for these persons.

H. Currently able to use psychiatric medications as needed
I. Currently able to recognize and avoid common hazards and danger-ous interpersonal situations (traffic and smoking safety, being vic-timized, exposure to elements, and so on)

Risk Factors

J. Current risk for physical violence toward others
K. Current risk for committing sexual offenses (sexual violence, sexual threats, exposure, stalking, harassment)
L. Current risk for deliberate self-harm (self-injury, suicide)
M. Current risk of significant consequences from other unacceptable behavior (illegal or socially disturbing behavior such as victimizing others, property damage, harassment, theft, or arson)
N. Current risk of harm due to substance use
O. Current risk of leaving services prematurely (stop attending needed services, wandering from home or program, escaping from secure settings, and so on)
P. Current risk of harm due to poor impulse control

Appendix B

CERF-R Rating Scale

Ratings of Functional Abilities (Items A to I)   The language of the scale point anchors for functional abilities is designed to emphasize the client's strengths. Some items cover more than one skill, and occasionally a client will be stron-ger with some skills than with others covered by the same item. In such cases, base the rating on the skill where the client needs the most assistance.

Fully Able. The client currently demonstrates complete independence and full personal responsibility for the area of functioning specified. A rating of 1 on any given item is completely independent of ratings on any other item. Therefore, even CERF-R profiles with many 6 ratings almost always contain one or more 1 ratings.

Mostly Able. The client currently demonstrates a willingness and ability to be independent and self-sufficient for the area of functioning specified most of the time, but benefits from occasional assistance such as advice or periodic prompts. Individuals functioning at this level often recognize when assistance is needed and seek the help accordingly. In the general population of all people living in the United States, many persons with no diagnosed serious mental illness would likely receive a rating of 2 on at least one CERF-R item.

1. *Somewhat Able.* The client often demonstrates the ability in question, but lapses are frequent enough that regular assistance is desirable. Such a person benefits sufficiently from structure and interpersonal supports that external controls are not needed, but shows less initiative

than is needed for a rating of 2. Someone living in the general population who was not receiving these services would probably call attention to themselves in daily life for this particular functional ability.

2. *Marginally Able*. The client may have some skills in this area, but frequently needs close supervision and verbal redirection before actually using them. In the absence of such help such clients are unlikely to seek it, which makes it probable that in time they will come to the attention of the authorities for lapses in this particular functional ability. However, this person consistently responds to verbal redirection, unlike the person rated 5.

3. *Rarely Able*. Regardless of whether or not this person has any skills in this area, the person shows such poor judgment or rejects help so frequently that verbal redirection or guidance is not always sufficient to maintain well-being in this one area alone. External controls are generally needed to maintain the safety or well-being of the client. However, ratings do not reflect whether the person is currently receiving any specific services. Rather, the rating is an assessment of what would be appropriate to maintain well-being based on current behavior and mental status. It is the person's ability that is being rated, not the caregivers' response to the ability. A person living alone without services may still be rated a 5 or 6.

4. *Not Able*. This rating reflects a complete inability to care for oneself in this one particular ability area. As a result, such clients are completely dependent on others to meet their needs adequately in this area, such as being hand-fed by others (Item B, Nutrition), bathed by others (Item A, Hygiene), having a financial custodian or guardian (Item C, Personal Finances), or requiring near-constant visual surveillance to avoid accidental harm (Item I, Common Hazards). However, it is the ability that is being rated, not the type of services already in place. For example, if you believe a client with Alzheimer's disease needs constant supervision to prevent wandering, but the client is currently living independently without services, the correct rating is still 6.

Ratings of Risk Factors (Items J to P)

1. *Not an Issue*. This person does not pose a risk in this one area, and if such people have impulses to behave in risky ways they are able to control them without assistance. This may be because they are not prone to this particular type of risky behavior. It may also be because they are only prone to this particular type of behavior under certain conditions that are not current. For example, someone who shows

risky behavior during manic or psychotic episodes, but who is *currently* stable, would receive a rating of 1 if the person were able to control his or her behavior *without any assistance* from others. Ratings on each item are independent, and it is extremely unusual for an accurate CERF-R rating to have no ratings of 1 for any risk factors, even for extremely dangerous individuals. For example, dangerous sexual predators are rarely suicide risks, and lethally suicidal individuals are rarely rapists (although exceptions surely exist).

2. *Minimal Risk.* This person currently demonstrates the ability to use internal controls to prevent risky behavior in this area, but may seek occasional help to bolster his or her efforts. The initiative shown in seeking help is important in distinguishing 2 from 3. As with Functional Abilities, many people in the general population would receive at least one rating of 2 for risk.

3. *Low Risk.* This person is usually able to use internal controls, but frequently needs external assistance such as prompts, external structure, or other community or professional help. There is less initiative shown than for 2, but no need for the close supervision that 4 describes to control the risk. Someone in this range who lived independently in the community would be likely to have life difficulties. Such individuals might or might not come to the attention of caregivers or the authorities, but in the absence of supports, they might act in extremely risky ways.

4. *Moderate Risk.* This person is likely to exhibit risky behavior in the absence of close supervision or redirection as needed. Active intervention by others is needed to maintain safety. The distinction between 4 and 5 is that a person rated 4 will usually respond to verbal redirection, and will rarely need any kind of physical intervention for lapses in this one area alone.

5. *High Risk.* Regardless of whether or not these individuals have insight in this area, they act in risky ways in spite of external controls. Such controls might be environmental (such as locked doors) or interpersonal (close supervision). Unlike 4, verbal redirection or guidance is not always sufficient to maintain safety in this one area alone. The types of external controls may include those discussed for 6, but they are generally effective in controlling the risky behavior. What is important is not the person's current level of care, but rather that the rater believes that external controls are warranted to maintain safety based on current behavior and mental status. It is the risk to self or others that is being rated, not the caregivers' response to the risk. A person living alone without services may still be rated 5 or 6.

6. *Extreme Risk.* This person is an extreme danger to self or others for this one type of risky behavior alone, and is likely to act in ways that have serious medical or legal consequences in spite of external controls. If receiving care, such individuals are likely to need frequent 1:1 supervision, physical or chemical restraints, restriction to locked care settings, or other similarly intense interventions to maintain safety.

2

Do You Hear Voices?

Problems in Assessment of Mental Status in Deaf
Persons With Severe Language Deprivation[*]

Introduction

When people undergo an emergency psychiatric evaluation or are admitted
to a psychiatric hospital, the clinicians evaluating them will try to determine
whether they have a mental illness. They will perform a "mental status exam"
to see whether the patient has a thought disorder, one indication of mental
illness. The mental status exam is essentially an attempt to get inside the head
of the person and understand how he or she thinks. The clinician will draw
conclusions based on observations of behavior, reports from others, and, most
importantly, by listening to what patients say and how they say it. Among
other things, the clinician will be looking for evidence of *language dysfluency*,
of odd, unusual expressions of language, because these are often indicators of
mental illness.

What happens when the patient is a person who became deaf at birth or in
the first year or so of life and who did not receive adequate exposure to American Sign Language (ASL)? This person will probably show a great deal of language dysfluency in their best means of communication, usually sign, and far
worse language problems in a spoken language like English. How do mental
health clinicians make sense of the language patterns of these patients? How
can they determine whether language problems are due to mental illness, language deprivation, both, or some other factors?

Example: A Psychiatric Patient With Severe Language Problems

Juanita is a 23-year-old deaf, mild to moderately retarded woman who was
placed in the Westborough (Massachusetts) State Hospital Deaf Unit after
demonstrating severe behavioral problems in her group residence. She grew
up in a developing country where, as far as we know, she received little education or sign language exposure. Upon arrival in the United States at age 13,

---

[*] An earlier version of this chapter was printed in Glickman, N. (2007). Do you hear voices?
Problems in assessment of mental status in deaf persons with severe language deprivation. *Journal of Deaf Studies and Deaf Education. 12*(2), 127–147.

she was placed in a residential program for deaf persons with emotional and behavioral problems where staff used ASL. We know she experienced physical and sexual abuse as a child.

On arrival to the Deaf Unit, Juanita is interviewed by the clinical team which includes deaf and hearing clinicians with extensive experience in treatment of deaf people. The team also includes expert interpreters, trained in mental health interpreting, and a Deaf communication specialist, a near-native signer who works as a Deaf interpreter, simplifying sign language and gesture for deaf persons without full ASL abilities. When the team interviews Juanita, they notice right away that her sign language is poor. It is very difficult, even for the communication specialist and top level interpreters, to understand her fully.

At a later point in her treatment, the team decides to get a language sample to study in more depth. After securing the needed permission, the communication specialist and interpreters interview her and videotape her responses.* She is interviewed about her family and life, and at one point the interviewers deliberately ask her abstract questions with vocabulary they know she does not know. Their purpose is to see how she handles a question she does not understand. For instance, does she sign, "I don't understand. What do you mean?"

Interviewer:	What's your favorite food?
Juanita:	H-I-A-T-H-T-I-A-H-T-I FISH R-I-C-E, R-I-C-E HOT P-E-P-P HOT LEMON *mash fold in palm* BANANA, O-I-L, O-I-L, *flip, flip put in palm smash.*
Interviewer:	Do you vote?
Juanita:	NO.
Interviewer:	Why not?
Juanita:	ME GO GO SUPPOSE SUPPOSE SUPPOSE SUPPOSE GO MEET MEET MEET MEET ME ME ME NAME FAMILY FAMILY FAMILY ME FAMILY C-A-M-G-I-D-E-R GO T-X-I-A-X-I-T DRIVE DRIVE DRIVE HOME VISIT HAPPY ME MY GO HOME LOOK LOOK LOOK LOOK BUY BUY BUY BUY CLOTHES SHIRT SHOES FOOD SHOP HAIR FINISH BRAID DIFFERENT DIFFERENT DIFFERENT *counts off 1-2-3- on open hand beginning with middle finger.*
Interviewer:	Are you Democrat or Republican?
Juanita:	ME GO FRAMINGHAM (sign) NOT FAR OVER-THERE (to her left) THEY SAY MEET ME MEET HEY HEY HEY ME HOME

---

* Her signing and gesturing is transcribed as literally as we can though the transliteration into written English is itself very difficult and problematic because ASL lacks a written form and Juanita is not communicating in clear, standard ASL. Conventions used: *Italics* indicate mime or gestural communication. CAPITAL LETTERS indicate signs. W-O-R-D indicates fingerspelling. "?" indicates viewers' guess of what she means.

BACK (signed toward Framingham) visit P-A-P-A-P-A MAMA PLANE (take off) *ticket have passport have* SISTER, SON 5 SON 5-SON (# incorporation) 5-SON 5 JOSE JOSE JOSE 2 JOSE SISTER SISTER SISTER SON B-O-R-N-E FOSTER 5 5 *holding luggage and putting it down* ARRIVE BACK FRAMINGHAM NOT FAR HOTEL HOTEL HOTEL RIGHT THERE RIGHT THERE RIGHT THERE (Framingham space) FINISH BACK (Framingham space) PUERTO RICO VISIT FOOD PLAN FOOD DELICIOUS NICE BELT BUCKLE WALK CAN'T BELT BUCKLE BETTER FOOD WAIT WAIT WAIT *leaving food on tray* ARRIVE FOOD FINISH BACK WALK ARRIVE BACK FINISH GO EAT FINISH *giving tray back pushing cart* ARRIVE PLANE FINISH HI SAY HI NICE HI CUTE MEET HAPPY HUG FRIEND FOOD R-I-C-E NEW (using fingers to indicate triangular shape) SMELL SMELL SMELL GOOD NEW NEW NEW *slice drink* MATCH SPARKLER (thrown in air) STARS STARS STARS STARS STARS (fireworks?) STARS STARS STARS PRETTY SUN RAIN NONE NO RAIN HAVE HOME BEAUTIFUL SUN GOOD OUTSIDE BOAT (signed as if it is a powerboat) PRETTY FISH EAT DELICIOUS BOAT ROW *carrying sack over shoulder picking up fish? Throwing in something twice* FINISH *scraping fish? (scaling?)* KNIFE *scrape* THROW FINISH.

Juanita is using a combination of signs and gestures but this is not fluent ASL. Her language is "dysfluent," meaning that it is severely impaired in ways that we will analyze shortly. When the Deaf Unit team showed this videotape to a competent psychiatrist who is not trained in working with deaf people, and transliterated it just as we did here, his conclusion was that Juanita was probably psychotic. He knew that mental illness can create language problems, and without much experience working with persons with extreme language deprivation, this was the natural conclusion for him to draw. The Deaf Unit team knew, however, that Juanita's poor language abilities in her best "language," ASL, could also be explained by an impoverished educational environment and severe language deprivation. In addition, Juanita is mentally retarded and may have other kinds of brain pathology. How could the team judge whether she was, indeed, thought disordered?

Selected Literature Review

The problem of evaluation of "mental status" in a deaf person without fluent language skills has been addressed before (Evans & Elliott, 1981, 1987; Gulati, 2003; Kitson & Thacker, 2000; Pollard, 1998a) but mostly with regard to pointing out potential dangers or mistakes clinicians may make. The easiest and most glaring mistake is to draw conclusions about mental illness on the basis of the spoken or written language skills of the deaf person. For instance, Evans and Elliott (1987) write:

> The cultural language of the deaf community, American Sign Language (ASL) is not readily translatable into syntactical and grammatical English. Consequently, to the examiner unfamiliar with ASL, the written language of many deaf adults appears fragmented, confused and primitive. Such English language deficits may give the appearance that deaf ASL users think in vaguely holistic and concrete terms, and their written communications may strikingly simulate a severe thought disorder. (p. 84)

Pollard (1998a) elaborates on the dangers of drawing conclusions based on deaf person's English language skills and then addresses the larger problem that language dysfluency in deaf persons usually has different causes from language dysfluency in hearing people. Language dysfluency in deaf people is usually related to severe language deprivation; a problem that may be confused with, or confounded by, mental illness that develops later.

> Because deaf individuals' knowledge of English vocabulary and syntax is frequently limited, written communication, if essential, must be kept at very modest difficulty levels. Idioms and expressions are particularly to be avoided, as these are frequently the last and most difficult aspects of language usage to master. The most extreme caution should be exercised in conjecture about the person's education, intelligence, and thought processes on the basis of their writing. The risk of overpathologizing is very great, even when writing samples appear to be severely limited or disorganized. This is not at all uncommon and usually, but not always, evidence of educational or experiential limitations, not psychopathology. (p. 176)

> Essentially, disrupted communication fluency in hearing persons is indicative of psychosis, aphasia, dysphasia, or related serious mental disorder. Yet, the majority of deaf patients who demonstrate gross limitations in communication fluency (in ASL, English, or other modalities) do so for reasons other than neuro- or psychopathology. Expert consultation is needed to identify neuro- or psychopathology based on communication impairment in deaf people. Interpreters are not typically qualified to render such opinions, as their education does not address the nature of psychotic or aphasic disruptions in sign language. (p. 177)

As Pollard explains, disorders like schizophrenia may cause disruptions in thinking and language expression, and the English language output of deaf persons whose primary communication is through a sign language should never be used to draw diagnostic conclusions. Psychotic disorders can disrupt thinking in known, predictable ways, but one needs to observe this in the *native* language of the patient. Evans and Elliott (1981) performed pioneering work examining well-known criteria for schizophrenia and analyzing which of these criteria were applicable to 13 deaf adults with schizophrenia diagnosed at the University of California San Francisco Center on Deafness. Thacker (Kitson & Thacker, 2000; Thacker, 1994, 1998) built on their work to record and analyze the sign language output of deaf persons diagnosed with schizophrenia. These important studies found that formal thought disorders may manifest in sign language in ways that mostly parallel their appearance in spoken languages.

Some of these examples of language dysfluency related to thought disorder (LDTD) that Thacker (Kitson & Thacker, 2000; Thacker, 1994, 1998) observed were as follows:

1. Cross-linguistic contamination between British Sign Language (BSL) and English. For example, the patient signs SOUL (spirit) and then points to the sole of her feet, making the nonsensical comment TWO FEET JUMP IN MY MOUTH.
2. Bizarre sign production errors such as fingerspelling or signing backwards or using the wrong handshape or sign location.
3. Attending to the shapes of signs rather than to their meaning. This is equivalent to the phenomenon known as *clanging* in which words are linked based on their sound, not their meaning.
4. Switching abruptly from one topic to another especially when it is difficult to see any link between the topics.
5. Repeating the same sign or theme unnecessarily.
6. Visual-spatial behaviors unique to signers such as assigning different personalities to two hands and using different locations and time lines on the two sides of the body.

Thacker also looked at the sign errors made by deaf persons without psychiatric history or symptoms. For instance, nonmentally ill deaf persons also switched or dropped topics, repeated signs or themes, and even *clanged* or rhymed signs. The three kinds of errors she found that were made only in her deaf subjects were incoherence, visual-spatial anomalies, and paraphasias (incoherent arrangement of words or signs). Thacker reports that her comparison sample of nonmentally ill deaf persons were fluent users of BSL (Thacker, 1994). She does not describe what language dysfluency in deaf persons looks like when it is due to the most common reason deaf people have this problem: language deprivation.

Language Dysfluency in "Traditionally Underserved" Deaf Persons

Because most deaf people grow up in hearing families and communities, they usually do not have the same easy acquisition of language as hearing people.

The only languages that deaf children can acquire naturally and effortlessly are sign languages. Deaf or hearing children raised by parents who sign fluently will, unless there is some gross learning or brain problem, sign fluently themselves. They will have *native* signing skills. Unfortunately, huge numbers of deaf children grow up without adequate exposure to the local sign language, and many deaf people never acquire native fluency in any language. Their language output, in their best language or communication modality, will exhibit language dysfluency related not to a thought disorder, but to this language deprivation.

In Chapter 1, Patricia Black and I reviewed the literature on psychiatric inpatient care of deaf persons as well as the literature on the "traditionally underserved" deaf group. We saw that poor language skills are the chief defining characteristic of this group along with problems in educational, social, vocational, and independent living skills functioning. We argued that it is this group of deaf persons that most confounds clinicians, rehabilitations specialists, and educators. In this chapter, I examine the nature of language dysfluency in more detail, highlighting how easy it is to misdiagnose deaf persons based on misunderstanding of language dynamics.

Poor language skills per se do not usually bring someone to the attention of mental health providers, but because language can be a visible manifestation of thought, it is a domain that clinicians attend to closely. Gulati (2003) notes that "most Deaf people have firsthand knowledge of language deprivation, having seen it all around them. For many hearing people, however, and in the general psychiatric literature, the nature and severity of this condition is generally unrecognized" (p. 62).

Based on the research reviewed and presented in Chapter 1, there are good reasons to conclude that large numbers of deaf persons served in inpatient psychiatric settings do not have the psychotic disorders like schizophrenia that predominate among their hearing peers. Rather they are persons from this traditionally underserved group who exhibit language dysfluency along with developmental, behavioral, mood, and personality disorders. As many clinicians in the deafness mental health field have already noted (Denmark, 1994; Gulati, 2003; Pollard, 1998a; Vernon & Daigle-King, 1999), they may look, to clinicians untrained in deafness, like persons with psychotic disorders, but this is fundamentally because their language skills and deficits are not properly understood.

The therapeutic challenge in evaluating and treating deaf psychiatric patients is therefore much more complicated that simply providing ASL translations. Beginning with the assessment process itself, clinicians are challenged to parse out much more carefully whether the language patterns of dysfluent patients reflect mental illness, language deprivation, or some neurological disorder. The conclusions that are drawn have great import for how patients are treated not just in the hospital but for the rest of their lives.

This clinical problem is complicated enough but one also must acknowledge that there have been *political* barriers to addressing this issue well. For the past 30 years, the political need to validate ASL as a language guided socially aware clinicians and teachers in the deafness field. Along with Deaf people themselves, deafness professionals have rejected the mistaken belief that ASL is a substandard communication system, a kind of elaborate gesture, or a simplification of English. In the social and political context in which professionals have needed to affirm ASL and Deaf Culture, it has been difficult to recognize that many deaf people are not, in fact, fluent users of ASL; that they *are* language impaired or, *language dysfluent,* in their best language, ASL.

Further complicating the difficulty of making such judgments is that so few hearing clinicians are truly fluent in ASL. Tackling this latter problem presupposed an exceptionally high level of sign language skill in the clinician or clinical team as well as an extensive knowledge of psychological and language development in deaf people. Most hearing people in the deafness field communicate in more English-like variants of sign, and this is also true of many deaf clinicians working at the master's and doctoral levels. For non-ASL-fluent signers, especially if they are hearing, to make judgments about language dysfluency in deaf people looks a great deal like the old prejudicial judgments about deaf people not having a language or having "poor language." It echoes the oppressive dynamic in which hearing people, who were poor communicators in sign, made negative judgments about the poor language skills of deaf people. After all, it is fair to say that these hearing signers are also language dysfluent in ASL. Their problems, however, are those of persons trying to master second languages, not those of persons without mastery of a first.

What Is a Thought Disorder?

The *Diagnostic and Statistical Manual-IV* (American Psychiatric Association, 1994), the standard reference manual for mental health professionals doing diagnostic assessment, discusses the term "psychotic" as follows:

> The term psychotic has historically received a number of different definitions, none of which has achieved universal acceptance. The narrowest definition of psychotic is restricted to delusions or prominent hallucinations, with the hallucinations occurring in the absence of insight into their pathological nature. A slightly less restrictive definition would also include prominent hallucinations that the individual realizes are hallucinatory experiences. Broader still is a definition that also includes other positive symptoms of Schizophrenia (i.e., disorganized speech, grossly disorganized or catatonic behavior). Unlike these definitions based on symptoms, the definition used in earlier classifications (e.g., DSM-II and ICD-9) was probably far too inclusive and focused on the severity of functional impairment, so that a mental disorder was termed

"psychotic" if it resulted in "impairment that grossly interferes with the capacity to meet ordinary demands of life." Finally, the term has been defined conceptually as a loss of ego boundaries or a gross impairment in reality testing. (p. 273)

As most commonly understood, there are three components of psychosis or thought disorder. These are hallucinations, delusions, and disorganized thinking, language, and behavior. We consider each in relation to the difficulty of diagnosing these in deaf persons with language dysfluency.

Hallucinations

Can deaf people have auditory hallucinations? Can they "hear voices"? This question seems to intrigue hearing clinicians. Within the limited literature on the subject, there is near consensus that some deaf psychiatric patients report, or are observed, to have auditory hallucinations, although probably less commonly than with hearing psychiatric patients (Altshuler, 1971; Evans & Elliott, 1987; Gulati, 2003; Kitson & Thacker, 2000; Pollard, 1998a). Denmark (1994) argued that auditory hallucinations "would not be expected to occur in preverbally profoundly deaf schizophrenics" and that "visual and haptic (tactile) hallucinations are common" (p. 62). However, there are many questions about which deaf psychiatric patients "hear voices" and what exactly they experience. There are many also many concerns regarding how clinicians or interpreters translate the concept of "hearing voices" and how deaf psychiatric patients with language dysfluency, who may not understand the concept of hallucination, understand the question.

Most deaf people are not born deaf and hear some sounds. They may hear speech but be unable to understand it. It would not be so surprising to learn that those deaf psychiatric patients who have had some experience of spoken language could appreciate clearly the concept of auditory hallucination. Audiological assessment is not done as part of a psychiatric evaluation of deaf persons and clinicians do not normally ask deaf persons what they actually can hear. On the Westborough State Hospital Deaf Unit, for instance, some deaf patients have reported auditory hallucinations and some have been observed communicating with apparent hallucinations. Both occurrences are highly uncommon, however, and even in these instances, staff do not normally enquire about degree of hearing loss. "Deaf" may be distinguished broadly from "hard of hearing" but this is almost never done by actually measuring hearing loss. Feu and McKenna (1996, 1999), by contrast, present evidence that "profoundly deaf schizophrenic patients, who may never have experienced spoken language, report hearing voices to much the same extent as hearing patients. They also experience other auditory symptoms. Explanations in terms of misattribution of other symptoms or restriction of the symptom to those who were not prelingually deaf are insufficient to account for this phenomenon."

Pollard (1998b) questions whether the high reports of auditory hallucinations in deaf people result from the fact that this question is asked so often without questioning how the deaf patient understands the question. "The sheer frequency with which mental health professionals ask the question, 'Do you hear voices?' when evaluating patients (hearing or deaf), and the possibility that an affirmative answer might be spurious or even learned, could play a significant role in such situations. The voices question, unelaborated, is not recommended. Instead, more open-ended investigation of atypical perceptual and ideational experiences is preferred" (pp. 178–179).

Atkinson, Gleeson, Cromwell, and O'Rourke (2007) studied the characteristics of reported hallucinations in deaf psychiatric patients and attempted to relate these to the nature of the person's hearing loss and other factors. They found that they could organize the deaf patients' experience of auditory hallucinations into five groups.

1. In the first group, the voices were reported to be *nonauditory*, clear and easy to understand. Participants reported seeing an image of the voice communicating in their minds' eye. The members of this group were severely to profoundly deaf and became deaf at birth or before age 2. One exception was of a person totally deafened at age 6 who reported no auditory memory of sound.
2. In the second group, participants had the experience of hearing speech and using hearing aids. The members of this group were confused about whether their voice hallucinations were auditory in nature. They gave unclear descriptions of the phenomena they experienced.
3. Persons in the third group were born deaf in developing countries, spent their early years without hearing aids or formal language, and acquired signing skills only after moving to Britain after the critical period for language learning. These persons were language dysfluent. The researchers believed these persons had enough language to convince the researchers that they experienced language but not enough language to describe what they experienced.
4. The fourth group comprised people born moderately or moderately severely deaf who used hearing aids. These people reported that they heard sounds when the voices were present.
5. Two members fell into a fifth group in that they experienced true visual, auditory, olfactory, and gustatory phenomena in addition to voice hallucinations. These phenomena included tinnitus, seeing a dark shadow dart through peripheral vision, strange smells and tastes. Both of these persons were profoundly deaf. One was postlingually deafened at age 12.

The conclusion of these researchers is that the characteristics of hallucinations in deaf people maps closely their actual communication experiences. Persons born profoundly deaf, for instance, did not report unambiguous auditory hallucinations. Unambiguous auditory hallucinations were reported only by people who had the experience of hearing. However, two of the groups of deaf persons lacked sufficient language to describe their experiences clearly. This was due to language dysfluency but also the difficulty of finding words or signs to describe a very subtle experience. Thus, inadequate language skills bring us to the heart of the diagnostic dilemmas.

An enquiry into auditory hallucinations is a routine and expected part of a mental status exam and psychiatrists will generally assume that their patient at least understands the question. This assumption should not be made with deaf psychiatric patients, especially those from the traditionally underserved group. As Pollard noted, sometimes these people have been asked this question so often that they learn to respond "yes" without understanding the concept. This may reflect the "empty nod" problem, the fact that many deaf persons routinely answer "yes" to questions they do not understand so as not to appear ignorant. Sometimes the clinician, who is unfamiliar and uncomfortable with the communication dynamics, takes the "yes" answer at face value rather than probe into language and psychological domains they are unprepared for.

With some language dysfluent, psychologically unsophisticated (Glickman, 2003) deaf patients, it may not be clear how they understand the question. Do they distinguish hallucinations clearly, for instance, from thinking, speech, dreaming, or environmental sounds? Do they understand that the clinician is referring to hearing voices when there is no "real" speaker? If they do not have the language skills, these distinctions are difficult to make.

There is no standard way to sign auditory hallucination in ASL. There is an English sign for hallucinate, which is useful only if the patient knows that sign and concept. To convey the concept in ASL, the clinician or interpreter usually has to act out the process of hearing a voice that is not there. The person might sign VOICE or SPEAK and then use a classifier to show SPEAKING in the visual field. The person would also have to assume the role of someone having a hallucination, look here and there in response to this stimuli, perhaps sign NOTICE or indicate it with eye gaze, perhaps respond back to the unseen voice. The person might add the sign for IMAGINATION or note that there are PEOPLE NONE in the actual area. This might have to be acted out and described several times with the concept developed in interaction with the deaf patient. This sign interpretation of "hear voices" itself calls for considerable ASL skill. Less linguistically sophisticated clinicians or interpreters may simply sign HEAR VOICE or HALLUCINATE, an ambiguous and unclear idea that can easily be understood by the deaf person as a reference to his or her ability to hear speech. Indeed, asked in this unsophisticated manner, one can readily expect an answer such as "NO, ME DEAF."

There are other reasons the patients' self-report of hallucinations alone should be taken skeptically. On the Westborough Deaf Unit, staff members have seen patients report that they hear voices but provide no behavioral evidence of it. When people are hallucinating or "responding to internal stimuli," there are usually behavioral clues. They seem distracted. Their eye gaze darts around. Sometimes they communicate back to the perceived voice. We have also had patients whose pathology consists of imitating the pathology of others. These patients report voices after seeing someone else do so. These same patients may also develop an "eating disorder" after observing a peer display this problem.

Some patients tell staff what they think staff want to hear, and because of language and cultural differences develop confused perceptions of what they think staff expect from them. Sometimes the language output from hearing staff is as bizarre as any that might come from deaf patients. The worst example of this we have come across was that of a deaf psychotic woman whom a colleague and I interviewed on a hearing psychiatric ward where no one signed well. She was observed signing to a staff person "YOU KILL ME" repeatedly, and the staff person, who did not understand her at all, nonetheless smiled brightly and nodded her head up and down in an apparent effort to show support. One trembles to imagine how the deaf patient made sense of this "insane" behavior from her staff. Her answers to questions raised during our clinical interview were very confused, but given her environment, who is to say what is *normal*?

The problem of how the deaf patient understands the questions being asked must be attended to with a diligence that most hearing nondeafness specialists are unaccustomed to. They usually have no reason to question whether the concept of hallucinations is understood, and they are used to interviewing at a pace that does not permit close attention to *the interviewers'* language. Skilled deafness interviewers know that close, careful attention must be given to how concepts are conveyed, especially with regard to phenomena, such as auditory hallucinations, which may be unfamiliar and difficult to interpret. *This should be an important topic of discussion whenever clinicians untrained in deafness are working with sign language interpreters.*

Evans and Elliott (1987) note that deaf psychiatric patients may also confuse sounds associated with tinnitus (ringing in the ears) with hallucinations.

They also believe that deaf people who report auditory hallucinations are most likely postlingually deafened. "In our experience, auditory hallucinations occur rarely in pre-lingually deaf persons; if they occur, they are more frequently found in persons who became deaf after language was established. Visual and haptic (tactile) hallucinations occur more often than auditory hallucinations in the mentally ill deaf patients we have seen" (p. 86).

What about visual hallucinations? Besides Evans and Elliott, Critchley, Denmark, Warren, and Wilson (1981) present a study of 10 profoundly deaf patients with schizophrenia who, they say, experienced visual hallucinations. However, their study is filled with caveats regarding their uncertainty about what role unclear communication may have played in the assessment. They add that, "as with other schizophrenic patients, it is not always possible to separate hallucinations from bizarre delusional experiences and this fact adds to our confusion" (p. 32).

The presumption made in this earlier literature that deaf schizophrenic patients would be more inclined to experience visual hallucinations seems very unlikely given current understanding of the major causes of visual hallucinations. "Seeing signing" is not a phenomenological equivalent of "hearing voices." Visual hallucinations, when they occur, suggest organic brain pathology like dementia or substance use/withdrawal (Pelak & Liu, 2004). Without those kinds of problems, clinicians should look beyond self-report for behavioral evidence of visual hallucinations. Staff on the Westborough Unit had one instance in which they concluded that a patient was probably having visual hallucinations but they could not be sure. This deaf, language dysfluent woman with schizoaffective disorder complained continuously about voices, was seen on a daily basis talking and signing back to unseen presences, was clearly distressed by this experience, and got better with a change in antipsychotic medication. The patient was prone to stopping in the midst of some activity, turning abruptly to her side, signing and yelling SHUT-UP or FINISH. She would say she was talking to a family member. This patient could not explain or label her experience but her behavior and report provided considerable evidence for hallucinations. Whether they were visual, auditory, or just "felt," was not clear.

The writer has been the unit director and psychologist on this Deaf Psychiatric Unit for, at the time of this writing, more than 11 years, and during this time has seen very few cases of unambiguous hallucinatory experiences of any sort in deaf patients. I agree that the phenomenon occurs, but more often than not I believe misjudgments are made by clinicians who do not attend sufficiently closely to the language dynamics. By contrast, unusual and bizarre beliefs, to be discussed shortly, are seen more commonly.

What should staff conclude when they observe patients signing to themselves and "laughing inappropriately?" It is customary for nursing and clinical staff to interpret this as "responding to internal stimuli," which is shorthand for psychosis. One assumes that in nondeaf settings, there would be few people who would challenge such inferences. Extra caution should be taken, however, in drawing this conclusion with deaf persons with extreme levels of language deprivation. A small number of the patients seen on the Deaf Unit were functionally nonverbal and relied on visual-gestural communication and home signs. Two of these persons treated in recent years were frequently observed gesturing to themselves, smiling or laughing for no reason that staff could perceive. One of these patients had been, in fact, treated with Haldol (haloperidol), an older antipsychotic drug with unpleasant side effects, for many years, but after he was on the Deaf Unit several months, staff concluded he was not psychotic. For such language deprived and isolated people, how can we say whether "talking to oneself" is abnormal? From a human perspective, their life experience is so abnormal that it becomes impossible to determine what constitutes a sane response.

It is safest to evaluate conservatively, to look for multiple indicators of thought disorder. Gulati (2003) emphasizes this important point. "In diagnosing psychosis, it is safest to rely on unambiguous evidence such as religious delusion, spontaneous statements of hallucinations, documented bizarre behavior, and the presence of ideas of reference, particularly in patients with non-fluent language. It is essential to assemble the broadest base of information and the assistance of collateral contacts" (p. 72).

In summary, the question of whether deaf people have hallucinations must be broken down into more detailed questions:

1. How are the concepts being conveyed into sign or gesture? How confident can the clinician be that the concept of auditory hallucinations is understood by the patient?
2. Might the deaf patient (especially the patient with language dysfluency) be answering yes to cover up a lack of understanding or because of confusion about what is being asked?
3. How does actual degree of hearing loss and onset of hearing loss relate to the ability to experience auditory hallucinations? The data from the Atkinson et al. (2007) study cited above suggests that profoundly deaf people who became deaf at birth or in their first few years are very unlikely to experience true auditory hallucinations. Their experience of "voices" is likely to refer to something nonauditory that still has the experienced quality of a message being communicated.
4. Might the patient be confusing tinnitus-related experiences with hallucinations?
5. What is the normal thinking experience for deaf persons with severe language dysfluency and communication isolation? If these people "talk to themselves," what does this mean?
6. Is there evidence for auditory hallucinations beyond the patient signing or saying "yes" in response to the question? For instance, is preoccupation with internal stimuli observed?
7. How does the degree of experience that clinicians have with deaf people relate to the kind of diagnostic conclusions they make?
8. When deaf people actually report visual hallucinations of people signing, is this really a visual phenomenon or something else, more akin to daydreaming?

Mental health clinicians need to be more cautious in drawing conclusions about psychosis in deaf people than with hearing people. As Pollard noted above, one cannot take, at face value, a "yes" answer to the voices question. One needs a lot more information about the patient's language abilities, intelligence, and conceptual world. When deaf patients cannot describe clearly what they experience, clinicians should look for behavioral indicators of hallucinations, such as eyes darting away inappropriately or the person signing or speaking to an unseen presence, before concluding that hallucinations are occurring.

Delusions

Delusions are described in the DSM-IV as "erroneous beliefs that usually involve a misinterpretation of perceptions or experiences." The most common delusions are persecutory or referential. In persecutory delusions, "the person believes he or she is being tormented, followed, tricked, spied on or subjected to ridicule." In referential delusions, "the person believes that certain gestures, comments, passages from books, newspapers, song lyrics, or other environmental cues are specifically directed at him or her." The DSM-IV acknowledges that "the distinction between a delusion and a strongly held idea is sometimes difficult to make and depends on the degree of conviction with which the belief is held despite clear contradictory evidence" (p. 275). When deciding what is a delusion and what is a personal or cultural belief, clinicians are urged to consider culturally attributed meaning of phenomena. For example, the idea that one is "possessed by the devil" may be delusional in one context, normative in another.

Clinicians who work with deaf people understand now that the Deaf Community is a subcultural group with its own language and normative expectations. Culturally Deaf and hearing people would tend to hold different beliefs about some issues such as the meaning of deafness itself, and one hopes that even culturally insensitive hearing clinicians would not describe as delusional a deaf person who supports the cultural view of deafness. But consider what the reaction of hearing clinicians untrained in deafness might be to deaf people who espouse beliefs within a Deaf culture frame of reference: beliefs that deafness is good, speaking is unnecessary and oppressive, signing is preferable to speaking, hearing aids and cochlear implants are oppressive attempts to fix something that is not broken (or, more extreme, forms of cultural genocide), a deaf child is preferable to a hearing one, and hearing people have been victimizing deaf people for generations. These may be extreme reductions of complex issues, but many deaf people (and hearing advocates) argue these points. To culturally hearing clinicians hearing these beliefs for the first time, they may seem, if not delusional, at least peculiar.

The danger of misdiagnosis is not mostly likely to occur when articulate deaf people espouse politically unpopular views. It is more likely to occur with socially isolated, language deprived deaf people with poor social skills and poor understanding of larger socially sanctioned shared meanings. For example, the Deaf Unit has treated persons arrested and charged, and sometimes convicted, of sexual crimes when they approached people in an inappropriate way asking for sex. Deaf people who communicate mainly through visual-gestural communication may be graphic in their solicitations of sex, and this can frighten hearing people who call the police for assistance. Socially isolated and unskilled deaf people are very vulnerable to having their intentions misunderstood and finding themselves in a psychiatric hospital or, worse, a jail after such incidents. When these deaf persons were hospitalized on the Deaf Unit, the "treatment" really consisted of the social skill education that they should have received at home and in school. It also consisted of educating players in the patient's network about his or her language and social deficits and advocating for appropriate interventions.

Delusions that are considered "bizarre" are thought to be diagnostic of psychosis. The person who believes, for instance, that the FBI is sending messages to him through the television is, by definition, psychotic. Deaf Unit staff do see deaf persons with bizarre beliefs like this. One deaf patient believed that Osama bin Laden was sending him personal messages. Another insisted he was the king. When people avoided him because of his provocative behaviors, he thought they were afraid of him because of his power as the king. Another patient believed so passionately that God was sending him on a mission to marry a particular person that he stalked and harassed her, leading to his arrest for this crime. In the hospital, he attributed his arrest and subsequent hospitalization to trials that God put before him to test his faith, like Job. He saw all of the mental health people as essentially in league with the devil to foil his God-sanctioned marriage plan. Another patient saw special messages embedded in the captioning on the television. Another marched around the unit, pointing angrily at staff and signing, YOU-KILL-ME, DIE, HEAVEN, GAY, RUSSIA, COMMUNIST. These persons, the staff felt confident concluding, were psychotic. I would add that Deaf Unit staff see these kinds of delusional symptoms in deaf patients far more often than they see hallucinations.

Even more common than bizarre delusions, in deaf and hearing people, are systematic mistakes in interpreting or judging reality so that patients attribute hostile intent when there is none. Deaf people are making these judgments, it must be remembered, in a context of not being able to determine what hearing people actually are saying. They also quite frequently have a much poorer fund of worldly information, including common understandings of human psychology. The concept, for instance, of "point of view," and the idea that we can disagree but both have reasonable opinions, may be alien. Staff often have to teach patients the idea that thoughts, feelings, and behaviors are different. The idea that one can feel angry without becoming aggressive may be entirely new to them and quite difficult to accept.

We know that nonverbal communication rules differ for culturally Deaf and culturally hearing people. Hearing staff need constant reminders that deaf patients are attending closely to their body language. But even patients who have a clear idea about Deaf culture may not necessarily understand the concept "cross-cultural conflict." Given all these information and skill deficits as well as cross-cultural differences, it may be quite easy for a deaf person to misattribute a hearing person's lack of eye contact, turning away, or facial grimace as evidence of hostility. Hearing people who do not appreciate the social and power differences between hearing and Deaf people, and between staff and patients, may be quick to draw conclusions about paranoia, but sometimes hearing people *are* talking about deaf people and not always with the deaf person's best interests at heart.

The worst example I have seen of this was that of parents that hid antipsychotic medication in the food of their language deprived deaf adult son. This son hated the medication and came to be suspicious of his mother's cooking, hovering over her as she prepared his meal. Attributions that he was "paranoid" were included in the psychosocial information the Unit received, and he was, indeed, quite reluctant to take any medication and very difficult to reason with (his lack of language skills making this even worse). He was not, however, clinically delusional. He was just hyperattentive to the possibility (which happened to be true) that people were placing medication in his food.

The deaf patient placed in an all-hearing psychiatric context should not be considered delusional for feeling unsafe because such environments *do* put deaf people at high risk for misdiagnosis, mistreatment, and interventions like restraint and seclusion ((National Association of State Mental Health Program Directors Medical Directors Council, 2002). Even "high functioning," college educated, English fluent deaf people can be victimized in these settings (DeVinney, 2003). The perceived "paranoia" of some deaf patients must always be understood in the context that sometimes "they" do not understand you, are not sympathetic to you, and *are* inclined to interpret your behavior as pathology.

In a Deaf psychiatric treatment setting, where Deaf and hearing staff and patients interact each day, the opportunities for cross-cultural conflict are enormous. If the program is fortunate enough to employ articulate and thoughtful Deaf persons, then some of these differences may be exposed. For instance, a Deaf style of discourse is often described as "blunt," but to hearing people this bluntness can appear harsh. When Deaf people are communicating with deaf persons with poor language skills, the need for clarity and bluntness is even stronger. For example, a deaf patient with poor language skills complains that she is not getting enough food, and the Deaf direct care worker points out that she is eating so much she is getting fat. A culturally naïve hearing clinician reprimands the Deaf staff person for being insulting and then tries to correct the problem by meeting with the patient and "beating around the bush" about the patient's weight problem. The Deaf staff person knows that the patient will not understand this subtle *hearing* discourse style, but does that mean that bluntness is always appropriate? What if the bluntness is insulting, as calling someone *fat* can be? An easy cross-cultural conflict for Deaf and hearing people to have is for the Deaf workers to argue that a blunt style is culturally appropriate and for the hearing workers to argue that insults, justified as bluntness, are never therapeutic. This argument can easily take the form of Deaf staff arguing they are oppressed by culturally insensitive hearing clinicians, and hearing staff arguing that the Deaf staff are clinically unskilled. These subtleties also make cross-cultural supervision particularly complex.

We have seen this cross-cultural conflict also occur in the area of name signs. Deaf people sometimes give each other name signs based on some prominent physical characteristic. This can include unflattering physical characteristics such as weight, baldness, scars, or unusual facial features. I have seen hearing persons take great offense at these name signs which seem, to the hearing person, like the equivalent of calling a person "fatty." Deaf people argue back that the signs are really more neutral, that Deaf people do not take the same kind of offense, and that in any case it is not for hearing people to proscribe for Deaf people the cultural rituals around naming. On the Deaf Unit, after many heated discussions, we have come to a shaky truce on this matter, with people agreeing to be more careful in the name signs they choose for persons who do not yet have name signs.

It is very easy for hearing people to judge Deaf people as paranoid because, unless they have had a great deal of sensitivity training, hearing people do not see their own biases and do not perceive how their own well-intentioned behaviors may *not* be benign. Indeed, hearing people who work with "the deaf" often like to think of themselves as kind, giving people (Hoffmeister & Harvey, 1996) and can be shocked and astounded to discoverer that Deaf people do not perceive them that way. A deaf patient placed in a hearing psychiatric setting, or a deaf staff person working alone among hearing peers, is vulnerable to being perceived as hostile merely for not appreciating sufficiently the efforts hearing people think they are making to accommodate the deaf person. If the deaf person assertively insists on communication inclusion, this can become very threatening to hearing people especially when they realize that communication inclusion asks more of them then procuring an interpreter. Real communication inclusion will require hearing people to communicate differently. As with any minority–majority group dynamic, the power differences influence perceptions of reality; but it is generally the dominant group that defines reality, such as deciding who is paranoid.

Delusions are misperceptions and misinterpretations of social reality that are not corrected through reason. On the Westborough Deaf Unit, staff see patients who are clinically paranoid, who have delusions of reference or persecution, much more frequently than they see persons with bizarre delusions or unambiguous hallucinations. The symptoms are more commonly subtle than obvious. Although some patients make the claim that "you are all trying to kill me!" more often we see patients sign to us that "you are mad at me," when staff are not. They may think that staff are having meetings to plan ways to trick or control them when staff intentions, from their perspective, are innocent. Some patients isolate themselves in their rooms, avoiding therapeutic activities, and some are guarded and defensive when attempts are made to probe how they feel. One patient who was constantly losing or giving away her clothing was just as constantly accusing staff and other patients of stealing from her. Her belief that a peer was stealing her clothing actually led her to attack the peer. If this happens repeatedly and if the patient cannot be reasoned with, a conclusion about paranoia is justified. In a Deaf treatment setting, where there are articulate Deaf clinical staff able to challenge hearing assumptions and biases, these conclusions are likely to be drawn more carefully. In hearing psychiatric settings, conclusions about paranoia flow easily from a culturally hearing perspective about deafness. Conclusions drawn without cross-cultural understanding are as dangerous in a Deaf-hearing context as they are in any other cross-cultural situation.

An interesting phenomenon occurred when the Deaf Unit had to admit some hearing patients onto this signing milieu. As many hearing patients in the hospital are clinically paranoid, staff were sensitive to the fact that they might find an environment where people are signing to be more threatening. We talked to administrators about being careful which hearing people are assigned to the Deaf Unit because of the danger of increasing their paranoia. This was not hard for our hearing administrators to understand. They could empathize with the hearing client placed involuntarily in a program where most people were signing. This same empathy may be more difficult to muster, however, for the experience of the deaf patient placed in a hearing setting. In this instance, any expressions of paranoia are more likely to be considered clinical symptoms. This all speaks to the fact that our attributions grow out of our psychosocial and cultural experience. The problem is that hearing people usually do not realize that, *as hearing people,* they also have a cultural viewpoint influencing their perceptions of what is pathological.

Disorganized Thinking, Language, and Behavior

The most difficult symptom to evaluate in deaf patients with language deprivation is that of disorganized thinking and language. Psychiatrists judge the quality of patients' thinking based on their language output. Language dysfluency in deaf people can be related to language deprivation or thought disorder or both, and it can also be related to brain disorders such as aphasia (Poizner, Klima, & Bellugi, 1987), and as a field we are at very beginning stages of parsing out the differences.

The kind of thought disorder commonly found in persons with schizophrenia is well summarized by E. Fuller Torrey (2001) as "a frequent inability to sort, interpret and respond" (perceptual phenomena) (p. 42). He compares what happens in the brain of the person with schizophrenia to a switchboard operator who does not connect the right caller with the right receiver. There is a disconnection between what the individual perceives through any of the senses and how the person makes sense of these perceptions. The person can then not organize thoughts into an organized, logical sentence structure. Torrey gives this example of a sentence, written by a person with schizophrenia, showing disconnectedness and loose associations:

> *Write all kinds of black snakes looking like raw onion, high strung, deep down, long winded, all kinds of sizes.* (p. 47)

This sentence shows language dysfluency, but it is not a sentence one would expect to see written or signed by a deaf person whose language dysfluency relates to language deprivation. The sentence, for all its illogic, is still grammatical. One would not think, hearing or reading this sentence, that the speaker does not know English, but rather that something is wrong in the person's mind.

There are other well-known kinds of language dysfluency related to thought disorder seen in persons with schizophrenia:

1. Loose associations: there is only a marginal connection between one idea and the next
2. Concreteness: an inability to appreciate abstract thought
3. Impairment in logical, cause and effect reasoning
4. Neologisms or made up words
5. Clanging: making connections between words based on sound rather than meaning
6. Thought blocking: the flow of the person's thinking stops because he or she becomes stuck on a word or idea

Because psychotic persons are not organizing and integrating their experiences well, there is often a disconnect between what they say and their emotions and emotional expression (their *affect*). The person may say he or she is happy but have a sad or anxious facial expression. Emotional expression may be minimal (*flat* or *blunted*) or rapidly changing (*labile*) and not seem to fit with the experience being described. When you interact with a person who is psychotic, you can have the experience that the person is not "grounded" or "there," and therefore that his or her behavior is unpredictable. Deaf people who are severely language deprived live in a very different conceptual world but they are not psychotic. For example, their ability to experience and express emotions and the quality of their human relatedness, their ability to form emotional bonds with other people, may be excellent.

To analyze the language patterns of deaf psychiatric patients better, we have been, with the appropriate permission, videotaping them and then analyzing their language output. Our intent is to study the kinds of language errors the patients made, just as Thacker (1994, 1998) did in her studies, but with more attention to the differential diagnosis of language dysfluency related to thought disorder versus language deprivation. Returning to Juanita, the patient presented at the start of this chapter, we found these kinds of language errors in her signing:

1. *Vocabulary.* Very limited (impoverished) vocabulary, with many signs used incorrectly. Juanita's vocabulary is largely limited to concrete objects and actions and descriptions she has experienced directly but even here it is surprisingly limited. For instance, she knows the signs for only some of the food she herself eats. She knows the signs for FISH, MOTHER, BANANA (although she cannot distinguish it from a plantain) but not more abstract concepts like GOVERN-MENT, VOTE, INDEPENDENT, INTERPRET, ASSESS or even such a common sign as DECIDE. She uses the sign "IF" as a gesture to mean UMMM or I'M THINKING or I KNOW WHAT TO DO. She overgeneralizes the use of the sign SORRY saying it so often that it appears to be a learned response, like the "empty nod," rather than an expression of regret.

2. *Time.* Juanita uses almost no time indicators. She does not know the days of the week or months of the year. She has memorized the year of her birth but she does not now how long ago that was. She does not understand YESTERDAY or TOMORROW or MONTH or YEAR reliably. To use a calendar with her, you point to today, indicate the sun going up and down or her sleeping and waking up, then gesture the number of times this happens, to help her see the immediate future or past. She certainly does not use ASL number incorporation like TWO-WEEKS-FROM-NOW or FIVE-YEARS. She does not establish tense and communicates mainly in the present tense. Sometimes she will use general signs for PAST and FUTURE but she cannot break this down further. She will sometimes sign FINISH to indicate "all-done" or "all-over" but not to establish the past tense. Her stories have no sequential organization to them. She jumps back and forward in time without any logical reason and does not appear to understand she is doing that.

3. *Spatial organization.* Juanita does not make correct use of the visual field, organizing information spatially. In her story, she established the town of Framingham in one place but never referred to it again only to use the same spatial location to talk about Puerto Rico. She attempted to list family members on her fingers but repeated the

same finger for different people, moved the people on to different fingers, skipped fingers and never referred back to anything she established. She can use very simple sign directionality (YOU-GIVE-ME, YOU LOOK-AT-ME) and she will "give the finger" to a person set up in space, but after establishing a person in space, she "drops" them. This is equivalent to the pronoun "he" disappearing from an English sentence. She does not use more complex spatial modifications like I-GIVE-TO-EACH or I-GIVE-TO-ALL. She has difficulty indicating plurality. She does not use space to indicate more than one. She does not sign, for instance, 7 CHAIR or CHAIR 7 (seven chairs) or even use the sign for chair with a classifier marker to indicate many. If she indicates plurality at all, it would be by signing CHAIR repeatedly. She rarely uses a classifier. She can count only to 12 and cannot manipulate numbers.

4. *Syntax.* She does not use the ASL topic-comment structure. She does not establish subjects and then comment on them. She does not use pronouns or use any consistent Subject–Verb–Object (I GIVE-YOU BOOK) or Object–Subject–Verb (Book I-GIVE-YOU) structure. Because of the absence of time, space, and grammatical features, she cannot give an organized narrative or story. She is quite difficult to understand, even for fluent signers, until one gets to know her and learns her limited repertoire of topics. Juanita has a small number of concerns that she repeats regularly.

5. *She mixes sign with gesture and pantomime.* For example, when talking about cutting up vegetables or dancing, she will act it out. Because she relies so heavily on gesture or nonverbal communication, English translations are very approximate.

Overall, her communication appears to resemble a series of pictures presented in the present tense, organized loosely as a kind of collage. Her language is almost stream of consciousness (that is, Picture, Picture, Picture) with minimal organizing principles. While she incorporates sign in brief phrases or sentences, and even an occasional English word (for example, fingerspells R-I-C-E), her language is almost completely devoid of grammar. In particular, her sign order (syntax) is confused and key grammatical features are missing. By inference, we assume her thinking is similarly unstructured.

Does this language problem represent a thought disorder? Is Juanita psychotic? Although Juanita's narrative is confused, what is most striking is the lack of formal grammar. Hearing persons who are psychotic can be very disorganized but they do not typically lack language markers such as tense or time vocabulary. Their sentences will usually contain subjects and verbs, if not other structures. Their vocabulary might be simple or extensive, depending mainly on what their vocabulary was like before they became sick. A highly educated psychotic person is likely to still have a rich vocabulary. When you listen to psychotic hearing English speakers, you do not imagine they do not know English. You recognize that their thinking is *off*. A fluent signer watching Juanita, by contrast, will immediately recognize that she is a poor user of sign language.

Can Juanita's language pattern be accounted for in another way? Might it stem from her cognitive limitations such as her mental retardation? Juanita has had cognitive testing numerous times and the results have been reasonably consistent. She tests in the mildly to moderately mental retardation range using nonverbal intelligence tests. Her cognitive functioning is fairly uniform, suggesting global impairment (mental retardation) rather than specific learning disabilities. We know from cognitive testing that Juanita's brain has difficulty putting things in order by time or space. We know from looking at her sign language use that she has trouble telling a story sequentially and in manipulating the signing spatial field. This brain pathology likely contributes to her language difficulties. However, psychological assessment cannot tell us what caused her language problems, only that she has language and other cognitive problems.

Another important diagnostic clue is that Juanita's problem is *developmental*. She did not have better language skills and then lose them. This fact weighs against the conclusion that her thinking is caused by mental illness or an acquired aphasia. If we observed a dramatic decline in language functioning, this would certainly suggest a psychiatric or organic disorder.

Juanita's behaviors give us other diagnostic clues. Her emotional expression is appropriate. Her behaviors can be impulsive and dangerous but they are not bizarre. Indeed, even her disruptive behaviors are remarkably predictable after you get to know her. Most importantly, she appears to have a quality of "relatedness" with people. She forms friendships. She has appropriate relationships with staff. When you interact with her, you have a sense of a very simple or childlike person, but one who has a stable personality structure and behavior pattern. She does not "feel crazy."

The cognitive limitations as demonstrated by psychological assessment, the language problems as demonstrated by detailed linguistic analysis, the fact that her problems are developmental, and the absence of disorganized behavior or inappropriate affect, together lead to the conclusion that her language dysfluency is not likely to be due to mental illness. *To conclude that she is mentally ill, we need evidence besides her language difficulties, and the evidence is not there.*

Other Language Examples

Even though Juanita has mental retardation, her language sample is fairly representative of what we see in patients we have come to conceptualize as "language dysfluency due to language deprivation." For example, here is a sample of language from another patient of near average intelligence.

Question: YOUR FAMILY. DEAF. HEARING. WHAT? EXPLAIN. (Tell me about your family? Are they hearing or deaf?)

Patient: HEARING, MY FATHER LIVE (wrong handshape for live) MY FATHER LIVE M-A-S-S. (points right) B-E-V-L-Y, NEAR BOSTON (points right) MOTHER LIVE LIVE MOTHER W-O-R-C-T-E-R W-O-R-C-T-E-R M-A-S-S (points right, same as before) BROTHER BROTHER T-O-M- T-O-M LIVE, M-A-N-A-I-E-D FIELD NEAR P-A-T-R-I-O-T FOOTBALL FOOTBALL THROW-FOOTBALL (points right, same as before) S-T-A-D-I-U-M (points right again) THROW-FOOTBALL.

So far this patient is not communicating well but he is understandable. He is using short sign phrases and sentences. He repeats signs unnecessarily, uses an incorrect handshape for a common sign (LIVE), uses signing space incorrectly (placing BOSTON and WORCESTER, which are at different parts of the state, in the same signing space, and then puts the stadium in the same place), and of course misspells the English names for two cities (which is a reflection of English language skills). He does not give the English name for the football stadium in Foxboro, Massachusetts but correctly identifies it as the place that the Patriot's team plays. When he signs, FOOTBALL FOOTBALL THROW-FOOTBALL S-T-A-D-I-U-M THROW-FOOTBALL, he is basically naming or identifying the stadium. His meaning is clear even though his vocabulary is poor. The segment appears to represent ASL language deficits but not a thinking disorder. Shortly afterward, however, we find this language segment:

Question: YOU HERE HOSPITAL FOR-FOR? (Why are you here in this hospital?)

Patient: E-X-GIRLFRIEND CRISIS, LIKE S-E-P-H-I-C T-A-N-K, MOVE TRUCK, ROUND, LEAKING, FOSTER HOME CHURCH. I VOLUNTEER PROGRAM. (looks down at striped, colored Koosh® ball he is holding) GREEN. MERRY CHRISTMAS. HAPPY NEW YEAR. HOTEL WEDDING THINK MAYBE PARTY.

In this segment, he is unable to make himself understood, and staff have to probe to obtain a coherent story from him. It is not clear what he is talking about. Most notable is the "loose thinking." He jumps from talking about his girlfriend and something that happened involving a septic tank and a truck to memories of foster home and church. He then gets distracted by the green stripe on the Koosh ball and associates it with Christmas, New Year, and a party at a hotel. This segment does not illustrate just impaired language. It also illustrates tangential thinking and loose associations. It is suggestive of psychosis, though one needs additional data before drawing conclusions.

In another interview (not videotaped), the interviewer showed the patient a series of pictures that showed a person putting laundry into a washing machine and the machine overflowing with sudsy water. The pictures occur in a sequence representing a simple story, and the patient was asked to tell the story. The patient began by describing/miming clothing being put in a washer, and then she switched to an apparent dialogue between a parent and a child. The parent scolds, FIGHT. STOP. FIGHT. The child responds, I-LIKE ICE-CREAM. This is a tangential association from the pictures. Describing the picture of the washing machine overflowing, she laughed and signed OVER-FLOW, NOT PAY-ATTENTION. OVERFLOW. At another point, shown a picture of a man sitting in a chair reading a newspaper, she signed RELAX WAIT TIME 30 MINUTES. In both sentences the subject or topic is missing. Grammatically correct sentences would be *WATER SOAP MIX* OVERFLOW. *MAN* NOT PAY-ATTENTION and *MAN* RELAX WAIT TIME 30 MINUTES. Also, in the best ASL, the 30 MINUTES would have started the sentence.

Beyond the language behavior, however, the patient demonstrated some significant nonverbal behaviors. She was highly distractible and used some nonsensical comments. For instance, at one point she looked past the interviewer to the electric socket on the wall behind him, pointed at it, and appeared to be miming getting an electrical shock. She looked away frequently and her eyes darted around wildly. At one point, she glanced at her stomach, pulled up her shirt to show her stomach, and signed "BABY," then a classifier handshape that may have meant umbilical cord, then "MOTHER FATHER" while looking very frightened. Her affect was exaggerated and grossly inappropriate for either a deaf or a hearing person. At an earlier point, asked how she feels, she signed HAPPY MUCH but her facial expression was one of sadness.

There is evidence here of language dysfluency related to both deprivation and psychosis though the overall presentation makes the psychosis more salient. We see evidence of thought disorder in her inappropriate affect, tangential comments, extremely high distractibility, and nonsense and bizarre comments. Language deprivation is seen in her impoverished vocabulary, short and simple sentence fragments, and lack of pronouns. Her signing was also mixed with gesture and pantomime, something that deaf language deprived people frequently display.

In the next example, a deaf patient signs the story of a relay race he observed. There are four players on the team. They run around a track and pass a baton to each other. Finally, one crosses the finish line.

He begins by gesturing *passing baton* and fingerspells R-E-Y, apparently intending *relay*. He then signs 4, 4 PLAYER (indicated with left index finger pointing to floor on right thigh; right hand U-handshape fingertips to floor diagonally and forward of the right knee) PLAYER PLAYER (signing "AGENT" touching his own body). He gestures again *passing baton*. He signs PLAYER 4, points in spatial locations, but creates a visually confused picture. He signs 4, then uses the right closed 5 handshape, drops it down as if gesturing "GO," changes to the right index finger and pulls it into an X handshape as if gesturing a gun going off, then, using the G handshape, signs ZOOM and mouths *pow* two times to indicate the starting gun going off. He then uses a 5 clawed handshape, fingertips to floor, as in MARCH (wrong handshape and palm orientation) to represent the classifier of runners moving around the track. He then uses 2 C-handshapes to create a pipe (baton) and then gestures a runner handing it off to another runner. However, his hands get tangled up as he strives to gesture the baton passing. He cannot quite represent it on himself. Finally, he signs, COMPETE COMPETE COMPETE DON'T KNOW. He signs LINE at his own chest and then leans forward to show a runner breaking through a finish line. He signs WIN, then SEE AGAIN SEE AGAIN and an additional gesture/sign that is not clear. He mouths *over*.

This depiction of a relay race is organized and logical. However, it is poorly told. There are a very limited number of signs actually used. He uses PLAYER when he means RUNNER. Classifier handshapes are used incorrectly. He relies mainly on gesturing, embedded in a story with some signs, but even his gesturing is awkward. He does not really show what passing the baton from one runner to another would look like. He attempts to use the spatial field of the signer but his placement of the runners is visually confusing. There are no real sentences. The viewer can guess his meaning based on pieces of information. He is not using facial grammar. His body movement is used inconsistently and unclearly to indicate shifting characters.

All of this reflects language impoverishment. There is nothing crazy or illogical in his depiction of the story but he lacks the vocabulary and language structure to articulate it.

Another patient was a 30-year-old deaf man, also from a third-world country, who, as far as staff knew, had no formal education. He communicated with family members using a combination of home sign and gesture. The Unit's best Deaf communicators could not easily understand him. His brother communicated with him better than anyone, using the same home signs and gestures, but even there the communication was imprecise. We videotaped him telling a story. His communication is almost entirely mime and gesture.

Staff: NAME YOU WHAT? (What is your name?)
Patient: (Name sign T on forehead) T-O-M-A-S
Staff: WORK BEFORE YOU? (Have you worked?)
Patient: GHANA FLY FLY ME (Puts on leg braces starting at the foot up to the hip) WORK GHANA (putting on and strapping leg braces foot to hip and adjusting the straps, tightening and cinching at the

waste and shoulder harness). CRUTCHES (Making crutches step by step process in intricate detail). CRUTCHES WORK WORK FINE WORK CRUTCHES ME SMART (making the handles, screwing on wing nuts by hand, adjusting, measuring the length, hand screwing) ME THUMBS-UP GOOD WORK SMART HOSPITAL (unconventional sign G handshape making shape of the Cross on upper left arm) (putting on and strapping leg braces, foot to hip and adjusting the straps, tightening and cinching at the waist and shoulder harness, using cane to walk) LEARN (throws cane away).

This mostly mimed sequence is logical and organized. The patient is recounting the story of making crutches. He shows how they were made in detail. He repeats himself and adds comments like ME SMART (that is, I know how to do it). While his signing skills are very poor, his visual-gestural communication skills are excellent. This presentation does not suggest psychosis.

On the Unit, this man was frequently seen "talking to himself." He sat at the window, gesturing and mumbling to himself, and other deaf people could not understand him. A psychiatrist (new to deafness), who walked by, saw the patient communicating to himself, could be forgiven for interpreting this behavior to be evidence of psychosis. But is talking to yourself *normal* for a deaf person who grew up without a formal language system and without the experience of linguistic communication with people outside his immediate family? We do not know. How can we judge what is normal for a person with a life experience that is so abnormal? We certainly do not have enough data to be confident about such an inference. Our conclusion has to be: there is not enough here to suggest psychosis. We need more data before drawing such a conclusion.

Language Dysfluency: Language Deprivation Versus Thought Disorder

Our knowledge of differential diagnostic assessment between language dysfluency caused by mental illness and language dysfluency caused by language deprivation in deaf people is still rudimentary, but we can advance this knowledge by first recognizing the issue. Observation and study conducted with deaf inpatients at the Deaf Unit at Westborough State Hospital, and review of prior literature, especially the important contributions by Thacker (1994, 1998) suggests some guidelines.

The language skills of deaf persons who are language dysfluent related to language deprivation will vary enormously. The most severely language deprived will communicate with visual-gestural systems, including home signs, and no formal language at all. At the other extreme will be deaf persons with a great deal of sign vocabulary and some grammatical features. The language deficits seen will reflect inadequate learning. Vocabulary is poor with sign and sign features formed incorrectly or used with the wrong meaning.

Basic elements of clear communication, such as the topic-comment structure, or the presence of clear referents (who did what to whom), or time vocabulary and indicators, may be missing or used inconsistently and incorrectly. In the absence of grammar, signs may be repeated unnecessarily. Isolated signs or short sign phrases will be present rather than full sentences. Even the correct grammatical use of the signing spatial field, which one might suppose would be natural to deaf persons, is likely to be impaired. The person may act out scenes, like the patients described above acting out the process of passing a baton in a relay race or constructing crutches, but this is not the same as using the grammatical features of ASL to construct a story in the visual field.

We have also observed a number of language dysfluent persons refer to themselves in the third person. They will say, for instance, JOE ANGRY rather than ME ANGRY.

A deaf person who is a native, competent user of ASL and who is language dysfluent because of a thought disorder will not make these types of language errors. Although language skills that deteriorate markedly from a previous level are important clues of possible thought disorder, psychotic persons do not lose their native language. Rather, they may make loose or bizarre connections between one idea and another. Their ability to attend to and follow through on a task may suffer, and they can become easily distracted. They may get caught up with the structural qualities of signs (such as handshapes or sign locations) rather than the meaning of signs (clanging). Most likely, along with language dysfluency one will observe a disconnection between thought, emotion, and behavior that one would not expect to see in deaf persons with language deprivation only.

The real diagnostic dilemmas will occur, of course, with deaf persons who are language deprived and may also have a thought disorder. Some symptoms such as concreteness and poverty of content are clearly related to both causes. A neologism or made up word may be easy to confuse with a home sign that only a few persons understand. Impoverished vocabulary may look a lot like thought blocking. Inappropriate dress and behaviors may be related to inadequate development of social and personal care skills as well as mental illness. Behavioral problems frequently occur in both conditions. Eye contact behavior is highly dependent on cultural and personal experience. It is very difficult to enter the conceptual world of a person with severe language skills and to begin to imagine what is normal and healthy for someone with such an abnormal life experience. Behavior such as "talking to oneself" is ambiguous. It also requires an exceptionally high level of sign language skill to even break down the nature of the signing errors that are occurring.

Loose and tangential associations are harder to categorize. Both language deprivation and mental illness can prevent a person from telling an organized story, giving a clear account of who did what to whom over time. Generally, the "looser" and more bizarre the connection between ideas, the more this suggests a thought disorder. Recall the deaf patient, presented earlier, who gave a coherent and organized account, in mostly visual-gestural communication, of how he built leg crutches. His "language" had almost no formal grammar, but his account was organized and sequential, and his affect and interpersonal relatedness were normal. By contrast the deaf patient who jumped from talking about pictures being displayed to miming getting a shock from the electronic wall socket to showing her stomach and conveying something about an umbilical cord and a baby, all the while with poor eye contact and very strange facial expressions, was clearly psychotic.

We have also concluded that clinicians should be slow to make inferences about hallucinations and delusions, especially when they are not directly observed or are nonbizarre. There are so many potential problems in translation between languages and conceptual worlds that great humbleness is called for in the clinician.

With all these difficulties, there are still clues that point the diagnosis toward thought disorder rather than language deprivation:

1. Inappropriate (for Deaf Culture) facial and emotional expression.
2. Language content that is not merely off the point but actually bizarre. As noted above, the looser the connection between thoughts, the more this suggests a thought disorder.
3. Nonverbal behaviors suggesting hallucinations (eyes darting, preoccupation with phenomena unseen to the clinician).
4. Guardedness, suspiciousness, and volatility. Clinicians communicating with psychotic persons often feel that they may explode any moment. There is a sense that they "aren't there." One does not usually experience this with language dysfluent, nonpsychotic persons.
5. In language deprived persons, the language problems have been longstanding. There was not a point when the person communicated better than now. In a thought disordered mentally ill person, there is usually a worsening of communication skills from a previous baseline.
6. The personal appearance and behavior of psychotic persons are often striking and abnormal for their cultural context. Self-care is often poor. The person may wear clothing inappropriate for the weather. There is no reason I can think of why a language dysfluent person who is nonpsychotic would wear winter clothing in the summer, dress only in black, or refuse to take off heavy boots when going to sleep at night. These are behaviors we observed in a deaf man with schizophrenia.
7. In most cases, when a patient's language is disorganized due to psychosis, the language will improve as psychiatric medication clears up the thought disorder. When the language is disorganized due to language deprivation, medication will not correct the problem.

Interpreting for Language Dysfluent Persons

Most hearing clinicians performing diagnostic assessments of deaf persons will be working with interpreters. The clinician without specialized training in deafness will have no understanding of the language dynamics and will just expect the interpreter to translate. Interpreters who are not trained mental health interpreters may be unprepared for language dysfluency in their clients. To do this work well, the clinician and the interpreter need to be familiar with the kinds of language dysfluency that may occur, and they must have some agreed-upon strategy for handling this dysfluency. They must also be talking with each other about the choices the interpreter is making in the interpretation process.

Karlin (2003) described the dilemmas faced by the mental health sign language interpreter when interpreting for a client with a thought disorder. She gives examples of dysfluent communication that may be related to mental illness. She notes, for instance, that mentally ill persons may be incoherent. Their "grammar and syntax are deficient." This is true, but this incoherency is more likely to be a result of language deprivation. Karlin notes that interpreters need to be trained how to respond to these instances of language dysfluency. She quotes the RID Standard Practice Paper, "Interpreting in Mental Health Settings," which says: "The interpreter can provide information and opinions related to the communication process, but not on the therapeutic process." The interpreter might state, for instance, about the client's communication that "her signing is less coherent than when I was here last Monday. The signs are not as well formed and her grammar is poor." The clinician must draw conclusions about what this means.

Sometimes with language dysfluent clients like Juanita, a second, relay interpreter, called a Certified Deaf Interpreter (CDI), is brought in to assist the hearing interpreter. Because hearing clinicians not trained in work with deaf people generally have limited experience with severe language deprivation, the need for a second relay interpreter can be puzzling. Clinicians usually assume that the language challenges are no more complex than that of interpreting from one language to another. It is difficult to understand the need for a CDI without knowing what language deprivation in deaf people looks like. CDIs are especially talented in communicating in visual-gestural communication and very simple, clear ASL. The clinicians are told that the first interpreter will interpret from English to some kind of more formal sign language, and the relay interpreter will "bring it down" to the level of the client. The translation process now goes through two people, at least one of whose job is to simplify the content. The clinician needs to understand the actual language patterns used in order to form clinical judgments, but in the interpretation process there is a significant chance that language dysfluent communication might be "repaired" in the interest of clarity. Top level mental health interpreters will not do this, but interpreters not trained in mental health work, or simply less experienced interpreters, might. CDIs are even more likely to change the content in some way which is clinically significant. The most likely danger is to present dysfluent communication as clearer and more coherent than it really is.

Interpreting dilemmas also occur in translating from the clinician to the deaf language dysfluent client. We have already discussed the difficulty that can arise in translating the concept of auditory hallucination. Similar interpreting challenges arise with abstract questions like these: *Is there any history of mental illness in your family? What has your mood been like over the last week? Did you ever experience physical or sexual abuse?* Interpreting dilemmas occur even when the clinician does not make gross errors such as asking for translation of English idioms. The author read one report where a psychologist without deafness experience asked the deaf client to repeat back "no ifs, ands, or buts," an idiom which makes no sense in sign and which cannot be translated. The deaf client in this situation did not have comprehensible speech and had very minimal knowledge of English. The clinician also asked the client to spell *world* backward and to define "season." The client knew the sign for WORLD but very possibly not the English word. The client did not know the word "season," which is not surprising given that the concept is translated into ASL as WINTER, SPRING, SUMMER, FALL. If the clinician were linguistically informed and the interpreter were appropriately trained for handling language dysfluent communication, then the two of them would have discussed the nature of what is occurring in the translation process.

The Deaf Wellness Center at the University of Rochester Medical Center has developed a curriculum for training mental health interpreters (Pollard, 1998b), which includes instruction on handling language dysfluent communication. However, the dysfluent communication refers to "times when mental or physical illness disrupt the structure of a person's language" (p. 94) and not necessarily to language dysfluency related to language deprivation. Nonetheless, two of the strategies presented represent best practices. The first is for the interpreter to describe what he or she observes (for example, "she is signing very fast. There is no subject so I don't know who she is referring to. She is repeating the sign MOTHER many more times than is necessary. She is not using the spatial field accurately so it isn't clear to me who gave what to whom"). The second is to describe and gloss, or present translations of individual signs without trying to make sense of them as a whole. The language samples presented in this chapter are glosses. Pollard gives the following example of glossing:

> Mother ... went (somewhere) ... devil with red eyes glaring, coming ... (something about) shouting and hitting ... mother was a girl a long time ago ... the devil won't, won't ... (I missed some there) ... you know the devil ... I'm 50 years old. (p. 95)

There are very few mental health clinicians in the deafness field today who have both the clinical and communication expertise to make sense of language dysfluent communication in deaf persons. Even when the clinician signs, this work usually requires a team consisting, at a minimum, of the clinician and a trained mental health interpreter. Specialized settings like the Westborough Deaf Unit may have a Communication Specialist on staff whose job is to analyze the communication patterns of patients. The key idea for these team members to remember is that they are a team, and that they need to have open communication about the communication process itself. The interpreter can and should comment on language and interpreting dynamics, but it is the clinician who must decide whether a client is mentally ill.*

Conclusions: Look for Redundancy in Evidence

Mental status assessment of deaf persons is more complex than that of hearing persons. One reason is because many Deaf people have ASL as a first language and are nonfluent in the spoken language of their hearing community. They are language minorities as well as cultural minorities, and culturally informed assessments need to occur (Glickman & Gulati, 2003; Glickman & Harvey, 1996). In recent years, this fact is receiving more widespread recognition. Another complication that is rarely recognized by nondeafness mental health specialists is that many deaf persons have experienced severe language deprivation. Language dysfluency is the core characteristic in the large group of deaf persons most commonly referred to as traditionally underserved deaf, and these persons are highly likely to be referred to any specialized educational, rehabilitation, or mental health service for deaf persons (Dew, 1999; Long, 1993; Long, Long, & Ouellette, 1993). In these settings, someone will inevitably be asked to provide a clinical assessment, and this person will come face to face with the diagnostic dilemmas associated with language dysfluency. As we saw, it is exceptionally easy for competent mental health clinicians without extensive training in deafness to assume that language dysfluency is due to a thought disorder.

The opportunities for misjudgments about deaf patients are many. They include misunderstandings related to conveying the concept of hallucination, culturally naïve and biased determinations about apparent delusions such as paranoia, and failure to recognize and evaluate carefully for the possibility of language deprivation. For clinicians with no knowledge of ASL, additional sources of error are embedded in the issue of whether the interpreter is skilled in mental health interpreting and whether the interpreter and clinician know how to collaborate on this task (Karlin, 2003; Stansfield, 1981; Veltri

---

* See Karlin (2003), Pollard (1998a), Stansfield (1981), Veltri and Stansfield (1986) for more on this. Discussions with interpreters about the patients' communication abilities should always occur in private, not with the patient present.

& Stansfield, 1986). Because the likelihood of diagnostic error is so great, it is recommended that clinicians be conservative in their evaluations. That is, clinicians should hesitate to draw conclusions about psychosis unless the data are unambiguous (for example, a bizarre delusion, a readily observable hallucination) or there are multiple indicators of psychosis (Gulati, 2003). Clinicians should be especially careful not to draw conclusions based solely on the patient's language. Gross (and in this day and age unforgivable) errors occur when basing these judgments on the spoken or written language of the deaf patient, but the same care needs to be applied when analyzing the quality of the patient's signing. When an interpreter is being used, clinicians should discuss with the interpreter how the interview questions are being translated and the kind of language output the patient is producing. Interpreters cannot diagnose thought disorders, but they should be able to discuss with the clinician the nature of the patient's communication skills.

On the Westborough Deaf Unit, the majority of patients are language dysfluent (see Chapter 1). As people without intact full language, they often develop behavioral problems or, as mental health clinicians say, behavioral *disorders*. These traditionally underserved deaf persons are highly likely to make up a significant portion of the clientele served by identified deafness mental health and rehabilitation programs, and they are highly likely to present the greatest clinical challenges. Treatment models in which an interpreter is placed in a hearing treatment center will most likely fail with such clients, and the staff, unfamiliar with this kind of language dysfluency, will not understand why (Glickman, 2003).

For decades now, Deaf people and their advocates have fought for the recognition of ASL and genuine communication inclusion of signing Deaf people. While this battle is far from won, we have an even greater challenge, which is to find ways of educating and serving signing deaf people who are not fluent users of any language. On the Westborough Deaf Unit, staff see every day the terrible implications of growing up deaf without full access to natural sign languages like ASL. When these patients are referred for psychiatric crises or severe mental illness, their problems will be confounded by the implications of this language deprivation. This chapter addressed some of the implications for assessment. Chapters 4 through 7 address the equally compelling implications for mental health treatment.

Acknowledgments

The author thanks the following people for their assistance with this chapter: Wendy Petrarca, Susan Jones, and Michael Krajnak for their assistance in communication assessments; Michael Harvey, Robert Pollard, Philip Candilis, and Marc Marschark for their helpful reviews of this chapter; Pat Black for her research on the Westborough Deaf Unit that highlighted the significance of language deprivation in our clinical work.

3

Language and Learning Challenges in Adolescent Hearing Psychiatric Inpatients

JEFFREY J. GAINES, BRUCE MELTZER, AND NEIL GLICKMAN

Many hearing psychiatric inpatients have significant language and learning challenges (Jaeger, Burns, Tigner, & Douglas, 1992). These challenges interfere with their ability to use standard talk- and insight-oriented therapies. The majority of patients on the University of Massachusetts Medical Center (UMMC) Adolescent Continuing Care Units at Westborough State Hospital in Westborough, Massachusetts have such challenges. These language and learning challenges range from moderate to severe and take a variety of forms. They have many and overlapping causes such as genetic factors, chaotic upbringings, education deprivation, and medical and psychiatric symptoms.

The lead author of this chapter is a neuropsychologist at Westborough State Hospital. He performs neuropsychological evaluations on all the patients admitted to the two adolescent units. He has also worked with the third author in performing psychological and neuropsychological evaluations of deaf patients on the hospital's Deaf Unit. The second author is a psychiatrist and medical director of the adolescent units. The adolescent and Deaf units are in close proximity in the same building, and over the years, the three of us have had conversations in which we found similarities between the language and learning challenges of deaf patients and those of hearing adolescent patients treated at the hospital. With both groups of patients, the problems that brought them into the hospital were not limited to the occurrence of major mental illness such as schizophrenia. Rather they have a variety of developmentally based problems which could broadly be defined as deficits in psychosocial skills. Most have severe behavioral problems, either hurting themselves or other people frequently, and significant numbers have experienced multiple kinds of trauma. When they have major mental illness, it is usually in addition to these developmental and trauma-based problems. The challenges of helping them are not simply the severity of these problems but the accompanying cognitive and language deficits which make learning new skills difficult for them.

Unlike the deaf patients, the hearing adolescent patients all have a native first language. Nonetheless, most are unskilled language users with poorly

79

developed logical reasoning abilities. A small number have language skills that are so poor that they are functionally nonverbal. The purpose of this chapter is to discuss the language and learning challenges our hearing adolescent patients face and their implications for mental health care. Our Deaf Unit patients also have these problems, though in the face of the extreme language deprivation so many of them have endured it becomes difficult to parse out the causes. For example, many of our deaf patients have attention and behavioral problems and readily apparent difficulties learning new information. Great caution should be observed, however, before jumping to conclusions about, say, attention-deficit/hyperactivity disorder or specific learning difficulties because these problems have many possible causes, the most obvious of which is the impact of this severe language deprivation (Gulati, 2003).

Overview of Our Adolescent Hearing Population

Our adolescent units treat chronically hospitalized psychiatric persons, aged 12 to 19. The units house both male and female patients. Approximately 80% of our patients have a history of physical and/or sexual trauma. Our patients commonly show disorganized, agitated, aggressive, or self-injurious behaviors that have proved difficult to manage in the community or short-term psychiatric settings. They come to us if they need continuing assessment, treatment, and stabilization prior to reentry into the community or a less restrictive institutional setting. Patients often stay a year or more. They attend a specialized school on grounds, receive intensive psychiatric and psychological services, and are discharged when judged adequately stable for extended stay outside the hospital.

We can classify our patients as falling into one of two groups. The first group has generally intact, even strong language and learning skills. This minority of our patients usually have primary diagnoses like major depression or an eating disorder. The second group includes those with distinct language and learning challenges. This majority of our patients usually carry primary diagnoses such as bipolar disorder, schizoaffective disorder, schizophrenia, pervasive developmental disorder, mild mental retardation, and neurological complications like fetal alcohol syndrome or stroke with psychiatric symptoms. This chapter focuses on the last group, whose psychiatric and cognitive deficits are pronounced and interdependent. We explore the cognitive deficits in this majority group and their implications for psychotherapeutic treatment.

The Neuropsychological Evaluation

In this chapter, we consider language and learning challenges the way a neuropsychologist does, by reviewing different aspects of brain (or cognitive) functioning. We consider each kind of cognitive function and discuss how it is impaired in so many of our clients. Our aim is to give a more detailed account of what we mean by "language and learning challenges" using nontechnical terms to the extent possible. This chapter complements the discussion of language dysfluency related to language deprivation presented in Chapter 2 though that is, of course, rarely an issue with hearing persons.

Different areas or circuits in the brain are responsible for different functions. For example, the left side of the brain in over 90% of people is largely responsible for understanding spoken, written, and signed language, and for producing speech (Poizner, Klima, & Bellugi, 1987). The right side of the brain is largely responsible for using visual information (such as reading a map, organizing things in one's room, understanding the meaning of facial expressions and other social cues, and so on; see Gazzaniga, 2000).

Neuropsychologists give tests measuring basic intelligence and other cognitive skills. Intelligence is a construct that summarizes a number of cognitive skills such as vocabulary, verbal reasoning, visual-spatial skills, nonverbal reasoning, attention and working memory, speed of information processing, academic abilities, and learning. We consider now each area of functioning, what impairment there looks like, and give clinical examples. We also discuss the ways in which major mental illnesses affect language and learning.

Intelligence

We measure intelligence with IQ tests. Intelligence, like personality, is an abstract psychological construct. It can be defined in different ways depending on what specific skills it is thought to include (Gardner, 1993; Goleman, 1996). We measure intelligence by breaking it down into smaller skills, assessing these, and then considering the overall pattern of cognitive abilities. The components of intelligence we review here are vocabulary, verbal reasoning, visual-spatial abilities, attention, working memory, and speed of information processing.

Vocabulary

Vocabulary is a good indicator of language skills and a reasonably good measure of educational achievement and overall intelligence (in hearing people). Is the person's vocabulary limited to common objects like "chair" or does the person understand more abstract concepts like "consequence?" A word like "consequence" is used often in behavioral therapies but we have hearing clients who do not know the word and do not understand when staff use it unless considerable time is spent explaining it.

Matt was a 17-year-old boy admitted to our program after a lengthy series of hospitalizations and out-of-home placements. At age 16, he was in the seventh grade, or fully 3 years behind his peers. He experienced physical, emotional, and sexual abuse by his mother's very violent boyfriend, severe neglect, and a head trauma with loss of consciousness from an automobile accident. His family members had an extensive history of mood disorders, alcohol abuse, and cognitive problems. When he came to us, he had a nearly lifelong pattern of aggression, explosive behaviors, suicidal thinking and gestures, self-harming behaviors, and poor peer relationships. Although this was his first hospitalization admission to the UMMC Adolescent Continuing Care Units, it was his twelfth psychiatric admission overall.

Matt had enormous difficulty using words to describe his feelings or thoughts. Like many Deaf Unit patients, he expressed himself with behavior, not language.

On a test, Matt was asked to look at a picture of a cord in the middle of a floor and describe what was dangerous. He could identify the cord as dangerous but could not say why (that one might trip on it or use it to harm oneself). He knew the value of individual coins but he could not add coins or make change. He required a paper and pencil and assistance to subtract 50 cents from $1. He had difficulty writing his address and was unaware of his home city, state, or zip code.

Matt was able to bathe and groom himself and clean his room. He could not use words to express and cope with feelings and certainly not to negotiate with other people. He had great difficulty stating what he wanted or needed. To complete tasks, he needed clear, simple, one-step instructions (for example, "put the spaghetti in the pot"). He did much better in gross motor leisure and sensory tasks (sport activities, exercise, playing with animals).

When we studied Matt's history, we found a clear relationship between worsening aggression and certain medications he was prescribed. He experienced a symptom called akathisia, which refers to an uncomfortable, restless, anxious feeling. Matt could not tell us about that feeling so it was some time before we understood that the medication was causing some of his behavioral problems. When we finally understood this and changed the medication, his behaviors improved. Unfortunately, Matt literally did not have words for his experience and therefore could not collaborate well with his doctors.

Neuropsychologists also give specialized receptive and expressive language tests, assessing abilities not covered by most verbal IQ measures. One of these abilities is *naming*. The ability to easily name objects in the surrounding world is something many of us take for granted. Asking patients to name natural and manufactured objects, as depicted in simple line drawings, generally tests this ability. Our patients struggle on this type of test. For example, most would be able to name an object they use every day such as a *pen*. However, they would struggle to name less common objects shown in pictures such as a *billboard*. This is consistent with their generally low vocabulary, and has similar implications for treatment. It means that staff must be careful about the words and names we use. When we use words or names that are too sophisticated, patients will not benefit fully from instruction, conversation, or counseling. One unfamiliar word or name can throw off their understanding of an entire message, resulting in confusion and/or feeling overwhelmed. Many patients on our units are embarrassed by their inability to understand certain words, names, or phrases. They pretend to understand, nodding their heads and trying to cover up their lack of knowledge. This behavior is so well known in the Deaf world that we actually have a sign for it, translated roughly as "the empty nod."

Verbal Reasoning

Using language to reason includes such abstract thinking skills as understanding how one thing is similar to another, seeing patterns, and identifying cause and effect. Abstract thinking deficits are common in our patients. If we asked them, for instance, how "fear" and "anger" are alike (that is, they are both emotions and both generally unpleasant), they would not know. Their thinking is *concrete*. That is, they take events or experiences as isolated events. They do not connect them to see patterns. They do not see how one thing may represent an instance of a larger category. A patient might understand, for instance, that punching a wall is not allowed and threatening peers is not allowed, but not see that both of these are forms of *aggression* falling into the category of *unsafe behaviors.*

We have many patients who want to increase their level of independent privileges (clearance to attend certain programs, go out on grounds with staff or family members). One patient requested increased privileges to go on community outings. However, he had also been touching other patients inappropriately during day program. Staff explained to him that inappropriate touching represented a lack of self-control, and that he needed to demonstrate better self-control before staff could allow him access to the community. He struggled to make the mental connection between lack of self-control in the day program and anticipated lack of self-control in the community. He did not see how they represented the same concern.

This problem will, again, be very familiar to people working with language and learning challenged deaf clients. Patients who do not readily see patterns (for instance, between events in the past and current emotions, or between behaviors, emotions and thoughts) can be said to lack *insight.* As discussed in Chapter 4, this becomes a formidable barrier to insight-oriented therapy. Sometimes disagreements between staff and patients over, for instance, whether or not they have been *safe* are really because the patients do not relate specific behaviors (unwanted touching of a peer, banging a wall) to the abstract category of safety. Thus the disagreement really stems from conceptual misunderstanding.

Visual-Spatial Skills

One of the authors remembers a time when he hired a mover. The man arrived with a small truck into which he had to fit several rooms of furniture and accessories. To the author, this seemed like an impossible task, but the mover then did an astonishing job of fitting hundreds of items of all shapes and sizes into a very small space. That mover had superb visual-spatial abilities. Other examples of this ability include organizing one's bedroom, repairing a bicycle, finding one's way around a residence or neighborhood, and reading people's facial cues and body language. These kinds of skills are as important for daily living as are verbal abilities.

Commonly used intelligence tests such as the Wechsler scales measure several visual-spatial skills. They measure the ability to assemble things according to a plan, see complex visual patterns, and use reasoning based on pictures (for example, identifying what is similar between different pictures as in "these pictures all show things that float"). Most of our patients do well on the test that measures their ability to assembly patterns based on abstract designs. This is consistent with the observation that many do relatively well with hands-on, multimodal learning (using movement, touch, vision), especially when guided by models. They also tend to do well at a task that asks them to identify which of a group of common objects does not fit with the others (for example, a kite, a bird, a plane, a hamburger). On the other hand, as the visual patterns they are asked to work with become more unfamiliar, complex, and abstract, their abilities fall apart. When the amount of visual information they have to take in, understand, and act on becomes complex, they have difficulty coping.

Staff see the evidence of poor visual-spatial skills often. They see it with patients whose bedrooms are impossibly messy. The problem is not just, as staff sometimes think, that these patients *will not* straighten out their rooms. It is that they *cannot* without a great deal of assistance. They are just overwhelmed by the mess and they cannot figure out how to begin. Similarly, patients may have difficulty finding their clothing and getting to groups on time. Staff may conclude wrongly that the patients are lazy when really the problem is poor organizational skills. An occupational therapist might be teaching these skills through a water painting project. The patient may have no idea how to organize the workspace so that the cup of water is not knocked over on to the paint or the drawing, creating a sloppy mess. The occupational therapist helps the patient think about how to organize the workspace so the art project can be accomplished and frustration avoided.

Nonverbal Learning Disabilities

Increasing attention is being paid in the psychological literature to what is called "nonverbal learning disability" (Kronenberger & Dunn, 2003). Although this is not yet a diagnosis found in the *Diagnostic and Statistical Manual of Mental Disorders* (latest version: DSM-IV-TR), there is evidence to support the existence of such a syndrome, as an area of special deficit even when other cognitive domains are relatively preserved (Forrest, 2004). Individuals with nonverbal learning disability have difficulty seeing how parts fit into a whole. They have the related difficulties in organizing a workspace, a room, their appearance, and their movement through space. They may position themselves too close to other people without realizing they are intruding on the other person's "space."

Nonverbal learning disability is also associated with difficulty reading facial expressions, body language, and other social cues. Consider how we communicate to someone we are talking with that we want to end the conversation. We may look away, move backward, check our watches, or finally say, "Excuse me, I need to go." People with a nonverbal learning disability may misread these social cues. This contributes to other people misjudging them (concluding, for example, that they are overly aggressive or intrusive) and to social problems.

To address this problem, we have developed a "social cues" group wherein patients are asked to bodily express emotions such as "feeling frightened" or "feeling happy." Our staff were surprised to see how many patients struggled with depicting emotions through their facial expression, posture, and body movements. Many patients were said to simply "draw a blank" when asked to depict these emotions. They also had difficulty reading the emotion a staff member was trying to depict, even in the most unambiguous fashion.

Many of our patients have both language-based and nonverbal skill deficits. Some of the patients with excellent verbal intelligence nonetheless have very poor nonverbal abilities. Charlene was an example of someone in this latter group.

Charlene was a 17-year-old girl who was admitted with the chief complaint of "I want to stop feeling this way. I want to go home and lead a normal life and do the things I used to do. I want to be safe and healthy." She had tried to hang herself twice, had a long history of cutting herself, abusive dieting, overeating and then purging, along with very unstable mood. She experienced at least two incidents of sexual abuse as a child and young teenager. She had at one time been functioning as a straight A student at a private school, but over the 18 months prior to admission, she began abusing alcohol and drugs, became sexually promiscuous, started her pattern of binging and purging, became self-abusive, and finally made serious suicide attempts.

Although Charlene's language skills were excellent, she showed nonverbal learning problems in her poor ability to read social cues and manage interpersonal relationships. She could not identify her own emotions and was even less skilled at reading the emotions of peers. This interfered with her ability to empathize with others and make friends. Her nonverbal learning disability, experience of sexual abuse, and upbringing in a chaotic family all contributed to her great confusion regarding social rules and expectations and interpersonal boundaries. She did not know what she believed, and was completely at a loss when faced with the common therapeutic task of identifying her feelings. She knew she was smart, but she could not identify anything else that was positive about her personality. She had no sense of her own "voice," self, or identity; and therapeutic conversations aimed at exploring these were unproductive. Because of her difficulty in understanding and processing social interactions, she felt that family therapy was "pointless." Having no language for her own experience, she did not believe that her parents, or anyone else, could understand her either.

Charlene was extremely good at being able to complete cognitive tasks like homework. She was extremely poor at most of the social tasks she faced: making and keeping friends, recognizing and handling emotions, responding to rules and expectations, participating appropriately in social events. Most of her interactions with people were superficial and driven by what she wanted at a particular moment. Her language skills were excellent as long as she was feeling no strong emotion. In the face of strong emotion, her language literally crumbled, and she found herself at a loss for words. These deficits made contexts such as counseling, in which she is invited to talk about her feelings, very unpleasant, so she avoided or sabotaged efforts to engage her therapeutically.

Attention and Working Memory

Attention and working memory are important (and interrelated) abilities. Attention is the ability to focus on information coming in, such as a task one is doing. We use attention when we listen to a conversation, read a street sign, watch a television program, play a game with friends, and so on. It is a critical cognitive ability, serving as a building block for all others. If one cannot attend properly to information—and sometimes more than one type of information at a time (as in "multitasking")—one cannot function adequately in the environment, learn or recall things properly.

"Working memory" is the related ability to hold new information in mind long enough to use it (as when we are told a phone number, and without writing it down go to a nearby telephone and call the number). Working memory is also a foundational skill for learning. We need to be able to hold new information in mind long enough to attach meaning to it, engrain it for easy recall, and act on it as necessary.

Attention and working-memory deficits are very common in psychiatric inpatient populations (Iverson, Lange, Viljoen, & Brink, 2006), and our adolescents are no exception. When these skills are impaired, it is difficult for people to make any gains in their recovery. If patients cannot attend properly to what is going on around them, including treatment information/guidance, they will not be able to fully process or retain pertinent information of any kind: verbal, visual-spatial, social, and so forth. Our patients perform poorly on all tests which measure these skills, and we staff see evidence of the real-world consequences daily. Patients have difficult attending to and retaining important information such as that pertaining to medication, treatment, privileges, unit policies and rules. For example, a patient might be asked to bring her laundry to the laundry room. She becomes distracted on the way to get the laundry by conversations with peers or a note on the bulletin board. She forgets about the laundry and walks into another room to watch television.

Even if she made it to the laundry room, she might forget on arrival what she is there to do. Staff see incidents like this, in which patients forget what they were supposed to be doing, frequently.

These skill deficits have huge implications for teaching and counseling. They require staff to present information in ways that increase the likelihood it will be received and processed. Instructions usually have to be broken down into simple, declarative statements supported by gestures or other visual cues—for example, "Please push the button here (teacher points), that pops out your disc … put the disc in your folder like this (demonstrated with teacher's disc/folder) … and push this button (teacher points) to turn off your computer." This direction may need to be repeated often and in exactly the same way.

Speed of Information Processing

Information processing speed is another very basic ability that involves the *rate* at which one takes new information in, makes sense of it, and acts on it. Imagine listening to a recording that is speeding up. As the speed increases, our ability to understand decreases until at some point we cannot follow at all. If you have had the experience of trying to learn a new language, you may have had the sense that people were speaking (or signing) that language too rapidly. Usually, they are conversing at a natural pace, but to a new learner it appears to be very fast. Most people know that when they speak to a new learner of English, they should slow down, enunciate clearly, and perhaps select simpler words. We understand intuitively that we must present information slowly to people who do not know a language well.

The ability to process information at a certain speed is necessary to keep pace with everyday situations and tasks. Processing speed is consistently lower in psychiatric inpatients than in the general population (Iverson et al., 2006). Our patients do poorly on formal tests of information processing speed and on tasks occurring across multiple contexts such as therapy groups, school, and in the treatment milieu. Patients with this difficulty are often labeled "slow learners."

Staff note that the typical patient on our units requires information presented at about *half* the speed one uses when interacting with the general population. Staff must learn to speak slowly, use smaller words, and give information in smaller "chunks." One must also prompt patients before they are asked to do something. They need time to get ready to do a task. For instance, reminding patients 5 minutes before a group increases the likelihood they will get there.

A new psychology intern discovered this problem upon her arrival at the hospital. As one of her first duties, she began interviewing patients for a research study concerning patients' view of how they came to be at the hospital. She started by asking questions at a rate she would normally use with persons in the general population. Even though content of the questions was relatively simple, she could not be understood by many patients at the hospital because the rate at which she asked the questions was far too fast. Many patients did not follow what she was saying until her supervisor advised she speak at a slower, more measured pace. At that point, patients were better able to follow the questions and could participate in the study.

Clinicians who are in a hurry, who have a long list of questions to ask and not enough time, tend to overlook the speed of information processing issue. They want quick answers. We have seen this happen when clinicians seek to gather a history. The amount of time they have allotted to the task, or was allotted for them in managed care contexts, is unrealistic. This is a huge issue when they are interviewing language and learning challenged deaf clients and going through one or two interpreters. Doing this work well takes more time, often substantially more time. We can avoid unnecessary stress if we give ourselves the time to accommodate to the speed and manner in which clients process information.

Academic Abilities

Basic academic skills include reading ("decoding," or ability to recognize and pronounce or sign words; and reading comprehension, the ability to understand the meaning of what one reads and answer questions about it), writing (including spelling, proper punctuation and grammar, development of ideas in writing, and so forth), and written math skills (basic calculation using addition, subtraction, multiplication, division, and so forth). Patients on our units receive schooling while here as well as academic-level testing within the neuropsychological battery.

Results from academic testing done as part of the neuropsychological evaluation show that our patients' sight reading or pronunciation of single words is fairly low, about fourth grade level when most of the students are well beyond fourth grade age. Reading comprehension skills (reading and answering questions about grade level passages) are much lower, about second grade level. Patients' basic math skills are also quite low (about second grade level). These results show that many of our patients will require substantial academic support throughout future schooling. Their relatively poor academic skills will have a negative impact on the development of skills for working and independent living. They are likely to struggle in the future with reading more complex materials, such as employee manuals, and with mathematics for managing household expenses.

Poor reading abilities affect our ability to use written materials as part of the counseling process. There is a great deal of psychoeducational material available for people who read. Clients who cannot make use of these have fewer resources for their recovery.

Learning and Memory

Neuropsychologists have traditionally placed a lot of emphasis on long-term "new learning and memory" ability and for good reason. Learning and retaining new information over the long term (past the few seconds required for "working memory," and into minutes, hours, weeks, and so on) is crucial for adapting to a complex and changing world. We rely on new learning/memory ability when we meet new people, read a story that interests us, attempt to master a new task, or navigate a new environment. Conditions such as Alzheimer's disease and severe alcoholism are well known for their devastating impact on new learning/memory, leaving this ability almost entirely lacking in affected individuals. However, new learning/memory is also often compromised in psychiatric inpatient populations (Kato, Galynker, Miner, & Rosenblum, 1995).

Our patients have difficulty learning new verbal and nonverbal (visual-spatial) information. They show these difficulties on formal memory tests. For example, they typically learned only about 8 of 16 words from a list repeated to them five times, where the average individual learns about 12 of the 16 words. They also had difficulty recalling more than 7 words from the list after 30 minutes, where the average individual can recall about 12. When given words to recognize from the list, mixed with words not on it, our patients often appeared overwhelmed with the choices and tended to say "yes" to any word presented. They had the same learning and memory difficulties when presented with groups of shapes. The testing shows that our patients become easily overwhelmed when presented with too many items to remember. Staff on the units and in the classrooms see this also.

Our teachers need to compensate for the learning/memory deficits common in our patients by repeating the material frequently and by using several modalities (for example, using simple language, animated gestures, pictures, charts, and interactive exercises). Teachers note that these patients do best with rote or repetitive learning, slowly building on familiar material by very gradual addition of the new. Patients quickly become anxious if too much new material is introduced at once.

We receive reports that some of our patients were berated or teased by family members, previous teachers, and peers during schooling. Therefore, they react negatively to phrases such as "How many times do we have to go over this?" from staff who have unrealistic expectations. These patients also have difficulty retaining the few basic school rules (for example, come to school fully dressed; no swearing; no touching; no sharing, since sharing items can have negative repercussions in the classroom; and no walking out of class without permission). For example, one patient requires repetition of the "no walking out of class without permission" rule in each and every class—not because he is oppositional, but because he has difficulty remembering the rule, and will simply get up to walk out of class when needing to go to the bathroom, for example. However, staff report that our patients can practice and learn a rule by having it modeled for them repeatedly and consistently, and by acting it out, even if they cannot explicitly state or recall the rule in verbal terms. *They learn better from watching models and practicing than from listening or talking* (Daprati, Nico, Saimpont, Franck, & Sirigu, 2005). This has important implications for counseling.

Executive (Advanced Thinking) Skills

The more advanced thinking abilities are collectively referred to as executive function. This includes some of the cognitive skills already discussed such as speed of information processing, attention/working memory, and verbal abstract reasoning. It also includes cognitive skills such as sequencing tasks in time and space, inhibiting one's own responses (for example, not acting on an impulse to harm oneself or others), understanding the reasoning of others, and complex problem solving.

Executive function is commonly associated with integrity of the brain's frontal lobe and related neurological circuits. Executive function becomes impaired in a variety of psychiatric disabilities, including mood/psychotic disorders, post-traumatic stress disorder, eating disorders, attention-deficit/ hyperactivity disorder, and so forth. Executive function skills need to be nourished and developed. Children raised in conflictual, dysfunctional, and violent environments, where good executive function is not modeled by adults, fall behind in their own development of these skills. The adolescent patients we see almost always have weak executive function skills. Generally speaking, they are not good thinkers or problem solvers. They act impulsively, without careful consideration of consequences, and without the skills to implement more adaptive strategies. While this is somewhat true about adolescents generally, it is true for our patients to an alarming degree.

An example of executive skill is the ability to learn and execute sequenced tasks such as dressing, cleaning a room, or cooking a meal. Impairment of this ability is seen in patient behaviors in the program and also measured by neuropsychological tests. For example, many of our patients have difficulty following a daily routine, and they need many prompts to stay on task. Staff may interpret this to be laziness or lack of motivation, but it occurs in patients who are actually very motivated to keep a schedule. Some of our patients have difficulty reading clocks, either analog or digital. This contributes to their difficulty managing tasks over time. Despite carefully displayed personal schedules and frequent staff prompting, they learn daily sequences/schedules very slowly. As a consequence, they often miss group activities or are late for them.

Occupational therapists are particularly good at helping clients with learning sequencing skills. One of our occupational therapists runs a macaroni cooking group that among other things teaches this skill. A typical patient will take about 8 months of weekly sessions to learn a 15-step process of cooking macaroni (for example, set up bowl and measuring cup, measure water needed, pour water in pot, turn on stove, boil water, mix ingredient packets in bowl, pour in macaroni, cook for 6 minutes, drain, lower heat, put pot back on stove, pour in mixed ingredients, stir for 5 minutes, turn off burner, move from burner and let cool). By the end of the eighth month, typical patients could complete this task approximately 80% of the time, provided nothing unexpected occurred (for example, a public address announcement broke their concentration, and they lost their place in the cooking sequence).

Occupational therapy staff note that if any of these highly structured sequencing activities were changed in terms of pace, complexity, or amount of interruptions, the activity could easily fall apart, as if the patient had never learned it at all. Although such activities as cooking simple dishes *could* transfer to the community postdischarge, they appeared easily lost without ongoing refresher support, especially as concerns safety aspects (for example, turning off burner after cooking is complete).

Another basic executive ability is response inhibition. This refers to the ability to stop oneself from responding impulsively or habitually and instead consider options and choose a skillful response. Lack of impulse control in our patients is probably due to a combination of factors, such as chaotic upbringing, psychiatric (for example, mood/psychotic) symptoms, and generally low cognitive functioning. For many of our patients, developing this skill is a central treatment goal.

We observe patients display impulse control problems frequently. For example, on a community outing by van, many of our patients call out to passengers in other cars (for example, female patients calling out to a group of males in a passing car), despite knowing the rule not to do so. They make inappropriate gestures or start rocking the van as a group. One patient showing poor impulse control can contaminate the group as peers imitate the impulsive behaviors. Staff may have to stop the van to keep the group from calling out to strangers, rocking, or other dangerous behaviors. Staff must remind the patients about the rules and help them understand why the rules are important. Staff report that it takes most of our patients significant time to understand the rules governing behavior on and off the wards. It takes them even longer to practice and consistently enact the rules.

Problem solving is another basic executive skill. It involves the ability to acknowledge that a problem exists, see the nature of the problem, generate a variety of solutions, choose what appears to be the most appropriate solution, and finally to verify whether one's solution worked. Daily problems can be of a purely practical nature (for example, how to arrange one's belongings in the most efficient fashion in a room), or a social nature (for example, how to resolve a longstanding conflict with a peer), and so on. We all use basic problem-solving skills every day, with more or less success. We try to solve problems on our own, and sometimes consult with others concerning how best to solve a given problem.

Our patients have difficulty with more complex aspects of daily problem solving, and very often with understanding another person's feelings and point of view. This can lead to social confusion on the patient's part, along with misinterpretations of other's behavior. For example, one therapist on our units spoke of a patient who had a physical fight with a peer, and expressed a desire to press charges against this peer. At the same time, this patient asked her therapist if she and the therapist could meet with the peer to discuss the situation and process feelings about it. The therapist stated this was possible, but also mentioned unit policy that if charges are currently being pressed, therapists cannot mediate until these have been settled. The patient said she understood and would comply with the policy. However, she had already pressed charges, without telling the therapist. The mediation meeting took place, without the therapist knowing unit policy had been violated. When the therapist later attempted to explain to the patient how this was a violation of their prior agreement and the kind of behavior that could compromise the therapeutic relationship, the patient had difficulty understanding this perspective.

The therapist went to great lengths to explain her perspective in language the patient could understand. When asked to explain in her own words what the therapist had said, the patient was only able to state, repeatedly "This means everyone on the unit hates me." The therapist was struck by the patient's inability to take another person's perspective. This also represented a failed attempt at social problem solving by this patient. She wished to process with a peer feelings related to their conflict, and hopefully help resolve the conflict in this way, while at the same time pressing charges against this peer. She did not understand how these two approaches to the problem were incompatible, or how pursuing both avenues at once would violate an agreement with her therapist that could compromise the patient–therapist relationship.

Maria is an example of a patient with many kinds of language and learning challenges. She is 16 years old but appears and acts younger, in part because of her extremely simple and childlike use of language. In fact, her simple use of language makes her sound as if she were mentally retarded. As a result of her expressive language difficulties, her intellectual capacity was often underestimated and her academic opportunities limited. In fact, initial IQ testing showed normal (low average) verbal reasoning ability, and while on our units she showed increasingly sophisticated math skills.

Maria was lost in activities that were not structured and goal directed. She had great difficulty learning new tasks unless they were modeled and she could practice with support. She could not follow directions that had more than three steps. She could fix a cold snack or sandwich for herself but was completely overwhelmed by the tasks involved in preparing macaroni from a box.

Her learning difficulties were well represented by the challenge of learning to make chocolate chip cookies. After practicing this task for several months, she could still do it only with a great deal of support. She obtained all the supplies and ingredients independently. She needed assistance to operate the oven and read and follow directions. She could identify measuring tools but not use them without assistance.

She could not remember safety rules. She worked at a steady pace but became overwhelmed easily. When overwhelmed, she would become silent and withdraw.

Maria could initiate grooming and bathing but she needed prompts to clean all the parts of her body. She could dress herself but not coordinate clothing selection. A large wardrobe with many choices was overwhelming to her. By simplifying her wardrobe she was able to avoid the embarrassment of needing assistance with clothing selection.

Her table manners were reasonably good but she had difficulty understanding the idea of sharing limited quantities of food or following diet restrictions for her health. She was able to prevent frustrations in food preparation by precutting food, allowing two to three times the usual time to eat, and being assisted in opening packages. She was able to negotiate liquids and prevent spilling by filling cups half full and to avoid burns by restricting access to hot food and fluid until it was cool.

Maria would take prescribed medications when given to her but she could not organize even a few medications on her own. She could not remember when to take which of two pills without using a pill organizer. She learned to avoid the risk of running out of medication by checking on her supply and renewing prescriptions with prompts, such as marking a calendar.

Maria was able to manage very simple day-to-day money transactions. She could shop for small, familiar items, quote and slowly calculate correct change with pencil and paper or a calculator, but could not determine whether she had enough money for all the items on a shopping list, and could not do comparison shopping.

She was able to do familiar laundry by hand and use a washing machine, but she was not able to sort clothing. When walking to and from buildings on hospital grounds, she often got lost and was unable to find alternative routes. She needed an escort to be with her several times before she could remember a particular route around the campus. When she was overwhelmed, she could not do problem solving and would choose the first option available, whether or not it was the best one. She also needed supervision because she simply would not look both ways before crossing the street, even with multiple reminders.

Her weak planning skills led to problems in social situations. For example, she frequently had toileting emergencies on recreational activities until staff realized they had to remind her to use the bathroom before leaving. She needed two to three times the usual time to bathe, groom, and get dressed in order to get to school on time.

The Interface of Language and Learning Problems With Major Mental Illnesses

Language and learning challenges are also caused or worsened by psychotic or mood symptoms. Most individuals, when under stress, experience difficulty thinking clearly, articulating their thoughts, understanding what someone else is saying, or using skills they have learned. This is an even greater problem with psychiatric patients. Many of our patients with basically intact IQ and academic skills still suffer from cognitive disorganization (for example, loose or tangential thinking, with associated attention and memory difficulties) during periods of aggravated psychotic or mood symptoms. Psychosis can include hallucinations or delusions. When such symptoms are active, they can easily derail or distort cognitive processes. For example, our teachers describe working with one patient of average baseline IQ, who is essentially incapable of learning when he becomes psychotic. The patient wants to attend school, and is allowed to do so even when he is completely immersed in his own thoughts. At these times, he pays little attention to safety and shows poor judgment and impulse control. He requires constant supervision. For instance, in a cooking class, he might reach for a hot baking pan without using an oven mitt. This could be due to a "command hallucination" telling him to reach for the baking pan, or to such extreme disorganization and confusion that he is not attentive to basic measures to assure his safety.

Another patient who showed disorganized thinking was Jonathan, a 16-year-old Chinese American boy admitted after a very carefully thought out suicide attempt in which he stabbed himself twice in the chest with a knife. In this effort, he punctured his left lung, barely missing his heart. He collapsed, bleeding, in the snow behind his house knowing that no one would be home for 3 hours. Unexpectedly, his mother returned home early, found him, and called 911.

Jonathan's mother reports that he stopped taking his medication immediately after his discharge from the hospital 3 months earlier. He began hearing voices and dressing and acting bizarrely shortly thereafter. When asked what he has been doing lately, he replied, "I am a lover of the undercover." He believed he was an agent of a White Supremacy group devoted to ridding the United States of Asians (he and his entire extended family are Asian). His speech is marked by incoherence and rhyming. On the Unit, he is always seen carrying a book called *The Hitchhiker's Guide to the Galaxy* but never noticed to be reading it. He has a white towel draped across his shoulders "so the space ships will recognize me and pick me up when they come. So I won't be left behind."

Other types of thought and/or emotional disturbance can affect our patients' ability to communicate and learn. Depression is well known for its negative effects on motivation, language, and learning (Shenal, Harrison, & Demaree, 2003). Depressed patients often lack motivation for activities and treatments. They have difficulty initiating conversation and other activities. Their thinking and speech become slow and labored. If something is even modestly difficult, they will often not make the effort to do it on their own. In these cases, frequent encouragement, prompts, and praise by staff can be very useful in helping patients engage in even brief back-and-forth conversation, get started on tasks, and continue tasks to completion.

On the other end of the emotional spectrum, we find patients that are too energized to converse or behave in an organized way. This occurs, for example, in manic states, wherein patients appear "high" or agitated in their thinking/behavior. Other signs and symptoms of mania include overtalkativeness to the point that it may seem impossible to get a word in edgewise. Manic people are often hypersensitive to the point of being irritable, angry, volatile, or explosive. This may be over something as minor as being asked to wait their turn. They perceive this as insulting or unfair. Often, in the midst of a manic episode, patients will have a significantly decreased need for sleep, often as little as 2 hours per night for several nights. Despite this decreased sleep, they wake refreshed and will state that they "never felt better." Manic people often engage in risky behaviors such as driving too fast or visiting dangerous areas because they feel "on top of the world" or "invincible." People experiencing mania often experience feelings of increased sexual interest, exhibit increased sexual talk, or engage in increased sexual activity. Similarly, they may be tremendously interested in other activities that have a high potential for harm such as gambling more than they can afford to lose or spending more than they can afford.

Frederick was a patient who cycled between depressed and agitated/manic states. When he first came to the units he was depressed, withdrawn, often wore sunglasses (even indoors), and spoke slowly and very sparingly. He would only speak when spoken to, and offered little information about himself or his treatment preferences. He had difficulties with attention and memory, and he would give up easily when thinking clearly became a challenge. Several months later, this same patient began to experience a manic episode. His speech became rapid and he could not get to the point. He was always on the go, flitting from one activity to another in rapid succession, as things in the environment caught his attention. His memory became poor again, not (as before) because he was depressed and could not muster the effort to remember things, but because his mind was moving too fast to receive new information for any length of time. In both depressed and manic states, he had great difficulty learning any new skills, and even sustaining normal conversations. He could hardly tolerate a short academic group or recreational activity and was completely unable to sit with his counselor for any sustained discussion.

Data on Language and Learning Challenges in Our Population

To better understand our patients not just individually but collectively, in terms of overall cognitive pattern (strengths and limitations), we studied their results on neuropsychological testing as compared to age- and gender-matched community-dwelling adolescents. In our study, 34 patients (23 female, or 67%; 26 White, 4 African American, 2 Hispanic American, 1 Asian American, 1 biracial ethnicity) with a mean age of 16.2 years were referred for neuropsychological testing. We compared their performance to that of 29 controls (19 female, or 65%; 15 White, 9 African American, 4 Hispanic American, 1 biracial ethnicity) with a mean age of 15.5 years, referred for neuropsychological testing due to marked learning difficulty in Boston area schools. Neuropsychological measures used included the following:

- Wechsler Intelligence Scale for Children (WISC-IV)
- Wechsler Individual Achievement Test (WIAT-II)
- Finger-Tapping Test
- Boston Naming Test (BNT)
- Verbal Fluency; Category Fluency
- Rey-Osterreith Complex Figure Test (copy and recall)
- California Verbal Learning Test—Children's version (CVLT-C)
- Brief Visuospatial Memory Test—Revised (BVMT-R)
- Delis-Kaplan Executive Function System (D-KEFS) Trail Making Tests
- D-KEFS Color-Word Tests
- D-KEFS Sorting Test

Tests were typically administered over three to four sessions. Group differences were examined using independent sample t-tests. All statistics were evaluated using a $p <. 05$ threshold. Results indicated that Full Scale IQ was equivalent for patients and controls, per the WISC-IV. Nevertheless, patients showed lower performance ($p < .05$) on certain WISC-IV subtests (including Comprehension, a measure of understanding/expressing social norms); on the Verbal Comprehension Index ($p < .05$); and on combined measures of information processing speed (Processing Speed Index difference = $p < .05$). Patients performed lower on delayed recall of the Rey-Osterrieth Complex Figure, a measure of visual learning/memory ($p < .05$). Patients also performed lower on CVLT-C Trials 1 to 5, a measure of verbal learning ($p < .01$); and on CVLT-C long delay free and cued recall, measures of word recall with and without cues, respectively ($p < .05$). These results are summarized in Figure 3.1, where the y axis represents standard scores.*

---

* Score of 100 equals 50th percentile for age. Standard deviation = 15 points in either direction.

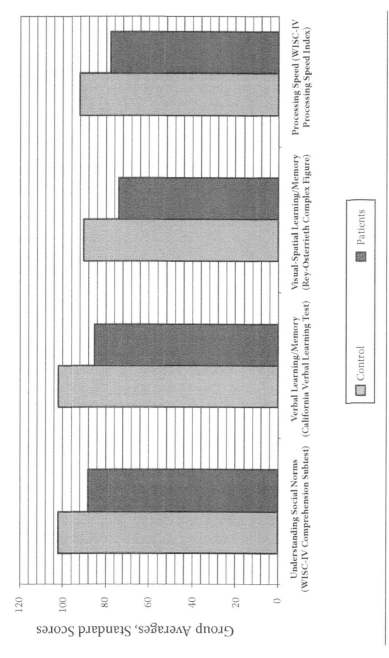

Figure 3.1 Adolescent controls versus patients on key neuropsychological measures.

This figure illustrates how, despite statistically equivalent Full Scale IQ, the hearing adolescent patients in our study showed significant language and learning difficulties per neuropsychological testing, as compared to community controls referred for testing. Their limited language skills, slowed information processing, and generally low recall capacity help explain why they struggle with traditional talk- and insight-oriented therapies. We believe such patients are better suited to a symptom management approach emphasizing *doing* over *talking* (for example, by modeling basic self-help skills).

Summary and Implications for Counseling

Most of our adolescent hearing patients have severe language and learning challenges. Their vocabulary and grasp of sentence structure is very limited. They have short attention spans. They cannot receive and process new information easily. They are poor students in that they lack strategies for learning. They have difficulty organizing and sequencing daily living tasks as well as academic assignments. They have difficulty with step-by-step problem solving, and especially in appreciating the perspectives and feelings of other people. They have difficulty noticing and controlling their impulsive and habitual ways of responding even when these behaviors have gotten them into significant trouble. They are prone to being restless and unfocused. Sometimes they are so preoccupied with psychiatric symptoms (such as racing thoughts, hallucinations, delusions, anxiety, and depression) that they cannot engage well even in the routine give and take of social conversations.

These language and learning challenges make traditional talk- and insight-oriented therapies impractical. As discussed in Chapter 4, traditional talk- and insight-oriented therapies depend on a dialogue requiring significant vocabulary, ability to grasp complex sentence structure, understanding of themes, memory for themes from session to session, ability to see patterns and make connections, and development of insight concerning one's own and others' emotions/behavior. Without these cognitive abilities, insight-oriented talk therapy is often an exercise in frustration for both client and counselor.

As a result, we have found that our counseling strategies have to be adapted to facilitate their engagement and learning. The following two stories represent counseling efforts that were successful with two of these clients.

A patient we will call Albert was a 13-year-old adolescent. He had a history of severe abuse and trauma-related symptoms, problems with attention and behavior, academic and social failure in school, and evidence of mood swings and delusional thinking that suggested bipolar disorder. He had several psychiatric hospitalizations prior to being on our unit. On admission, he stated, "I have trouble controlling my behavior … I get really hyper … but also, I'm really sad a lot." While his vocabulary was adequate, he could not attend and process information in a way that would make insight-oriented therapy useful. By the time Albert arrived at Westborough, he was quite hopeless about benefiting from further psychotherapy or medication. His anxiety and paranoia also prevented him from functioning well in groups.

Albert experienced disabling anxiety and phobias especially regarding discharge to a halfway house in the community. His fears sometimes took on psychotic proportions as when he would hear people outside his therapist's window talking about how he was in danger. He construed the world outside hospitals as unsafe and worried that if placed in the community an accident would occur, such as a tree falling on him or being struck by lightning.

The psychotherapy approach used with him focused on simple psychosocial skills, mainly implemented through therapeutic activities. Therapy was often conducted during walks on grounds or while playing simple card games with the therapist. This approach engaged him in a multisensory way that held his attention and helped discharge energy constructively. The use of games and sensory activities brought him into the counseling process.

One of the first psychotherapy goals was helping him develop skill in naming and identifying feelings. This goal is common to most psychotherapies but it was conceptualized here as a foundational skill leading to a variety of simple coping strategies. He was taught simple relaxation techniques such as distraction, seeking quiet time, positive self-talk, and diaphragmatic breathing.

When he reported hearing voices outside a window, the therapist took him outside to see whether anyone was there. He benefited from this type of active reality-testing. He also said that when he heard voices (often of "dead people talking to me"), he would "Just ignore them and walk away.... I tell myself they're not real and just walk away." The therapist recognized this as an example of a simple coping skill (self-talk) that he already had at least partially learned, and she encouraged its development and built on it. With consistent activity-oriented therapy, simple but steady skills building, and use of a few basic symptom-management techniques, this patient made consistent psychiatric progress and was judged transferable to a community setting in a little over 1 year.

Beatrice was another one of our language and learning challenged patients. She was a 16-year-old adolescent who experienced severe neglect and abuse at her home. She suffered from symptoms of trauma as well as severe depression. Beatrice was also mildly mentally retarded. She came from a home where both English and Spanish were spoken, and was only marginally skilled in each. She preferred to communicate in English, as this was the primary language for most of her peers, but had very limited English vocabulary. She could only understand very simple conversations and her own expressive language consisted mainly of one or two words, or short phrases, at a time.

On arrival at Westborough, her academic skills (including reading and writing) were second grade level at best. To learn new information such as Unit rules, she needed these told to her in simple sentences, repeated many times. Her attention and language problems, combined with dramatic mood swings in which she would shift from pleasant and sociable to explosively angry within minutes, made her unsuitable for insight-oriented psychotherapy. She made her own feelings about therapy very clear by yelling at and sometimes hitting her therapist.

Although her verbal skills were poor, she had nonverbal skills in the average range.

Neuropsychological testing suggested she would learn more effectively if she was taught by modeling and practicing rather than talking. This proved true. She was also helped by being given a vocabulary for very simple psychosocial skills. For instance, she learned the coping skill of "using my [calming] words when I get mad." Counseling sessions were limited to 15 minutes at most and focused on a single theme, such as "how to help myself" that was often repeated over numerous sessions. A successful counseling session occurred when she engaged in a short discussion, with role plays concerning a recent incident on the Unit. For instance, at one point, a peer took some of her clothing and she responded by punching her. The counselor asked simple questions such as: What happened? How did she feel? What did she do? What happened next? Did she get in trouble?* As Beatrice could not usually present an organized account of what happened, the counseling involved interviews with staff to help her construct the story. When Beatrice became aggressive, she would face an unwanted consequence such as loss of a privilege, and this helped motivate her to consider more skillful ways she could respond. She was gradually able to modify her behavior, by developing a repertoire of basic skills taught consistently in individual therapy and various groups (including occupational therapy groups such as cooking, exercise groups, music group, and so on). These basic skills included recognizing as early as possible when she was becoming agitated and repeating calming words to herself. If these were not effective, she learned to go to staff and ask for help, and either accept staff redirection or allow staff to help her use a skill.

Acquisition of such skills gave Beatrice more productive options for dealing with difficult situations, and was credited with improving her sense of self control, as well as her mood and behavior. As her mood and behavior improved, she also showed improved cognitive ability. She started doing much better in school. This increased her self-esteem. By the end of her stay at Westborough, she had increased her academic skills to the sixth grade level (moderately low for her age, but still a notable improvement). She clearly benefited from basic therapies emphasizing emotional coping and social skills. She was discharged with the recommendation that such basic skill building remain the mainstay of her treatment for the foreseeable future. Perhaps at some point much later she would be able to do insight-oriented work related to processing the traumas she experienced.

---

* This is a form of simple behavior analysis, discussed in more detail in Chapter 7.

Conclusions

Although this book concerns itself primarily with mental health care of deaf persons with language and learning challenges, we included this chapter because we discovered that many hearing psychiatric patients, such as the adolescent patients on these units, have similar developmental deficits which pose enormous barriers to the use of traditional talk therapies. While the hearing patients generally have native language skills, we saw that this was not really true of Beatrice, and that the overall language and learning problems these hearing adolescents face are quite formidable. Therapists on the adolescent units have had to be just as creative in adapting psychotherapy, and it has been useful to us to consider the adaptations we have made in common. Chief among these is the emphasis on skills rather than insight, on doing rather than talking, on conceptualizing skills in very simple terms, and in use of activities and games as the vehicle for treatment. The skills we focus on are the same. They include simple coping, conflict resolution, and symptom management skills. Development of a shared vocabulary for these skills, and for the process of growth and recovery, is a crucial part of helping these clients know what they need to do to move forward. The shared vocabulary about skills also provides clients with a simple, clear map for the treatment and recovery process. It is one crucial *pretreatment* strategy, discussed in the next chapter.

4
Pretreatment Strategies to Engage and Motivate Clients

Why Do So Many of Our Clients Appear Unmotivated for Mental Health Treatment?

Mental health treatment is collaborative, and that is its greatest virtue and most serious limitation. Mental health clinicians have an enormous amount to offer people in emotional distress if we can convince them to make use of our services. Because many people who need mental health care do not seek it out and may resist it, mental health providers must also develop skill in soliciting client engagement. We can call this phase of our work, when we try to educate and motivate clients into informed participation in mental health care, *pretreatment.*

Society has conflicting expectations for mental health programs and professionals. On the one hand, it wants us to manage and, where possible, cure psychiatric disorders and help consumers gain relief from psychological pain. On the other hand, it wants us to act as agents of social control and forcibly prevent people with psychiatric disorders from behaving in violent, antisocial ways. Society gives us the power to lock people up for short periods of time against their will and sometimes to force them to take psychiatric medications. Clinicians know, however, that there is usually great cost to our acting like police or judges; that when we force people to comply with *our* will, we usually lose them as partners in a process of recovery (Laurance, 2003). Even with these powers, we cannot, ultimately, force anyone to do anything. We cannot force people to behave appropriately. We cannot force them to keep taking medication after they leave inpatient facilities. We certainly cannot force them to make use of counseling. Even traditional behavior therapy, which seeks to change behavior by changing environmental responses to the behavior, is now understood to be a collaborative process. Clients can and do rebel against behavior plans that are not developed with their consent. Thus, whatever magic that people in society expect mental health providers to have, the truth is that no one gets better in mental health treatment unless the person becomes an active agent in his or her own recovery.

Mental health care begins when the client and the therapist or clinical team has a shared understanding of, and commitment to, treatment goals and process. It begins when the client and clinician/team make a relevant treatment plan to which the client says, "Yes, I want that. Let's proceed." The client says, "I want help with depression, drinking, relationship problems, trauma memories, unbearable internal pain, etc....," and the clinician/team says, "Here's how we can help you with that." A treatment plan is developed that may include medicine and will probably include some kind of counseling. There is a structure to this process, which the client understands and accepts. The client "buys into" the process at least enough to participate with some sincerity.

Medication is sometimes forced on people without their consent in psychiatric hospitals. Other involuntary treatments have included commitment to psychiatric hospitalizations, subjection to behavioral plans developed without one's knowledge or consent, and involuntary administration of physical treatments like electroconvulsive therapy, insulin shock therapy, and psychosurgery (Beam, 2001; Whitaker, 2002). These involuntary interventions, while administered by mental health practitioners, are more clearly thought of as acts of social control. I do not believe that any treatment applied involuntarily should ever be conceptualized as a therapy. In this book, when we refer to mental health care, we are referring only to that which we do in collaboration with clients. Because we do, like it or not, have a social control function, we should be honest and direct and label that aspect of our work as social control. A clear distinction between mental health treatment and social control also enables us to see that while we have many strategies for the former, we are stunningly inept at the latter.

A woman brings her husband in to see a counselor and complains that he drinks too much. He agreed to go to the session because she told him that she is unhappy in their marriage and they need help. He initially refused to attend but when she threatened to divorce him, he reluctantly agreed to come "one time." She said nothing about his drinking until they were in the counselor's office. Then, when the counselor asked, "What brings you here?" she launches into a tirade about his alcohol consumption. The husband, feeling ambushed, becomes very defensive. He insists he has no drinking problem. The only problem *he* has is a wife who nags him incessantly. He asks sarcastically if the counselor can help his wife stop being such a "bitch."

Is this man or woman or this couple ready for mental health care? The husband does not accept that he has a drinking problem. The wife is not ready to examine her dishonest communication with her husband. The couple is not ready to enter a counseling process to try to save their marriage. Each blames the other and wants the other fixed. As individuals and as a couple, these people are in "pretreatment." The counselor has a lot of work to do to establish a framework that, either individually or as a couple, they will accept as a basis for treatment.

Our work is much more difficult than that of the counselor in this example. The couple described above at least knows what counseling is. They somehow managed to get themselves into a counselor's office. They have a general understanding of counseling even as they insist it is not for them. They also have language. They may blame each other for their difficulties, but at least they can do so in full, grammatically correct sentences. They are also using words, however aggressively, instead of behavior to convey their feelings. They probably are at least high school graduates and may well have attended college and hold professional jobs. They probably pay rent or a mortgage, own one or more cars, manage a budget, read newspapers or magazines, and plan and take vacations. They have skills and resources well beyond that of most of our language and learning challenged (LLC) clients.

The majority of the LLC deaf clients we serve, especially on their first hospitalization, are not engaged, motivated, sophisticated consumers of mental health services. They do not arrive and joyously proclaim in sign, "At last, I have a signing psychotherapist! Now I can get the psychotherapy I've always wanted!" Much more typically, when they arrive they do not understand why they are in the hospital. Nor do they want to be there. They have no understanding of how psychiatric hospitals work or of how counseling can help people. They usually do not see themselves as having a problem; and certainly not *a mental health* problem, whatever that means. Their problem, as they see it, is usually that other people make life hard for them. They have been blamed, abused, mistreated, or oppressed. Life is not fair, and they have been given a bad deal. What they need is for other people to support and help them or perhaps to leave them alone.

Although hearing LLC clients do not have the language dysfluency problems associated with language deprivation, they have other language and cognitive problems as we saw in Chapter 3. These clients may be just as unprepared and unmotivated for any kind of counseling. Often our clients have experienced multiple forms of trauma, but that does not mean they come to us seeking treatment for trauma. More often, they come to us angry, resentful, self-harming, and engaged in a variety of dangerous and self-destructive behaviors. They come to us with the attitude that *others* are to blame for their problems. They may come to us with either no understanding of the counseling process or an aversion to it. This externalizing attitude and hostility to mental health providers can sometimes be a bigger barrier to their recovery than the challenges posed by any particular mental illness or disorder.

The concept of "pretreatment" has echoes in the mental health literature. For instance, the notion of "pretherapy" has been explored in relationship to culturally diverse clientele. Dolgin, Salazar, and Cruz (1987) designed a psychiatric inpatient unit for Hispanic Americans in which the staff provided an educational program called pretherapy. Staff in this program realized that many of their clients were unfamiliar with the concept of psychotherapy. In pretherapy, a therapist met with clients to provide an orientation to psychotherapy. Dolgin et al. reported that this pretherapy intervention helped clients feel more relaxed in discussing cultural, personal, and sexual problems. "It was our experience that pretherapy facilitated the psychotherapy process for both client and therapist" (p. 292).

Acosta, Yamamoto, and Evans (1992), in a text on psychotherapy with low-income and minority clients, argued that outpatient therapy clinics should develop client orientation programs, and they provide an example of one. A client orientation program would certainly be one approach to pretherapy. Sue and Morishima (1982) advocated for "pretherapy orientations" when working with Asian and Pacific Americans. Dialectical behavior therapy (DBT) is a cognitive-behavioral treatment program initially designed for clients with borderline personality disorder (Linehan, 1993a). DBT places a heavy emphasis on learning psychosocial skills and contains a curriculum for teaching these skills. Before clients begin DBT, they are given an orientation to the structured treatment protocols. Linehan, the developer of DBT, calls this phase of treatment "precommitment." It is also referred to as "pretreatment" (Koerner & Dimeff, 2007). Linehan (1993) explains,

> The use of pretreatment orientation sessions has been empirically linked to a reduced dropout rate in several treatment studies. Thus, the first several sessions of individual therapy focus on preparations for therapy. The goals of this stage are twofold. First, the client and therapist must arrive at a mutual, informed decision to work together on helping the client make changes she wants to make in herself and in her life. Second, the therapist attempts to modify any dysfunctional beliefs or expectations of the client regarding therapy that are likely to influence the process of therapy and/or the decision to terminate therapy prematurely. (p. 169)

In DBT, clients are oriented to the nature of this particular kind of therapy so that they can make an informed decision regarding participation. Clients who wish to have a less structured opportunity to "vent" with a therapist without pursuing specific goals of skill acquisition are referred elsewhere. The therapist says, in effect, this is the treatment that works, and this is the treatment that we offer. If you agree, you are signing on to this particular approach. Later, when clients protest that they want something else, they are reminded about the pretreatment commitment.

Meichenbaum and Turk (1987) tackle the issue of pretreatment from a slightly different angle, that of eliciting from patients compliance with treatment recommendations. Their book is designed to "bridge the gap between what patients are asked to do by health care providers and what patients actually do" (p. 12). They address problems such as patients not following advice regarding medication, physical activity, and diet. Their research is relevant to the issue of why some clients do not engage easily in psychotherapy. Some of the most important variables that they cite, which affect patient noncompliance, are as follows:

1. The patient does not know what to do.
2. The patient does not have the skills or resources to carry out the treatment regimen.
3. The patient does not believe or feel that he or she has the ability to carry out the treatment regimen.
4. The patient does not believe or feel that carrying out the treatment regimen will make a difference.
5. The treatment regimen is too demanding and the patient does not believe that the potential benefits of adhering will outweigh the costs.
6. Adherence is associated with aversive or non-reinforcing events or sensations.
7. The quality of the relationship between the patient and the health care provider is poor.
8. There is no continuity of care.
9. The clinic is not mobilized towards facilitating adherence. (Meichenbaum & Turk, 1987, p. 68)

Our Clients Frequently Do Not Understand or Embrace Insight-Oriented Treatment Models

One of the variables cited by Meichenbaum and Turk is particularly relevant to the challenge of engaging lower functioning clients in counseling. This is the variable of the "explanatory model of the disorder," or how clinicians explain the nature of the clients' problem and the nature of treatment. Meichenbaum and Turk explain that:

> patients' representations of illnesses include their beliefs about the cause of the illness, expectations about its duration and course (acute, chronic, cyclical), beliefs about its consequences, and potential responsiveness to treatment. Even serious, life-threatening disorders do not insure adherence if the patient does not share this perception and the accompanying intention, ability, and perceived benefit for adherence behavior. (Meichenbaum & Turk, 1987, p. 48)

Mental health care is a field of medicine barely 100 years old. Psychotherapy really did not enter the culture until after World War II, and as a means of helping sought out *voluntarily* by clients it is still mainly the province of educated middle and upper class persons of European descent (Gladding, 1992). The idea that one seeks help for mental and emotional problems by talking to a mental health specialist is perceived as bizarre by people in most of the world's cultures. In these cultures, problem behaviors and unpleasant emotional experiences are not attributed to mental illness. Consequently, mental health personnel are not sanctioned as helpers or healers. To value and benefit from mental health care, the explanations and models of mental health care must make sense at cultural and personal levels. They have to be consistent with one's worldview and belief system.

When people seek out a psychotherapist for help with a personal problem, it is because they have come to believe there is value in talking about their feelings and experiences. They value exploration of their "inner worlds" and treatment strategies, which boils down to talking and trying to understand themselves better. They have been acculturated into a belief system in which mental health practitioners are legitimated as socially sanctioned helpers.

The clients we are addressing here do not usually attend as we would want to their inner experiences. They tend to have a focus on the external world rather than their inner experience. They tend to understand their problems as reactions to what other people do to them. If people are mean to them, they feel angry. If people are nice or desired things happen, they feel happy. They have problems now because other people gave them a hard time. They often complain that what has happened to them is not fair.

Insight-oriented counselors believe that talking about yourself and your life will help you understand yourself better, and with this understanding you will be able to make changes that you want. Most mental health professionals, by the nature of our work and the acculturation process we undergo in our clinical training, value insight and what we sometimes call *psychological mindedness*. This refers to the capacity to explore one's inner world and the valuing of that process. *We* value insight, and we think that other people should as well. The pursuit of insight can become such a core value for us that we forget that there is nothing inherently superior about this *internal* orientation toward life. This way of thinking is just as much a social historical development as ways of thinking that root problem solving in efforts to please one's ancestors or the gods.

Besides insight, a second key value of traditional psychotherapy is the importance of the therapeutic relationship. Most models of psychotherapy posit that a strong therapeutic alliance is necessary for change, and some models, like person-centered therapy, argue that this relationship, if it meets certain conditions, is sufficient for change (Rogers, 1951). The research on treatment efficacy makes clear the central importance of the therapeutic relationship to positive outcome (Wampold, 2001). Most counselors work exceptionally hard to establish these relationships, sometimes to the exclusion of other therapeutic goals. Many counselors believe that if they can just establish the therapeutic alliance, all else will fall into place. Clients will know how to use this relationship, or will at least be receptive to suggestions from the clinician. This is hard to do when clients do not come to us, as they might a religious or community leader, with an internal map for what the process of healing consists of. When people are not seeking a therapeutic relationship, and they lack a map of how therapy works, we are offering an intervention that is culturally inappropriate.

Viewed from other cultural and historical vantage points, therapeutic relationships are actually quite peculiar. These are relationships in which one person, the client, talks about himself or herself, while the other, the counselor, for the most part does not. They are relationships which generally occur in professional settings like offices, clinics, and hospitals. They are relationships which have odd rules and peculiar boundaries, and where concrete advice from the clinician is often discouraged. People may talk with someone who is nice to them and seems to care about them, but this does not at all mean that clients will use these relationships as opportunities for self-exploration. Even if they like the counselor, the idea of self-exploration can seem quite bizarre to them. *Why should I talk about my feelings and my life especially when you don't give me suggestions on what to do? And why are feelings so important to you?*

Another framework to understand this dynamic is one that focuses on the clinicians. When clients do not value what we are selling, we feel deskilled and helpless. We therefore blame them for lacking the skills to make use of our procedures. Would it not be more reasonable to fault us, as supposed experts in the inner worlds of human beings, for failing to devise treatment methods that meet our clients in their own conceptual worlds?

Steve de Shazer (1988) uses other metaphors to describe the willingness of clients to make use of therapy. He refers to clients as either *customers, complainants,* or *visitors.* A client is a *customer* if the client and therapist are working collaboratively to solve a problem. Clients are *complainants* when they blame other people for their problems and expect the therapist to do something to change the people responsible for their problems. *Visitors* to therapy show up because someone else told them to come but they are unable to identify any issue to discuss or problem to resolve. Most of the LLC clients we work with initially come to treatment as either complainants or visitors. When counselors sell insight as a treatment goal, these clients do not buy. They do not become customers. In fact, they flee the store.

Our Clients' Language and Cognitive Impairments Make Verbal Counseling Strategies Difficult

Besides a lack of cultural and personal belief systems consistent with a psychologically oriented worldview, our LLC clients have cognitive deficits which make verbal oriented psychotherapy difficult.

In deaf LLC clients, it is not merely language deprivation that causes language and cognitive problems. There may also be an organic cause. Many of the diseases that cause hearing loss are also leading causes of neurological damage affecting other parts of the brain (Vernon & Andrews, 1990). Children who became deaf because of prenatal rubella are more likely to have lower IQs, poorer educational performance, poorer psychological adjustment, and have language aphasias than the general population of deaf children. Meningitis is the leading postnatal cause of profound hearing loss and it is also a leading cause of brain damage. Children who become deaf prelingually because of meningitis also show lower intelligence, poorer educational performance, greater language problems, and other disabilities. Medical advances have allowed more children born prematurely to survive but these children also tend to have a variety of cognitive, language, and learning problems.* Many of our clients are persons whose deafness was caused by disorders like these. The language and learning problems they have are likely caused by these disorders also.

In practice, it can be very difficult to isolate one cause for a deaf child's language and learning problems. There are commonly multiple causes. A neurological problem associated with prenatal rubella, early childhood meningitis, prematurity, or some other cause of deafness may be a factor. The child may *also* have been raised in an environment that is linguistically inappropriate for a deaf person. There may be physical and sexual abuse and other trauma. The child may come from an impoverished family that does not have the resources to obtain the appropriate medical care and education. The family may be recent immigrants, legal or illegal, who are struggling to survive and wholly unprepared to raise a deaf child in a new country and culture. Some of our clients were abandoned by their families, raised in a succession of foster homes and residential schools, and have emotional wounds that may never be soothed.

In Chapter 2, some of the language deficits that have been observed in LLC clients treated on the Westborough Deaf Unit were described: These include:

1. Limited vocabulary with many signs incorrectly formed or used inappropriately.
2. Limited ability to use tense or time referents. Difficulty conveying the linear narrative of a story.
3. Poor use of the signing space to establish pronouns and relationships resulting in confusion over who did what to whom.
4. Confused and incorrect syntax (sign order).
5. Difficulty conveying plurality.
6. Use of idiosyncratic "home signs" only familiar to a small group of people.
7. Mixture of formal sign with gesture and pantomime.

As discussed in Chapter 2, these are language deficits seen in clients who do not suffer from a major mental illness. Those with major mental illnesses show additional kinds of language dysfluency such as these problems identified by

---

* A much fuller discussion of the causes of deafness and their implications for cognitive, educational, social, and psychological functioning is found in Vernon and Andrews (1990).

Thacker in a population of British deaf psychiatric patients (Kitson & Thacker, 2000; Thacker, 1994, 1998):

1. Contamination between English words and signs from British Sign Language.
2. Bizarre sign production.
3. Connecting signs based on their shapes rather than their meaning ("clanging").
4. Jumping from topic to topic in a disorganized manner.
5. Unnecessary repetition of signs.
6. Unique visual-spatial behaviors that are not part of British Sign Language.

In Chapter 3, Jeffrey Gaines, Bruce Meltzer, and I discussed language and learning challenges in hearing adolescent inpatients. Our deaf clients have these also. They include:

1. Limited vocabulary, including difficulty finding the right word or name.
2. Poor ability to use language for reasoning.
3. Concrete thinking. Difficulty with abstract concepts and relationships such as difficulty seeing patterns, relating one domain (like an experience in early childhood) to another (like a current behavior), limited insight.
4. Impaired attention and memory.
5. Poor visual-spatial abilities, understanding of nonverbal social behaviors and social norms.
6. Slow information processing. Clients are slow thinkers. Information must be presented to them slowly and simply and they need time to "take it in" and apply new learning.
7. Poor problem-solving skills (e.g., the inability to identify a problem that needs to be solved, identify a range of possible solutions, evaluate, select, and implement a particular solution).
8. Poor ability to notice and inhibit their own impulses.
9. Poor academic abilities like reading, writing, and mathematics.

Thus, the linguistic and cognitive demands of verbal counseling may exceed the abilities of our clients. Counselors often know this but they do not know how to adapt to provide treatment more consistent with client abilities.

One counseling theorist who offered treatment considerations relevant to this problem is Allen Ivey. He developed a style of counseling called developmental therapy in which the treatment approach is matched to the cognitive-developmental stage or orientation of clients (Ivey, 1971, 1986, 1991; Ivey, D'Andrea, Ivey, & Simek-Morgan, 2002). Basing his model on Piaget, who described how thinking in children develops as they grow, Ivey described how cognitive abilities affect one's ability to make use of psychotherapy. In Ivey's model, the earliest stages of cognitive organization are called, after Piaget, *sensorimotor* and *concrete operational*. Understanding sensorimotor and concrete operational thinking is important because so many of our clients, lacking fully intact language structures, think in these ways. We *will need to provide them a treatment style that is also mainly sensorimotor and concrete operational.*

According to Ivey, people whose thinking is primarily sensorimotor in quality do not think about the world in any logical way. They may know words or signs but they cannot tell stories in which information is organized. Their cognitive structures are fragmented. They experience the world mainly through their senses, not through beliefs or ideas. This model fits for very young children, people who are actively psychotic and deaf clients who have experienced severe language deprivation. The discussion in Chapter 5 about sensory modulation interventions and the use of pictorial aids is designed to meet the treatment needs of clients with severe language dysfluency.

Most of our LLC clients have some language skills and are more accurately thought of as concrete-operational thinkers. They think in terms of stories with an emphasis on concrete details, not on what things mean. They are not motivated to acquire insight into what things mean partially because they lack capacities for much abstract analysis. They tend not to think, for instance, in terms of patterns, or in terms of how a behavior can be an instance of a larger problem. They may also have difficulty with hypothetical questions (i.e., if you felt this, what would you do?). This is why we completely miss them when we try to engage them in the task of finding deeper meanings or viewing things from multiple perspectives. For these clients, our model of treatment must itself be simple, clear, and concrete. Storytelling can be an effective technique because it is interesting and because it helps concrete operational thinkers organize their experience.

Ivey has pointed out how most counselors and psychotherapists, concerned with helping clients develop insight into what things mean, into patterns and relationships, think in highly abstract ways. This can become so much second nature for mental health professionals who have high levels of education that they lose the ability to converse in more developmentally simple ways. Indeed, very little time is spent in mental health graduate programs preparing clinicians to work with developmentally disadvantaged people. By the time people complete medical school or a doctoral program in psychology, their language patterns may have become so complex that they talk over the heads of people with less education who are the majority of their clients. Sometimes they talk over the heads of people with normal intelligence and intact cognitive functioning. Consider whether you have had the experience of not understanding your doctor when the doctor is telling you something you are highly motivated to understand. Then consider what the experience must be for the LLC clients we are discussing. Is it any wonder, then, that they would appear unmotivated to involve themselves in an activity like psychotherapy dependent on language and thinking skills they do not have?

Thus, there can be a poor match between the worldview of mental health professionals, rooted in the value of insight into one's inner life, and the worldview more typically found in clients that values concrete problem solving in the external world. When our clients also lack language skills, and have cognitive deficits such as limited capacity for abstract thinking or problem solving, we might as well be asking them to perform higher level mathematics. This does not make them bad candidates for psychotherapy. It makes us bad candidates to become their therapists.

Our Clients Resist the Disempowered Client Role and Story

One of the attractions of working in the helping professions is that people tend to assume you must be a good person. Professional helpers such as nurses, doctors, and counselors may be drawn to their fields by the reward that comes from helping others. Part of this reward is the identity. If you are a helper, you are presumed to have positive qualities, to be kind, generous, and caring. Helping others provides the very definition of goodness.

It is far less rewarding to be the recipient of help. People who receive help are more likely to be presumed deficient or lacking. They may be seen an unhealthy, handicapped, or morally wayward. People giving help can imagine themselves right with God. People receiving help must come to terms with the fact that they are inadequate in some way and dependent on others. The psychiatric clients we work with have had a lifetime of being in the dependent role, the person receiving help. Most have had few achievements and many failures. They are used to working with professional helpers who have authority over them. Sometimes they have unexpressed feelings about being in this dependent role. Clients often express the desire for independence. They express frustration that they are not permitted the same freedom as staff. Accepting help may mean for them continuing to live this negative identity of *a person with problems who needs help.*

To complicate matters, helping is not always what it is supposed to be. Sometimes the line between *helping* and *controlling* is hard to find. Psychiatric hospitals, or as they used to be called, *asylums,* have historically been places where help took the form of staff asserting paternalistic control over all aspects of the lives of patients. The history of psychiatry, in fact, is filled with horrible abuses of patients (Beam, 2001; Masson, 1988; Whitaker, 2002). Westborough State Hospital in Massachusetts, like many other hospitals, has in recent years made huge efforts to change its culture from an asylum to a rehabilitation facility. Key components of this change have been the empowerment of clients, the move to a more respectful, collaborative problem-solving model, an appreciation of the impact of trauma on clients, and a focus on skill development. Yet even in such progressive hospitals and other social service organizations, one can still find examples of staff who are very controlling, and sometimes demeaning, of clients. They usually have the best of intentions, but people can convince themselves that almost anything they do is morally right. Slaveholders, for instance, usually considered themselves good Christians carrying out God's plan (Finkelman, 2003). Current events demonstrate that people can commit mass murder by, for instance, blowing themselves up while in a crowded market, while believing themselves morally righteous. Psychiatry itself, as Beam (2001) graphically showed, promoted enormous abuses, with self-deception in psychiatrists dwarfing any delusional system patients could muster. By comparison, believing oneself to be helping clients while one is really deriving personal satisfaction from one's position of authority, the power one wields, and the dependency of other people, is a relatively facile form of self-deception.

Staff power in psychiatric hospitals is justified by concerns that patients may harm themselves or other people. It is tied to our responsibilities as agents of social control to keep people with dangerous behaviors safe. Staff power is reflected in the fact that clients may be hospitalized against their will. They can request to leave at any time, but their psychiatrist can petition for their commitment. The power of staff over clients is reflected in all aspects of client care. Clients earn "privileges" such as the ability to leave the unit unsupervised based on staff assessment of their safety. The official account of what happens to a client in a psychiatric hospital is the story recorded by the staff in the client's medical records. In this story, clients are given diagnoses, and their behavior is commented on. Judgments are made about whether they are cooperative or resistant and whether their mental health is improving. Usually clients' account of their stay is neither articulated nor recorded. This is especially the case when clients have language and cognitive dysfunction.

In my experience, one can go to virtually any psychiatric or rehabilitation program and find staff acting out arbitrary power against clients. Staff direct clients where to go and what to do. They send clients to time out. They set rules such as to when clients can have snacks, go out for smokes, or go to bed. Clients are routinely put in the position of having to ask for privileges such as coming and going as they please. All too often rules are arbitrary and unexamined aspects of institutional culture that are there more for the convenience of staff than the benefit of clients. For example, for years Westborough State Hospital had an unstated rule that whenever patients filed a petition for discharge, they had to be restricted to the unit "for observation." There was another unstated rule that clients were automatically restricted to a unit (they "lost their level" in hospital jargon) following any kind of restraint. We impose schedules and rules about when snacks are offered and what snacks are permitted. Seclusion and restraint of patients used to be commonly accepted and unexamined practices. In theory, patients were restrained only when their behavior was unsafe. In practice, this was always a judgment call, and needless to say it was not the patients making the judgments.

These power dynamics are not limited to psychiatric facilities but occur in any setting where organized education or treatment occurs. They are reflected in the *stance* that staff adopt toward clients. The stance is the attitude toward power that staff assume. A "one-up" stance occurs when staff act from a position of authority, making decisions unilaterally.

Unless trained otherwise, staff will generally fall back on a default one-up stance. They will tell clients what to do. They will advise, direct, and do their best to persuade. When clients behave "inappropriately," staff will "set limits." They will remind clients of the rules and procedures. They may advise clients of the consequences of not following the rules. They will give warnings. They may give direct feedback that was not solicited. The movie *One Flew Over the Cuckoo's Nest* shows a paternalistic, one-up mental health culture at its worst (Forman, 1975). Contemporary American psychiatric hospitals, to my knowledge, no longer engage in the gross abuses depicted in this movie (such as ward attendants beating patients up, forcing electroshock treatment without anesthesia, administering psychosurgery as punishment), but subtler forms of paternalistic control are much harder to eliminate.

Staff also use a one-up stance when they offer praise and make decisions that clients are happy with. A one-up stance is based on how people use their authority and power, not on whether their decisions are pleasing to other people. Some staff are very kind, but they are nonetheless making decisions without collaborating with clients.

The psychological *pull* on staff to work from a one-up stance is enormous. First, staff are also in a hierarchy so they report to "superiors" who make demands on them. Their own jobs and belief in themselves as competent may be dependent on how well they can influence clients to behave in desired ways.* Second, their jobs can be very stressful and dangerous. Clients are sometimes aggressive and abusive toward staff and peers, and responding to them takes enormous skill. Third, staff usually do want to help. Many are there because they take pleasure in the helper role. They do not always consider whether they are "teaching someone to fish or catching a fish for them." Fourth, people follow the models they have been exposed to. Most people's model of helping is that of authority directing people. We experience this in our families and in virtually all institutions in our society. We do what we know.

One can also see staff demonstrating a one-up authority stance in rehabilitation facilities such as residential treatment programs. Just ask the clients for examples of staff behavior or attitudes they do not like. A client who must be supervised at all times complains that when he asked the staff person to

---

* This is reflected in our language. Staff efforts to influence patients are called "helping." Patient efforts to influence staff are called "manipulation."

go out with him for a smoke, the staff person "gave him an attitude" and told him he was too busy. Another complains that the staff person is constantly harassing him to clean up after himself even though it is his body, room, and dishes. Another complains that staff control the television so that she is forced to watch the programs staff want to watch. Another complains that staff are always talking among themselves or on their pagers or the Internet. It usually is not hard to draw such examples out of clients. Indeed, we need only consider our own experience as a recipient of medical care or social services to find instances of what appear to us to be staff abusing their power or authority.

We are trying to engage our clients in treatment, but they are always react-ing to us and to the treatment settings. To the extent they experience staff as exhibiting arbitrary and abusive authority, they will resist our efforts at engagement. It does not matter whether their perceptions are fair or accurate. It is the same with us. How readily will we work with a doctor, nurse, or coun-selor who strikes us as disrespectful or bossy?

Accepting the client or patient role also means engaging in discussions about one's problems, illness, or deficiencies. Higher functioning people can see illness or problems as departures from their normal state of being. They may seek out a doctor or counselor because they are unhappy with problems that are keeping them from their desired state of life. For many of our cli-ents, however, their normal state of life is one of overwhelming problems and personal failure. They do not necessarily want to talk about how badly they are doing, and they can see invitations to use counseling as just that. Many behaviorally disturbed clients, when confronted about problem behaviors, have told me that was all "in the past," and they don't want to talk about the past because it brings them down. "The future is different," they say. They "won't do it again."

Our LLC clients usually cannot describe these power dynamics. They can-not articulate theories and they often cannot give coherent explanations for their resistance to treatment. They may just say that they "don't like to talk about the past," or they may just react to staff that they believe are pressuring or bossing them. Even when staff are "nice," they remain, from the client point of view, people who tell them what to do. This is true regardless of the set-ting: hospital, group home, day or work treatment. Indeed, much of the efforts of recent culture change in such institutions are designed to help staff move from acting like police persons to acting more like skill coaches (Regan, 2006). From LLC clients' perspective, the whole mental health enterprise, from the social control functions of the institutions in which they receive care, to staff who reflexively act in authoritarian manners, to the narrative about their problems that is told in treatment, can reflect disempowerment, whatever our noble intentions. This is often the unstated context in which we ask clients to engage in treatment.

Pretreatment Strategies

The pretreatment strategies described below are culled from a variety of counseling and psychotherapy models, chief among these being the constructivist narrative CBT framework of Meichenbaum (1994, 1996, 2001). There is overlap between pretreatment and treatment strategies. We can say that all pretreatment strategies, designed to elicit treatment engagement, are also treatment strategies, designed to develop client skills or stories. However, the reverse is not true. Not all treatment strategies work as pretreatment strategies. For instance, specific skill training groups, or strategies involved in relapse prevention, assume that clients have agreed to participate. Giving clients the opportunity to explore their thoughts and feelings can be good treatment but assumes the clients see this as a meaningful task. When clients are not willing or able to do these treatment activities, it is an exercise in frustration to offer them. A pretreatment orientation brings a more clear and relevant focus to clinical thinking.

In practice, there is no clear line between pretreatment and treatment. These are not developmental stages and the movement from one to another is not linear. Rather, the concept of pretreatment is useful to clarifying our thinking around the challenges of soliciting client-informed engagement. In practice, clients often agree to some kind of therapy contract one moment only to drop it the next. They cycle in and out of commitment. More psychologically sophisticated clients can also reject their treatment and turn on their therapist even when they are well into the process. The notion of pretreatment is designed to bring our focus to the fact that mental health care must be collaborative, and that there are specific kinds of interventions that bring LLC clients into the treatment process and others that are unproductive. The discussion offered below is focused primarily on engagement of this group of LLC clients. Their "resistance" to mental health care is based mainly in their lack of understanding and skills to use such care rather than on resistance related to a psychological dynamic like denial or transference. To be sure, the latter may also be at play, and all of these strategies help with those dynamics as well. The attention we give to pretreatment stems from recognition of the extraordinary efforts we must make to bridge the chasm between the conceptual worlds of our clients and that of psychiatry, psychology, and the mental health field.

The key elements of our pretreatment efforts are the following:

1. Presenting a clear and compelling map of treatment by defining recovery in terms of skills.
2. Noticing and labeling the skills that clients already use.
3. Demonstrating empathic understanding.
4. Working skillfully from one-down and collaborative stances.
5. Engaging clients in collaborative problem solving.

BOX 4.1   PRETREATMENT STRATEGIES

Mental health treatment begins when client and staff have a shared understanding of, and commitment to, treatment goals and process. Until that happens, clients are in pretreatment.

Pretreatment strategies are motivational and educational. They are designed to elicit engagement in the treatment process.

All the strategies listed below can also be used in treatment once clients have agreed to focus on psychosocial skill enhancement.

We work simultaneously to help clients develop skills and construct a new story about their skills. We help clients link instances of skill use into a pattern or story about their new abilities.

1. Provide a path or map of recovery. *Treatment is developing skills.*
    - Activities of daily living (ADL) skills for care of oneself and one's physical environment.
    - Coping skills for managing feelings, thoughts, impulses, and bodily sensations.
    - Conflict resolution and problem solving skills.
    - Relapse prevention skills for managing problem behaviors and symptoms.
    - Health consumer skills: understanding mental and physical health and illness, medications, how to work with treatment providers.
2. Notice and label the skills clients are already using.
    - *Strength-based treatment.* Whatever happens, find the skill.
    - Notice when clients use any positive skill.
    - Find skills when the problem is absent, less intense than previously, or in the recovery from the problem.
    - Use everyday language to describe skills (e.g., calm down skills, talk skills, think skills).
    - Develop an extensive vocabulary for skills. The particular names are not important.
    - *Attend continuously to skills clients are using, and keep discussing these with them. It is far more important that staff notice and label their existing skills and strengths than that staff notice and attend to their problems.*

3. Empathy and validation.[1]
   - Make sure you understand how the client feels and thinks before attempting any intervention aimed at change.
   - Say back to them what you just heard: "You seem to feel/think ____. Have I got that right?"
   - Show your understanding of how clients' behavior makes sense in light of their history or the current circumstances.
4. Work "one-down."
   - Invite participation.
   - Ask permission to discuss difficult issues.
   - The message is always: "We value your input. We want to solve this together."
   - Helpful phrases: "I wonder if ..." "I'm worried/fearful/anxious that ...," "Can you help me with...."
5. Collaborative problem solving.[2]
   - Treat problems as opportunities to help clients develop skills.
   - Avoid arbitrary limit setting and making decisions for clients. We only resort to authoritative one-up stances when (a) clients will not or cannot collaborate and (b) clients' behavior is unsafe.
   - Steps of collaborative problem solving: (a) Empathy, (b) defining the problem, (c) brainstorming and evaluating solutions.
   - The solution has to work for all parties. Negotiate.
   - Staff should be flexible within reason.
6. Address problems by promoting client self-evaluation.
   - Explore client feelings, ideas, experiences, perspectives. Show interest in them.
   - Clarify client goals.
   - Ask questions that help clients evaluate their own problem behaviors.
   - Ask: "What are you doing? Is it helping you reach your goals?"
   - Use self-monitoring procedures if possible.

7. Make treatment fun.
   - Use games and fun activities.
   - Role play is better than talk.
   - Tell stories and elicit stories.
   - Use movies and television shows that teach important lessons.
8. Whenever possible, put clients in the helper/teacher or consultant role.
   - The best way to learn a skill is to teach it.
   - You cannot be a good teacher unless you are a good student.
   - People who refuse to accept help are often very willing to give help to others.
   - People often learn more by giving than by receiving.
9. Attend to and develop the client's "story" of strength, resiliency, recovery, and skillfulness.[3]
   - Selectively attend to skills and strengths and highlight them.
   - Every success is a moment in the strengthening of the story of recovery or developing ability.
   - Ask questions that help clients discover their abilities, "How did you do that? When else have you used these skills?"
   - *Skills linked by a story create an identity.*

Notes

1. Carl Rogers described three essential conditions for psychotherapy: accurate empathy, unconditional positive regard, genuineness. He highlighted the centrality of empathy to psychotherapy. Marsha Linehan emphasizes the skill of emotional validation in DBT.
2. Ross Greene developed the approach of collaborative problem-solving with "explosive" children and clients.
3. Donald Meichenbaum's constructivist narrative cognitive-behavioral therapy attends to both psychosocial skills and the construction with the client of a story about recovery, strength, skills, and resiliency.

6. Promoting client self-evaluation.
7. Using treatment interventions that are compelling and fun.
8. Putting clients in the helper, teacher, or consultant role.
9. Developing the client's story of strength, resiliency, recovery, and resourcefulness.

Presenting a Clear and Compelling Map of Treatment by Defining Recovery in Terms of Skills

As discussed above, one barrier to client engagement is their not understanding or valuing what mental health providers do. But what is it that we do? Can we explain in simple clear terms what mental health treatment means? Put another way, if we consider ourselves to be professionals marketing a service, then what exactly are we selling?

One simple model is that we help people understand themselves better. With new *insight*, they will be better able to handle life challenges. This model suffers, as we saw, from the limitation that many LLC clients do not value insight and may lack language and other cognitive abilities that foster the development of insight.

A second model is that we offer support, a special *relationship*. This model suffers from the fact that by *relationship*, we mean something peculiar. We do not mean friendship. We do not mean love. We do not mean joining our family. We mean a relationship with the strange rules and boundaries discussed above, which the client, or some other source, pays money for. Besides that, how exactly is this relationship supposed to help? It is quite hard to define in a compelling way unless you fall back on the idea that the relationship helps you understand yourself better. Then you are back to the limitations of promoting insight as your means of soliciting clients.

A third model is that we provide treatment for psychiatric disorders. We treat mental illness. This is certainly true, but explaining to our clients that we will help them with their mental illnesses is hardly a way to elicit their engagement in treatment. This model has the severe disadvantage of being associated with the stigma of mental illness. In our experience, psychoeducation is indeed an important part of mental health care, but it is a huge mistake to begin with it. Such psychoeducation, properly adapted for the language skills of clients, is very important once we have a therapeutic relationship and they are engaged in treatment. One could hardly, however, come up a strategy more likely to foster resistance than to begin by insisting that they accept help because they are mentally ill.

Fortunately, there is another model that is clear, simple, compelling, and associated with the established best practices in the mental health field. That model is that we *help clients develop skills*. Reduced to its essentials, cognitive-behavioral therapy (CBT) is about teaching skills. The skills we teach are psychosocial skills. They are skills for dealing with one's inner life (thoughts, feelings, impulses, sensations, experiences) and skills for dealing with one's outer life (interactions with other people; responding to environmental challenges). They are skills for self-care and skills for managing problems. Our first pretreatment strategy is to give clients a usable language or map for the treatment process. We do this by developing our vocabulary for talking about skills and sharing this vocabulary with them.

There is yet a fifth model for what we do. This model is that we help people change their stories. This model comes from the constructive narrative tradition associated with Michael White and others (White, 1995, 2007; White & Epston, 1990) and is also an important part of Meichenbaum's perspective. The word *story* has a particular meaning here. Essentially it refers to how one thinks about oneself. We help people change their stories or beliefs about themselves. Rather than struggle to explain this very abstract idea, it is simpler to remember that changing how one thinks is also a skill. It is the cognitive part of CBT. The narrative therapy tradition, in the process of talking about *metaphor* and *story*, offers many strategies to help people think differently. When we talk about skills, we mean these thinking skills also, but introducing the model of storytelling in the pretreatment stage only muddles the issue for our LLC clients. It is best to stay with skills.

Conceptualizing treatment as learning skills takes us into the world of CBT. It takes us into the world of empirically validated best treatment practices. Before it became *cognitive*-behavior therapy, behavior therapy was concerned chiefly with motivation, not skills. Meichenbaum was the earliest researcher and clinician to change the paradigm to its current skill focus, and in that process create what we now refer to as CBT. Later influential researcher/clinicians such as Marsha Linehan (1993a, 1993b), Ross Greene (Greene, 1998; Greene & Ablon, 2006), and G. Alan Marlatt (Marlatt & Gordon, 1985) elaborated skill-based treatment strategies and created DBT, collaborative problem solving therapy, and relapse prevention treatments, respectively. The work of Meichenbaum, Linehan, Greene, and Marlatt is presented in Chapters 5 through 8.

Skill training as a model has "face validity," for clients and staff. That is, it makes sense fairly easily. Skill training is nonstigmatizing. Staff and clients need the same skills. We can talk with staff about *their* use of coping and conflict resolution skills, using the same language for clients and staff.* Psychosocial skills, such as coping, nonviolent conflict resolution, symptom management, communication, problem solving, taking care of one's body and physical environment, are directly relevant to our clients' problems. This kind of language is relatively easy to understand and in this way contrasts very favorably with such abstract psychodynamic notions as unconscious, defense mechanisms, transference, object relations, self and self-object.

---

* See Chapter 8 for a discussion of how this is done.

In our work with LLC clients, the language we use is very much an issue. We can talk about skills using everyday language, avoiding the special jargon that the CBT world can also fall prey to. The clinical challenge for staff is first to develop their vocabulary for skills and second, as we discuss next, to help clients discover the skills they are already using.

Noticing and Labeling the Skills That Clients Already Use

CBT gives us the framework for talking about skills, but this is not enough. Although our clients have many problems, we are more likely to bring them into treatment by talking not about these problems but about the skills they already are showing.

A 16-year-old deaf boy we will call Tom has been hospitalized on our unit after attacking staff and their property in a residential school program. His program staff have questions about his psychiatric diagnosis and need for medication, but the hospitalization is primarily a result of this assaultiveness. On admission, he is initially cooperative but he insists he does *not* need to be in the hospital. He agrees to stay for a day or two but no longer. He says that *he* does not have a problem. It is just that the rules at his school are too strict. A day after his admission, I sit with him to discuss his hospitalization. I want to see how difficult it will be to engage him in treatment about a problem *he* has such as aggression. I am very aware that this is a pretreatment conversation, that he has not accepted that he needs our help, and that he does not necessarily see me as a credible helper. I am going to use our skill framework and try to catch him using skills. I will be looking for some examples of skill use to comment on.

Once sitting down with me, Tom insists he is ready to leave. He has been safe, he says. I ask him about his behaviors at the school, but he is unwilling to discuss them. That is all in the past, he insists. He is in control now. I commend him for being in control but point out that we have a problem. The school is not ready to take him back. He punched a staff person and damaged a staff person's car, and the school needs to be sure he is safe before he returns. Tom says that he is safe, and complains that the staff person would not let him go outside. He blames the staff person and the school and insists again that he is safe and does not need to be in the hospital. So far, this is a pretty typically unproductive conversation. I say to Tom that he has the responsibility of convincing the school and us that he is ready to return. Just saying he is safe while blaming other people will not convince anyone. The way to convince us is by using skills.

Tom then tries a variety of other strategies to persuade me to let him leave now. He begs to leave, looking as pathetic as he can muster. Then he cries. Then he puts his head in his shirt for 10 minutes. Because he is deaf and a signer, this ends communication between us. I just wait him out. When the shirt technique does not work, he starts more aggressive posturing. I am concerned that he may get aggressive with me, but I try to stay as emotionally connected with him as I can. His manner gets more hostile but he does not attack me. At a certain point, he just gets up to leave, storming out, but not, to my surprise, slamming the door. He then goes to his bedroom and cries for half an hour.

Actually, Tom gave me the opening I was hoping for. He adopted a slightly hostile posture but he did not verbally threaten me. He did not hit me and he left without slamming the door. He also stayed and talked with me for almost an hour, though a good part of it was spent with his shirt over his head. There is enough here for me to find some skills.

Next day, we meet again. I begin by commending Tom for the control he showed. I point out that I had heard stories about how violent he is, but yesterday he did not threaten or hurt me and he did not slam the door. I acknowledged his feelings of anger and frustration, and I ask Tom why he did not blow up.

He replies, "If I blew up, I'd have to stay here longer."*

"Exactly right," I say, "and very smart of you to figure that out. Actually, I don't know if you know it, but you were using an important coping skill there. Do you know what skill you were using?"

"No. What?"

"To stay in control, even though you are mad. You stayed in control so you must have been using a coping skill. Coping skills are skills for managing your feelings and your behaviors, like staying calm even when you are mad. I'm wondering if you know how you did it?"

"No. I don't know."

"Well, you just said that you knew if you blew up, you'd stay here longer. That means you were thinking. You used your brain. You thought about the blowing up, and what would happen if you blew up. You thought 'I'd have to stay here longer. I don't want that.' So you stayed safe. Wow. I'm impressed."

Tom looks puzzled. He does not know what to make of this.

"Uh-huh."

"Where else do you use that skill? Can you tell me about another time where you stayed in control because, say, you did not want to get in trouble?"

He thinks for a moment and then tells me about one time when he cooperated with staff. Now we are having a conversation about skills and successes. This is just the opening I was hoping for.

"So sometimes you think, and sometimes you stay in control. I know you have at least one coping skill, thinking, that you use sometimes. Maybe you have other coping skills. I don't know. Do you use this thinking skill all the time?

---

* In Chapter 2, I used "glossing" to more closely approximate the signing and gesturing actually used, but even this is not an accurate or exact representation of the language used. Tom is a relatively good signer, but others that follow are not. For ease of reading, and because there is no written code for the signing apart from technical systems developed by sign language linguists, I present these English approximate translations.

"No," he shakes his head.

"Suppose you did use thinking skills all the time. Whenever you are mad, you think first. You stay calm. You decide what to do. If you did that, would your life be the same or different?"

"Different."

"How would it be different?"

"I wouldn't be in this stupid hospital. I want to get out of here."

"Exactly right, " I say. "You wouldn't be here. What else?"

"I wouldn't be in trouble. I'd be able to spend more time with my family."

"More clear thinking. You seem to have some skill at thinking. If you were really good at thinking skills all the time, and maybe really good at other coping skills, you wouldn't be in the hospital. You'd be with your family."

"Yes."

"Well, I wonder," Long pause here because the most important question is coming. "Do you want help with that? Do you want your coping skills to improve?"

Tom nods yes, though I'm not convinced he understands what he's agreeing to.

"Well, that's good news, because we can help you with that."

Tom may not understand it, but we have just made an initial contract for treatment. This might be the initial movement from pretreatment to treatment, but probably it is not. Probably we are going to have some variant of this conversation again, maybe several times. In fact, it is just a few hours before we have another behavioral incident with Tom which provides another opportunity to search for skills even when he appears out of control.

Later that afternoon, Tom wants to use the staff tty (text telephone). He does not want to use his own money on the client pay phone tty. Staff tell him he has to use the client pay phone, at which point he becomes more agitated. He starts grabbing and throwing things, rips several pictures off the wall, and attempts to destroy the ping-pong table. The nurse gives him a choice of calming down or being restrained. He yells and signs "No!" at which point he is restrained until he can calm down.

There is a meeting the next morning with his parents, school officials, and Tom. We certainly have plenty of problem behaviors to talk about, and nobody but Tom thinks he is ready to be discharged. Our challenge is to set some limits while trying to engage him in a treatment plan focused on learning skills to manage feelings. If we start talking about his recent behavioral explosions, Tom will probably not even stay in the room, and he may well have another explosion. At the same time, we are not going to pretend the problem behaviors have not happened. We begin the meeting by asking Tom to discuss how he demonstrated good thinking skills and keeping in control. We talk about his staying in control for the first 2 days of his hospitalization even in the face of feeling angry and not being permitted to leave. We label the skills he used (self-talk, thinking, distraction), and we applaud him for it. I talk about how he stayed in control with me even when I gave him news he did not want to hear. Then we ask him to comment on the phone incident when he did not use the same skills. Tom says very little, so we describe, as objectively as possible, what happened. Tom wanted to use the staff phone. Staff said no. Tom damaged some unit property and would not calm down. The nurse gave him a choice but he said no. He became very angry, and staff were afraid he would hurt someone, so we restrained him. Then Tom calmed down.

This part of the conversation is hard for Tom. He complains that he did not have any money, and the phone rule was stupid. He insists on leaving the hospital, but all the adults present are in agreement that he cannot leave yet. We set a limit, working as we must at this point from a "one-up" authority position. His complaints are cut off and the meeting is ended. Tom starts to cry, and we let his mother comfort him while everyone else leaves.

A few hours later, I approach him again and ask if he is willing to talk. He agrees, and I start by empathizing with him. The meeting must have been tough for him. He really wants to get out of this place, and everyone said no. I tell him I know he is upset, and I am sorry to see him unhappy. Then I commend him again for staying in control that morning in the face of everyone telling him he had to stay in the hospital. Again, I ask him why he did not blow up today, and again he answers, "If I blow up, I'll have to stay here more. I want to get out of this f…ing place." I point out again the thinking skills he is using, commend him for it, and then ask him again how he is doing using that skill in other situations. He looks away. "So what about the plan we talked about of helping you improve your coping skills?" He is no longer arguing but neither is he fully signing up for skill training.

This is a fairly representative pretherapy conversation except that many are much harder because other clients have much poorer language skills than Tom. The team does set necessary limits but we also look for skills even when ostensibly bad behavior is being shown. We focus our conversation around the skills and then invite the person to consider the advantages of becoming even more skilled. Throughout this process, it is not usually necessary to say the words "counseling" or "therapy." We're just inviting someone to learn more skills.

The skill framework provides a relatively clear, concrete roadmap for treatment. However, we still need to engage in conversation clients who do not necessarily want to talk to us about their problems. These clients are often expecting criticism, or they interpret discussions about their problems as criticism. The best way to engage them is to initially confound this expectation by focusing conversations on skills they are already using. The skill for staff can be thought of as turning your brain around (this is how we sign this) so that staff notice when the problem behaviors and symptoms are *not* occurring, and then infer a skill that the client must be using to stay in control.

Even clients with the most serious behavioral problems are not dangerous most of the time. In fact, most of the time, they are doing rather mundane things such as eating, talking/signing, playing games, and watching television. Sometimes they have appropriate social conversations, using skills like good eye contact, turn taking, listening, and appropriate space. Sometimes, when someone picks on them or sets a limit, they do not blow up. The skill of "talking to yourself" or "considering consequences" or "thinking" is pretty commonly used but one has to know how to look for it. Through the process of breaking down coping, conflict resolution, and other skills, staff develop the skill vocabulary that enables them to recognize skills in routine and innocuous behaviors. Thus, the fact that Tom did not blow up when he did not get his way, at least in two meetings, suggests he must have been using skills. In situations like this, skills like "thinking," "distraction," "rocking in a chair," or "walking away" can almost always be found or inferred. Again, we avoid using specialized vocabulary for skills because it can interfere with finding the skill in everyday behaviors.

Examples of skills staff must learn to recognize include:

- Any use of distraction
- Any use of reasoning
- Any physical/sensory action to calm down
- Any reliance on a "higher power"
- Any prosocial behavior
- Any effective problem solving and decision making

Finding skills when someone is showing negative behaviors is like an exercise in figure-ground, when one shifts one's gaze to another part of the picture. As a treatment milieu becomes more oriented around the concept of skills, this figure-ground shift becomes easier. Skills talk becomes the language of a program. Some ways to make this shift include:

- Focusing on when the problem behavior does not occur
- Focusing on when the client shows a lesser degree of intensity or duration of the problem behavior (why client was less violent, more in control, this time)
- Focusing on skills used before the problem behavior (client stayed in control much longer this time and used several coping skills before blowing up)
- Focusing on the recovery process and on positive behaviors that occur after the negative behaviors (the client calmed down much quicker and discussed the behavior in a productive, responsibility taking manner; the client apologized and set a new goal)

In the following example with a much more language dysfluent deaf client, the staff use the strategy of locating the skill in why the client's behavior was not worse.

Priscilla is a 25-year-old deaf client with borderline personality disorder, low intelligence, and a history of self-mutilation and aggression. She signs in short phrases at best, often repeating back much of what is signed to her. Staff doing ward checks find Priscilla in her room using a scissor to cut her nails. In our locked psychiatric inpatient unit, clients are not allowed to have "sharps" unsupervised; especially clients with a history of cutting themselves. Staff approach Priscilla, remind her of the policy, and ask for the scissors. Frustrated, Priscilla takes the lock from her locker and hurls it at the locker, denting it. With much show of exasperation, she hands over the scissors to the staff person.

How should staff respond to her? Without a great deal of training, the first response of most staff persons will be to focus on her negative behaviors. She brought a scissor to her room and was using it unsupervised. She threw a lock and damaged hospital property. She was "angry, out of control, un-cooperative and argumentative." It's not inconceivable to think that in some settings she might be restrained for this.

But there is another way to look at this. Priscilla made a choice to not throw the lock at the staff person, and instead to throw it at the locker. She was using self-control even as she was "blowing up," in that she kept her aggression within certain limits. She must have been using a skill to accomplish that. We want to talk to her about her aggression, but the conversation will not be therapeutically useful unless it becomes one in which she is seeking ways to control her own behaviors. She probably expects a scolding or punishment, and probably does not relish the idea of "processing" the incident with us. At a later point, when she was calm and willing to talk, the conversation between the staff person and Priscilla proceeded like this:

"Remember yesterday? You were cutting your nails. I asked you for the scissors? You gave me the scissors and threw the lock? Remember? Seems you were mad?"

"No, not mad."

"You seemed mad. You threw the lock. But, wow, you showed skill also. What skill did you show?"

"No, don't know."

Staff repeat themselves until Priscilla knows what they are talking about.

"I was mad. Staff watching me. Staff are nosy."

Staff reflect empathically. "You think, staff watch you all the time. It's not fair. You feel mad."

Priscilla nods yes.

"You did throw the lock but at the locker, not at me. You didn't hurt me. Why?"

"Don't know."

"You did show self-control. You didn't throw the lock at me. You controlled yourself. How'd you do it?"

Priscilla just nods. She cannot answer this. Staff offer her some possibilities. "Maybe you thought, 'I don't want trouble'?"

Priscilla nods her head, yes. She signs, "No trouble." It is very possible she is just agreeing with whatever was suggested, but it is good enough for now.

"Seems you used your thinking skills. You thought that you don't want trouble. That's thinking skills. Good job!"

Priscilla smiles.

"Now there is one more hard question. Are you ready?"

She nods.

"You didn't throw the lock at me. That was a skill. Can you do even better?"

Priscilla thinks. "Don't throw lock. Talk."

"YES! YES! RIGHT!" responds staff enthusiastically. For Priscilla, this was an impressive moment of what could be called *insight*.

The staff solicited a therapeutic conversation by using the relatively simple skills framework and noting some positive skills even at the moment of aggression. Staff also used some other pretreatment skills, to be discussed shortly, notably, empathy, a "one-down approach," and promoting client self-evaluation. It is a relatively small step from this pretreatment conversation to treatment contracting over how she could become even more skillful. The goal we eventually set with Priscilla was MAD? PRACTICE TALK.*

With a little playfulness, one can easily extend this strategy. A school counselor once asked me about a student with an unusual and troubling behavioral problem. This student had a prosthetic leg and whenever he was upset, he would take it off and throw it at staff. The counselor asked what the staff should do. She noted that one staff person had the idea that they should hold on to the leg to "teach him a lesson." This is a punitive response that is only likely to increase conflict. Besides, the student has already demonstrated willingness to give up his leg. A better response is to focus on the times when he does not throw his leg. In fact, while he sometimes does throw his leg at staff, usually he keeps his leg attached. Staff should notice and comment any occasion that he is upset and does not throw his leg and label what he is doing as "leg keeping skills." They can then engage him in a discussion of how he is dealing with his feelings more skillfully, including using his "leg keeping skill." When he is ready, other coping skills besides "leg keeping" can be introduced.

Demonstrating Empathic Understanding

Probably the most powerful technique for creating an alliance with a person who resists working with you is to convey to that person an empathic understanding of his or her world. The central importance of empathy to psychotherapy was first highlighted by Carl Rogers (1951) who claimed that accurate

---

* On the formal treatment plan, this goal can be written up as, "Patient will notice mood states such as anger and practice use of coping skills such as talking about her feelings."

empathy, along with unconditional positive regard and genuineness, were the three essential conditions for successful psychotherapy. The style of counseling Rogers developed, person centered counseling, has as its hallmark the cultivation by counselors of this empathic connection with their clients. Rogers believed that accurate counselor empathy, unconditional positive regard and genuineness were all that was needed for clients to grow in psychotherapy. For him, these conditions were both necessary and sufficient.

Few counselors will disagree with Rogers that it is necessary for counselors to develop an empathic understanding of clients, but many will disagree with him that these conditions are sufficient. Two approaches that have embraced Rogers while also extending his approach are motivational interviewing and nonviolent communication (NVC). Motivational interviewing is a style of counseling designed by William Miller and Stephen Rollnick (2002) for work with clients who are not yet ready to behave differently. These include people ambivalent about change (e.g., an alcoholic who knows drinking is destructive but cannot imagine life without alcohol) and hostile to change (e.g., the client mandated into treatment by a judge). The most important component of motivational interviewing is demonstrating empathic understanding of a client's reluctance to change. NVC (Rosenberg, 2003) is a method of conflict resolution developed by Marshall Rosenberg. In NVC the core skill is also conveying empathically that one understands the feelings, beliefs, and frame of reference of all parties to a conflict.*

Motivational interviewing is essentially a strategy for pretreatment counseling, and it is striking how heavily it relies on empathy. Students learning counseling in graduate school often learn person centered counseling strategies first because they are so foundational to all good counseling. Empathy is conveyed through reflective listening in which one states back to clients what they are saying and what they appear to be feeling, experiencing, and meaning. Corey (2005) writes that "empathy is a deep and subjective understanding of the client *with* the client" (p. 173). He cites Watson (2002) who stated that "60 years of research has consistently demonstrated that empathy is the most powerful determinant of client progress in therapy."

The power of empathy to disarm resistance is enormous. A counselor using motivational interviewing engages a client by seeking to understand their ambivalence about change and recovery. For example, motivational interviewers do not try to convince an addict of anything. They do not confront addicts about their drinking, insisting they face their denial. That would only promote deeper opposition. Rather, the counselor attends well and reflects back to clients the ambivalence they express. If the client says, "I'm only here because my wife threatened to divorce me unless I got help for drinking," the counselor may reflect back, "you really don't want to be here. However, it

---

* NVC is discussed in more detail in Chapter 6.

seems like you do want to save your marriage." The counselor then helps the client express the concerns that he does have. As this happens, the client may, on his own, start to discuss the impact of drinking on his relationship with his wife. The counselor reflects this also. "You've told me you enjoy drinking with your buddies, but you are also saying that after you drink, you and your wife fight, and your relationship has suffered so much that you are beginning to wonder whether the drinking is worth it." The reflection is of both sides of the client's ambivalence, but the emphasis is helping the client explore the reasons for changing. Because the counselor conveys understanding, there is nothing for the client to resist. The result is greater willingness for a client to explore a problem.

There are many tense moments in psychiatric hospitals when clients appear ready to hurt themselves or other people. When I approach these crisis situations, I have learned to think aloud to myself, "empathy, empathy." I am reminding myself that the single most helpful intervention I can make is to convey to the person who is escalating that I want to understand how he or she feels. I am also aware that my self-talk will affect my stress and functioning. This may not be sufficient to end a conflict or crisis, but it is rare that a conflict or crisis is resolved well without staff conveying empathy.

A mentally retarded, linguistically impaired client on the Deaf Unit wants to go on a shopping trip but there is no such trip scheduled for that day and her request cannot be accommodated immediately. Multiple attempts are made to engage her in other activities but none of these succeeds. She insists on going out on the trip that will not happen, and she begins to show warning signs of escalation into her pattern of assaultive behavior. Staff have seen these signs before: pacing, sitting by the plants and tearing up the leaves, pulling papers off the walls and tearing them up, disengaging from conversation. Staff are doing all they can to interrupt her escalation but this is a client who lacks the language and cognitive capacity for much reasoning. She just does not accept that there is no trip today. The reasons there is no trip are irrelevant.

A Deaf social worker with whom she has a relationship approaches her to try her hand at disengagement. She knows that she cannot use much language, and that her nonverbal communication will matter more than her signs. She keeps a respectful distance, makes eye contact, leans forward, and signs softly. She asks,

S.W.: What's the matter? You seem angry.
Client: Shopping trip.
S.W.: You want to go on a shopping trip. I understand. I'm so sorry there is no trip today.
Client: Home. Discharge. I hate hospital.
S.W.: Are you angry or sad?
Client: Discharge. Home.

S.W.:   I know you are sad. You miss your parents. You miss your family. I'm sad too. (The social worker is conveying support and empathy nonverbally as well. The client is listening and she has stopped ripping papers. She looks more sad than angry. She looks down and away.)

Client: Discharge.

S.W.:   You are sad. You want to see your parents. I'm sad. All of us are the sad same as you. (The social worker notices that the client is calming down, and this provides an opportunity to incorporate the strategy of helping the client notice skills that she is already using. This is, of course, tougher to do with someone with so little formal language.)

S.W.:   You are calming down, using calm-down skills. Good for you. Thank you.

This interaction is followed by various staff attempts to distract the client with other activities. The client declines these and goes off to sit by herself. About 15 minutes later, the crisis is past, and staff can approach the client to praise her further for using "calm-down skills."

In motivational interviewing, one works to get one's client to argue the reasons for change. One does this by empathically eliciting from clients the pros and cons of changing and then asking them questions that get them to elaborate on the reasons for change. When the client who loves to drink with his buddies also notes that his marriage is in jeopardy, the counselor, after reflecting back how he enjoys this camaraderie, will shift the focus to his concerns about his marriage. "What happens when you come home after drinking with your friends? How does your wife react? What effect does this have on your marriage? How important is saving this marriage to you?" These kind of questions *pull* for the client to argue the reasons to stop drinking.

Tom was the adolescent client presented earlier who was helped to see the skill he used in tolerating staying in the hospital longer. After some skills were identified, he was asked if he used these skills at other times. He was then asked to speculate on how his life would be better if he did use these skills. He replied, "I wouldn't be in the hospital," and "I'd get to spend more time with my family." Once he is describing advantages of better behavior, the counselor need merely reflect it back or encourage elaboration. "And you'd like to spend more time with your family?" The more Tom elaborates on this, the more *he* is presenting the reasons for change.

Human beings crave to feel understood. When another person approaches us in the spirit of trying sincerely to understand our feelings, perspective, and needs, the result is almost always helpful. If this empathic connection is even partially skillful, we relax. We calm down. We stop arguing and fighting. We engage with the interviewer. We are brought into the process. Indeed, empathic understanding is so reliably successful at creating positive connection that one has to wonder why it is not used more often. Why do we, as a species, persist in trying to dominate each other into submission when respectful, engaged empathy creates alliances and cooperation even when people are initially adversaries?

One answer is that we have deficits in our own skills. We do what we were taught, and unfortunately the default model that most of us learn is to manage people through domination and submission. Our least-skilled leaders model this at the highest levels of government and industry. There are wise people like Mahatma Gandhi, Martin Luther King, Jr., and Marshall Rosenberg throughout world history who teach other peaceful means of conflict resolution, but they are not yet the dominant voices. You have to search them out, but they are there.

Whatever the techniques one uses to solicit engagement from clients, the main factor determining whether they succeed or fail is probably whether they are done with empathy. Staff may ask clients to complete a self-monitoring form and review it with them, for instance. If the staff person treats this as an obligation or chore and does it mechanically, the client will likely conclude it is a waste of time. If the staff person shows genuine interest in the client, and uses empathic listening skills, the technique is much more likely to succeed. All the pretreatment techniques discussed here can be done mechanically, and they will fail. It is the practice of empathic tuning in to other people that creates relationships and allows the other techniques to work.

Working Skillfully From One-Down and Collaborative Stances

Unless trained to do otherwise, mental health professionals and paraprofessionals commonly work from the "one-up stance" described earlier. This means they assume the stance or attitude of the expert and their interventions are directive. This does not mean they are not kind or helpful; only that they work with the understanding that they know what is best. This stance is commonly seen, for instance, in substance abuse treatment where providers confront the denial of substance abusers. It is seen in any setting where staff diagnose problems and recommend treatment approaches without considering the suitability of such assessments and recommendations for particular cultures and clients. It is seen when staff take a problem focused treatment approach, but it is also seen when staff reward clients for behaviors staff consider desirable. The key sign that staff are working one-up is that they consider themselves to be the experts.

One-up stances are being challenged even in physical medicine where a scientific basic for standards of care is easier to come by (Meichenbaum & Turk, 1987). Consumers increasingly expect doctors to be collaborative, and they expect to be the decision makers about their own treatment. The expertise of mental health and rehabilitation professionals is expected to extend not merely to a body of knowledge about illness and disability but to human relationships. Professionals and paraprofessionals who can strategically alter their stances, choosing to act one-up, one-down, or collaboratively as fits circumstances, do not lose any expertise by so doing. Indeed, they show even greater expertise. This expertise is in human relations and pertains to the ability to engage diverse clientele into treatment.

When taking a one-down stance, staff treat the client as the expert and put the client in the power role. This may involve playing dumb, as seen in the television character Columbo who is often cited for his expertise in getting persons to confide in him precisely because they do not take him seriously (Meichenbaum, 1985; Meichenbaum & Turk, 1987). One-down stances need not involve playing dumb but rather working from a stance of "not knowing" (Anderson & Goolishian, 1992), described below. There is overlap between one-down and collaborative stances, but in the latter clinicians are less likely to act like they do not know. In a collaborative stance, the power is shared more equally between clinician and client with each having expertise in their respective domains.

Gerald Corey, a leading authority in counselor education, described the strategy of "not knowing," as developed by Anderson and Goolishian (Corey, 2005). Corey writes,

> It is therapists' willingness to enter the therapeutic conversation from a "not-knowing" position that facilitates this caring relationship with the client. In the not-knowing position, therapists still retain all of the knowledge and personal, experiential capacities they have gained over years of living, but they allow themselves to enter the conversation with curiosity and with an intense interest in discovery. The aim here is to enter a client's world as fully as possible. Clients become the experts who are informing and sharing with the therapist the significant narratives of their lives. (p. 387)

This is to say, when the therapist stops assuming the posture of an expert on the client's life, the therapist is more able to empathically tune in the world as the client sees it. This in turn will facilitate a deeper level of engagement and therapeutic conversation.

I think of one-down stances as often beginning with the phrase, "I'm concerned that ..." or "I'm worried that...." The counselor says, "I'm worried about what will happen to you if you continue to hit people," or "I know you want to get your own apartment. I'm worried that if you keep hurting yourself, you won't be able to live independently." Counselors also show a one-down stance when they ask permission to talk with a client, ask about a client's willingness to do something, ask for help from a client, or invite clients to join with them in completing some task. One-down stances often take the form of requests and invitations.

What happens when the client says "no" to these requests? First, from my experience, that does not happen nearly as often as people seem to fear. Indeed,

I believe we get more "no's" when we take a one-up stance than we do from a one-down stance. But clients certainly do say no, and in extreme situations may continue to show unsafe behaviors. What should counselors do then?

One response is to commend them for saying "no," and point out the skill they are using in clear communication or assertive statements of their needs. We might say, "I appreciate your ability to say no, to communicate what you want really clearly. I will respect your wishes, but I may ask you again at a later time."

Counselors face many instances when clients will not collaborate and persist in doing very unsafe behaviors. For instance, a client who meets criteria for borderline personality disorder is struggling constantly with staff. He has a history of suicide attempts and of self-mutilation through cutting. On one occasion, he almost died from an intentional overdose of medication. On most occasions, he cuts his arms enough to bleed but not enough to put himself in danger. This client is challenging and provocative to staff. He insists there is no reason to keep him restricted to the unit. He complains that staff watch him unnecessarily and try to control his every mood. Staff are making him miserable, he cries. He demands to be let off the unit. His history, however, is that when unsupervised, he hurts himself. Staff do not believe he can be trusted. They set the criterion that he must show no unsafe behavior for 3 weeks before he is given privileges to leave the unit.

Anyone who has worked in a psychiatric hospital will recognize this client and scenario, regardless of whether or not the client is deaf. Here, staff respond to the client's unsafe and provocative behaviors by setting limits and raising expectations for safety before granting any privileges. This is their default one-up stance, motivated by concern for the client but also about worry for their own liability. Staff know that if they just believe the client's assertions that he will be safe in the face of extensive evidence to the contrary, then they will be faulted should a bad outcome occur. Staff then set up an arbitrary criterion for privilege increases (i.e., no unsafe behavior for 3 weeks), believing this will protect *them*. The client responds to these restrictions by losing hope, becoming angrier, and challenging or threatening staff further. A vicious cycle follows: unsafe and challenging behaviors are responded to with restrictions that are responded to with more unsafe and challenging behaviors. This is a formula for client regression and staff burnout. It is a very common treatment scenario.

In this struggle, staff have lost sight of the pretreatment issue. They get caught up in their efforts to keep the client safe without the client's agreement to stay safe. Without this treatment alliance and agreement, mental health staff have very little power. Again, we do not do the agent of social control job very well. We fall back on arbitrary restrictions and complain about how difficult the client is. In mental health work, our only real power comes from successfully engaging our clients in treatment. We have a lot to offer engaged clients and very little to offer those who are not engaged. It is helpful to remember that in this situation, we have a pretreatment problem. Our challenge is not fundamentally to keep the client safe. If that were our sole intention, we could keep him on 24-hour supervision in a locked setting. Even this does not stop people who are really determined to hurt themselves. Our challenge is to engage him in the project of keeping himself safe. That will require a different stance from us.

The way out of this downward cycle is to move into a one-down stance. Instead of deciding on their own what is best for the client, staff could *share the dilemma* with the client and solicit his participation in problem solving. This *one-down stance* might look like the following:

Staff: We have a problem and we need your help. Is it ok if we talk with you?

Client: I don't care!

Staff: I'll take that as permission to talk. Thank you. Here's our problem. When you cut yourself or threaten to hurt us, we get nervous about safety and then we restrict you further. But it seems when we restrict you, you just get more unsafe. How are you feeling about what is happening here?

Client: I hate it. You don't trust me. You don't believe me. You boss me around. I told you I would be safe. You are violating my rights! No one here cares about me. You are all assholes!

Staff: So you are feeling pretty frustrated also? You feel like no one here supports you or cares about you. We're just mean to you. You feel like you are battling with us?

Client: Right. It's a war. How do you expect anyone to get better when you treat people this way?

Staff: We get it, but here's our dilemma. Believe it or not, we really don't like controlling you. Telling you what you can and can't do. Restricting you. Holding you back from things you want to do. Acting like a parent. *Fighting a war.* We know you hate it, and you may not believe it, but we hate it too. We really want to be able to back you and to trust you. We want to feel like we are working together as a team, helping you get better control and reach your goals. Do you feel like we are one team, working together, or two teams, fighting each other?

Client: I just told you. It's a war. You don't support me at all.

Staff: Well, if this is a war, we want you to win. We don't want to fight. We want to be on the same side.

Client: Then just give me back my privileges.

Staff: We're willing to take that risk but only if we really are a team. *We need your help!* We ask you to understand that when you are not collaborating with us, not honest; when you say you will be safe but then aren't safe, you don't give us much choice but to say "no." If we can't believe you, we worry that you won't be safe. The question for us is,

"Do you get this? Do you understand?" If we can come up with a treatment plan that makes sense to us all, and if we are really working on it together, then we can and will take more risks, but it all depends on how well we're talking together; how open and honest you are; how reasonable you are. Do you follow this?

Client: I just think this is more bullshit!

Staff: So here's the problem. When you talk like that, when you fight us, we have to say "no" to you. We can't take the risk that you will hurt yourself. So we're stuck. We say no. If you want to get your privileges back, we need your help. We need to make peace.*

Client: Can I have my privileges?

Staff: You have more power in this than you think, but you have to stop fighting, at least a little, and try problem solving with us. Do you think that's possible?

Client: (Thinking) What do you mean?

Staff: Great question. I appreciate you being willing to consider what we are saying. The problem is you want privileges and we want to be reasonably assured that we are working with you on learning skills to stay safe. They go together: privileges, safety, working like a team. How can we meet all of these goals?

This conversation begins one-down and moves into an invitation toward what Greene and Ablon (2006) call collaborative problem solving. Clients may or may not "buy" this, or they may appear to collaborate only to hurt themselves again. If that occurs, the natural consequence, at least temporarily, is staff falling back into the one-up role and setting limits. But as soon as possible, the client must be approached again, invited to discuss what has occurred, and invited again to collaborate. The message is, "Each day, we'll try again to have a more collaborative relationship with you. We'll keep at it until it happens." This may need to occur many times before clients get it, and there are clients who do not ever seem to get it. But most, from our experience, eventually move to a more collaborative position. With people who have severe character pathology, this may take quite a long time. But the meaningful treatment goal is not "keeping the client safe," but engaging the client in the process of keeping himself safe. That cannot be done without taking some risks (and documenting one's reasoning for purposes of risk management), and continually soliciting collaboration, even in the face of many setbacks.

The above conversation occurred with a client who had fluent language skills and was capable at that moment of rational thought. The challenges are much more formidable with clients who are language dysfluent, cognitively

---

* The staff person is working with the metaphor of "war" that the client offered. This narrative therapy strategy is discussed in Chapter 5.

impaired, or psychotic. Nonetheless, the challenge is still the same, to find a "language" that will enable staff and client to collaborate on grounds closer to that of equals. If one looks, there are many opportunities to approach a broad range of clients from a one-down stance.

A decision is made by the medical team to limit the number of times clients can call out for pizza and fast food due to nutritional concerns. Staff could inform clients that they can now order out only on Mondays and Fridays (one-up) or staff can explain the problem and ask clients' help in selecting which two days will be the order out days (one-down).

Staff are concerned about the increasing incidents of racist language coming from clients. Staff can set up a rule that any racist language will be responded to with loss of points or privileges (one-up) or staff could engage clients in a discussion of racism and other forms of prejudice, including prejudice against people like them, and ask for help on how we can make the program more respectful for everyone (one-down).

Two clients are arguing over what DVD to watch. Their argument appears to be escalating into a battle. Staff can intervene by telling them both to go for a time out (one-up) or deciding on a solution like which DVD will be watched first and which second (one-up). Staff can also seize this as an opportunity to engage clients in a task of skill building. Staff can invite the clients to find a solution peacefully. Are they willing to try? If so, what do they suggest (one-down)?

A client is constantly seeking staff attention, and staff are becoming resentful and avoiding her. Staff can set up a rule such as "we meet for only 15 minutes each shift" (one-up). Or staff can ask the client for help, explaining that they really want to spend time with her, but when they never get a break they become tired and burnt out. Can the client help set up a plan so that they all get what they need (one-down)?

Asking Permission as a One-Down Strategy There is a fairly simple technique, consistent with working from a one-down stance, that is surprisingly helpful in soliciting engagement. This is to *ask permission* to talk with a client about a particular issue. This is an especially useful strategy if the topic one wishes to address is an uncomfortable or provocative one. For example, suppose there is the need to give bad news to a client. The news is likely to provoke an angry or hostile response. The client is someone who is easily "disregulated," that is, who does not cope well with strong emotions and is likely to lose behavioral control. The treatment goal for the client may be for the client to learn "distress tolerance" (Linehan, 1993a) or coping skills. Staff need to give clients news that can easily trigger the problem behaviors that the client was hospitalized for.

We need to approach Juan, a highly explosive deaf male client, with the news that he did not get the advance in LOS (level of supervision or privileges) that he sought. He did not get this advance because his continuing behavioral problems have led staff to be concerned about his safety outside the unit.

Someone on the treatment team is given the unenviable task of giving him the bad news. In this case, it is me, and I will draw heavily on the asking permission strategy. I want to get his permission to have the conversation before we have the conversation in order to create a mental set most likely to lead to a positive outcome.

"Juan, is it ok if we talk? There is something I want to tell you, and how you respond is very important."

Juan shrugs. "Did my LOS (privilege level) go up?"

"I want to talk to you about that. Are you ready to discuss it?"

He nods yes. I want to start by pointing out, if possible, a skill he is already using.

"That's great. I like talking to you. Sometimes you do a great job at talking, expressing your feelings, and staying safe. Remember the conversation we had yesterday?"

Juan gives me a puzzled look.

"You wanted to order out food, but food ordering nights are Friday and Sunday. We had to say 'no.' You didn't like it. You were angry. But you stayed calm and you talked to staff. Remember?"

"Yes."

"Well, we'd call that 'expressing feelings skills' and 'staying safe skills' and you did both. That was great. That's just the kind of skill you need to practice more to get out of here."

"Can I order food today?"

"Today is Friday so it's the right night. Yes. You put off ordering food and coped with the frustration until the right day, today."

Juan smiles.

"Now I have to talk to you about something else. I have to give you some other news you may not like, and it's really important to show the same coping skill. Do you know why?"

Juan shrugs.

"Why is it important to cope with bad news, to stay calm, even when you are angry? Just like you did yesterday. Why is that important?"

"What's the bad news?"

"When you hear bad news, you still need to be calm. It doesn't matter if the news is bad, you still stay calm. If you can do that many times, that shows real improvement. Then your LOS would go up."

"My LOS didn't go up?"

"No, it didn't go up." I try my best to look supportive.

"Why? I've improved."

Juan is at the point of deciding whether he will stay in control or not. I step back and talk *about* the conversation again.

"Are you calm? Can we still talk?"

"Yes."

"Good. Please take some slow breaths." I model this for him, and he takes a few half-hearted deep breaths.

"Are you ready to talk some more?

Juan nods. Rather than remind him of the unsafe behaviors he showed yesterday, I will try to draw these out of him.

"You did a great job using your coping skills when you had to wait to order food but later on, did you and Bob get into a fight? What happened?"

"Bob provoked me. It's his fault!"

"Ok, Bob provoked you? How did you respond? What did you do?"

Juan thinks for a minute, looks angry, but then walks away to his room. He knows what he did and does not need us to discuss it at that moment. Even though it took a lot of coaching on my part, Juan stayed calm and used the appropriate coping skill of going to his room. Later on, we will give him credit for using *go-to-room skills*. We will even give him credit for the half-hearted breathing skills. We will notice these skills and invite him to consider the advantages of using them more frequently.

Asking permission of clients to have conversations has several advantages. It can, as in the example cited above, help ease a confrontation. The two-step process—asking permission to have the conversation, then having the conversation—helps people mentally prepare. It also, as in this example, creates the opportunity to talk about the conversation before it occurs, thus fostering other goals, such as the ability to discuss safely a topic that provokes a strong emotional response. It increases the chances that a successful conversation will occur and that a client will show some positive skill. This will give us something to reinforce later. I have found that when people give their permission to discuss a topic, they are more likely to demonstrate the coping and social skills called for. Giving permission is implicitly consenting to handle the situation skillfully. In my experience, it is rare that people do not agree to have a conversation when asked in this way, but should the client say "no," I would much rather know that before I start. That way I can praise the client for using "saying no skills" and suggest that maybe I will ask the person again tomorrow. With this kind of prelude, it is rare indeed for the client not to agree to the conversation on the next day.

In a parallel way, in group treatment we often set up the rule that if people do not want to speak, they can "pass." We make this explicit to give clients an easy, safe way not to participate. It also sets them up to succeed because whether they speak or do not speak, they are using skills. Clients often choose not to speak at a particular time. When staff recognize the skill they are using in deciding not to speak, we foster an environment which fosters greater client participation in the long run.

Asking permission to talk also models the treatment contracting process. Clients who have agreed to speak are already, to some degree, engaged. They are at least willing to have a conversation. If the conversation goes well (or even if it does not), there will be positive skills to comment on, and a greater likelihood that additional conversations will be agreed to. The agreement to talk about something sets the stage for the agreement to do something. It might be considered a "foot in the door" technique in that, after agreeing to talk, a client has already moved toward treatment engagement.

Collaborative Problem Solving

Greene (Greene, 1998; Greene & Ablon, 2006) has developed a method of treatment of "explosive" children and adolescents which he calls collaborative problem solving. He understands behavioral problems in youth as caused by psychosocial skill deficits, not by lack of motivation and certainly not by bad personalities. He understands explosiveness as occurring in a context. Youth with skill deficits become explosive in response to adults with their own skill deficits. They become explosive when faced with demands they cannot meet and in response to one-up, authoritarian styles of parenting, education, and clinical management.

In his first book, Greene (1998) helped parents put their concerns for their children into what he called Baskets A, B, and C. In his second book (Greene & Ablon, 2006), the three baskets had morphed into three plans. Basket A refers to parental concerns that are nonnegotiable or, in a treatment program, "bottom line" rules around behavior that staff will insist on. Plan A means these concerns will be enforced by rule or fiat, no matter what, even if enforcing them triggers a blowup. Basket C refers to matters that are not important enough to struggle over. Plan C is essentially to let the youth have his or her way on that issue. The goal in collaborative problem solving is to put most matters into Basket B where plan B strategies of negotiation and conflict resolution are engaged in.

Greene understands that one-up, plan A behaviors from parents, teachers, and staff may result in compliance or defiance but they rarely result in treatment engagement or skill acquisition. Most of the coping and conflict resolution skills that we would want our clients to acquire can occur through the process of collaborative problem solving.

We consider this process in more depth in Chapter 6 when we examine skills of conflict resolution. The point here is that Greene's work is consistent with the other pretreatment approaches we have considered. Clients become engaged much more readily when staff approach them in a one-down or collaborative spirit. So much of the culture of traditional clinical, rehabilitation, and educational settings is reflexively one-up that staff are not even aware of how their attitudes and manners promote disengagement, resistance, and even explosiveness in their clientele.

For instance, the house manager of a residential program for deaf adults complains to me that the clients in his program are not cooperative with the schedule or the rules. When I ask how the schedule and the rules were made, he explains the careful consideration that *he* gave to setting these up. He thoughtfully considered each client's need to be in particular places at particular times and he scheduled his staff accordingly. "Did you share with your clients your thinking on this and ask for their input?" I ask. "No," he replies, because the clients only think about what they need, not what their roommates need. I ask him to consider whether his not including them might be a factor in their resistance. Would they cooperate with the rules and the schedules more if they were involved in constructing them? And if they lack skills in empathy and perspective taking, how are they to develop those skills when decisions like these are made for them? In addition, is his job to manage his clients or to help them develop skills? Will both managing them and developing their skills be fostered by a strategy of solving problems collaboratively with them?

Promoting Client Self-Evaluation Through Skillful Questioning

The pretreatment approach presented here places great emphasis on finding positive skills already used, even in the face of flagrantly dysfunctional and dangerous behaviors. Sometimes people learning this approach object that it is naïve and Pollyannaish, as if the clinicians are colluding with clients in denying or minimizing the seriousness of their behaviors. When a patient throws a chair, these clinicians have a hard time seeing the fact that the patient did not punch someone as an example of a skill or strength. If we just stopped at noting skills and strengths, that criticism would be valid. The reason for the focus on skills already demonstrated, it must be remembered, is to elicit treatment engagement. After our initial conversations about client skills, and after we have begun developing an alliance by empathic listening and working one-down, we proceed to invite clients to look at their problem behaviors. This is not done by confronting the negative behaviors, but by maintaining our one-down stance and inviting clients to evaluate themselves. We then use skillful questioning to guide them to productive self-examinations.

The clinical stories presented above included some initial efforts to elicit self-evaluation. Tom, the 16-year-old boy hospitalized after attacking staff and destroying property at his residential school, was asked whether he uses the coping skills he used in our meeting elsewhere in his life. He was also invited to consider how his life might be different if he were always as skilled as he appeared to be during that interview. This question could be asked in slightly different ways.*

- Let us suppose you were just terrific at talking yourself through difficult situations. And let's suppose you were really mad because Joe picked on you, but you were determined to respond to him skillfully. What would that look like? What would you get out of it?

---

* Knowledgeable readers may recognize these questions as emerging from the solution-oriented brief therapy style of questioning (de Shazer, 1985, 1988).

- When staff and your parents see you using these skills, how do you think we would react? Is that what you want?
- Would you be interested, then, in working with us to get your coping skills stronger? If you are willing to do it, we have a lot we can offer you. It will not be easy, but as you become more skilled, what would be the benefit for you?

Similarly, Priscilla, the client who threw the lock at the locker, not at the staff person talking to her, was asked whether she could express her anger in an even more skillful way. The next questions follow logically: "And if you did that, what would be different for you?" "Is this something you want help with?" If the client answers yes, we have moved a step from pretreatment to treatment.

The treatment contract at this initial point is usually weak. Even if clients agree that, yes, it would be a good idea to learn more coping skills, that does not mean that tomorrow they will remember what they said or still feel this way. In all likelihood, variants of this conversation will need to occur many times. Clients agree today to work on learning coping skills only to change their mind the next day. This is normal and to be expected, and staff will cope better if we understand this. When more aggressive or self-harming behaviors occur again, or when clients resume an oppositional stance with staff, it is very easy for staff to lose patience and conclude that this strategy "isn't working." Staff need to be cautioned to avoid the magical thinking that one smart intervention is going to result in a quick cure for someone with longstanding behavioral problems. They need to remember that there is as yet no treatment contract, that we are still trying to get to the starting gate. Our goal so far has just been to move the client from pretreatment to treatment. The pretreatment phase may be the longest and most difficult aspect of the treatment program.

Good clinical questions promote client self-evaluation as well as treatment engagement. Questions are relatively easy to ask from a one-down stance that minimizes client resistance. Skillful questioning is an important part of many contemporary psychotherapies. Solution-oriented counseling (de Shazer, 1985, 1988), constructivist CBT (Meichenbaum, 1994, 1996, 2001), motivational interviewing (Miller & Rollnick, 2002), and reality therapy (Glasser, 2000; Wubbolding, 2000) all rely heavily on a particular style of skillful questioning. Meichenbaum (1994) describes himself as having a "fetish" for good questions. He collects good clinical questions and guides clinicians in what he calls the "art of questioning."

> The art of questioning provides patients with an opportunity to discover, rather than for the therapist to didactically teach. Such questioning fosters patients' understanding as patients are more likely to remember and apply those ideas that they discover by their own reasoning processes than the information and observations that are offered by the therapist. (Meichenbaum, 2001, p. 147)

Meichenbaum's texts present hundreds of good clinical questions he has culled from diverse psychotherapies. Many of these questions assume higher level language and reasoning skills than the group we are addressing possesses. He has questions that elicit client problems and others that elicit skills and other resources. He suggests that therapists are most skillful when they ask questions that pull clients to give their own suggestions for what they should do. This idea is also an essential component of motivational interviewing (Miller & Rollnick, 2002).

For our language and cognitively impaired clients, we will need to draw on very simple and concrete questions. I have found the style of questioning used in reality therapy (Glasser, 2000; Wubbolding, 2000) especially helpful for these clients during the pretreatment phase of work. Reality therapy, now called choice therapy, is a style of counseling originally developed for work with oppositional adolescents. Clients are helped to articulate their goals and values and are then pressed to see the relationship between what they profess to want and care about and what they actually do. The focus of reality therapy is helping clients examine the choices they are implicitly making through their behaviors. The strongest element of reality therapy, I believe, is this focus it places on promoting skillful self-examination.

The fundamental reality therapy questions are "What are you doing?" followed by, "Is what you are doing helping?" "Will what you are doing enable you to meet your goals?" These questions are easily asked from a one-down stance. They are also easy to translate into simple ASL. Deaf clients are asked, simply, GOAL WHAT? (What is your goal?) or WANT WHAT? (What do you want?). Then they are asked what they are doing. NOW DO-DO?* Finally, they are asked if what they are doing matches their goal or wish. For instance, HOSPITAL LEAVE, WANT? TODAY BLOW-UP, HIT STAFF. YESTERDAY BLOW-UP ROOM MESS-UP. BLOW UP. BLOW UP. BLOW UP. HOSPITAL LEAVE, BLOW UP, MATCH? ("*You want to leave the hospital. Today you exploded and hit staff. Yesterday you trashed your room. You have many explosions. Does this show you are ready to leave the hospital?*") Much of this can also be acted out for clients who have severe language problems. These clients can then be asked if the behaviors are GOOD or BAD (THUMBS-UP or THUMBS-DOWN). Usually, they answer correctly, and this leads to a simple discussion of what else they could do that would be good.

Counselors trained in reality therapy become skilled at the kind of Socratic questioning that pulls clients to notice and consider their actions and make other choices. Taking responsibility for one's behavior is the heart of what we intend when we guide clients from pretreatment to treatment.

---

* DO-DO is a common gloss for the sign translated roughly as "what are you doing?"

Reality therapy questions that have to do with values and the purpose of life can be very abstract and difficult to use with some LLC clients. Nonetheless, the strategy of asking clients questions, from a one-down stance, about what they are doing and whether their behaviors are helpful is often quite achievable. For instance, suppose one of these clients became angry and threw a chair across the room. After the crisis is past, a staff person engages the client in a discussion.

Staff: It looked like you were angry before. Is that right?

Client: Yes. John wouldn't let me go out.

Staff: You wanted to go out, and John said no. So you were angry. I understand. But what did you do?

Client: (looks away)

Staff: What did you do?

Client: I threw the chair.

Staff: Right. You threw the chair. Being honest is a great skill. But now what? What happens when you throw chairs or break furniture?

Client: My LOS (privileges) drops.

Staff: Yes, your LOS drops because throwing chairs is not safe. Did you want your LOS to drop?

Client: No.

Staff: Do you want your LOS to go up?

Client: Yes.

Staff: Ok, then, here's the hard question. Are you ready? You have to use thinking skills for this. Suppose you are angry. You don't like the rules. You want to go out and staff say 'not now.' You are angry. But you think, 'I want my LOS to go up.' If you stop and think and remember what you want, then what do you do?

Client: Talk.

Staff: Exactly! But maybe you talk and still you can't go out. What do you do?

Client: Accept.

Staff: Sometimes, yes, you need to accept the rules. That shows great coping skills. If staff see you accept the rules, not blow up when you are angry, what will staff think?

Client: I'm safe.

Staff: You got it! And if staff see you being safe, what happens?

Client: My LOS goes up.

The Socratic questions here guide the client to useful conclusions. Taking this one step farther, staff could next invite the client to actually practice the skill. We conceptualize clients who are actively practicing skills as in treatment.

Promoting Client Self-Evaluation Through Self-Monitoring   After we have begun asking questions that prompt clients to evaluate themselves, we often find it useful to ask them to formally rate themselves on a daily basis.

One way to do this is to invite them to complete a self-monitoring form. This is a form on which they are asked to evaluate themselves in several areas such as:

- Mood
- Behaviors (positive and negative)
- Attitude (positive and negative)
- Thoughts
- Symptoms
- Skills used
- Activities completed

Staff can *request* client cooperation with these self-monitoring forms.* Requiring them to complete these forms would result in lower compliance. At the Westborough Deaf Unit, at the end of the day and evening shifts, staff meet with clients to review their self-monitoring forms. After this process is established as normal, it becomes a group norm, and most clients comply. When clients refuse, staff accept their refusal (and may even comment on their skills in saying no safely). Some of the ways we solicit client compliance with this request are as follows:

- "It would be helpful to us to get your opinion every day on how you are feeling and the skills you are using."
- "I wonder if you would be willing to fill our a simple form every day which gives us feedback on how we are doing in helping you and how you are doing with your problems and skills."
- "We can see you are using many skills but I'm not sure you see it. I'd like to ask you to check off each day the skills you are using and how you are feeling and how you are doing with your goals. Your ratings would be a way for all of us to measure your progress. Also, if we are not being helpful, we'd get immediate feedback."
- "You'll see that we ask most of the clients here to complete these forms. It's a way for us to see how you are doing and to know if there are any problems."

Some of these forms use words, some use pictures, and some use both. Some clients are offended by pictures but others, who do not read well, appreciate them. We design the form so that it is most likely to be used. We have to consider what domains to cover (e.g., moods, behaviors, attitudes, symptoms,

---

* A fuller discussion of guidelines for conducting self-monitoring activities can be found in Meichenbaum (2001).

skills, and so forth), and what kind of rating scale to use. The simplest rating scale would be thumbs up to thumbs down or smiling or frowning faces. More complex scales involve numerical ratings and request clients to comment. All this should be developed in conversation with the client.

It is most useful clinically for the forms to include a rating of the target problems. This could be symptoms such as depression, hallucinations, or self-harm or behaviors such as hitting others. Asking clients to evaluate whether or not the target problems are occurring is an easy way to educate clients about the treatment focus and to pull them into considering whether they are improving. For clients with Axis II personality disorders such as borderline personality disorder, their attitude and relationship with the staff is usually an important issue. They often find fault with the staff and are unhappy with various aspects of the program. Asking them to evaluate their own attitude toward their treatment is a one-down way to put the attitude issue on the table. Before we ask these clients to rate themselves, however, we should give them an opportunity to rate us. If they have a space to find fault with us, they may be more amenable to looking at themselves more critically. A sample attitude rating scale, for a client with reasonable ability to read English, might be this:

Rate your attitude: 0 (I do not think this) to 10 (I think this a lot)

1. Staff is helping me.
2. Staff respect me.
3. I am making an effort to help myself.
4. I am following my treatment plan.
5. I am participating well in treatment groups.
6. I am arguing with staff.
7. I am attending to my attitude.
8. I feel hope for my future.

Self-monitoring forms can be completed daily with direct care staff. This is designed to structure a 5-minute therapeutic conversation between direct care staff and their assigned clients in which staff ask them how they are doing. It is also designed to move direct care staff out of the role of unit police persons and into the role of skill coaches. They are encouraged to invite the clients to discuss their self-monitoring forms. Staff are encouraged to approach this task with an attitude of respectful interest in the clients, not as a duty or chore, because clients often cooperate or not based on the attitude staff bring to the task. People do not want to talk about their day with a bureaucrat who is just filling out forms. The self-monitoring forms can also be reviewed by counselors with their clients. They should be reviewed with someone so clients perceive that staff really are using this information.

Simple self-monitoring can be added to a group or activity to help clients discover that what they do influences how they feel. Our occupational therapist

Diane Trikakis used self-monitoring for this purpose in an art activity she was leading. She offered the art activity, and everyone joined except for one client who complained that she "stunk in art" and "couldn't do it." Diane asked her to rate her self-esteem, 0 to 10, as she experienced it at that moment. The client rated it as a "2." Diane then prevailed on her to do the art activity for Diane's sake, as a favor, and so she could give feedback to Diane on how to improve the group. The client begrudgingly joined the art activity, and before long became engaged, worked hard at it, and appeared pleased with the result. Diane then asked her to rate her self-esteem at that moment. The client rated it a "10." Diane then scratched her head and wondered out loud how the client was able to get her self-esteem from 2 to 10 in so short a time. When the client responded that she improved her self-esteem by doing art, Diane skillfully led her to draw the desired inferences. "So you mean you can improve you self-esteem by doing things? That's very interesting. I wonder what other activities might help you improve your self-esteem." When the client responded that she did not know, Diane said that she did not know either. Would she like to find out?

Self-monitoring activities are important for many reasons. First, they are designed to help clients attend to the thoughts, feelings, symptoms, and behaviors that have usually been automatic or habitual. People cannot change a dimension of their experience until they notice it. The first step of treatment is stopping and noticing, the red light on the traffic light tool discussed in Chapter 5. Second, the process of self-rating rather than staff rating helps elicit engagement. It fosters a collaborative relationship. Third, clients are brought into the process of judging for themselves whether an intervention is working. If they are the judges they will often be more engaged in the treatment process. Fourth, the degree of engagement in self-monitoring provides the staff a good measure of the clients' readiness for active treatment. A client unwilling to complete the form is usually not ready for more active forms of treatment. Fifth, sometimes the mere process of observing a problem can motivate the person to begin to change. For instance, when people are asked to monitor what they eat, *but to change nothing*, they often respond by beginning to make changes in their diet. When this occurs, the counselor can help clients notice skills they are already using, *even without prompting*. Finally, self-monitoring forms set the stage for an advanced form of treatment, relapse prevention, because in relapse prevention clients are asked to anticipate problems before they occur. To do this, they must monitor the feelings, thoughts, and behaviors that precede the target problem. Clients who have been completing self-monitoring forms are already used to this to self-examination process. They move on more easily to using self-monitoring as a conscious tool to produce behavioral change.

Figure 4.1 through Figure 4.3 present a few examples of pictorial self-monitoring forms. There are more on the enclosed CD-ROM, which also contains pictures that can be used to construct new forms.

Figure 4.1 Sample pictoral self-monitoring form.

Making Treatment Interesting and Fun

Counseling games are commonplace in child psychotherapy, but they are used much more rarely in counseling with adults. Clinicians often assume that adults do not need games to make use of counseling, and that they may

Patient: _____   Date: _____

EVERYDAY ADL's

SHOWER	BRUSH TEETH	WASH HANDS	MAKE BED
YES NO	YES NO	YES NO	YES NO

CLEAN CLOTHES	COMB HAIR	CLEAN YOUR ROOM
YES NO	YES NO	YES NO

WASH CLOTHES
PUT CLOTHES AWAY
YES   NO

CHANGE BED SHEET
(WEDNESDAY)
YES   NO

Figure 4.2 A self-monitoring form of activities of daily living.

reject the use of games as childish. This may well be true with psychologically sophisticated adults who seek out counseling and have internal motivation to talk about their problems. These clients are not our subject here. I have not found the use of games to be a barrier to work with LLC adolescents and adults. Indeed, I have been astounded to discover how much easier it is to engage these clients if one can present treatment in a game format.

I first came to appreciate the power of therapeutic games with adults while working as the director of a psychiatric partial hospital treatment program. I was learning about cognitive therapy at the time, and I wanted to engage these clients in a typical cognitive therapy task of completing a "mood log." (J. Beck, 1995; Burns, 1999). In this activity, people list stressful activities, their emotional reactions, and their thoughts. They then analyze the thoughts

Please rate your mood right now:

NOT HAPPY	1	2	3	4	5	6	7	8	9	10	VERY HAPPY
NOT SAD	1	2	3	4	5	6	7	8	9	10	VERY SAD
NOT ANGRY	1	2	3	4	5	6	7	8	9	10	VERY ANGRY
NOT NERVOUS	1	2	3	4	5	6	7	8	9	10	VERY NERVOUS
SHAME	1	2	3	4	5	6	7	8	9	10	PRIDE/CONFIDENCE

OTHER FEELINGS: _____

Please rate your behavior during the last 8 hours:

BLOW UPS	1	2	3	4	5	6	7	8	9	10	SAFE
CALLING PEOPLE BAD NAMES	1	2	3	4	5	6	7	8	9	10	RESPECT
ARGUE	1	2	3	4	5	6	7	8	9	10	COOPERATE
SKIP GROUPS/ MEETINGS	1	2	3	4	5	6	7	8	9	10	JOIN GROUPS
LEARN NOTHING	1	2	3	4	5	6	7	8	9	10	LEARN NEW SKILLS

Please rate your attitude:

DEAF UNIT HELPS ME	YES	NO	MAYBE
I TRY TO IMPROVE/BEHAVE	YES	NO	MAYBE
I BLAME OTHER PEOPLE FOR MY PROBLEMS	YES	NO	MAYBE
I GO TO MEETINGS/GROUPS	ALL	SOME	NONE

Skills practiced today:_____

Date/Time: _____

Staff:_____

Figure 4.3 A self-monitoring form in simple English.

by finding common thinking errors such as "all or nothing thinking." Finally, they write out more adaptive thoughts and rerate their emotions. This is a wonderful therapeutic task for people with the motivation and cognitive abilities to do it. I had previously used this task with clients like this in my private practice, and they found it very helpful.

In the day treatment program, working with hearing psychiatric patients most of whom had very severe forms of mental illness, I had a different experience. As I began to write down the mood log structure and explain how it was used, I noticed that hardly anyone in the room was paying attention. One or two restless people were walking aimlessly around the room. Another person was sleeping. A few others were making bizarre, tangential comments. A few persons were attending for moments but then disengaging. This occurred at a time before I thought about pretreatment and before I attended intentionally to clients' readiness for change. Consequently, I became very frustrated. Here I had this wonderful therapeutic technique, and hardly any of the clients were interested. I figured the clients were "not ready for psychotherapy." The problem, I figured, was with them, not with my therapeutic techniques.

Around this time, I also had attended a workshop by Lawrence Shapiro on the use of games in psychotherapy with children (Shapiro & Shore, 1993). Shapiro showed the audience how to use a simple board game structure to engage clients in a therapeutic task. The structure of a board game is simple and familiar. One roles dice or flicks a spinner, and then moves forward or backward on a game board. Along the route of the game board, one can place challenges representing any therapeutic concept or skill. For instance, one might land on a penalty space (e.g., "you skip work for a week and the boss fires you; go back five spaces") or one might land on a space where one is required to pick a "coping skill card" (e.g., "you seek out a friend to talk with; go ahead 3 spaces"). Other cards might pose questions for one to discuss (e.g., "what is one positive thing to do when you are angry?").

Using this basic structure, I drafted a "get out of the hospital game." It had a game board, dice, pieces to move along the board, and cards for topics like "know your medicine," "coping with stress," and "dealing with other people." I brought the game into the day treatment group and to my astonishment and delight, almost everyone in the room sat down to play the game! Even some clients who were psychotic were interested. That was an "aha!" moment for me when I realized games were not just for children. Games were in fact a wonderful way to engage "resistant" clients (Glickman, 2003).

In the next few chapters, I describe ways of using games to teach coping, conflict resolution, and relapse prevention skills. One simple technique we have used hundreds of times is to put the skills one wishes to teach onto "skill cards" and then have clients "pick a card." The treatment method presented here uses very simple and concrete depictions of psychosocial skills. These skill cards are available on the accompanying CD-ROM. One can, of course, put the names of skills on a board and then try to discuss them. One can accomplish the exact same thing by having clients pick a card and then having them discuss, role play, or play a game related to that skill. The invitation to pick a card is an invitation to play. It conjures up the spirit of childhood when learning occurred effortlessly through play.

The kinds of therapy games one devises are limited only by one's creativity. Many professionally produced psychotherapy games are commercially available. Many were pioneered by Richard Gardner (1986) and Lawrence

Shapiro (Shapiro & Shore, 1993) and are available through the Childswork/Childsplay Company. I have found, however, that even those games designed for children contain complicated boards with lots of writing. They use stacks of cards that clients are assumed to be able to read. The pictures created by Michael Krajnak contain, at most, simple English captions, and many are available without any captions. Over time, we have become less dependent on board games and more interested in using the pictures as prompts for role-playing games described in the next chapters.

In an earlier publication (Glickman, 2003), I describe how we invented a game to engage Jonah, a 16-year-old deaf client. Jonah was refusing to take any part in anything called "therapy." He was also refusing group treatment such as the 10:00 coping skills group. Seeing Jonah in the hallway an hour before the group, I handed him a stack of poker chips and asked, "Would you bring the chips to the 10:00 meeting?" He looked surprised and asked what they were for. "We need them for the game," I replied. Showing his usual oppositionality, he handed the chips back to me and said, "I don't need to bring the chips. You bring them." "OK," I said, "see you at 10:00." When 10:00 came, Jonah was the first person in the room.

We then assigned point values to white, red, and blue chips and to various coping skill activities. Easy coping skills, like distraction, earned lower numbers of points than advanced coping skills like "thinking about consequences." We then picked cards, role-played the skills, and competed to earn the most points. At early stages in the engagement process, we also give out prizes to the person with the most points. Jonah did not suddenly become a fully cooperative, engaged client, but he participated in a group he would have otherwise refused. He was also introduced in that group to much of our skill-building vocabulary, terms that became part of our therapeutic dialogue with him.

Thus, we have found it useful, when clients are refusing treatment activities, to ask ourselves whether the activities are too boring and to search for ways to teach the same concepts through games.

*Put Clients in the Helper, Teacher, or Consultant Role**

Jason was admitted to the Deaf Unit because his noncompliance with his diabetic diet was putting his health at serious risk. Jason was a young deaf adult, newly diagnosed with diabetes, from a professional family that had always exerted a lot of control over their handicapped son. Now, at the moment when he was tasting his first moments of relative independence, he was hit with a devastating medical problem that required him to follow a whole new set of

---

* This is another best practice discussed by Meichenbaum (Meichenbaum & Biemiller, 1998).

rules for eating and for managing his life. He was tired of listening to rules and guidance from all the well-meaning family members and professional helpers. He decided he would eat and do what he wants. Within a short time he became seriously ill, and after his medical condition was stabilized he was hospitalized psychiatrically for treatment of his self-destructive behavior.

The usual treatment in circumstances like this is more one-up educational interventions designed to help clients understand and manage their problems. This usual treatment would represent more of the same for Jason. However well intended, he would experience it as more attempts to control him and keep him in a dependent role. He was almost guaranteed to resist such a strategy. Staff decided they would try the intervention of asking him to help them. Our nurse clinical leader explained to him that we have many patients in the hospital with diabetes. We had a problem because most of the staff did not know much about diabetes. Since he "knew so much," would he be willing to teach the staff? We would love to set up a class for him to teach the staff about diet and symptom management in diabetes. Would he mind working with the nursing staff to prepare this presentation for us?

Jason wanted to see himself as competent like his professional family. He loved the idea. He agreed to meet with a nurse for a series of meetings in order to prepare his presentation. The meetings, of course, actually constituted the psychoeducation regarding diabetes management that we had wanted him to accept. They discussed the nature of diabetes, how one measures the level of sugar in one's blood, the kinds of foods that need to be avoided, how one self-administers insulin injections, and other lifestyle issues that assist with remaining healthy. We knew these meetings were his primary therapy, and they were documented in his medical record accordingly. However, staff were careful not to speak to him about the meetings as anything other than preparation for his lecture. Eventually, Jason gave a nice presentation which consisted of telling his personal story including what he has learned about managing diabetes. He made the same presentation prior to discharge to his community workers and astonished parents.

Many of the Deaf Unit clients have been discharged into newly developed specialized Deaf group homes. At the time of this writing, the largest provider of these group homes is an organization called Advocates Inc. After leaving the hospital, many clients still resisted suggestions that they go to "therapy." They were introduced to the skill-building model of treatment in the hospital, but they were discharged into community settings where some staff still think that treatment consists of sending them to insight-oriented psychotherapy. When their coping, conflict resolution, and relapse prevention skills are not reinforced in the community setting they are likely to continue to display the severe behavioral problems that led to their hospitalization.

The leadership of Advocates recognized that it had to bring a skill-building focus to its group homes. It also had to train its staff in this model. To foster these aims, the Advocates leadership agreed to an innovative project in which it would hire its own clients to develop videotaped teaching materials in sign. The Advocates leadership and I met with the clients, inviting them to meet weekly to practice the skills in preparation for making DVDs *to help other deaf people*. The meetings were a job, we explained, for which they would be paid. We would develop stories about real-life situations in which people had to cope, solve conflicts, and manage problems, and we would use the stories to teach the relevant skills. As this was a job, we were interested only in people who could come each week and make a commitment to follow the project to its conclusion.

In the months that followed, we had a group of about 10 Advocates clients attending weekly "practice sessions" to prepare for the filming. In these sessions, I followed many of the same teaching strategies outlined in the next few chapters, but mainly we identified simple, concrete skills and then practiced them in role plays of real-life stressors. We created three stories. The first story was of one client, playing the role of a newspaper reporter, interviewing various people on the street about how they coped with stress. The second story was about a mischievous person determined to provoke his housemates into rages. He explains to the camera that he enjoys causing trouble, and then he goes from person to person doing something to annoy each. Unfortunately for him, each person uses a different coping skill to stay in control. He eventually gives up, realizing their coping skills are too strong, and commenting to the camera on how they all won. The third story was of a group of people on an airplane traveling to their vacation. While en route, the plane encounters turbulence, and everyone becomes frightened. The camera pans the group as each passenger demonstrates a different coping skill. One uses deep breathing. Another tells himself everything will be OK. Another visualizes walking on the beach. Another prays. Another rocks in his chair. One person plays with his toy train and others play cards. The finest moment of the DVD is the final scene where all the clients line up together and take a deep bow, wide grins on their faces.

The filming was followed by a "movie premiere" night in which staff, family, and other interested parties were invited for a public viewing. Before the viewing, several clients got up to explain their work. Of course, they received enormous praise. Some of these clients went on to present their work at a conference of the Massachusetts Psychiatric Rehabilitation Association. With minimal assistance from me, they went through a Power Point presentation consisting of pictures of various coping skills, discussed the skills, showed the DVD they had made, and then took questions from a very impressed audience.

Another way of using clients as teachers is when staff and clients switch roles in a role play. Staff become the clients showing their problems and clients role-play staff.

For instance, after a series of incidents on the unit where several clients were caught in lies, we started a group by asking the clients to help us with a problem. Then one staff person accused another of stealing his soda, money, and clothes and then made up an elaborate lie to tell staff about it. We asked the clients to consult with each other in a treatment team meeting and then come back to help the *liar*. The clients did that and they responded, as expected, with a confrontational and punitive stance. As *staff*, they confronted the *client* about his lies and then told him the negative consequences of his behavior. The *client* then responded by saying "I don't care. You can drop my level. I can stay here and not be discharged. I don't care." We persisted in asking the clients to stay in role and deal with his attitude. One client told the staff person that God was watching and he would go to Hell if he was not honest. Another client said, "If you lie, no one will trust you." A third said, "You will lose friends." The *client* then repeated all this and said, "Well, I want to have friends. I want people and God to trust me. I will try to improve." The *client* then thanked the *staff* for their assistance, and we ended the role play.

In this reverse role play, with clients consulting in the staff role, everything we wanted to bring up about lying was brought up by the clients themselves. They were also far more engaged than they likely would have been if the subject had been, directly, their own lying. In this way, they are placed in the expert and helper role and then validated for their excellent performance in that role. Having clients lecture staff about the reasons not to lie is an example of the motivational interviewing strategy of having clients argue the reasons for change.

In a Deaf treatment setting, where all the treatment programming is geared toward client skills, there are endless opportunities to put even very low functioning clients in the teacher role. One of the Unit's lowest functioning persons, a woman with moderate mental retardation and very poor language skills, took pride in being the person who explained the rules to the group at the start of our Unit meeting. She did not do this task particularly well, frequently omitting rules or getting them wrong, but that never really mattered. She would have her 3 minutes in the front of the group, as an authority, explaining "yes, do this" and "no, don't do this." The only real problem was when other clients wanted their turn to do the same thing.

When deaf clients are placed in hearing treatment or rehabilitation settings, it is much more difficult to find such opportunities to put them in teacher or helper roles. Deaf clients in these settings are at such a huge disadvantage in communication access that they are lucky if they receive half the same information as their hearing peers. Their own communication and other skills will not be seen by the hearing community, and they will remain people struggling to get access, not contributing in their own right.

Developing the Client's Story of Strength, Resiliency, Recovery, and Resourcefulness

As narrative therapists (Freedman & Combs, 1996; Morgan, 2000; White, 2007; White & Epston, 1990) and solution-oriented therapists (Berg, 1994; de Shazer, 1985, 1988; O'Hanlon, 1994) have explained, clients always have at least two stories. There is the story of their problem and the story of their recovery from the problem or successes in spite of the problem. Meichenbaum (1994, 2001) refers to the latter as "the rest of the story." Counselors working in this narrative or constructivist tradition see themselves as helping clients construct new stories in which their abilities and successes are highlighted. Whether the story told in counseling is one of problems or one of recovery, resiliency and skill have direct bearing on the pretreatment challenge, especially for language and cognitively impaired clients. These clients usually are living a "problem-saturated story," and may resist counseling efforts that they believe amount to further elaboration of these negative stories. When they see that the story we want to construct is one of their abilities, they will be more likely to participate.

A client gets some disappointing news. She then goes to her room, takes her clothing out of her dresser, and throws it all over the floor. She rips some drawings off her wall and tears them up. She slams her door. She takes the mattress off her bed, and turns the bed frame on its side. She then covers herself in blankets and pillows and sits in the corner of her room crying.

What story will the staff tell about this incident? How will the incident be reported in the nursing shift report? How will it be documented in the chart? How will it be discussed with the client?

Will the staff say that the patient "blew up," "trashed her room," "regressed," "relapsed," or was "out of control?" Will she be restricted to the program because of her negative behaviors? Will she lose passes and other privileges? Will staff approach her to discuss her *negative* behavior?

There are other important pieces of information relevant to this incident. The week previously, the client also threw her clothing and bed linen all over the room, but at that time she took a shirt and tried to strangle herself with it. She also accused staff of not caring about her, called them "idiots" and "assholes," and tried to punch a staff person who was trying to help her calm down. The previous week's incident lasted about 2 hours. This week's incident lasted about 15 minutes, and she made no gesture of harm to herself or others. She also calmed herself down by the sensory process of throwing her belongings onto the floor and then wrapping herself in blankets and pillows. When staff suggested she write down her feelings so that she would have them ready to discuss with her therapist, she did so. A few hours later, she discussed the incident well with her therapist, and left the meeting in a good mood. She even apologized to staff for her behavior and said she acted "stupidly."

Does "the rest of the story" get into the staff narrative? Will staff comment on how much more skillfully she acted? We have discussed the strategy of noticing skills clients already use. After we note the skills, we need to help clients link them to create a narrative about skill use. Each example of skill use is a moment in time. Skills connected by a story become something much more profound. Skills connected by a story become an identity.

The client described above certainly displayed some negative behaviors and maladaptive coping. She also displays a pattern of growth. In this particular incident, her "acting out" is much briefer and less serious and her recovery is much quicker and more profound. She will see herself as growing or regressing dependent on how we construct the meaning of her behavior. If she sees herself as growing, as developing new skills, there is far more likelihood she will continue on that trajectory. A problem-saturated conversation (e.g., "What caused you to regress in this way?") may foster a story about hopelessness, even in the face of evidence for significant change. A self-story about hopelessness will foster more self-destructive behaviors.

When we discussed the incident with the client, we commented first on the relative strengths she was using by managing to be *so much safer* this time. We then asked her to evaluate how satisfied she was with her own use of skills. That led to a productive discussion of how she could have been even more skillful. The incident was discussed in a way that avoided all possible shaming and actually fostered skill development.

This same client told me, at another time, that she hated herself because she "was the kind of person who did bad things." When I asked her how she came to that conclusion, she told me about an incident in which she hurt someone she cared about. Fortunately, this client, a bright hearing woman with good language skills, readily understood when I put this behavior in a wider perspective. I explained that this incident reflected one moment in the complex story of her life. She was basing her identity on her behavior in this particular moment. In reality, her behaviors were much more diverse. They consisted of helpful and nonhelpful, kind and mean, acts, and it would be more objective to fashion an identity based on all of what she does. In other words, like all of us, she is complex and imperfect. However, if she wants to be so "narrow minded" as to fashion her identity just on one particular behavior, why not at least select a positive behavior? She got the point.

Clients with severe language and cognitive limitations may not be able to understand this discussion, but the principle still applies. If we work to help them see themselves as people with skills, their identities also change. With this changed belief about their own abilities come more adaptive behaviors.

Betty, a young adult LLC deaf client, is admitted to the Unit after cutting herself, assaulting staff, and destroying property in her home. Her first few days on the unit provide the "honeymoon" period in which she shows no dangerous behaviors. The metaphor of a "honeymoon" is commonly used by psychiatric hospital staff and reflects their expectation that negative behaviors are soon to occur. The danger of using this metaphor is that it is part of a story about the inevitability of finding pathology in clients. We could also construct her first few days of positive behaviors as examples of her competencies. Perhaps we should infer that Betty showed her "true self" during this initial period.

Staff knew to seize the initial positive behaviors and comment to her about the skills she was using. However, on her third day in the hospital, Betty took a tab from a Coke can and scratched her arm. She then announced that "I can't control myself" and "I will hit staff tonight."

Staff became concerned, of course, that she was telegraphing her intent to become assaultive. I also became concerned not because I believed she was "out of control," but because she was telling herself the story that she was out of control. In this particular moment, sitting calmly and telling staff she was going to explode hours later, she showed no evidence of being out of control. However, she was constructing this story about her own powerlessness in the face of impulses to hurt herself and others. If she told herself this story, she might well create a self-fulfilling prophecy. We needed, therefore, to do something right away to challenge this story. We needed to help her discover evidence that she *can* control herself.

Taking a one-down stance, staff expressed worry and concern about what would happen to her if she did lose self-control. They discussed possible consequences including a loss of privileges, a delay in discharge, damaged relationships with staff, as well as the possibility that she might be restrained. Staff then, feigning puzzlement, asked her how she managed to stay in control her first 2 days here. Was she not upset at being hospitalized? Is she not the same person yesterday as she is today? If she was able to do so well these first few days, how can it be that she is "out of control"?

In this instance, Betty did stay in control. The next morning, when I arrived on the Unit, she waved to me and signed, "I safe all night." We sat down to talk and I asked her how she did it. She signed "staff support me" and "I don't want my level to drop." I reframed this as skills she has used. "You used staff support. You used your brain. You thought, 'If I stay safe, my level won't drop.'" She nods yes. "You used good skills," I replied, but then I resumed one-down puzzlement. "But I'm confused. Yesterday, you told me you can't control yourself. All night, you were safe. I don't understand." "I can control myself," she replied. Her story has been repaired.

Suppose, however, that Betty did assault staff and thereby confirmed for herself the story of her being "out of control." Suppose the next morning, when I arrived, she told me that she "couldn't help it," but she "blew up" and "hit staff." The therapeutic challenge is the same. We could help her identify the consequences of her behavior and ask her if she wanted these consequences. When she replies that she "couldn't help it," we could contrast this behavior with other instances in which she did show self-control. We could ask her to comment on whether she is "in control" now, in this very moment we are talking, and explore that with her. We could ask her to self-monitor how much in control she feels and then have her evaluate how particular activities or interventions effect this sense of self-control. We could also ask her if she wants help using the "self-control skills" more effectively. If she says yes, she has just contracted for treatment, and we move on to the treatment strategies described in the next few chapters. We are interested not merely in helping her develop skills but in constructing with her a story about how she can be in control. Each instance we can find of her using skills successfully helps us create this new story.

While the theoretical rationale for such "narrative therapy" emerges principally out of the work of Michael White (White, 1995, 2007; White & Epston, 1990), many of his therapy techniques, such as the use of "externalizing conversation" in which clients are helped to locate the problem outside of themselves, are ill suited for many LLC clients. Meichenbaum's narrative constructivist work is more useful because, unlike White, he never loses sight of the CBT emphasis on skills. Our clients need new skills and new stories. Psychosocial skill building is deepened enormously by occurring in a narrative framework. Narrative therapy, in turn, is enhanced when the new story being constructed concerns skills.

The process of helping clients construct a new story is somewhat like the game of connecting dots. Each example of skill use is a dot, and the lines connecting them are the new story, the new identity.

Conclusions

Awareness of pretreatment has the effect of simplifying mental health counseling. I am always aware that I cannot make anyone do anything. The best I can do is to invite a person to join what I sometimes think of as a special kind of dance. When clients refuse to work with us, we have no magic that will make them change. I find that knowing this is very comforting. It takes the pressure off. There often are many people with unrealistic and unfair expectations that we *fix* this person. They may think that just because we sign, this gives us the power to change people against their will. Sometimes the pressure on mental health people can be so great that we forget that we are not all-powerful. We do not have proven treatments for every problem, and we can do almost nothing when working against a person's will. What we can do, however, is recognize that we have a pretreatment problem. The strategies presented in this chapter are some of the best ideas we have for eliciting meaningful client involvement. The next few chapters describe some of what we can accomplish if our pretreatment work is successful and our clients join the dance.

5
Coping Skills

What Are Coping Skills?

All humans face hard times and suffer. We live in a world of profound inequality and injustice, but a life of privilege is no more a guarantee of happiness than a life of poverty is of misery. How well people function, the quality of our lives, is enhanced by external resources such as money, access to education and health care, a supportive family and friends, and a tolerant and humane society. These external resources help foster inner resources like intelligence, language skills, creativity, flexibility, a sense of humor, and self-confidence. External and internal resources reinforce each other. Nurturing, supportive family and social environments produce more psychologically healthy people. War, tyranny, and deprivation produce more people suffering with mental health problems. While all human beings suffer, we vary enormously in our capacity to manage adversity. Some people have the ability to survive catastrophic challenges. Other people seem to fall apart when faced with minor inconveniences.

Mental health professionals have the responsibility of helping people develop psychological resources to manage life challenges. We help people develop the resources to manage both internal experiences like depression, anxiety, and anger and external experiences like human relationships. Coping skills are important inner resources. Coping skills can be understood to mean the strategies that people use when faced with unwanted, unpleasant circumstances or strong, overpowering, and usually unpleasant emotions. Coping with anger, anxiety, and depression are examples. Coping skills also include strategies people use to manage experiences associated with wanted, sought-after goals such as climbing a mountain or getting a doctorate. For the sake of simplicity, we can say that coping skills are strategies used to respond to one's inner life (for example, feelings, thoughts, physical sensations, memories, etc.) whereas social skills, such as the conflict resolution skills discussed in the next chapter, are strategies to respond to one's outer life, especially demands imposed by other people. In practice, these categories overlap as people cope both by managing emotions and by drawing on social supports.

In this chapter, I present first a theoretical and practical framework for helping clients develop coping skills. I take this framework principally from the work of Donald Meichenbaum, which he called *constructivist narrative cognitive behavioral therapy* (CBT) (Loera & Meichenbaum, 1993; Meichenbaum, 1977a, 1977b, 1985, 1994, 1996, 2001, 2007). I also borrow from Marsha Linehan's *dialectical behavior therapy* (DBT) (Linehan, 1993a, 1993b), Ross Greene's *collaborative problem solving* (Greene, 1998; Greene & Ablon, 2006), and a number of occupational therapists, especially Karen Moore (2005), who have pioneered sensory modulation strategies for coping. The chapter begins with a theoretical discussion of coping, drawing on these approaches. The chapter goes on to discuss various domains of coping: through thinking, acting, sensory modulation, problem solving, various DBT skills, and construction of new meaning to experiences of adversity. I also discuss counseling strategies derived from these various theoretical approaches, especially Meichenbaum's early development of self-instructional training and stress inoculation therapy and his later narrative focus on questioning, metaphors, and storytelling techniques. While drawing on these theoretical and clinical approaches to coping, our goal is to develop a simple menu of coping skills which are represented in pictorial form for people who do not read English well. Because this book concerns itself with mental health treatment of clients with language and learning challenges, I pay special attention to the issue of finding coping strategies that are simple, clear, and compelling. I place heavy emphasis on sensory modulation strategies which are minimally dependent on language, the simplest form of cognitive therapy found in self-instructional training, the use of engaging psychotherapy games, and narrative techniques such as storytelling. A central concern throughout is helping these clients become intentional and self-directed in their development, and this involves providing them a map and tools that they will want to use.

Meichenbaum's Early Work on Coping Skills

One of Donald Meichenbaum's initial contributions was to bring to the field of behavioral therapy a focus on helping people develop coping skills. Traditional behavior therapy sought to influence client motivation through manipulation of reinforcers. Rewarding a behavior would presumably lead to more instances of the behavior. Meichenbaum (1977a) had an insight that has since become the hallmark of most CBT. This was that motivation was insufficient in the absence of skills. A child, for instance, may be motivated to behave well by the presence of rewards but still unable to behave because the child lacks the skills to handle stressors. In his book on cognitive behavior modification, Meichenbaum initiated the paradigm shift within psychology from the previous emphasis on reinforcers to the new emphasis on skill development. He called the most important skills *coping skills.*

Almost all contemporary CBT concerns itself in some way with teaching psychosocial skills. Skill training is certainly at the heart of DBT and collaborative problem solving therapy, to be discussed shortly. If the hallmark of psychodynamic psychotherapies was insight, and that of traditional behavior therapy was motivation, then the CBT paradigm finds its center in this teaching of skills. Emotional and behavioral problems are understood in this model as occurring because people lack psychosocial skills such as the ability to cope with emotions and deal with other people.

Meichenbaum went on to present a framework for teaching coping skills. He called his framework "stress inoculation training" (SIT) (Meichenbaum, 1977b, 1985). Essentially, SIT is a treatment approach designed to prepare or "inoculate" people so that they are able to cope with stressful situations. Counselors inoculate people against stress just as a doctor would against disease.

In SIT, one does not just talk about skills. The goal is not for clients to understand they lack skills but for them to develop the skills. Skill development takes practice. One practices skills with clients in situations in which there are progressively greater levels of challenge or provocation. For example, we may be working with an "explosive" (Greene, 1998) client on coping skills for managing anger. The client is easily provoked by stressors that more healthy people would consider minor, such as having to share or to wait. After identifying the stressor, we help the client select some coping strategies. We might have the client practice "red, yellow, green" or "shield" (Glickman, 2003; Jacobs, 1992). When the client is ready, we increase the intensity of the provocation. We ask the client to wait longer or we say "no" to some request that matters more to the client. We also coach the milieu staff so they are ready to seize opportunities that present in the treatment milieu to practice with naturally occurring provocations. With more practice and demonstration of successful coping, the client becomes increasingly *inoculated* against these stressors. This increases the likelihood that the skill will actually become learned.

Stress inoculation training is not a specific technique of stress management such as relaxation training. It is a framework for creating a program of coping skills training. Meichenbaum argues that there are countless means of coping with life problems, and it would be arbitrary to decide, for instance, that sensory strategies are superior to cognitive strategies, or that everyone "should" develop a sense of humor. Coping skills programs should be individually tailored. For some clients, merely understanding the concept of coping skills and then selecting something concrete like "watching TV" to distract themselves may be a treatment goal. Others will be capable of changing thoughts and beliefs. For one of our most cognitively impaired patients, her main coping skill when upset was tearing apart pieces of paper. Accordingly, staff had a box of papers ready for her, and when she was upset she was encouraged to sit with the papers and tear them apart. This *sometimes* helped deescalate her. A hearing adolescent client could only be soothed by swinging on a swing, listening to music, and singing. These were her coping skills, and staff built them into her daily structure.

Stress inoculation training has three phases: conceptualization, skill acquisition, and application. The conceptualization phase is designed to ensure that clients understand the nature of the treatment and are collaborating mean-ingfully. It corresponds to our notion of pretreatment. It is the step of solicit-ing "buy in" to the program. As discussed in Chapter 4, engaging language and learning challenged (LLC) clients into meaningful participation in treat-ment is often our greatest clinical challenge. More than any other objective, we strive to help them become active agents in their own development. Once they are engaged, actually providing the treatment is relatively straightfor-ward. We just have to adapt treatment to their level of understanding.

In the skill acquisition and rehearsal phase, Meichenbaum (1985) stresses that "the coping skills repertoire is tailored to the needs of the specific pop-ulation" (p. 54). There does not need to be a specific coping skills training curriculum (a specific contrast, as we shall see, with Linehan) but rather the counselor needs to offer clients a menu of coping skills techniques from which the two of them can, together, construct an approach that is suitable. The pic-torial skill cards presented here provide such a menu of coping skills for LLC non- or semiliterate clients.

Meichenbaum describes in detail specific means of teaching relaxation training, various cognitive restructuring procedures (that is, ways of helping people change thoughts and beliefs), and problem-solving training. He argues that it does not matter what specific approach is used as long as the client is practicing approaches that he or she finds useful. The practice can occur in imagination and then through role play, with the counselor modeling effec-tive coping. Meichenbaum mentions the value of having client and counselor reverse roles. The client becomes the skills coach and the counselor pretends to be a client with the same problems as the real clients.

The reverse role play technique is often used with deaf mental health and rehabilitation clients. Many deaf clients enjoy role play. American Sign Lan-guage (ASL), with its use of role shifting to convey points of view, may lend itself to role play. Role playing is also active, engaged treatment. It is concrete and immediate. One is not talking *about* a problem but instead is acting out the problem. Role playing is thus a form of stress inoculation or exposure. When our deaf clients cannot provide us with a coherent narrative, we must role-play for linguistic reasons. The role playing also works, however, because it exposes the client to stress and teaches coping skills for responding to this stress.

CBT therapists worry about skill *generalization*. That is, will the skill prac-ticed in therapy generalize to new situations? Will it actually be learned and used? To foster skill generalization, the skill practicing needs to occur not merely with the counselor in an individual or group treatment setting but with the staff in the treatment milieu. It also needs to occur with staff or fam-ily who will be with the client in the next living or treatment setting. In other words, skill practice has to become the common language of treatment, prac-ticed in every venue.

The application phase of treatment (that is, practicing the skills in real life) should include relapse prevention skill training because it is important that clients be prepared for new stressors and some failure in their coping skills strategy. Relapse prevention skills build on coping and conflict resolution skills. We consider relapse prevention separately in Chapter 7.

Cognitive Therapy With Language and Learning Challenged Clients

Imagine you are driving along a highway and a man in another car drives up beside you and swears at you. How you feel, cope, and what you do is very connected to how you interpret the meaning of his behavior and what your internal dialogue looks like.

1. You could think that this man is an immediate threat to you, that nobody has a right to treat you like that, and that you should teach him a thing or two. If you think like this, you will feel angry. These beliefs may lead to aggressive behavior especially if you believe that he behaved in this aggressive fashion on purpose.

2. You could think that you must be doing something wrong because you always do something wrong. No matter where you go and what you do, you make other people upset. This man yelling at you is further proof of what a deficient and worthless human being you are. If you think this way, you will almost certainly feel depressed, and you may put yourself at risk for doing something to harm yourself.

3. You could start imagining what this man may do. Maybe he will become violent. Maybe he has a gun. Maybe he is going to follow you and then harm you. Maybe he will then kill everyone you love, and so on. If you think this way, you will almost certainly feel anxious. If you characteristically think this way about whatever happens, you probably are hypervigilant and have an anxiety disorder. You may put yourself at risk for withdrawal and social isolation.

4. You could recognize that this man is angry, think rationally about protecting yourself, and not attribute additional meaning to his behavior. You could think, "This man may be having a hard day but that shouldn't affect me. I'll just let him go ahead of me and avoid him. I don't need his anger or his stress to rub off on me. I need to be alert to protect myself, but the wisest course is not to provoke him further." If you think this way, most likely your emotional state will be reasonably calm. You will be coping well, and you will be able to make rational decisions to stay safe.

Thus, the way we appraise a situation (such as what the other driver's behavior means) and our appraisal of our own ability to respond (whether we can handle this) influence our emotions, behaviors, and overall coping. Cognitive and cognitive-behavioral therapies all seek to help people think in ways that promote psychological health. Along with Meichenbaum, the two other originators of cognitive therapy are Albert Ellis (1962) and Aaron Beck (1976). All three of these men designed treatment strategies which help clients cope by changing how they think but not all of these treatment strategies are suitable for LLC clients. Ellis in particular made a distinction between rational and irrational thinking, and both Ellis and Beck believe that "thinking errors" contribute to emotional problems.

LLC persons make the same kinds of "thinking errors" as people with PhDs. They may think in "all or nothing" terms (for example, "I always fail at whatever I do"). They may blame themselves or others unfairly (e.g., "You made me mad. You deserve to get hit"). They may misunderstand and mislabel the motivations of other people (for example, "He has a bad attitude. He's trying to mess up my life. He's doing this on purpose"). Their dysfunctional thinking may be similar but their resources to understand and change this thinking are fewer. It may be difficult or impossible for them to attend to their thoughts at all. They may have great difficulty learning to distinguish a thought from a feeling or a behavior, much less to analyze "thinking errors," a common cognitive therapy task. An important concept like "point of view," and the idea that there may be many valid ways to view a problem, may be beyond their grasp.

Most of the coping skills associated with cognitive therapies require some ability for people to *think about thinking*. The cognitive developmental psychologist Piaget (1963) called this "formal operational thinking." Yet there is research that finds that only 30% to 35% of adults in the general population attain formal operational thought (Kuhn, Langer, Kohlberg, & Haan, 1977). Does this mean that cognitively based coping strategies will be unavailable to our LLC clients?

It is possible to help LLC clients change their beliefs and thinking patterns, but we need strategies that do not require them to think about thinking. This rules out some forms of cognitive therapy. For instance, Ellis (1962) likes to teach clients to analyze irrational beliefs and replace them with rational beliefs. He frequently equates psychotherapy to the adoption of a new philosophy about life. Both Ellis and Beck (A. Beck, 1976) like to have patients identify cognitive distortions and thinking errors and perform personal experiments to evaluate whether their thinking is sound. These are often effective interventions for clients who can do them, but many people cannot grasp these ideas. Meichenbaum offers teaching and counseling strategies that are more concrete and accessible.

Meichenbaum has written about the characteristics of expert teachers and counselors (Meichenbaum & Biemiller, 1998). He discovered that experts teach by modeling and by making their thinking and problem solving transparent to students. From his earliest work, Meichenbaum studied the thinking processes that facilitate coping and problem solving. As a counselor educator, he exposes students to his internal thought processes as he counsels clients with difficult problems (Meichenbaum, 1996).

This thinking-out-loud demystifies the counseling process and makes learning much more accessible. Much of his early CBT work is focused on helping clients talk to themselves or think-out-loud in ways that help them complete tasks or solve problems. He called this technique "self-instructional training" (Meichenbaum, 1977a).

Meichenbaum's work on self-instructional training was originally developed to help children with problems like attention-deficit/hyperactivity disorder. These children were taught to coach themselves through tasks. Meichenbaum gave the following example of self-talk modeled for children struggling to complete the task of copying line patterns:

> Okay, what is it I have to do? You want me to copy the picture with the different lines. I have to go slowly and carefully. Okay, draw the line down, down, good, then to the right, that's it; now down some more and to the left. Good, I'm doing fine so far. Remember, go slowly. Now back up again. No, I was supposed to go down. That's okay. Just erase the line carefully.... Good. Even if I make an error I can go on slowly and carefully. I have to go down now. Finished. I did it! (Meichenbaum, 1977a, p. 32; Meichenbaum & Goodman, 1971, p. 117)

Self-instructional training is a very useful cognitive intervention with our LLC clientele, both children and adults. One of the most popular coping skills used on the Deaf Unit is something we call "traffic light" or "red, yellow, green" (Glickman, 2003), to be described shortly. The green light, "think then act," calls on clients to coach themselves through the current challenge. Here we use self-instructional training. If a client feels provoked by a peer, the counselor may model the following self-talk: "OK, I'm angry. I don't like her pushing me like that, but I have to think about myself. If I blow up, then my privileges will drop. My pass will get canceled. My discharge will be delayed. If I stay in control, staff will be proud of me. They will say I'm mature. I've improved. If I blow up, he wins. If I stay in control, I win." We model this for clients, and we literally ask them to repeat after us. Then we ask them to add to it, saying it on their own. We do this numerous times. The modeling and the active practice through role play are essential.

Meichenbaum (1985) does not propose that in self-instructional training, a ready-made script be given to clients. Self-instructional training is not a form of mere "positive thinking" and it certainly is not meant to consist of repeating memorized phrases like "I'm getting better and better every day." Rather, the counselor and the client jointly construct a set of relevant coping statements and the client is encouraged to elaborate on these. This is what we strive for, but we have also found that many LLC clients cannot initially add much to the coping script we give them. We have found that sometimes we literally do have to provide some clients with such a script. Over the course of training, we try to fade our prompting and encourage clients to embellish on the original script.

We have found "thought bubbles" to be useful tools to help clients identify their thinking. When clients reveal their thinking, counselors draw a thought bubble and put the thoughts inside the bubble. They then ask, "Is this what you think?" Putting thoughts inside a thought bubble helps clients to "externalize" their thinking (White & Epston, 1990). It puts client thoughts outside of themselves, as if they are disembodied and do not belong to the thinker, and makes it easier for them to see these thoughts as something they can change.

One can also draw a second thought bubble with more adaptive thoughts and ask clients to compare them. Which way of thinking will help them feel better? Which way will help them cope and stay safe? Of course, this presupposes the ability to read and practice at least simple words. Figure 5.1 and Figure 5.2 provide an example of adaptive and nonadaptive thoughts within thought bubbles.

Figure 5.1 Showing maladaptive thoughts with a thought bubble.

Figure 5.2 Showing adaptive thoughts with a thought bubble.

Thoughts written in a bubble on a blackboard can be erased or crossed out and new thoughts written over them. Erasing and rewriting exemplifies concretely the process of changing thoughts.

Thought bubbles can be used to test out the clients' ability to recognize their own thinking patterns. If they grasp the idea, one can test out more complex cognitive coping strategies. One can then explore with them the connections between these thoughts and their mood and behaviors. One can ask them to answer back to the thoughts or role play a counselor trying to show a client with these thoughts how they are not helpful. One can even see if they can identify "thinking errors" like all-or-nothing thinking. Clients who read can be given cards with simple coping statements. More commonly, we give clients pictures of the particular skills we want them to practice. Staff model these coping statements and skills, and reminders, in the form of coping skill cards, can be posted throughout the program.

Cognitive therapy strategies work at varying levels of sophistication. It helps to understand this and to test out what clients are capable of. One should not assume that clients are not capable of thinking about thinking but neither should one despair if one discovers they lack this ability. Self-instructional training gives us a simple, powerful cognitive therapy technique, and we have many other kinds of coping skills to choose from. We have to make the same selection of appropriate skills when considering a sophisticated treatment program such as dialectical behavior therapy (DBT).

A Complementary Approach: Linehan's Dialectical Behavior Therapy

It is useful to contrast Meichenbaum's early CBT for coping skills with another approach, Linehan's DBT (Linehan, 1993a, 1993b), to help us appreciate the kinds of training options we have, and to be able to best match our treatment approach with the abilities and deficits of our clientele. Both approaches are variants of CBT. Both concern themselves with teaching psychosocial skills. Both are considered "best practices" in the psychotherapy field. They vary widely, however, in their suitability for LLC deaf and hearing clients. Studying DBT enriches counselors and greatly expands our skill set with clients, but many DBT strategies themselves need to be simplified considerably before they can be used with this LLC clientele.

DBT is a model of treatment initially designed for clients who are chronically suicidal or self-harming or who have borderline personality disorder. DBT includes a formal curriculum for teaching psychosocial skills. A unique contribution of Linehan was to combine CBT strategies designed to help people change (that is, learn skills) with mindfulness strategies taken from Zen Buddhism to help people accept themselves. Mindfulness refers to a state of nonjudgmental awareness of self and environment. It is a state of tuning in, of experiencing whatever one feels directly, without thoughts telling you what is good or bad or what things mean. One practices mindfulness as a form of profound self-acceptance.

The term *dialectic* refers to the movement between these ostensibly opposing change and acceptance strategies. *Dialectic* can be understood by drawing on the metaphor of a person holding a Slinky® in both hands and alternatively raising one side and then the other. One hand represents change strategies. The other hand represents acceptance strategies. The moving Slinky represents the ebb and flow of the dialectic as the therapist shifts between acceptance and change strategies. Dialectical thinking also involves integration of opposing ideas. We shift the Slinky back and forth, now emphasizing change, now emphasizing acceptance, but we aim for both. Psychological development occurs through a movement of self-acceptance and change, and it is Linehan's genius to articulate a therapy that promotes this process.

Linehan realized that if one offers persons with borderline personality disorder only change (skill building) strategies, they will feel invalidated and disrespected. They will complain

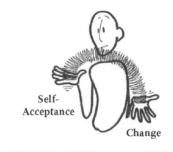

Figure 5.3 Simple model of a "dialectic."

that they are not being accepted. However, if one offers them only empathy and self-acceptance strategies, such as one finds in client-centered counseling (Rogers, 1951), they will complain that they are not being helped to change. Therefore, the treatment must offer both change and acceptance strategies in a kind of dance. This is, in my opinion, a brilliant insight that is readily applicable to all psychotherapy. People change when they feel accepted. Good CBT skill-building treatment must occur in the context of an empathic, supportive relationship.

The skill-training component of DBT occurs mainly in the context of four psychoeducation treatment "modules" for which Linehan provides detailed syllabi. The skills learned in groups are coached and reinforced by individual therapists in outpatient work and milieu staff in hospital settings. The first module is called "Core Mindfulness Skills," defined as "psychological and behavioral versions of meditation practices from Eastern spiritual training" (Linehan, 1993b). Linehan is one of a number of contemporary clinicians integrating mindfulness into CBT. The first was Kabat-Zinn (1990) who developed a "stress reduction program" at the University of Massachusetts Medical Center, which treats persons with chronic pain and serious medical problems. In this program, patients are taught mindfulness meditation through sitting and walking mediations, body scans, and yoga. Kabat-Zinn's program influenced the development of DBT and spawned mindfulness-based cognitive therapy for depression (Segal, Williams, & Teasdale, 2002). Unlike these other two approaches, the mindfulness practice in DBT is not centered on formal meditation practice. Rather, through education and activities, clients are helped to bring this quality of nonjudgmental awareness to all their daily activities.

Mindfulness can be a very challenging idea to teach LLC deaf clients. Linehan breaks it down into what she calls "what" skills (observing, describing, and participating) and "how" skills (taking a nonjudgmental stance, focusing on one thing in the moment, and being effective). Mindfulness is a core element of DBT. It is the first skill taught. It is the heart of the acceptance component of DBT, and it is the balance for all the skills associated with change. One cannot argue one is using DBT if one omits mindfulness.

We have not yet found a way to teach most of our LLC clients mindfulness sufficient for them to use it as a major coping skill. We have taught approximations, or perhaps developmental precursors, of mindfulness. We have done this by helping clients practice slow, diaphragmatic breaths and other relaxation exercises. These are not the same thing as mindfulness as their aim is relaxation or composure and mindfulness is more about tuning in, a process that is not necessarily calming. The best way we have found to approximate mindfulness is to work on the skill of "stop and notice." The red light in our traffic light skill means "stop and notice." *Right now, what are you doing? What are you feeling? What are you thinking?* Some clients may grasp the idea that you can allow yourself to feel something, observe the feeling and not act on it.

Many of our clients have impulse control problems, and it would be very useful indeed if they could learn to observe their impulses and *do nothing*.

A concrete way to teach this is to have them observe their responses to a piece of candy or other food sitting on their tongue. Do they have the impulse to bite, chew, or swallow? Can they just observe that impulse and leave the food on their tongue? If they can do that, they have already demonstrated mindfulness. Observing one's impulse to harm oneself or others or one's cravings for alcohol or drugs, yet doing nothing, is fundamentally the same skill. Yet generalizing this skill of self-observation to more demanding provocations and urges is notoriously difficult even for linguistically competent people. Almost all of our LLC deaf clients need a more concrete strategy to *do something*. This is one reason adopting DBT wholesale has not worked for us. For practical purposes we draw more on coping skills that involve *doing something*.

The second and third modules are called distress tolerance and emotional regulation skills. Linehan appears to have a preference for sophisticated vocabulary. The word "dialectic" is very hard to translate into simple sign or even to explain in simple English. With LLC deaf clients, the language one uses matters, and simplicity and clarity are crucial. *Distress tolerance* refers to skills "concerned with tolerating and surviving crises and with accepting life as it is in the moment" (Linehan, 1003b, p. 96). *Emotion regulation skills* are designed to help people identify and manage emotions when not in crisis. For our purposes, both modules teach what more simply can be called "coping skills."

The fourth module refers to interpersonal effectiveness skills. Again, I see no advantage to using this kind of vocabulary when "social skills" has the same meaning. Linehan's interpersonal effectiveness skills module emphasizes skills associated with assertiveness. Although assertiveness skills are important, I believe our clients have a greater need for the social skill of nonviolent conflict resolution. This key social skill is discussed in Chapter 6.

Another hallmark of DBT is the detailed class syllabi and curriculum. Linehan organizes a solid program for learning these skills. DBT purists become very concerned with teaching these skills exactly as Linehan intends. Meichenbaum, as we saw, is not concerned with presenting a particular curriculum for skills training but rather with helping clients create a menu of skill options. He believes that counselor and client should collaboratively construct a plan for learning particular skills. His stress inoculation training framework provides a commonsense structure for skill development.

In DBT, skills are taught by an expert in a classroom. The teaching model is formal and didactic. Meichenbaum recommends a more Socratic teaching style in which counselors ask clients good questions, and guide clients to discover the usefulness of developing certain skills. Research indicates that discovery-based instruction is more likely than didactic instruction to lead to generalization or transfer of training across settings (Meichenbaum & Biemiller, 1998). Our experience is also that formal, classroom like instruction is often rejected by our LLC clientele. We need to fashion treatment that is simple, clear, and compelling. As brilliant and therapeutically powerful as DBT can be with more sophisticated clientele, on the test of simplicity, clarity, and compellingness, with most of our LLC clientele, it bombs.

I have found the study of DBT enormously helpful, and I borrow from it whenever I can. I like the systematic organization of psychosocial skills, along with a training curriculum, that Linehan has developed, but I believe we need a much simpler set of skills and a different way of teaching them. Many Deaf Unit staff have studied DBT, but as we struggled to apply it we ultimately produced not a new or adapted curriculum but rather a menu of coping skills that are easily represented in pictorial form. We do not teach these skills through organized lesson plans such as one finds in DBT. Rather, the skills become our vocabulary for talking with clients about what they are already doing that works and what they could do that would help them reach their goals. When clients agree to learn new skills, Meichenbaum's model of stress inoculation is the best procedure. Essentially, we role-play and practice and practice and practice. Our skill-training program does not consist of organized lesson plans but rather a variety of fun, engaging, and easy-to-understand activities described below.

Coping Through Distraction and Pleasurable Activities

One set of skills taught in the distress tolerance module of DBT concerns distraction. LLC deaf clients may understand distraction as "keeping busy, doing things." One skill card for distraction shows pictures of diverting activities such as watching television. A second component of distraction that is a bit more abstract is that one does something *to get one's mind off of something else.* It is not the act of watching television that makes it a coping skill, but that one watches television to put off, for the moment, dealing with unwanted emotions and stressors or to create a positive mood state.

Distraction does not solve a problem but it is, as Linehan describes, a useful means of coping with distress in the moment. Because virtually any pleasant activity can be used as a distraction, this opens up the potential to frame a great many behaviors clients already engage in as examples of skill use. Our clients already watch television, play games, and enjoy other pleasant activities, and we can introduce the idea of coping to them by noting their effective use of these activities. By conceptualizing their engagement in activities that foster positive moods as skills, we help them discover a variety of coping skills they already use.

In DBT, distraction is taught with the mnemonic: wise mind ACCEPTS. The ACCEPTS stands for

- Activities
- Contributing (to others or a community)

Figure 5.4 Distraction.

- Comparisons (to people with worse problems than you have)
- Generating opposite Emotions to current mood states
- Pushing away (leaving a situation or blocking it from one's mind)
- Thoughts (distracting with other thoughts)
- Sensations

The widespread use of mnemonics in DBT is actually a barrier for work with people not fluent in English. Mnemonics, like jokes, often do not translate well. Some of the skills represented in the ACCEPTS list are, nonetheless, useful, especially those that involve behaviors. If we translate the ACCEPTS mnemonic into a simple coping skills menu, we would get

- Helping others (also a social skill)
- Doing Other fun things to feel better (games, sports, arts and crafts) that help you feel better
- Thinking about pleasant things (another simple cognitive intervention)
- Sensory activities that feel good (to be discussed shortly)

I have highlighted letters from this simpler list to create another acronym, HOTS, for those clients who would benefit from this.* We have skill cards for each of these, and we typically make reference to the pictures rather than acronyms (Figure 5.4).

Coping Through the Senses

People may use sensory-based activities as a means of coping and self-regulation more than cognitive strategies. Yet until recently sensory-based strategies were rarely incorporated into mental health treatment. With our LLC deaf clients, sensory-based strategies may be our principal means of intervention.

Peter was deaf, mildly retarded, and autistic. He expressed himself in sign, his best communication modality, in one to three sign phrases. He had sign

---

* I am grateful to Donald Meichenbaum for this suggestion.

vocabulary for simple, concrete things, activities, and concepts. We could sign "coping skills" to him, and he could sign it back, but he showed no evidence of understanding what it meant. He could identify good and bad behaviors. He could state the behaviors he should and should not show. He could say, "HIT, NO" and "SAFE, YES." He could not collaboratively construct a treatment plan, though when presented with a plan he would agree to it. His agreement was no guarantee of understanding or follow through.

Peter was hospitalized because he had become assaultive with his peers in his group residence. He could not tell us what he felt or why he was hurting people. We made some medication adjustments. We also put in place a traditional behavior plan in which he earned smiley face stickers every hour for showing none of the negative behaviors and all of the positive behaviors on a pictorial rating form. When he accumulated a certain number of smiley faces, he received another reinforcer. This behavior plan produced an immediate improvement in behavior, but nobody was confident his safe behavior would generalize to his group home placement. To solidify his progress, we needed to elicit from him skills that he and his staff could draw on. Sensory modulation strategies were the principal kinds of coping skills accessible to him.

Peter's favorite activities were drawing pictures and using Legos® to build complex structures. We started referring to these activities as his coping skills. Other activities we placed on his menu of coping skills included:

- Rocking in a rocking chair or glider rocker
- Tapping himself with a beanbag according to an established protocol
- Pushups on a table or wall
- Hot baths and showers
- Basketball, bowling, and ring toss
- Stretching
- Walking
- Stress balls and other things to fidget with
- Moving furniture and cleaning
- Ball tossing
- Rolling a heavy medicine ball over his body

These activities were Peter's coping skills. They provided distraction, enjoyment, and physical release. They helped him relax. They de-stressed him. Peter would seek out many of these activities on his own, and he would accept others when staff prompted him. He did not initially understand these activities as coping skills. After discovering what activities he enjoyed, our task was to call these activities his coping skills and praise him for using these skills to calm himself down. Our goal, of course, was to help him understand that he could *do something* to help himself. The behavioral reinforcement plan was helpful, but Peter would have a better chance of staying in control if he attributed his success to his own abilities (Meichenbaum & Biemiller, 1998). He would also be more likely to engage, at his level, in therapeutic conversations about what new skills he could develop. The skills he could understand and intentionally use, however, were mainly sensory-based activities.

For example, one afternoon Peter was showing some warning signs of impending assaultiveness. He looked tense. His eye contact was less frequent than normal. He made odd, unnerving facial expressions and was less responsive to conversation. Staff recognized the warning signs, and immediately invited him to do standing pushups against the wall. They took out a large, rubber elastic band called a Theraband®, and had him tug on one end while they tugged on the other. They then took out a jump rope and twirled it and invited him to jump. He jumped happily and staff cheered. They then took him outside to toss around a basketball. These sensory activities calmed him down, and when he was calm, staff talked to him about the coping skills he used. They said, "You were nervous but you used coping skills. You did pushups against the wall. You stretched the band. You jumped. You tossed the ball. You calmed down. Wow. Great coping skills!" Staff then gave him a smiley face sticker, not merely for "being good," but much more importantly for using his coping skills successfully.

In recent years, sensory modulation activities have received increasing recognition as mainstream psychiatric treatment strategies (Ayres, 1979; Champagne, 2006). Karen Moore, an occupational therapist, developed a program of sensory-based interventions for treating patients with psychiatric disorders (Moore, 2005), and we have drawn heavily on her approach in working with deaf psychiatric inpatients (Trikakis, Curci, & Strom, 2003). It is interesting that sensory modulation treatment comes out of the field of occupational therapy rather than psychiatry, psychology, social work, or counseling. Occupational therapy as a field concerns itself with helping people develop skills through meaningful, relevant activities. It is not problem-centered, the way most other mental health disciplines are, but strength, resource, and skill centered. In psychiatric inpatient units and day programs, the therapeutic program is often developed and run by occupational therapists. Over the years, I have worked with many occupational therapists, and I have been repeatedly struck by how much more engaged clients often are with them than with clinicians attempting to do traditional psychotherapy. This is especially true of the LLC clients who do not know how to make use of a talking therapy and of clients who are cognitively disorganized due to mental illness. The approach presented in this book, with its emphasis on engaging clients through activities that develop psychosocial skills, is heavily influenced by occupational therapy.

Moore's *The Sensory Connection Program* (2005) is a must read for mental health clinicians who want to use sensory modulation to help LLC clients with coping skills. Moore notes that the cognitive strategies used in DBT, such as mindfulness meditation, "presume a fairly high level of cognition and a state of mind that is essentially intact. Patients in psychiatric crisis are often unable to use mindfulness techniques and cognitive strategies for self-regulation" (p. 35). She contrasts mindfulness meditation with beanbag tapping, a technique in which "the patients use bean bags to give deep pressure touch input to the body as they tap firmly on hands, arms, shoulders, back, legs and feet. This sensory input produces a tingly and 'alive' feeling and puts people in touch, literally, with their body" (p. 35). Mindfulness meditation, she says, requires a state of self-control, has a high cognitive demand, requires concentration, works toward self-acceptance and aims for self-control through managing thoughts. Beanbag tapping, by contrast, creates the state of self-control, has minimal cognitive demand, does not require concentration, starts at self-awareness, and fosters self-control through physiological input.

Moore describes sensory modulation as a means of self-regulation through sensory input. Sensory modulation provides strategies for coping, calming, alerting, organizing, self-awareness, and environmental awareness. Sensory modulation programs typically focus on three problems:

1. Overresponsiveness (difficulties calming down and regaining self-control)
2. Underresponsiveness (difficulties meeting demands of the situation, poor environmental awareness)
3. Sensory defensiveness (overstimulated by sensory events others would ignore)

Interventions occur through the senses that are available to clients. We are most familiar with the external senses of smell, taste, vision, hearing, and touch, although external senses also include oral, motor, sensory input (a combination of flavor, texture, temperature, and movement of lips, jaw, and facial muscles). Moore describes activities that include these senses as "sensory snacks" in that they help us change our state or mood, but typically only as long as one engages in these activities.

More powerful means of sensory intervention occur through three less familiar internal senses:

1. Proprioceptive sense (muscle resistance, joint contraction, and compression)
2. Vestibular sensation (awareness of body position and movement in space; balance)
3. Deep pressure touch

Moore writes:

Input from these three internal senses provides the strongest powerhouses of lasting influence on regulation of sensory responses. This strong sensory input has a modulating effect on the nervous system, which is helpful in maintaining a state that is calm and organized, yet alert. Modulating sensory input comes from whole body actions involving walking, gardening and vacuuming. Exercise activities reward the body by releasing "feel good" chemicals such as the endorphins. Strong sensory input is organizing; it puts the person in better touch with the body. This input is important for individuals with low arousal, disorganization due to cognitive impairments, symptoms of dissociation, sensory issues due to abuse, and poor body and environmental awareness. Movement activities and heavy work activities are useful whenever patients have difficulties with sensory processing or problems with emotional regulation and self-control. (Moore, 2005, p. 8)

In other words, the most powerful sensory interventions will not usually involve sight, hearing, taste, smell, and touch but rather muscle resistance, movement, balance, and deep pressure touch. An exception might be music, which people often draw on to alert and soothe.

Trikakis (2003) described use of sensory strategies on the Deaf Unit at Westborough State Hospital. Deaf Unit staff welcomed these interventions initially because they were concrete, practical, effective, and minimally dependent on language. They offered a powerful means of assisting patients who lacked the verbal skills necessary to engage in dialogue-based therapy. On the Deaf Unit, sensory interventions are called SMI which previously referred to sensorimotor integration or sensorimovement interventions. Although the field no longer uses the term SMI, the term stuck. Most clients cannot say what it stands for, but they know it refers to fun activities that involve the body. SMI is presented to clients as one kind of coping skill. Figure 5.5 shows some of activities we consider SMI skills.

Other examples of sensory-based coping skills strategies used on the Deaf Unit include:

1. A client who wanted to cut her arms was encouraged, instead, to use a red felt marker and draw red lines on her arm. While this can also look scary, no skin was broken, and the client reported this did help her wean off of cutting.
2. A moderately retarded woman with poor language skills asks for a set of newspapers when upset, and with staff support tears them up and throws them out.
3. Clients cover themselves with heavy, soft blankets and rock in rocking chairs. They rub or tap themselves with brushes, beanbags, and other materials. They put on soothing lotion or dabs of a soothing smell.
4. Friendly dogs are brought to the program, and patients play with them or just sit and pet them. The calming effect of pets is well known. Pet therapy is a wonderful sensory intervention made all the more powerful when clients can take credit for their "playing with the dog" and "grooming the dog" coping skills.

Figure 5.5 Coping through the sensory activities.

5. Large stuffed animals are used with the stuffing replaced with seed corn, making the stuffed animals much heavier. These are placed on client's laps where they offer both a centering weight and a smooth, attractive surface to pet.

6. Clients are encouraged to exercise. Some will accept gentle yoga and tai chi. More will go for walks. Clients are given their own pedometers and prizes are given to those who walk certain distances.

7. Clients rock in comfortable rocking chairs or lie down on soft mattresses in specially designed "comfort rooms." The comfort room has a large, soft mattress, a beanbag chair, and a soft rocker. The walls are

painted with an attractive beach scene. The door of this room, in the past used for involuntary seclusion of assaultive patients, is always left open, so patients can enter and leave as they please.

8. Volunteers water the plants.

9. Clients with urges to self-harm are shown how to use beanbag tapping referred to above to settle their senses. Others place a rubber band around their wrist and snap themselves whenever they feel like cutting.

10. Sensory activities are used as warm-ups for treatment groups. For instance, medicine balls are passed around, beanbags are tossed into targets, or light balls are tossed.

11. A sensory cart is made available for clients in distress (see below).

Moore describes one purpose of her sensory connection program as the creation of success experiences. She writes, "It is amazing how many patients have told us that their seemingly trivial triumphs in the target games of the Level 1: Sense-ability Treatment Group made them feel good about themselves for the first time in months. It is my conviction that 'success leads to success.' If patients allow themselves to be proud of one small accomplishment, a positive trajectory of self worth begins" (Moore, 2005). Success does indeed lead to success, especially if the success is defined as skill use, and the clients are given credit for using the skill in order to help themselves. For instance, clients who put themselves in a better mood by tossing a ball can be credited with using "play skills" as means of coping. With the LLC clients toward whom this is directed, this reframing is usually accepted. They are made even happier by appreciating that they are happy due to their own behaviors.

Since the publication of the chapter by Trikakis, Curci, and Strom (2003), the Massachusetts Department of Mental Health (DMH) has embraced sensory modulation strategies as principal means of reducing/eliminating the use of restraint and as means of instituting treatment approaches sensitive to experiences of trauma by patients (Champagne & Stromberg, 2004; LeBel et al., 2004). Occupational therapists have brought sensory modulation strategies to inpatient units throughout Massachusetts and have taught nursing staff how to implement them with patients. Common interventions include a protocol for rigorous brushing, weighted blankets, stuffed animals and elastic wrist bands, aroma, color and music therapy, deep breathing, and multisensory treatment rooms where patients can retreat to "chill out." The occupational therapist on the Deaf Unit, as well as many others, put together a "sensory cart" that includes multiple items from a sensory menu. These include massagers, weighted objects, Therabands and other objects for stretching, jump ropes, DVDs containing tranquil or stimulating sounds and sights, books with pictures of landscapes and animals, objects for squeezing, rolling, playing; brushes, beanbags, different aromas, coloring and other art supplies. Staff work with clients to identify sensory interventions that are helpful to them and record these in client crisis plans. They are then brought out when needed.

Sensory-based interventions have an obvious appeal for LLC clients but they are, of course, applicable to everyone. I like to ask higher functioning people what strategies they use when they are depressed, anxious, angry, or stressed. Inevitably, the list will include activities like exercise, going to the gym, yoga, meditation, walking, music, playing with animals or children, sports, art, and so on. Healthy people have a repertoire of such interests but may not think about them as coping skills. Because sensory activities are usually pleasurable, people may not credit themselves with doing something healthy when they engage in them. People may think it is not really treatment unless it involves enormous effort or suffering. They may not consider engagement in these activities to represent skills because these come relatively easily. Counselors who are primed to find skills in such ordinary activities have a larger bag of tools for pretreatment and treatment. Sensory-based interventions are scattered throughout the DBT modules but they are not used in a systematic way or exploited for all they have to offer. With LLC clients, for whom sophisticated cognitive treatment strategies may be unavailable, the ability to find skillfulness in sensory-based activities is essential.

Coping Through Problem Solving

For the most part, this discussion of coping skills is focused on what is called "emotion-focused coping;" that is, managing one's emotions. People also cope by doing active problem solving, what is referred to as "problem-focused coping" (Snyder & Dinoff, 1999). To engage in problem-focused counseling, one has to conceptualize one's emotional responses as a reaction to a problem that needs solving. One has then to consider possible solutions and eventually choose and implement one. This process would appear to require composure under stress as well as analytic abilities. One would expect to see problem-focused coping in higher functioning, resourceful people. Can we nurture this ability in our LLC clients?

Meichenbaum's early work in CBT includes training clients in problem solving, and such training is widespread within the CBT field. A representative text is *The Handbook for Communication and Problem-Solving Skills Training: A Cognitive-Behavioral Approach* by Bedell and Lennox (1997). This text presents a problem-solving training program. The authors break down the process of problem solving into seven steps:

Step 1.   Problem Recognition
Step 2.   Problem Definition
Step 3.   Generation of Alternative Solutions
Step 4.   Evaluation of Alternative Solutions

Step 5.   Making a Decision
Step 6.   Implementation of the Solution
Step 7.   Verification of the Solutions Effect

The text also contains lesson plans. Each step is broken down into simpler parts or principles to aid in instruction. The format for training is (a) instruction, (b) supervised practice, (c) feedback, and (d) independent practice. Seven guiding principles of problem solving are offered for consideration. These include the notion that problems are natural, most can be solved, and solving them requires taking responsibility. Exercises are offered to give people experience in applying the principles. Problem vignettes are offered, and people are coached in using the problem-solving format, first supervised and then independently.

The lesson plans in this excellent resource are clear and well organized. The theory is presented along with structured practice sessions. Supervision is faded out as student competency develops. The text presents a prototypical model of effective teaching. If clients are willing and able to make use of this training approach, it has to be recommended.

Our problem, of course, is that even this seemingly simple curriculum is well beyond the ability of many LLC clients who may not be willing or able to attend the sessions, much less engage in the analytic process required. Our teaching approach needs to be much more creative and compelling, and it needs to be even simpler.

As with all the skills taught in this book, counselors need to be thoroughly familiar with the components of problem-solving so they can recognize and label any of these skills, even in embryonic form, that clients show unprompted. Our clients actually engage in problem-solving efforts all the time, but their skills may be poorly developed. Sometimes staff mistake poorly developed skills for examples of pathology. Rather than seeing therapeutic opportunities in the fact that clients are making efforts at problem solving, staff may discount their efforts and discourage them.

For instance, when our clients attempt to convince us to behave in certain ways, we may label them as "manipulative" or "borderline." I observed a client making persistent efforts to get the attention of a doctor who was busy. The doctor commented that the patient was "pestering" her. She could just as easily have noted her "assertiveness." On another occasion, clients requested to go out on an outing to the mall, but there were not enough staff available and other tasks were priority. When the staff explained this to the clients, the clients made various suggestions. One suggested they go on a shorter trip. Another suggested they could go out with less staff. While these solutions were not practical, they showed efforts at problem solving. Rather than recognize this, staff just encouraged clients to *use your coping skills*," a praise that can become as meaningless as "have a nice day." On the other hand, with training staff get better at seeing embryonic skill use and noting these with clients.

An agitated client was pacing up and down the hall, banging his fist against the wall as he did so. An astute staff person recognized that the fist banging, while it might be a warning sign of an impending explosion, could also be considered an attempt at coping through getting sensory input. The staff person approached the client, asked to talk, noted that the client looked upset, and wondered whether the wall banging was helpful. The staff person said, "Sometimes people feel better when they bang something. I wonder if you are using that skill?" The client did not know but was engaged by the positive approach. The staff person then invited the client to try out some other sensory skills with her, and they went together to the "comfort room" to see if other SMI skills worked.

The collaborative problem-solving method of Ross Greene (Greene, 1998; Greene & Ablon, 2006) helps parents, teachers, and counselors to teach skills in the moments when problems or conflicts naturally occur. This method does not depend on clients going to structured group therapy. It promotes skill generalization because skills are developed in real-life contexts, not the pretend context of a therapy group. We consider this method in the next chapter, but offer an example of it here.

A client asked for a double portion of dinner. He saw that there was one extra food tray because another client was out on pass. He asked to be given her portion. Staff responded by presenting him with an opportunity for problem solving. "What if other people want the double portions? Won't they feel it was unfair that they weren't offered the extra food? Won't they become angry? We do have an extra tray, but how could we be sure that we give out the food fairly?" The client responded that the others did not mind. "*How do you know that*?" staff asked. The client decided to ask the other clients if they minded. The staff person said "*Good idea*," but accompanied him to be sure he was not unduly pressuring his peers. One peer said he would like some more food, and the staff person again posed the problem. "You both want the extra portion. What can we do?" The two clients came up with the idea of sharing the extra portion. That does appear to solve the problem. Staff then noticed and labeled the skills used: identifying a problem, brainstorming solutions, listening to other people, compromising. The client got part of the extra food as well as lots of praise for his effective problem solving.

Greene's approach complements the stress inoculation training developed by Meichenbaum as well as other versions of psychosocial skill training offered in structured groups or individual sessions. Collaborative problem solving is brought to the moments when conflicts or problems actually occur. If clients have previously learned some coping, problem-solving, or conflict resolution skills in group or individual treatment, that will only help, but the emphasis is on developing the skills at the moment when they are actually needed. When staff engage clients in this kind of "live" problem solving, and follow up by labeling the skills just demonstrated and offering lavish praise, it is far more powerful than any learning one would hope to accomplish in a group or individual session.

Thus, we can strive to teach formal problem solving in a classroom like format such as that offered by Bedell and Lennox, but when clients cannot or will not attend such trainings, we can still teach elements of problem solving. The best way is to note problem-solving skills when they naturally occur and then follow up with invitations to develop these skills further. How skillfully clients behave is at least partially in the eyes of the beholder. As staff become skillful at noticing skills, clients come to appear healthier. Staff who see client skills have an easier time engaging clients in treatment.

The most comprehensive treatment and rehabilitation settings should offer a program of individual, group, family, and milieu therapy all oriented toward the development of psychosocial skills. Meichenbaum made a huge contribution by creating this treatment paradigm, but he then went on to rethink some of his basic assumptions and move CBT in a very different direction. In the process, he revealed a whole new set of counseling strategies that can be very effective with LLC clients.

Meichenbaum's Later Work and the Development of Narrative Strategies to Assist With Coping

An important cognitive dimension of coping is the ability to find new meaning in adversity (Affleck & Tennen, 1996; Tennen & Affleck, 1999). For instance, people suffering from serious illness or from the suffering and death of loved ones may come to see themselves as stronger, develop a more profound appreciation for what is important in life such as a deeper connection to people or a higher power, or they may find the ability to live much more fully in the moment, appreciating the good things in life. A mother who loses a child to a drunk driver may find new meaning in joining an organization like Mothers Against Drunk Drivers. A parent who loses a family member in a war may become a peace activist. In effect, such individuals find or "construct" a new perspective on life, and this new perspective helps them cope or adapt to their new reality. Another way to conceptualize this process is that they are constructing a new narrative or story about their life. Were we to give this new story a title, it might be something like "How I became a survivor" or "How I came to understand what really matters."

Mental health counselors working with clients who are struggling to come to terms with serious adversity need to assist clients in the process of their creation (construction) of such new narratives. In the psychotherapy world, a school of constructivist or narrative psychotherapy has emerged associated with the work of Michael White and David Epston (White, 1995, 2007; White & Epston, 1990). This school of therapy works with the epistemological assumption that reality is socially constructed. Meichenbaum (1996) writes:

A constructivist narrative perspective (CNP) focuses on the "accounts" or "stories" that individuals offer to themselves and others about the important events in their lives. The CNP views humans as "meaning-making-agents" who proactively create their own personal realities or meanings. Constructivists do not believe people are depressed because they "distort reality." Moreover, it is not the job of the therapist to educate clients about how they distort reality. Rather, a constructivist narrative perspective proposes that there are multiple realities and one of the tasks of therapy is to help clients appreciate how they go about constructing their realities; how they "author their stories."

Clients need to tell their "stories," not only about the problems that bring them into therapy, but also about their strengths and resilience, what we have referred to as "the rest of the story." There is a need to help clients change not only their behavior, but also the accompanying narratives they construct. (Meichenbaum, 1996, pp. 18–19)

Meichenbaum concluded that it was not helpful to conceptualize thoughts as "rational" or "irrational" and to go on a hunt for dysfunctional thinking. This distinguishes his approach from the cognitive therapy of Beck (A. Beck, Rush, Shaw, & Emery, 1979; J. Beck, 1995) and Ellis (1962). Rather, like therapists in the narrative therapy school, he attends to clients' thinking as if they were telling stories. These stories are not true or false. They are helpful or unhelpful. Borrowing and extending on the work of narrative therapists, Meichenbaum developed a number of strategies that help clients change their stories. These are cognitive therapy strategies, but they do not require the ability to think about thinking or analyze beliefs. Like his early work in self-instructional training, these cognitive therapy strategies are suitable for LLC clients because they change thinking patterns without requiring clients to have strong capacities for rational self-analysis.

Even as a constructivist narrative therapist, Meichenbaum never loses sight of the goal of teaching clients psychosocial skills. That is why his work remains CBT. The combination of the traditional CBT emphasis on psychosocial skill training and the narrative therapy emphasis on changing clients' stories creates a powerful set of techniques well suited to LLC clients. As noted in the Introduction, we borrow from Meichenbaum the twin themes of skills and stories as the primary avenues for work with our LLC clients. The main narrative strategies Meichenbaum employs are skillful questioning, use of metaphor, and storytelling.

The Art of Questioning

Meichenbaum relies heavily on what he calls the "art of questioning."

The art of questioning provides patients with an opportunity to discovery, rather than for the therapist to didactically teach. Such questioning fosters patients' understanding as patients are more likely to remember and apply those ideas that they discover by their own reasoning processes than the information and observations that are offered by the therapist. (Meichenbaum, 2001, p. 147)

Several of Meichenbaum's works contain lists of questions. For example, in his 2001 text on treatment of persons with anger-control problems and aggressive behaviors (Meichenbaum, 2001), he presents 10 tables with lists of questions designed to:

1. Help patients define treatment goals.
2. Highlight situational variability as a way to nurture hope.
3. Help patients prioritize goals.
4. Enhance patient motivation to change.
5. Help patients get going.
6. Assess and bolster confidence.
7. Elicit commitment statements.
8. Elicit self-motivational statements.
9. Notice possible changes that they can bring about in the future.
10. Assess patients' understanding and comprehension of the treatment rationale.

Most of these questions require fluent language skills, but simple versions of these questions can be asked of people with language and cognitive limitations. One strategy is to ask questions about when the problem is not being exhibited. It is best not to ask "Why did you do so well?" but instead "What did you do that helped yourself?" For instance,

"You didn't blow up. You stayed calm. How? What did you do?"
"Today, you felt sad. You wanted to hurt yourself. You stayed safe. No cutting. Wow, that's terrific. I wonder what coping skill you used?"
"You went out on pass. You were with your family. Before, you and your mother would argue and you would drink. This time, you didn't drink. You didn't relapse. How did you stay sober?"

Skillful questioning leads clients to discover their own abilities. Whether we direct our clients' attention to their positive or negative behaviors influences the kind of narrative we construct together. Questions only about negative behaviors create a "problem saturated narrative." Questions about skill use and success influence the clients' story toward greater hopefulness. The most relevant question we can ask here is simply, "What coping skill did you use?"

Usually the first time we ask clients to account for how well they did, we get a shrugged shoulder. They literally do not have words to account for their successes. Because the language of our treatment program is skills, and pictures of skills are posted everywhere, clients eventually learn to speak this language.

They learn names for skills, and before long they are answering questions like this by naming particular skills (whether or not they actually used them). The task for staff then is to help them answer this question meaningfully.

A 17-year-old deaf girl with fair ASL skills, hospitalized after several terrible behavioral explosions, asks to use the videophone. Because the phone is located in a room where there are objects people can use to harm themselves, she has to be supervised, and staff are not available to supervise her at that moment. A staff person asks her to wait, and she becomes tense and agitated. She begins to argue with him. However, she manages somehow to walk away from the argument and go into the comfort room. She emerges about 2 minutes later, somewhat calmer, and asks again to use the phone. The staff person at this point has a choice. He can focus on her recurring demands and ask her to be more patient. Or he can notice her efforts to avoid aggression. Taking the latter course, he asks her a series of questions: *You seemed to be getting angry, but you walked away. You went into the comfort room. Wow. How were you able to do that? How come you didn't blow up? What skill did you use to calm yourself down?*

This patient does not initially have the language to answer these questions, but over time in a program in which skills are constantly identified and reinforced, she develops the language. For the moment, she just answers that she "went to the comfort room and calmed down."

The staff person wonders about skills she might have used (deep breathing, talking to herself, lying down, squeezing a ball, looking out the window). She listens and answers that she used "breathing" and "lying down skills." The staff person then ask her if she could use these same skills for a few more minutes until he can be freed up to supervise her. After she does this, he also asks her if she noticed the conflict resolution skills she was using (listening, waiting, compromising). This staff person is building her vocabulary and knowledge for skills, her belief in her own ability to use skills, and her story about her successes in using these skills.

Using Metaphors

Meichenbaum likes to "pluck" metaphors from clients and use them as ways of joining with them through their conceptual world. He uses metaphors to help clients understand the "cost" or "toll" for thinking the way they do. For instance, in a videotape he developed in which he demonstrates his constructivist narrative CBT (Meichenbaum, 1996), Anna, the client he counsels, describes her life as "a glob of misery" and a "total personal tragedy." Asked what she does with her feelings, Anna replied that she "stuffs them down." Meichenbaum plucks and reflects these metaphors and uses them as an opportunity to invite a collaborative process of examination of the impact or toll of the way she sees the world. He writes:

Whenever I hear a central metaphor such as "stuffed feelings," I ask the client a series of questions: "What is the impact...? What is the toll...? What is the price paid for 'stuffed feelings'?" In response to such queries, a client may answer, "I don't know," as Anna did. I then responded, "I don't know either. How can we find out?" This exchange conveys that therapy should be viewed as a collaborative process. (Meichenbaum, 1996, p. 36)

Do our LLC clients use metaphors that we can "pluck" as our treatment language? In my experience, clients who are severely language impaired use metaphors less commonly, though if you learn to listen for metaphors, you will still find them. Even when clients do not produce many of their own metaphors, they may be responsive to metaphors used by staff. When staff are able to pluck a client's metaphors, therapeutic pathways may appear. Sometimes we can create metaphors out of clients' interests.

Joe's main joy in life was basketball. It was almost the only thing he wanted to talk about, and he had a tremendous knowledge of the game. On arrival to the Unit, he quickly set up mock basketball court at different ends of the hall, with wastebaskets for basketball hoops, and a taped grid over the floor, and invited staff to participate. Joe also had a problem with aggression and was not interested in talking about it. The trick to engaging him in treatment around aggression turned out to be staff ability to use basketball as a metaphor for the treatment process.

We explained our privilege system to Joe by comparing advancement in privileges to moving down a basketball court. Hitting, threatening, throwing things, or kicking were examples of "fouls" that would result in a penalty. Staff were assigned different positions. We had a team manager, various coaches and assistant coaches, and the team doctor. The other clients were team players and his family was the home team. His provocative, in-your-face behavior was a "personal foul" and noncompliance with the rules was a "technical foul." These behaviors resulted in a "time out on the bench." While on the Unit, he was encouraged to participate in "training," which he did so he could earn points and "win."

After we found this metaphor, treatment compliance was much less of a problem. In fact, on return to the unit for a second hospitalization a year later, he immediately put himself back "on the bench" and requested the reinstatement of his basketball treatment plan. When any client requests *any* treatment plan, the client leaps from pretreatment into active treatment, and we are thrilled. In effect, basketball provided him a map for recovery. Staff just needed to pay attention to his metaphors as they revealed to us the language of his mind.

In a coping skills group, we were discussing intensity of emotions, and I was having trouble conveying the idea that emotions vary in strength. A deaf client named Sam, who had a gift for metaphors, ran to the locker in the room where he was keeping a set of weights. He took three different weights out and called a peer, who was having trouble grasping the idea, up to role-play. He asked him to show a little anger, and when the peer did so, he handed him the lightest weight. Then he asked him to show more anger, and when he did so, he handed him the next larger weight. And so on with the third weight. The co-leader and I then jumped at the metaphor offered and played with it. *"Show some improved coping,"* I said, and demonstrated with positive self-talk. When the client did so, we took the heavy weight out of his hand. "Show even stronger self-talk, even better coping," I urged. The client did so, and we took the second weight out of his hand. "Now show you are really coping well." As he did this, we took away the last weight.

Understanding dawned on the client's face, and I thanked Sam. I told Sam that he taught me something, and that I would proceed to share his idea with others. The idea that he was giving us treatment tools, that he had become a teacher, made this use of metaphor particularly sweet for all of us.

A client reported he feels "like a horse with blinders on." He signed and mimed this concept and may not have known the English phrase. He just acted out a horse that had blinders on and could only see ahead. This was a wonderful opening to discuss what he did and did not allow himself to see, experience, and think. Another hearing client reported that in his treatment, he felt like he keeps walking up a steep hill only to fall down the hill again. This remark led to a productive conversation about obstacles in his path and the process of relapse prevention. Another hearing client with mild mental retardation said, when discussing whether she can notice and manage her delusional fears, that she felt she only makes it to "first base." This led us to draw out a baseball diamond, clarify what she would achieve at first, second, third base, and at home plate, and then draw up a self-monitoring form in the shape of a baseball diamond.

Whenever we can find a simple visual metaphor to conceptualize coping skills, it always helps. Two metaphors that I have described previously (Glickman, 2003) that have been especially useful over many years are what we call "red, yellow, green" and "shield."

"Red, yellow, green" refers to the traffic light (Figure 5.6). Over the red light, we put the words "stop and notice." Patients readily grasp the "stop." It takes more work for them to notice the "notice." Most concretely, we want them to notice their behavior. Are they about to harm themselves or other people?

Figure 5.6 Red, yellow, green.

What are they doing that is risky? We also want them to notice their feelings and, if possible, their thoughts. With substance abusers, we want them to notice their cravings.

"Stop and notice" can be understood to be the first step of all CBT. Whatever the problem behavior or symptom is, we cannot change it until we notice it. If one wants to change one's eating patterns, one has to first notice how and when one eats. Keeping a food diary would be a logical first step. If one wants to stop smoking, one has to first notice when one smokes. We need to break habitual patterns and become self-conscious about anything we seek to change. Self-monitoring activities can be considered efforts to help clients stop and notice.

The yellow light corresponds to the admonition to slow down, become cautious, and prepare to change. The most concrete manifestations of yellow light work are slow, deep breaths. It might also refer to taking a time out. We made major advances with a client when he was able to notice his own stress, walk out of a meeting rather than blow up, and then return when he was ready. As part of yellow light work, we may ask clients to rock in a chair, use heavy blankets or weights for grounding, or go outside to "chill out." From a sensory modulation perspective, clients are not ready to change if they are too drowsy or too alert. They need to be at the "just right" level of alertness in order to be receptive to learning. These yellow light sensory modulation activities, as described above, help people calm or alert themselves, and get ready for the green light work (Trikakis et al., 2003).

People associate the green light with *going*. We usually advise that green light means "think, then act." Under green light, we coach clients on what they can say to themselves to stay safe. We may ask them to repeat ideas like "I can stay calm. I will not blow up. I can cope. I can handle this. It is not so bad," and then ask them to add their own words. This is, as mentioned previously, Meichenbaum's self-instructional training method. Green light might also be conceptualized as "use a coping skill" that was previously agreed on.

If clients object that red, yellow, green is for children, I tell them with honesty that I use this skill every day. This is honest because the format of stop and notice, get ready to act, and use appropriate skills represents a solid CBT approach to most any problem. While we initially used red, yellow, green for anger control problems, we quickly saw its applicability to self-harm, symptom management, substance abuse, and relapse prevention. Even higher functioning people often appreciate how a powerful treatment approach is conceptualized through this simple pictorial metaphor.

The other visual metaphor we draw on constantly is "shield." We borrowed this idea from a wonderful book of creative counseling techniques, including many other therapeutic metaphors, by Ed Jacobs (1992). Jacobs has developed what he calls "impact therapy" to engage clients rapidly and powerfully using creative techniques (Jacobs, 1994). His work is very applicable to LLC clients. Jacobs will use a prop representing a shield to help clients grasp the idea of protecting themselves from abusive words or behaviors from others. He will ask clients to role-play using the shield in situations where there is pretend provocation. We have found it useful to extend this technique a bit further. We purchased costume armor, including a vest, arm shield (Figure 5.7), and protective hat/visor. Wearing the hat/visor is especially important because it never fails to bring laughter from the group. With the armor on, we set up pretend provocation and ask the client to use the shield to protect himself or herself. After doing this a few times, we have the client take the armor off, and we role-play the provocation again. Pausing for dramatic effect, we ask the client again where the shield is. Concrete thinkers may respond that the shield is on the table or wherever we put it. We answer, "No. Think again. Where is the shield?" Sometimes the client will figure out the answer, perhaps with some hints. "The shield isn't on the table. It is in your brain. Your brain is your shield." Then we watch the moment of insight flood into their eyes.

Figure 5.7 Shield.

The shield skill is a developmental precursor to more advanced conflict resolution. For some clients, being able to shield themselves from a perceived provocation is the best they can do at this moment. When they are more confident, we would want them to put down the shield and engage the person who is provoking them in dialogue. When they can do that, they are ready to move from coping to conflict resolution.

Using Stories

In constructivist narrative therapies, stories are also considered metaphors because through stories one makes an implicit comparison between the world of the story and the world of the client. Stories are used with clients in many ways. Most simply, we can tell clients stories that convey messages we hope to teach. Burns (2001, 2005) edited books of stories that have various therapeutic purposes. In a coping skills context, one would want to tell stories that facilitate coping. I do not know who created the following short, powerful story which I have used successfully many times in counseling.

A man finds a cocoon with a caterpillar inside in the process of transformation into a butterfly. He puts the cocoon in a special place on his desk so he can watch the butterfly emerge. He watches for several days, and though he can see some movement inside, nothing happens.

He decides he needs to help the butterfly find its way out of the cocoon. He takes a knife and cuts a little slit into the cocoon and then opens it about half way. In a short amount of time, a little creature sticks something like a wing out, and drops out of the cocoon on to the desk.

The man waits for the cocoon to spread its big butterfly wings, but nothing happens. Instead of spreading its wings, the poor creature shrivels up and then dies.

Then the man realized something important. The butterfly had to make its own way out of the cocoon. By pushing against the walls of the cocoon and forcing them open, the butterfly pushes fluid into its wings so it can eventually spread them. If the emerging butterfly does not have the cocoon to struggle against, the wings never spread, and the butterfly never develops. The struggle against the cocoon was crucial to the life of the butterfly. When the man deprived the butterfly of the opportunity to struggle against the cocoon, he deprived it of the opportunity to live.

The story means that struggling is important. By struggling, you grow. Without struggle, you shrivel up.

Counselors can follow a story like this by asking clients to "tell me about your struggle." Because struggling has been defined as a positive value, clients may be more willing to disclose problems they are having. If they accept the metaphor of "struggling," the counselor may have an opening to the discussion of skills for winning.

I like to tell the following true story about my own use of coping skills.

I was traveling through Costa Rica with a tour when the group decided to go on a zip line canopy tour. These are tours of the jungle from the treetops. One puts on a harness and climbs up a wooden tower to the top of the trees. Then a guide attaches each person to a cable connecting the trees. We put one hand in a thick glove and hold it behind us, letting the cable wire slip though our grip. The other hand holds on to the harness. On the particular zip line tour my group went on, the cable hung several hundred feet above the forest floor. The platforms were built around the top of the tree trunks. They were about 10 square feet with no railing. Hundreds of feet separated one treetop platform from the next. There were 12 platforms, and after the first 4 there was no way down except to go forward onto the next cable. I have long had a fear of heights with occasional panic attacks, and I decided I needed to do this activity as part of my own therapy for myself. I was aware that I was giving myself an "exposure therapy," but I felt ready for it.

As the group members climbed up the first tower, I learned that other group members had also experienced panic attacks in their lives. A few group members started to hyperventilate and panic, and they turned back. The tour guides told us the first few cables were for practice. I thought that meant they might be 10 feet off the ground. I'll at least try the practice runs, I thought, but I discovered that even the first cable was hundreds of feet in the air. The walk up the wood steps to the first treetop platform was the most frightening part. I had no idea we would be so high up so quickly. On the top of the tower, I was so terrified that my legs buckled underneath me. I literally could not stand up. The other group members got attached up to the cable and lined up. Most of them appeared nervous but very excited and happy. They thought this would be fun, and they did have a lot of fun, a reminder to me how "attitude is everything." The tour guide hooked them to the cable, lifted them into the air, and pushed them out over the abyss. They slid forward hundreds of feet to a destination I could not see because of the coverage of the tree branches and leaves. The cable made a distinct whirling sound as each of my tour mates flew off into the distance. Some of them so enjoyed the experience that they allowed themselves to swing from the cable upside down as they zipped from platform to platform.

My attitude was different. I don't remember ever being so frightened in my adult life, but I had one important resource going for me. I knew about coping skills. I knew that what I said to myself would be a crucial determinant of how I coped so I didn't let myself indulge in catastrophic thinking about how I was about to die. I told myself that as scary as this was for me, this was a routine activity for the tour guides who do this hundreds of times a year. To them, this was just this morning's tour group. They probably had a second group booked for the afternoon, I thought. This was scary, but objectively I was safe. In the very unlikely event that I fell off the platform, I was always hooked up to the cable and would just have been helped up. If I didn't make it to the next tree platform, the guides would come and get me. They wouldn't leave me hanging hundreds of feet above the jungle floor. These were very experienced guides doing an activity that must be regulated by the government (though the thought did occur to me that Costa Rica might not have the same government regulations as the U.S.). I then reminded myself of the old saying, "This too shall pass."

I knew that above all else, I needed to take slow, deep breaths. As I waited my turn, I leaned in against a tree and noticed a string of ants marching up and down the bark. I recognized this immediately as a useful distraction, and devoted my attention to the ants. I became absorbed in their disciplined movements. Where were they going and why? How did they communicate to each other? I also made a joke to a tour mate about how this would be a good time to pray. The laughter helped. Finally, I got up, continued to breathe slowly and deeply, and walked up to the platform edge. The guide hooked me to the cable and asked me if I was ready. "Listo?" he asked. Looking straight ahead (not down) and breathing slowly, I replied "Listo!" and he pushed me off the platform.

All I can say is that, thanks to coping skills, I lived to tell the tale.

A good story is a powerful way to begin a group treatment session. It may grab the attention of members and elicit a discussion. All too often counselors, when starting treatment groups, use a dry psychoeducational method. They will write "coping skills" on the board and ask clients what this means. They may then ask for examples. The least skilled counselors/teachers may start lecturing. Imagine instead beginning the group with one of the two stories presented above. Imagine further than you are the client. Which teaching method would work better with you?

Sometimes we tell stories about unnamed previous clients who had problems similar to those of current clients. Common stressors and provocations can be role-played, helping the story to come alive in the current moment. For instance, the counselor tells the story of a client who was scheduled for an important meeting. At the last minute, the meeting was postponed, and the client, angry, "blew up." This kind of scenario will be familiar to many clients. We ask them to role-play with someone assuming the role of the client and others assuming the role of staff helping the client. Placed in the staff role, clients have to think of specific skills to coach those role-playing the clients. Pictures of many skills are on the walls in the room, providing visual prompts. One client, in the role of staff, coaches the other to take a time out and breathe deeply. Another suggests he go for a walk. A third suggests he talk to staff. Through this process, clients not only develop a vocabulary for the skills but they construct stories about persons like themselves using the skills.

Stories can also be developed through the "mutual storytelling technique" of Richard Gardner (1986). The counselor starts a story about a person who really wanted to attend an important meeting, waited and waited all day, and was then told that the meeting was postponed. The story can be passed around with each client adding to it. In other sessions, a few deaf mentally retarded clients and staff acted out plays they devised on the spot. The plays involved coping with the frustrations of waiting in long lines to buy tickets or enduring long traffic delays while the people in the cars around you blast their horns and make rude gestures. Another story, involving both coping and conflict resolution skills, involves responding to a roommate who wants to keep the light on and the window open while you want the light off and the window closed.

In treatment settings, there are many common stressors that can be used as fodder for storytelling and skill building. Many of these scenarios are included as "situation cards" on the enclosed CD-ROM. They may prompt practice of both coping and conflict resolution skills. Examples are:

1. People have different preferences for what television program to watch.
2. Someone changes the channel without asking.
3. Someone has kept their laundry in the washing machine all day. Someone else has taken out the wet clothing of a peer and left the clothing on the table. Some of the clothing has fallen on to the floor.
4. Someone took someone else's seat.
5. Someone is controlling the remote for the TV.
6. Some important personal possession is missing.
7. A person with a special diet wants to eat the same junk food and cake as his peers.
8. One person makes a mean gesture or facial expression.
9. An activity that people looked forward to, such as an outing, is cancelled.
10. Staff enforce an unpopular rule.

One can also use television and movie clips to show a story. For instance, one may show an excerpt from the movie *Home Alone* (Hughes & Columbus, 1990) in which a resourceful child outwits two bungling burglars. The child displays wonderful creativity in problem solving. In the movie *Cast Away* (Bradshaw & Zemeckis, 2002) the character played by Tom Hanks shows phenomenal coping and problem-solving skills after being stranded on a remote island. Portions of this movie show the protagonist problem-solving to get water, food, and clothing, and most of these scenes have no dialogue, making them very suitable for persons without abilities to read captions. Counselors can introduce discussions of coping by showing the movie clips and asking questions like "How did he cope? What skills did he use?"

Another very dramatic movie segment, illustrating good and bad coping in the context of a life threatening crisis, occurs in the movie *Simon Birch* (Steven, 1998). The film portrays the friendship between Simon, a boy who is about 2 feet tall, and his normal height friend Joe. Simon believes deeply that there is a special purpose for him, and in the movie's climactic scene he draws on this belief to rescue a busload of children whose bus is sinking into a frozen lake. The adult bus driver illustrates the contrasting poor, panicky coping by opening the bus door to save himself and allowing the bus to be flooded with frigid water. The scene is harrowing and highly visually engaging with minimal dialogue. The scene must be used sensitively, as it shows children in mortal danger, but it illustrates powerfully how people in the same situation cope differently. We have used the scene to provoke a discussion of coping. It helps challenge the belief that so many LLC clients have that how well they do in life is dependent on what happens to them, not on their skills, attitude, and behaviors. The fact that the hero is a handicapped child makes this lesson all the more relevant.

Using Games

Counselors readily incorporate games and play into treatment of children, but rarely use this approach with adults. With a little creativity, skills can be taught through a game just as easily as through a lecture or discussion.

The goal of a coping skills group is to have clients identify and practice particular coping skills. It helps to have pictures of the most common coping skills on a bulletin board in the room. We also have the coping skill cards laminated giving us a deck of durable cards. Before group, we can remove from the deck any cards which we think are not appropriate for this particular group. We have a second deck of cards which we call "situation cards (Figures 5.8 and 5.9)." These cards elicit scenarios where coping or conflict resolution is called for. When clients cannot draw on real-life conflicts that have happened recently, we bring out the deck of situation cards and ask them to "pick a card." In hundreds of group sessions, I have never had a group member refuse to pick a card. Even the most hostile, resistant, behaviorally disturbed adolescents will pick a card.

Groups generally begin with a warm-up, a short, fun and engaging activity. A popular example is to have the group in a circle around a table. Balls and soft objects of varying sizes are on the table. Starting with one object, we pass or toss it in one direction. Then we add more objects. We circulate some objects in one direction, others in the opposite direction. We vary the speed of the object passing. Sometimes we allow participants to toss the objects to the person of their choosing. We match the complexity of the task to the capabilities of the group members in order to assure the experience of being successful. Before long, we have the objects passing or flying in all directions. This frequently elicits laughter even in clients who are deeply depressed and raises the level of engagement in the tasks to follow.

We then seek to have members name and practice particular skills. This is usually best done in the context of a situation that demands coping. Although one can start by defining coping skills and giving examples, with LLC clients it is best to begin with a story, game, or role play of particular examples. If the group leader is a counselor in the treatment program, he or she may

Figure 5.8 Situation cards.

know of an incident which recently occurred and can ask members if they will role-play what happened. For instance, a client went to the candy machine, put in his money, but no candy came out. A client and staff were stuck in the elevator during a 5-minute electricity outage. Clients were disappointed because a planned trip had to be delayed.

Suppose there are five coping skills the counselor wants the group to discuss and practice. These might be (a) red, yellow, green; (b) shield; (c) distraction activities like watching television; (d) thinking skills; and (e) sensory modulation activities like taking a hot bath. Cards representing these skills can be selected and the clients are invited to "pick a card." This gets the same content into the discussion as writing the skills on the board would do, only it is far more engaging. One then invites clients to use these skills to respond to hypothetical or real stressors. If the clients are willing to discuss and role-play a real-life stressor, that is best. If not, one can draw on a situation card. Some clients will be able to make up their own situations. There are many variations on this theme. Members can be asked to guess the skill or guess the situation. The

Figure 5.9 Situation card.

group can be broken down into two competing teams. Points can be assigned. Poker chips can be used to represent points of varying values. When groups are new and motivation is tentative, it sometimes helps to offer prizes.

Using Clients as Teachers

Whenever we have a mixture of new and experienced group members, we will ask the experienced group members to help teach the new members. This puts them in the roles of helpers, coaches, and teachers and cements their learning. It is quite common to have group members have very different levels of language and skill competency. Working with a highly diverse set of clients is one of the constant challenges in most deaf treatment settings. We have sometimes finessed this problem by having the more competent members become coleaders. We also do this when clients are at the point of discharge to help cement both the skills and the story they tell themselves about their skills.

I remember many years ago, when I worked briefly as a nursery school teacher, having one 4-year-old girl recite, for the first time, the alphabet. The teachers all *kvelled* with praise for her, and one asked the girl if she would mind teaching the alphabet to her 3-year-old friend. I can still picture her saying "Okay!" with a huge grin and the two of them marching over to a corner for the lesson. The 4-year-old barely knew the alphabet, but there was no question in my mind she would know it solidly by the end of the activity of teaching it to her younger peer. Though this was nursery school, the same principles apply to adults. The best way to learn something is to teach it, and clients who refuse to engage as students are often willing to engage as teachers.

All of these techniques are designed to influence the story that clients tell themselves about themselves. When we notice clients demonstrating competence or set them up through a game or activity to demonstrate competence, we set the stage for them to construct a new story about themselves. Putting clients in a helper or teacher role can influence profoundly how they see themselves. I realized this one time we had a client develop a teaching videotape on the red, yellow, green skill. During a break in the taping, I said to him that he really was an expert in red, yellow, green. He looked away, and signed to himself repeatedly, "I'm an expert." That was a moment that I realized that cognitive therapy could be done with "low functioning" clients. His beliefs about himself were changing because we enabled him to become an expert on something, put him in a teaching role, and talked to him about his expertise.

Meichenbaum understood in his early work that skill training was the heart of psychotherapy. In his later work, he has come to understand that skills are strengthened when embedded in a story, and that our goals for clients extend beyond skills toward helping them construct a new narrative about themselves. Skills are the foundation, but skills linked by a story create an identity.

Summary: A Framework for Developing Coping Skills in Language and Learning Challenged Clients

Donald Meichenbaum's constructivist narrative CBT provides a broad framework and many useful techniques that are effective with LLC deaf and hearing clients. In developing our treatment approach for LLC clients, many of whom do not readily see much purpose in counseling or know how to use it, we look for ideas and approaches that are simple, clear, and compelling.

The elements of our treatment approach, pertinent to coping skills, which we take from Meichenbaum's pioneering work, are as follows:

1. The emphasis in psychotherapy on helping clients develop coping skills.
2. The use of the stress inoculation procedures, rather than specific coping skill curriculum, as the framework for skill training.
3. The importance of the conceptualization phase, which we call pretreatment, in which client engagement and collaboration is obtained.
4. The importance of working one-down, Columbo style.
5. Fostering clients' self-appraisal though use of self-monitoring.
6. The importance of developing a menu of coping skills that are clear and compelling for the clients served. With the assistance of a talented artist, Michael Krajnak, we create visual representations of these skills (that is, skill cards) to help concretize them.
7. The importance of active practice of skills with increasingly more difficult challenges and in diverse situations.
8. The use of self-instructional training to help clients change thoughts.

9. The concern with skill generalization, including the need to anticipate and prepare for relapses in client problems.
10. The use of skillful questioning, usually from a one-down stance, to guide clients to drawing new conclusions.
11. The use of simple metaphors, spoken and visual, to conceptualize treatment concepts and as means of engagement of clients. We also look for opportunities to "pluck" metaphors from clients when they offer them.
12. The use of stories, including those shown in television and movie segments, to engage and teach.
13. Attention to helping clients construct new stories about their own abilities. This is done by helping them "connect the dots" and see in themselves a pattern of skill use over time.
14. Setting up opportunities for clients to demonstrate skills use, for example, by helping and teaching others, and using these successes as elements of their newly constructed stories.

Two components of our program compatible with Meichenbaum's approach but not emphasized by him are:

15. A heavy reliance on sensory-based activities, especially as developed by Moore (2005).
16. Use of play and psychotherapy games.

The core challenge of counseling with LLC clients is to elicit in them intentionality regarding their own development. This can only be done if they are given tools and strategies which are simple, clear, and compelling. Counseling theory must draw us to see and promote what is healthy and healing in everyday life. Thus, our list of coping skills is very mundane. It can be found on the CD-ROM in the set of pictures given under coping skills. Examples are art, deep breathing, deep thinking, laughing, praying, shield, videogames, asking for forgiveness, and, of course, red, yellow, green. If an activity helps someone cope, then we count it as a skill, and we engage people in the counseling process by helping them discover skills they already use. Then we use every creative technique we can find to engage clients in the process of intentional practice. The two core components of the counseling are this practice of skills along with the construction with the client of a story about his or her developing abilities.

To do this work, it is not necessary for staff to master a particular curriculum for skill training but they do need to develop an extensive knowledge of and vocabulary for the skills. To recognize when clients use skills, staff must know the skills themselves. We have discovered that it does not matter what the skills are called. Indeed, specialized psychology jargon is an unnecessary barrier. It is better to use everyday language. "Self-talk," for instance, is just as easily called "thinking" or "coaching yourself." We will even resort to "watching TV skills" as in "Paul was picking on you. You used skills of walking away and watching TV. You kept yourself calm and safe."

For the most part, we find that the skill training curriculum of DBT imposes too many intellectual demands to be useful for our clientele. Studying DBT is enormously helpful for clinicians in that it provides a very detailed, empirically validated map for the treatment and recovery process. Linehan's notion of treatment as a dialectical process involving a dance between acceptance and change treatment strategies is broadly applicable. She also presents a model for a seamless treatment plan where individual and group therapies are integrated. Meichenbaum argues, and I agree, that it is not necessary to have a particular curriculum to teach coping skills. It is more useful to think of coping skills as emerging out of a treatment menu and for the counselor and client to select and construct those particular coping skills that are good matches.

The strategy presented here assumes there is an institutional treatment setting such as a hospital, day treatment program, rehabilitation or independent living center, where group and milieu treatment occur. We assume also that deaf clients have staff who can communicate well with them though we know from experience this is often not true. It is very hard to imagine implementing this model of treatment for deaf people in a setting where staff are not very attuned to their language skills and where there is not a critical mass of deaf staff and clientele.

Coping skills training can occur in individual and group settings. Innovative teaching strategies such as the use of stories, movies, games, and role-playing work best. Sensory modulation–based coping strategies are very accessible and minimally dependent on language. Counseling should occur in formal counseling venues but as Greene (1998; Greene & Ablon, 2006) emphasizes, we have to be able to seize therapeutic opportunities whenever challenges occur. This means that families, milieus, and residence staff must be taught the same framework for developing skills. Greene's collaborative problem solving is discussed in more detail in the next chapter.

A program where coping skills are taught in group, individual, family, and milieu treatment, in structured therapy sessions as well as when needed in the moment of crisis, is most effective. Creating such *seamless* programs is much easier said than done, especially considering the communication demands in working with LLC deaf clients, but with this vision we can construct elements of the program, piece by piece, and build what we can. I do not believe, however, that individual therapy alone is sufficient, most of the time, with LLC clients with severe emotional and behavioral problems *no matter how talented the clinician*. It helps when the individual therapist adopts a CBT focus on skills, but it takes a team to do this work well. In Chapter 8, we attend to the construction of such a clinically and culturally competent team.

6
Conflict Resolution Skills

If coping skills refer to abilities to manage one's inner world (that is, feelings, thoughts, impulses, cravings, bodily sensations), then social skills refer to the ability to manage one's outer world. The most important element of the outer world is other people. Social skills include the ability to meet people and develop relationships, assert one's own needs while respecting the needs of others, form relationships with different boundaries and levels of intimacy, solve interpersonal conflicts peacefully, and manage expectations and demands imposed by other people and the environment. There are books published with curricula for teaching social skills to distinct populations (Bellach, Mueser, Gingerich, & Agresta, 2004; McKay, Fanning, & Paleg, 1994). The distinction between skills for managing your inner and outer worlds is important in dialectical behavior therapy (DBT) where the former are subsumed under the distress tolerance and emotion self-regulation skills training modules and the latter are subsumed under the interpersonal effectiveness skills training module (Linehan, 1993a, 1993b). This chapter focuses on what I believe are the most important social skills for most of our language and learning challenged (LLC) clients. These are the skills of being able to solve conflicts peacefully.

Nonviolent conflict resolution skills are a more advanced set of skills than coping skills because they involve working with other people as well as oneself. To solve conflicts with other people peacefully, one has to be self-aware. One has to understand one's own wants, needs, beliefs, interests, and perspectives, and one has to manage the internal experience that occurs when one finds oneself in situations where these are opposed by other people. It is possible to have strong coping skills without strong conflict resolution skills but not the other way around. For instance, a person might have excellent skills for dealing with internal distress by using solitary activities like meditation or prayer but be very poor at dealing with other people. On the other hand, to manage conflicts with other people well, one has to simultaneously manage one's internal experience. One cannot become a skillful negotiator without the ability to self-observe and cope with anger and anxiety. For this reason, we usually teach coping skills before conflict resolution skills. We teach both of these before the even more complex and demanding relapse prevention skills, discussed in the next chapter.

Participation in peaceful conflict resolution requires the ability to become empathically attuned to the wants, needs, interests, and perspectives of other people. This requires good listening skills and good skills at joining or making connections with other people. This is difficult enough, but we have conflicts with people we do not like or with people we may construe to be enemies. Peaceful conflict resolution requires the ability to form empathic connections with them as well. Advanced skills include the ability to reconceptualize those with whom we are in conflict not as enemies but as people with needs similar to our own. Weeks (1992), whose work we review, suggests the term "conflict partner." He says one has to be able to find the humanity in one's opponents, to see them as people, not as monsters. All this must happen before we even get to the concrete negotiating and problem-solving skills.

Nonviolent conflict resolution can be an exceptional challenge for the best of us so how can we expect to find such abilities in the LLC clients with whom we work? A key pretreatment principle discussed in this book is to find and label the skills clients already use. It is unlikely that the LLC clients referred to us will already be showing advanced conflict resolution skills, *but they almost always show developmental precursors to these skills.* They may not, for instance, engage in complex negotiation, but they might well flip a coin, take turns, wait in line, or, using their hands, "shoot for it." Counselor educator Allen Ivey coined the term "microskills" to describe component skills of counseling such as asking questions, paraphrasing, summarizing, reflecting feelings, and interpreting meaning (Ivey, 1971, 1991; Ivey, D'Andrea, Ivey, & Simek-Morgan, 2002; Ivey & Ivey, 2003). He pioneered the process of teaching counseling by breaking it down into these microskills and teaching the skills one at a time. Similarly, we can develop conflict resolution skills in our clients by noticing and labeling the relevant conflict resolution microskills they already show. If we know how to identify such developmental precursors to more advanced skills, we can start positively, building on client strengths. We can then invite clients, using innovative and fun teaching strategies, to develop these skills further.

Drawing on the constructivist narrative perspective (Meichenbaum, 1994, 1996, 2001) we remember that counseling can also be conceptualized as the process of constructing with clients alternative stories about themselves. We remember that clients always have at least two stories; the story of the problem and the story of their abilities and resiliency, in spite of the problem. Each time we invite clients to name and reflect on skills they are using, we are helping them construct this new story about their abilities. Clients become engaged in the treatment process of skill building as they experience treatment as offering them this new hopeful story.

This chapter begins with a story about a very difficult to engage deaf adolescent who badly needed better conflict resolution skills. We consider both the pretreatment and treatment challenges with this boy who, for a prolonged period, remained stubbornly oppositional, refusing to negotiate. We also present the struggle staff faced as we moved between strategies of firm limit setting and collaborative problem solving. This is not a polished case where we did everything "right," but rather an instance in which we were uncertain which model to apply. I share some of my own internal dialogue during our treatment of this challenging young man in the hope that exposing what I think we did both skillfully and unskillfully will be useful to others.

I then review a few important approaches to conflict resolution with an eye toward eliciting an understanding of the relevant microskills. We draw especially on nonviolent communication (NVC) as developed by Marshall Rosenberg (Rosenberg, 2003, 2005) and collaborative problem solving (CPS) as developed by Ross Greene (Greene, 1998; Greene & Ablon, 2006). Because we need to understand the developmental precursors of nonviolent conflict resolution skills, we draw on several works that demonstrate how to teach these skills to children. Many methods commonly used with children, such as games, role playing, and storytelling, work well with our adult LLC clientele. Based on this literature, we produce a menu of conflict resolution microskills and present these in both verbal and pictorial form. Finally, we consider three strategies for developing conflict resolution skills in clients. These are (a) identifying the conflict resolution microskills clients already show and inviting them to develop these further, (b) turning each behavioral conflict into an opportunity for CPS, and (c) conducting formal skill training groups, but using innovative and engaging activities.

A Client Refusing to Collaborate

Tim was a 17-year-old deaf boy admitted to the Unit after he assaulted several staff at his residential school. We were told that he is normally argumentative and oppositional but not physically violent. However, a series of recent losses in his family plus a bad reaction to medication seemed to have compromised his coping abilities. He was hospitalized with the goal of completing a medication change and stabilizing his behavior. During his hospitalization, staff searched tenaciously for any and all signs of positive skills while Tim, just as stubbornly, remained hostile and oppositional for a long period of the time.

Tim's hospitalization occurred at a time when we were transitioning from an earlier focus on traditional behavior plans to our new use of CPS (Greene & Ablon, 2006) and a strength-based attention to skills the client already shows. Our earlier style of work involved greater willingness to work "one-up," setting limits around problem behaviors, and developing behavioral plans with minimal input from clients. Our new style was to search tenaciously for skills and strengths and to see every crisis as an opportunity for skill development. During this transitional period, many staff were not on board with our new approach. I was the cheerleader for the new approach, but Tim would give me many reasons to doubt the wisdom of these changes.

For his first week on the Unit, Tim's behavior was rambunctious but safe. It was difficult to believe the stories about his violent assaults. Gradually, he began to show us his dark side. He stopped attending therapeutic groups and activities, refused to get out of bed in the morning, cursed out staff who tried to engage him in anything, and when a nurse set a limit, punched him in the arm. After this assault, I arrived at work and encountered a team that was angry, scared, and demanding that I implement a behavioral plan. Their message to me was to "do something" about him. The consensus was we had to set firmer limits.

As the team psychologist, I drafted a behavior plan. Staff had noticed that he spent many hours a day on the play station even during times when therapeutic activities are occurring. The play station is there for recreation. We did not normally use it as a reward, but we decided to make it something he must earn. The behavior plan I drafted had three expectations of him: that he be safe, cooperative, and engaged in treatment. All of these expectations were defined concretely. I designed a simple rating chart that staff would complete in which he earned points which could be exchanged for time on the play station during nonprogramming hours. I prepared, with a mental health worker assistant, to review this plan with him. This plan was drafted without his participation. This was a classic one-up use of authority that I felt compelled to use because he would not talk to me.

When we approached him to discuss the plan, he refused to meet with us. He was sitting on a low rocking cushion, making silly remarks, and rolling backward over his head. He was not engaged. Finally, because he would not talk to us, I handed him the plan to read. He looked it over, crumpled it up in his hand, and signed "I-REFUSE" multiple times. However, at least we now had his attention. We explained our rationale and our concern that he punched a nurse. Hitting people was not allowed, I said. He argued with us, said the plan was "STUPID" and repeated that he "REFUSES." Then he stopped looking at me.

Though we were in transition between treatment approaches, I knew at the time this was not the way we wanted to be interacting with him. We presented him with a plan that we developed without his input that required him to earn points for something he already got for free. We were doing this to a 17-year-old boy we knew was oppositional, inflexible, and explosive. We were focusing on his problem behaviors rather than his strengths and skills. Was it not predictable that we would get this kind of response from him?

At the time, I felt stuck because Tim's dangerous behavior had escalated to the point of assaulting a staff person, assaultive behavior was the reason for the hospitalization, and he was refusing meetings with us. The refusal to have any discussions with us forced us, I felt, into this limit-setting mentality. If we could meet, I would have begun by finding strengths and skills to comment on and inviting him to evaluate his own behaviors. I would have asked him, one-down, how could he have shown more skill. His hunkering down into a belligerent defiance while escalating his level of dangerousness left me feeling I had few options. As Unit director, I was responsible for Unit safety, and staff were communicating very clearly to me how unsafe they felt with him. I told him as best I could in the 10 seconds of eye contact he gave me that if we could sit and talk, we could probably come up with a better plan. If he would not talk, then staff would make the plan for him.

A Deaf mental health worker joined the conversation, and Tim engaged a little more. He told us that the plan was *stupid*. I told him that the particular plan could be changed, but not the goals of safety, learning skills, and getting back to his normal life. If he had a better way to achieve these goals, we would like to hear it. He then started to tell us about a behavior plan used at his school. We showed interest and tried to draw him out. This school plan had him being rated by staff each hour on a slightly different set of criteria and earning points toward a list of reinforcers. It did not sound that different from our plan, and we encouraged him to say more. We wanted him to express his ideas clearly, answer our questions, address our concerns, and think together with us about how this plan could meet all of our objectives. However, this was expecting more than he could deliver.

Tim has reasonably good signing skills but he did not have the kind of language and thinking skills that would enable him to describe a complex behavioral plan lucidly. Many aspects of the plan (the point system, the reinforcers, the criteria for getting points, how they are given, how this would work in a hospital setting) were unclear, and when we tried to flesh these out, he lost patience and resumed insulting us. We pointed out that he was insulting us, and I told him I would not talk with him if his insults continued. He did not stop, and I ended the meeting. I asked him to leave the room where there are some dangerous items I did not want him left alone with. He refused, closed his eyes to end communication, and stopped looking or communicating with either the mental health worker or myself. He was forcing a confrontation. At that point we could have waited him out, but we had already been talking for over an hour, and I could not give more time to this. We had to stop, and he had to leave the room. I called for more staff support. When he saw other staff arrive, he stormed out of the room, and started threatening people in the hallway. The charge nurse saw this, and insisted that he go to his room or the "comfort room" to calm down. He refused and continued to threaten people. Now we were in a full-blown confrontation. Tim became more aggressive and probably lost what was left of his capacity for rational thought. Staff then restrained him (that is, they tied him down to a bed with straps), an experience that was horrible for all of us.

He was released from restraint immediately after he settled down, and staff did a good job of processing the experience with him. Later, he apologized to me for "not listening" and I apologized to him for restraining him. I told him this made me very sad. He asked then to use the play station, but I again said "no." The new behavior plan, the one that staff made, was in effect until he and I could collaboratively develop a better plan. The current plan said he has to earn play station time. He asked to try to make a new plan, and I said yes, we would do that tomorrow. He insisted we do it now. I said we would do it tomorrow. I wanted to reinforce strengths, but I would not let him bully me. He started to argue and sulk, and I walked away.

The next day, he asked to use the play station again, but we were still following the current behavior plan and he had not earned it yet. I said "no." I could not meet with him that minute, but I offered to meet with him shortly afterward to develop a new plan. He became angry and noncommunicative for the next 2 hours. He went to his bed to sleep. I woke him up, and told him I was ready to meet to develop the new plan. I said our meeting was as an opportunity for us to work to solve our conflict. The goal was for both of us to use good listening and talking skills and to make a plan together. He got out of bed, and came with me to talk, but after our bad experience the previous day, I wanted to establish the right framework. I wanted him to work at having a successful conversation with me. He had no patience for this talk about talking, and wanted to get right to the plan. He then proceeded to tell me again how stupid the plan was and he added that I was stupid as well. I made it clear that we could only have a successful meeting if we followed certain rules, like listening to each other without insults or threats. Could he do that now? He begrudgingly agreed, and we actually were able to have, from my point of view, a fair conversation that did produce a draft new plan. That enabled me to give him credit for specific conflict resolution skills which I named (listening, problem solving, compromising, and so forth) and to praise him. Now we were back on track, I hoped.

The new plan worked for 2 days, during which time he earned a perfect score and got lots of praise. On the third day, we had a problem. The plan goals were safety, collaboration, and engagement. He got a point for each hour. However, he decided to avoid some activities and went to bed. He expected not to get a point for engagement, but we made the decision that he could not earn points for safety and collaboration while was sleeping. We had not anticipated the issue of how to evaluate him if he was asleep. He was unwilling to get up to discuss it, so staff made the decision, one-up, without him. When he finally got up and reviewed his score card, he became furious that he received a "0" in all categories while he was sleeping. He asked to meet with me, and when I came out, he launched into a tirade about how unfair this was and what a jerk I was. At that point, I stopped the meeting, but he refused to stop talking. When I walked away, he physically blocked my exit. This was clearly not OK.

Staff intervened and held him while I left the unit. He struggled with staff who, using tremendous skill, were able to avoid using mechanical restraints again and let him walk down to his room. He stormed away, slamming his door.

Although we had a plan that had worked for 2 days, we had a new issue to discuss: what were the rules about getting points while sleeping? This would require a conversation, and it had to be a *civil* conversation without threats or insults. The next day, we met with him three times to attempt to negotiate this issue. We told him that until we negotiated changes together, staff rules stayed in effect, but his opinion mattered. We preferred to work this out together. However, meetings must follow basic communication and safety rules. The first meeting this day was to discuss how to have a discussion. That took about an hour. We finally agreed on terms, but he did not follow them and escalated to new threats and insults. Each of our three meetings this day ended by either his storming out or our ending the session due to his threats and insults.

Could we find skills in these "bad" meetings? He did not assault anyone. There were productive moments in the conversations that could be commented on. I looked for opportunities to point out to him any examples of good communication skills he used. Meanwhile, Unit staff were increasingly frustrated with me. They saw me as not being firm or clear enough. They thought that these time-consuming attempts at negotiation were only letting him "get away with" abusive behaviors. A constraint on my own efforts at problem solving was that I was also trying to help Unit staff feel safe and protected. I reminded them, and myself, of the treatment principles we were using:

1. This work is about developing his coping and conflict resolution skills. Setting limits does not teach skills, and it usually triggers more explosive behaviors. Each crisis is an opportunity, and the many conversations we are having with him *are* the treatment.

2. Tim was in a pretreatment mentality. He was minimally engaged. We would accomplish nothing with him unless we engaged him in his own treatment.

3. Our emphasis must, therefore, be on pretreatment strategies. These include empathizing with him to the extent possible, looking for strengths and skills to comment on, promoting his self-evaluation, and striving for collaborative goal setting.

4. We would do one-up limit setting if necessary, but not as a first step. We must continuously offer him opportunities to work collaboratively, but if he could not or would not and his behavior was unsafe, we would use our authority and set limits. This must always be done in a spirit of regret that we are not able to work collaboratively at that

moment (*for example, we want to make treatment plans with you, not for you. We hope you'll be willing to work with us tomorrow.*).
5. We had to be careful so our own stress, anxiety, and rigidity did not push us into unnecessary limit setting when there were more skillful options available to us.

After a weekend break, I returned to work with new resolve. I was determined to find and comment on his positive skills if it killed me. But I was not going to let him bully me or other people.

I arrived with this hopeful frame of mind. Five minutes before I walked on the unit, there was a fire drill. All patients and staff on the Unit *must* collect at one place on the Unit during fire drills in case of a need to evacuate the building. This is nonnegotiable. When I stepped on to the Unit, I heard Tim screaming. Two staff had grabbed him and were carrying him down to the designated place, with him kicking, screaming, and attempting to bite them. He had refused to get up and even talk to staff. They had no choice but to take him forcefully down the Unit.

I decided I would not focus on this dangerous behavior immediately although I would, if I got the chance, challenge him to think through his choices. He wrote down on the daily schedule that he wanted to meet with me and his favorite mental health worker later in the day, in a private room in the back. This was meeting on his terms, but I agreed provided he followed the communication rules we set up. I repeated to him that either one of us could end the meeting if we wanted, and he nodded agreement. There was to be no blocking anyone from leaving as he did to me yesterday.

Before we sat with him, I coached the mental health worker on how we would make empathic comments. We would tell him that we understood he was unhappy, thought the rules were stupid, and wanted to be more independent, and we understood that he was trying to stay in control. In fact, most of the time, his behavior *was* safe. He did use some coping skills. He used humor well. We could even see how sleeping, for him, was an attempt to stay in control. He listened to us, and then he brought up the subject of the fire alarm. He was having a nice dream when the alarm woke him up, he said. The alarm should not be sound based. It should be visual only. It was stupid to have fire alarms. We should just remind people what to do once a month. The escape route was on the wrong side of the hall. He knew it was not a real fire. The people who came to get him up were idiots. And so on.

We stopped and pointed out to him that he had resumed insulting people. We asked him to rate the meeting so far. He gave it a thumbs up. We both gave it a thumbs middle, and expressed our concern that the meeting was becoming unproductive. He continued arguing about the alarm, the Unit rules, our approach with him. I watched with amazement how determined he was to argue, no matter what we said or did. He even argued when we agreed with him. Finally, he escalated his insults. He told the mental health worker that he "should go back to school" and "get a new head." We labeled those as insults and left the room. The best I could say was that he allowed us to leave and did not blow up about it. That was the only progress I saw at that moment.

The next day Tim's behavior was even worse. He refused to join any therapeutic activities. He refused to talk with any staff person. He stayed in his room sleeping, and when staff came over he pushed them away and gave them the finger. He watched some television, but he would not engage with any staff person on any issue of importance.

My own credibility with my team and their openness to this new approach were sinking fast. They were increasingly vocal about the need to set clear limits, and I felt increasingly compelled to agree. Our attempts at collaboration were failing. Tim was not a partner. We therefore made a series of executive decisions without him. The decision that mattered to him most was restricting his privileges. He had barged into the kitchen, pushing aside two peers and disregarding staff directives, so we put the kitchen off limits to him. We dropped his privileges further. We told him again that he was refusing our efforts at collaboration, and we had no choice but to set these rules. We also told him again that we preferred we solve these issues together, and we would keep trying.

Tim's response to each new restriction was predictable. He argued fiercely that it was not fair. He insisted he had been willing to talk all along. He blamed other people. Because once he started arguing, he would continue endlessly, we had to end several conversations before he was ready. I ended two conversations when he would not stop arguing and insulting us. The first time I ended the conversation and walked away, he just let me. The second time, he grabbed a paper off the desk to tear up, stormed down the corridor to his room, threw a laundry cart down the hall, and slammed his door three times. We let him calm himself down. About a half hour later, he came out of his room into the milieu, and he was surprisingly pleasant the rest of the day. He was aware, at that point, that we expected him to engage with us, and that failing that, he had no privileges. He appeared to be making an effort.

The next day, suddenly, Tim moved from pretreatment to treatment. He got up on time, took his medicine without a problem, and joined therapeutic groups he had not attended before. In the groups he was silly and mildly disruptive but engaged. As he started showing some skills, staff pounced on these moments, noting the skills and praising him. At a coping skills group in which we played a game of "guess the coping skill" he role-played the difficult skill of "change your point of view." He role-played himself blowing up, then literally stepping outside of his skin to see himself blow up, and telling himself to calm down. It was an amazing display I never imagined he was capable of, suggesting intelligence beyond that reflected in his language skills. Naturally, we praised him lavishly for this skillful work.

Then we sat down to review a new plan, designed to be easy and maximize successes but still establishing expectations for safety, skill acquisition, and engagement. He argued for a while over some minor points and then agreed to the plan. Each time he showed more skills, we noted these, labeled the skills, and praised him. Within a day he had his privileges back and was set up for some more enjoyable activities with adolescent peers.

The new plan required him to take medicine, stay safe, engage in an agreed set of therapeutic activities, and avoid disrespectful behaviors. If he did this, he would get his privilege level back up quickly, and we would discharge him in 2 weeks, after a successful pass. The amazing thing was that Tim's attitude and behavior changed very rapidly at this point. For the next 2 weeks, he met all the criterion goals and was reasonably pleasant most of the time. He was discharged back to his program as planned.

What happened? Why did he change his behavior so rapidly? Tim thought it was the medicine but we knew it could not be. The medicine did not act that quickly. It might be his belief about the medicine, a placebo effect. We did not want Tim attributing his progress to anything but his own skills, attitude, and choices. We explained that it could not be the medicine, and he agreed. It must be his use of skills.

Many staff believed the decisive factor was our willingness finally to set firm limits with him. I agreed that he needed to be up against a limit, but I argued that limits would not have resulted in this turnaround if we had not tried so stubbornly to engage him in collaborative problem solving and reinforce every positive skill he showed.

In retrospect, I think we could have done even better by him. I think we could have done better work during his first week, when he showed more positive behaviors, of commenting on his skills and strengths. I think we could have avoided the restraint by not forcing him to leave the room when the meeting was over. If we had the patience, we could have just posted a person by the door, and he would have walked out on his own eventually. The problem at that moment was that I was too emotionally dysregulated to recognize the wiser course of action. I also think that we made a mistake by not initially giving him points for safety even while he was sleeping. We could have done that just once while raising with him the problem of how we define safety. Our behavior plan also made the mistake of forcing him to earn use of the play station, something which might have been his chief coping skill. Could we have built on that skill by, for instance, recognizing and naming it as a skill, and having him teach others the skill?* If he had agreed to that, then he would presumably have been demonstrating other social skills, and we could in turn have built on these. Even the fire alarm incident could have been handled differently, if not in the moment of the alarm, at least in the aftermath. When he

---

* I thank Donald Meichenbaum for this helpful suggestion.

started to voice his complaints about the procedure, perhaps we could have assisted him in sending his complaints to the hospital administration. That would have potentially turned this into an opportunity for him to do some assertive but nonaggressive communicating. The Deaf Unit team felt I was too flexible with him, but I felt I was too rigid. Tim's manner felt to most of us to be bullying, and this made it difficult to collaborate with him without thinking that we were allowing him to intimidate us.

What we unquestionably did well was to continuously strive for a collaborative process and only retreat from that temporarily, and with expressed regret. We kept returning to try again, giving him the message that *we will work with you as soon as you are willing.* Once he started showing positive behaviors, we pounced on these, affirming them, and this helped create an upward spiral of escalating improved behaviors. We started constructing the story together about his skills, his ability to control himself in spite of bad things that have happened to him and many staff behaviors he believed were unfair. With this positive framework established, his attendance to groups improved and his participation became more meaningful. He started using conflict resolution and coping skills groups to demonstrate skills. We then saw a change in his vocabulary. During his discharge conference, he spoke to his school personnel about coping and conflict resolution skills. He left the Unit with an experience defined by all of us as success, and with the language of skills to map the way to future progress.

The struggles we had with Tim were challenging mainly because of his stubborn unwillingness to talk. Otherwise, they were representative of the kinds of interpersonal conflicts that occur between staff and clients in mental health and rehabilitation programs, especially with oppositional adolescents. Tim's conflicts were mainly with staff, but other clients just as frequently have conflicts with each other. Clients may fight over a limited resource like television, the play station, or the videophone. They provoke and antagonize each other. Conflicts with staff are often over rules and expectations or are responses to staff limit setting (for example, *You didn't get the privilege you wanted. You can't be discharged right now. It's time to get out of bed*). Clients may perceive staff as arbitrary, unfair, strict, bossy, or mean, and sometimes there is truth in their perceptions. Often they misperceive staff intentions as do staff theirs.

Whether we make conflict resolution an explicit component of our treatment program or not, staff will be confronted with an endless series of these conflicts. In traditional paternalistic mental health settings, conflicts are resolved by staff using their authority. Staff settle conflicts over television shows and other matters. Staff set the rules, decide who is right and wrong, and reward desired behaviors. I think it is fair to say that most staff persons perceive these daily conflicts to be problems they wish would go away. They think that clients *should* behave themselves. Yet each conflict is an opportunity for skill building. There is the old saying about the importance of teaching a man to fish rather than just giving him a plate of food. Each time staff take the initiative to solve a conflict *for* others, they deprive them of this opportunity to "learn to fish." They also reinforce for clients the idea that they are powerless and dependent on other people. *Solving problems for people does not pull them into treatment. It pulls them into conflicts with the problem solvers.*

Helping clients learn skills takes much more competence than doing things for them. It also requires the psychological willingness to let people grow rather than keep them dependent. Teaching conflict resolution skills to LLC clients is a formidable challenge. In some ways, it is similar to the work of teaching these skills to young children except that our clients are older, bigger, stronger, more entrenched in bad habits, and able to do more damage. Adults also have more reasons *not* to work with us than children do.

Interpersonal conflicts are the stuff of life. Like emotions, they cannot be avoided. We sometimes tell clients that feelings like anger or depression are not problems if one has the coping skills to manage them. Similarly, interpersonal conflicts are not problems for people who are skilled in conflict resolution. In our treatment work, and in our lives, we will always face one conflict after another. But do we intentionally develop in ourselves and our clients the skills to manage this stuff of life?

Nonviolent conflict resolution can be broken down into "microskills" (Ivey, 1971). To understand these microskills, it will help to summarize several popular approaches to nonviolent conflict resolution. To understand how these skills develop, it will also help us to summarize some approaches to teaching these skills to children. This will enable us develop a vocabulary for conflict resolution and the ability to perceive the developmental precursors to more advanced skills.

Marshall Rosenberg: Nonviolent Communication

NVC, developed by Marshall Rosenberg (Leu, 2003; Rosenberg, 2003; Rosenberg, 2005) is an approach to conflict resolution that places heavy emphasis on helping people develop effective communication skills. Training in NVC is essentially training in good communication. People are helped to express their own feelings and underlying needs and hear those of people with whom they are in conflict. Communication patterns that interfere with a "compassionate connection with oneself" and an empathic connection with others are targeted for elimination.

The NVC process has four steps:

1. Observing without evaluating.
2. Expressing feelings and understanding the feelings of others.
3. Identifying the met or unmet needs underlying the feelings.
4. Making concrete, specific requests (not demands) for "that which would enrich life."

This is summarized even more briefly as: *observation, feeling, needs,* and *requests.* All four components require skilled communication.

The first skill is to communicate *cleanly,* in neutral language, without judging or labeling other people. In the words of Detective Friday on the old television sitcom *Dragnet,* we want *just the facts.* Rosenberg (2003) describes and gives examples of forms of communication which block compassion such as:

1. Language that leads to moralistic judgments:
   "She's lazy." "They're racist." "That's inappropriate."
2. Language that invokes comparisons:
   "John does that better than you."
   "I never had this kind of problem with Sally."
   "Nobody else has a problem with this."
   "Why can't you do as well as your sister?"
3. Language that denies responsibility:
   "You made me angry."
   "I had to do it."
   "I drink because I'm an alcoholic."
   "I hit my child because he ran into the streets."
   "I started smoking because all my friends did it."
   "I was overcome by an urge that I couldn't control."
4. Language that attributes problems to basic character traits, especially those implying goodness or badness:
   "He deserves to be punished."
   "She's a bad person."
   "You are just a psychopath."
   "He's a terrorist."

In psychiatric treatment settings, one can hear staff at all levels of the organization, until they have been sensitized to this problem, using evaluative judgments that block compassion for clients. For instance, staff report not on what clients have done but on what their behaviors apparently meant. Clients or their behaviors are described as "manipulative," "needy," "demanding," "controlling," "aggressive," "paranoid," "borderline," or "inappropriate." People are labeled by the name for their disorder—for example, a "schizophrenic" rather than a "person with schizophrenia," or (better), "a person who meets criteria for schizophrenia." The training staff are given to help them make observations and write clinical notes in a neutral, objective way also helps them develop the communication skills needed to resolve conflicts. For instance, an untrained staff person might write in a patient's chart, "At dinner, John was argumentative, hostile and paranoid." Staff with more advanced communication skills might write, "John complained that he didn't like the food served at dinner and he insisted on being served cereal. He then pushed by two staff people to get into the kitchen, grabbed the cereal off the shelf, grabbed milk from the refrigerator, and took these outside. When staff approached him, he closed his eyes and looked away, refusing to engage."

With clients this skill can be called *describe calmly what happened*. It is presented on the skill card with four additional pictures that advise (Figure 6.1): *no insults, no threats, no blame, no criticize*. Usually clients who are arguing use harshly judgmental language. The task for staff is to point this out to them and to coach them to use neutral language.

Client: Jim is a jerk. I hate him.
Staff: Do you want to tell me what happened? I want to know the story, what he did and what you did. I don't want to hear insults or criticism. Just say what happened and then we'll see if we can solve the problem.

This usually takes quite a bit of coaching, but when the appropriate neutral language is finally used, staff can point this out and label it.

Client: Jim stuck out his tongue, gave me the finger, and told me to "shut up."
Staff: Now you are describing clearly what happened. Now I understand.

DESCRIBE CALMLY WHAT HAPPENED

NO INSULTS   **NO THREATS**

NO BLAME   **NO CRITICIZE**

Figure 6.1 Describe calmly what happened.

The second step of NVC is expressing feelings, and listening emphatically for feelings in others, without attacking, blaming, criticizing, or devaluing them. It involves saying, "I feel angry" without adding "because you are obnoxious." It involves being able to hear the anger that another person expresses without immediately criticizing them (for example, *"That's ridiculous. You shouldn't feel that way. What a stupid idea!"*). Expressing and labeling feelings, as we saw, is also a core coping skill.

Most mental health professionals encourage clients to identify, label, and communicate their feelings. As I discussed in Chapter 4, this is a skill inherent in the value system promoted by the mental health industry. In conflict resolution work, we are not aiming for an emotional catharsis. We are not striving just for the skill of self-expression but rather for the skill of expressing feelings in a way that is safe and enables others to hear our concerns. This is definitely not about "letting it all out" but rather of communicating skillfully.

A sample skill card says *express feelings safely* (Figure 6.2). We adapt this skill to the developmental level of clients. For some clients, identification of basic emotions (happy, sad, angry, nervous) is the goal. For others, it is the development of a much larger emotional vocabulary. Emotions can be named or, more advanced, rated on a scale (for example, rate how happy you feel, 0 to 10). Identification of basic emotions can lead to identification of shades of emotions, many of which are conveyed in ASL through intensifications or modifications of the sign for the emotion.

This work also involves helping clients distinguish feelings like anger from behaviors like hitting. It is consistent with a message that we communicate that *feelings are to be accepted while behaviors are to be controlled.*

Besides naming one's own emotions, we want to promote the skill of recognizing and naming emotions in other people, especially people with whom one is in conflict. Recognizing emotions in other people is a foundational

EXPRESS FEELINGS SAFELY

Figure 6.2 A sample skill card.

microskill to the development of empathy, crucial for conflict resolution. Sometimes clients will show empathy for other persons without naming actual feelings. For instance, one person is crying and another offers some kind of support. This moment of empathy should be noticed and commented on. *It seems you noticed how John feels. How did you notice that? What do you think he feels? And then you gave him support, patting him on the back. You used skills in noticing someone else's feelings and giving support. Where did you learn those skills from? Do you know that those are exactly the skills we use in conflict resolution?*

The most common formula used in teaching people to communicate feelings better is called, "I statements" ("When you do X, I feel Y") (Figure 6.3). In this case, the behavior or trigger is described neutrally, and the feeling is also described, but without attributing causality. Embedded in this statement is the ability to recognize cause and effect, which clients may not have. Recognizing needs is the third step of NVC, and in NVC the "I statement" formula is extended to include needs. *When you do X, I*

Figure 6.3 Simple "I" statement.

feel Y, because my need for Z is or is not met. This is pretty sophisticated psychologically, and with some clients, the two step, *"When you do X, I feel Y"* may represent the limits of which they are capable.

Unfortunately, needs and wants are easy to confuse. Indeed, in Ellis's rational emotive behavior therapy (Ellis, 1962), clarifying how desires or wishes are *different from* needs is a key therapeutic strategy. Rosenberg believes that emotions are expressions of whether or not underlying needs have been met. NVC helps people clarify feelings from needs and then make simple, positive requests to have needs met. Some basic human needs that Rosenberg lists are autonomy, integrity, celebration, interdependence, play, spiritual communion, and physical nurturance. Rosenberg says that because all human needs are universal, it can be easier to solve conflicts if we can relate our emotions to these underlying needs. For instance, people in conflict may feel anger and fear toward each other. Simply expressing these feelings can be useful, but it is more likely to lead to conflict resolution if the underlying needs are understood. "I need to have control over my life, and when you behave in an aggressive manner with me, I feel fear that you are taking away my control. I then feel angry with you." *Other examples of this are as follows:* "I feel angry because when you insult me, my need for self-respect is frustrated." "I feel sad because when you ended our relationship, my need for intimacy was undermined." "I feel embarrassed because I have a need to think of myself as a person with integrity and you've exposed ways in which I've acted deceitfully."

The ability to distinguish feelings and needs and the ability to relate them and then express the connection clearly are advanced psychological skills. They require intact language and capacity for abstract, rational thought. Our LLC clients cannot usually do this in a sophisticated way but they may be able to demonstrate developmental precursors of this skill. If we listen well, we may sometimes hear "I statements" expressed unselfconsciously (for example, PICK-ON-ME FINISH. I DON'T-LIKE. *Stop picking on me. I don't like it*). Whenever our clients state in clear neutral terms what they do not like, without adding insults or threats, they are demonstrating simple variants of this skill. Our job is to help catch these moments, amplify them, and give them a name. The label of "I statements" can work well, if explained.

Amy was upset with Joe because she felt he was dominating the TV. He had the football game on for the last hour and she wanted to watch a movie. After stewing with her feelings for the hour, she went over to the TV and abruptly changed the channel. Predictably, Joe got up, grabbed the remote from her, and switched it back. It looked like a fight was about to start, but a skilled staff person intervened, calmed them down, and then asked them if they were willing to talk. After they agreed, Joe said that he was watching the TV, bothering no one, when Amy changed the channel without asking. Asked how he felt, he replied "mad." When it was Amy's turn, she signed that Joe watched the football game for an hour, and it was now her turn. She felt mad too. So far, they have each actually communicated with some skill. Both said what the other did that they did not like, and both identified how they felt in response. The staff person interrupted them before they started insulting or getting physical with each other, so he was able to praise them for showing "express feelings safely skills." He then asked them how they can solve this problem so both are happy.

The final step of NVC is to make requests for "that which enriches life." The most important elements of this step are to distinguish requests from demands and to phrase requests positively (what I would like you to do) rather than negatively (what I do not want you to do). In a typical conflict, participants usually make negative demands like "Stop bothering me!" "Stop your racist behaviors!" In NVC, the language is cleaned up to remove judgments, the underlying need (perhaps for safety, autonomy, or self-respect) is identified, and a specific positive request is made ("what I'd like you to do is listen to me, try to understand my perspective, and take some time before responding.")

The fourth step can be simplified as *Do not demand it. Ask for what you want. Say please* (Figure 6.4). Even when clients do not understand their underlying needs and confuse their needs and desires, they can still be helped to demonstrate the conflict resolution skill of requesting rather than demanding. They can be helped to request what they want others to do, not what they

DON'T DEMAND IT

ASK FOR WHAT YOU WANT
SAY PLEASE

Figure 6.4 Do not demand it. Ask for what you want. Say please.

do not want them to do. They can be helped to make specific, doable requests (*please listen to me when I talk*) rather than vague requests (*please support me*). Again, clients sometimes do this unprompted, and those opportunities should be seized.

The staff person cited above asked Amy to make a request of Joe. With some coaching, Amy was able to ask Joe for her turn with the TV. Joe's initial response was "no," but with some skillful coaching, they were able to negotiate a compromise. Then the staff person, sitting with Amy, helped her see how much more skillful her request was than just abruptly changing the channel. He also praised Joe for his listening, discussing, and taking turns skills.

Dudley Weeks: Conflict Partnership

Dudley Weeks (1992) developed a method of conflict resolution he calls the "conflict partnership approach." A hallmark of this approach is the attention paid to the enhancing of relationships of combatants through the conflict resolution process.

Weeks distinguishes three levels of conflict resolution. The top level "is reached when parties in conflict come to a resolution that meets some individual and shared needs, results in mutual benefits, and strengthens the relationship" (p. 10). This can be considered WIN-WIN-WIN with the third win referring to the enhancement of the relationship. The middle level, which can be thought of as WIN-WIN (Figure 6.5), "is reached when parties at odds come to some mutually acceptable agreements that settle a particular conflict for the time being, but that do little to enhance the relationship beyond immediate concerns." Each of the parties gets something, and in that sense *wins*, but their relationship is not changed. The least beneficial level of conflict resolution "is reached when one party conquers or submits to the demands

WIN-WIN SITUATION
"WORK TOGETHER FOR FAIR SOLUTION"

Figure 6.5 Win-win attitude.

of the other or when the relationship is dissolved with mutual damage." This level could be considered WIN-LOSE or LOSE-LOSE.

Weeks refers to participants in a conflict not as opponents but as "conflict partners." This reflects his framework of seeing people in conflict as involved in the task of enhancing their relationship as well as solving problems. Conflict partners are not enemies to be defeated. The framework normalizes conflict and sees it as an opportunity to develop skills. Conflicts, therefore, are not to be feared or avoided but rather are to be welcomed, provided people approach them with the right attitude and necessary skills.

For Weeks, the skills used to resolve a conflict are the same skills needed to develop relationships. They include the ability to listen well to the other party, discern each party's perceptions, feelings, and needs, and understand and validate the perception of one's *conflict partner*. As with NVC, really good listening is the core component of this. Conflict partners are also helped to focus on the needs they share and on what their relationship needs. For instance, labor and management share the need to work together in a peaceful, mutually respectful, safe, and productive environment. If either labor or management wins a lopsided victory that harms the other, their relationship will suffer as will the long-term viability of their worksite. Similarly, combatants in global conflicts share the need to live in peace after the war is over. History is filled with examples of lopsided victories in which one side demolishes the other only to have the vanquished side rise again and seek revenge. The Allies' defeat of Germany during World War I, and its infliction of revenge, comes to mind; and it contrasts with the Allies' defeat of Germany and Japan during World War II. In the latter instance, the Allies rebuilt defeated Germany and Japan, and the result was they became new allies.

Weeks wants conflict partners to develop *shared positive power* which is power *with* one's partner to solve problems in a mutually desirable way. Conflict partners are expected to work as hard for the interests of one's partner as for oneself. For example, people in conflict at a community project may bring their entire enterprise into disarray by trying to defeat the other. When they work in a mutually enhancing way, their larger enterprise will usually benefit. The process of really listening to, appreciating the point of view of, and respecting one's conflict partner can only enhance a relationship, bringing people together and creating opportunities for unforeseen benefits.

How do we draw on such a terrific, perhaps idealistic approach with our clients? The idea of WIN-WIN-WIN may be useful for those clients who can understand it. Less abstract is the concept of WIN-WIN. The conflict partnership approach may be helpful to staff in orienting them toward welcoming conflicts as opportunities for skill development in all parties. Much of the stress associated with conflicts has to do with the idea that there *should not* be conflicts or that they are caused by other people who are bad. Welcoming conflicts as opportunities for people to grow and get closer is difficult but not impossible and creates a much less stressful dynamic. Put most simply, conflicts are opportunities to use skills (and develop relationships). A positive attitude is crucial. This is reflected in the "We can solve conflict!" skill card shown below (Figure 6.6).

The conflict resolution process eventually gets down to practicalities like generating options (brainstorming) and developing what Weeks calls

See conflict, use skill to solve.

Figure 6.6 We can solve conflict.

"doables." Doables are actions that have a good chance of being accomplished, do not favor one party at the expense of the other, meet shared needs, and build trust, momentum, and confidence in the conflict partners (p. 206). Doables are considered "stepping stones" to making "mutual benefit decisions." Weeks's discussion of doables is comparable to Rosenberg's discussion of making requests for that which enhances life. These are the nuts and bolts of conflict resolution that more sophisticated people understand to be part of that process. With our clients, any suggestions that anyone has about how to proceed can be considered a developmentally simpler version of this skill. A client says, "We can take turns" or "We can put up a sign up sheet." The client has just demonstrated *good idea skills,* or in Weeks's words, doables.

Bernard Mayer: Attitude Is Everything

Bernard Mayer (Mayer, 2000) goes even farther than Weeks in stressing the importance of the attitude one brings to the conflict resolution process. He argues that the underlying attitude of the participants is much more important than any particular communication skill.

> Good communication stems from intention not technique. If people put their full and focused energy into communicating, they can make lots of mistakes and still be effective. Conversely, no communication technique will substitute for a lack of commitment and a desire to hear or to be understood. (p. 120)

Rather than focus on communication techniques, Mayer describes attitudinal principles that are the basis of successful communication:

1. Caring about what others are saying is the key to good communication.
2. There is always new information to learn from a communication.
3. Good communication requires focused energy.
4. Effective communication requires a joint effort between speaker and listener.
5. Communicating is different from persuading, evaluating, and problem solving.
6. Tolerance of people's difficulty in communicating (including your own) is essential.
7. The best communication occurs when people are genuine and natural.

Both Weeks and Mayer put more faith in the attitude one brings to conflict resolution than specific conflict resolution techniques. Many LLC clients have difficulty understanding these principles and stepping back from the conflicts to consider the advantages of conflict resolution. On the other hand, I have witnessed many instances in which very unskilled communicators solved conflicts to their satisfaction because they wanted to. Children do this when they flip a coin or use "rock, paper, scissors" with their fingers. They do not necessarily understand the underlying principles but they are motivated to solve conflicts with each other.

Three clients work out a solution for what store they will go to on a Unit trip. Another client agrees to a plan for four cigarette breaks rather than eight. Two roommates agree on how they will arrange their room. Two other clients are in conflict over who gets to sit in the front seat of the car. The staff gives them a gentle prod to solve this on their own, and they decide that one will have the front on the way there and the other on the way back. In these situations, clients succeed more because of their attitudes than specific skills. Our pretreatment work consists of noticing and capturing these moments of "primitive" conflict resolution, framing them as skills, and noting also the attitude that made such success possible. "Why did you solve this conflict? Because you wanted to! Did you notice the skills you used? You listened to each other, came up with a plan and agreed on the plan. You did this with a positive attitude. Awesome!"

Fisher and Ury: Getting to Yes

The conflict resolution skills we have reviewed so far are components of the negotiation that occurs, at much more sophisticated levels, in international business and politics. Although our interest here is on simple skills, it is helpful to understand more advanced negotiation. Fisher and Ury (1981) wrote a popular book on negotiations skills. One of their main distinctions is between positions and interests. Positions are what you say you want (for example, labor says it wants 5% increase in wages and management says it wants no increase and to pay less for employee health insurance). Interests are the underlying needs (for example, both labor and management have underlying needs for financial security and a stable, successful work environment). Good negotiators learn to separate positions from interests. This is very similar to Rosenberg's distinction between wants and needs. Conflict resolution is more likely to occur when people can step back from arbitrary demands and analyze what they and their conflict partners really need.

Fisher and Ury present a method that also helps negotiators deal with distracting personality problems. Conflicts occur not only because people and institutions have different interests but because people are unskilled. Personality and relationship problems become entangled with the real problems. Negotiation requires skill at sifting through these distracting personal difficulties to look objectively at how interests may be reconciled. They also advocate for generating a variety of possible answers before deciding (brainstorming) and using objective criteria for making resolutions.

Conflict Resolution Skills in Dialectical Behavior Therapy

Conflict resolution skills are addressed in DBT but indirectly, without being named as such (Linehan, 1993b). The interpersonal effectiveness skill training module, which could just as easily be called social skills training or assertiveness training, teaches clients a variety of strategies for "asking for what one needs, saying no, and coping with interpersonal conflict" (p. 70). This module is also "most properly considered a course in assertion, where the goal is for persons to assert their own wishes, goals, and opinions in a manner that causes other people to take them seriously" (p. 70). Linehan chose to emphasize assertiveness training as the key interpersonal skill rather than conflict resolution skills. Nonetheless, we can find embedded in her assertiveness skills many of the components of nonviolent conflict resolution. For instance, she organizes the main components of assertiveness under the acronym DEAR MAN.

Describe
Express
Assert
Reinforce
(stay) **M**indful
Appear confident
Negotiate

The DEAR components essentially refer to clean communication. It is another way of teaching people to describe in objective terms what is happening, say what they want or need, make a request for an action, and let the other person know why they may want to comply. She does not include the skills involved in listening well. With our LLC clients, we need to attend to developing their listening skills more intentionally than Linehan does.*

The next acronym Linehan uses is GIVE, referring to skills designed to preserve relationships.

(be) **G**entle
(act) **I**nterested
Validate
(use an) **E**asy manner

The GIVE skills' focus on relationship certainly coincides with the works of Mayer and Weeks. Linehan has incorporated many skills relevant to conflict resolution without making it her focus. Her emphasis on assertiveness training, as opposed to this emphasis on nonviolent conflict resolution, seems to me misplaced. As I discussed in Chapter 5, her approach, including this interpersonal effectiveness module, also suffers from unnecessary complexity. Rosenberg covers much of the same ground more clearly. Based on our review

---

* At a training session by Dr. Linehan that I attended in July 2007, she stated her intention to add "mindfulness to other people" to upcoming revisions of her skill training modules. This might well address this deficiency in her approach.

of this relevant literature, we can create an even more simple and straightforward list of the microskills of conflict resolution. We can get clues of how to do this by studying how it has been done with children.

Conflict Resolution With Children

Having surveyed some of the key ideas in nonviolent conflict resolution skill training with adults, we turn to explore how these same ideas are developed in children. In the next few works, we see that the focus is on developmentally simpler microskills and on the use of creative teaching and counseling techniques. This helps us appreciate the usefulness of a developmental approach to skill training with LLC clients. We conceptualize and teach the skills in a manner that matches their language and cognitive abilities.

Naomi Drew's *The Kids Guide to Working Out Conflicts* (Drew, 2004) is a self-help book directed at 10- to 15-year-olds. The book is organized into eight steps which are ostensibly about conflict resolution but actually cover a broader array of psychosocial skills. Like all good books directed at young people, it is formatted well with lots of pictures, cartoons, and other insets that break up the pages and make them more readable. Drew draws heavily on stories, includes many simple activities that promote self-examination, and presents many simple self-help tools such as self-monitoring forms.

The first two steps are the equivalent of pretreatment work. They focus, as do Weeks and Mayer, on the development of attitudes conducive to conflict resolution.

Step 1, *Open your mind*, involves fostering willingness to be a conflict solver. Common conflicts for boys and girls are listed; and the advantages and disadvantages of becoming a conflict solver are described. Readers are encouraged to examine their own blocks to becoming a conflict solver and then are asked to describe some of the common triggers to their conflict responses. The metaphor of deciding to be in either the basement (continuing nasty conflicts) or balcony (behaving with respect and dignity to solve conflicts) is given and is illustrated with pictures.

Step 2 includes more stories about effective and noneffective conflict resolution, encourages readers to examine further their typical response to conflict, and provides more reasons to become a conflict solver. Drew distinguishes the interventions designed for people who have not yet signed on to becoming conflict solvers from those designed for people who have. She understands that there is a separate process that needs to occur to engage, educate, and motivate students into this skill-building work. Teaching the actual skills depends on willingness of the students to learn them.

In Step 3, readers are taught the basic components of good listening. These include the nonverbal behaviors, communication styles, and attitudes that

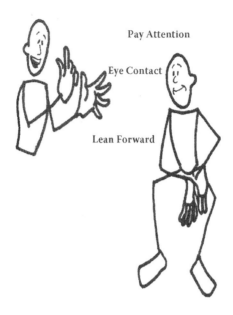

Figure 6.7 Nonverbal aspects of attending.

foster listening. Two games are presented to practice listening skills and more stories of good listening are presented. As with the work of Rosenberg and Weeks, communication skills are understood to be the core elements of successful conflict resolution. Nonverbal listening skills are also easy to represent with pictorial examples (Figure 6.7).

Step 4 presents much of the "meat" of conflict resolution. It presents six steps and five rules that provide a simple, clear WIN-WIN structure. Many story examples and practice exercises are provided including exercises to develop skill in making "I statements." Her WIN-WIN guidelines and rules, designed for young people, are well conceptualized.

WIN–WIN Guidelines

1. *Cool off.*
2. *Talk the problem over using I-messages.*
   How you feel.
   Why you feel that way.
   What you want or need.
3. *Listen while the other person speaks, and say back what you heard.*
4. *Take responsibility for your part in the conflict.*
5. *Brainstorm solutions and choose one that is fair to both of you.*
6. *Affirm, forgive, thank, or apologize to each other.*

WIN–WIN Rules

1. *Tell the truth.*
2. *Be respectful.*
3. *Attack the problem, not the person.*
4. *No blaming, no name-calling, and no negative face or body language.*
5. *Work together toward a fair solution* (p. 51).

Step 5 moves into basic anger management strategies, most of which we would include under coping skills. Readers are asked to examine how they typically handle anger and are educated about the fight or flight response. They are taught skills like *Stop-Breathe-Chill*, which is very similar to the *Red, Yellow, Green* skill discussed in Chapter 5. A key skill is stopping and noticing that anger has been triggered (the red light), breathing (the yellow light), and then considering how one can respond skillfully (the green light). The metaphor of "peace shield" and "light shield" is used to help people imagine themselves protected from other people's negativity. In Chapter 5, we discussed the use of a similar shield skill, developed from Jacobs (1992).

Step 6 connects stress management to conflict resolution and teaches a variety of basic stress management coping strategies: visualization, empowering imagery, physical exercise, activities that increase self-confidence, yoga, and meditation.

Step 7 teaches the difference between teasing and bullying, reviews the impact of bullying, encourages self-examination regarding whether one is engaging in bullying, and presents guidelines for responding to bullying in others.

Step 8 presents a day-to-day action plan, encourages people to strengthen their "courage and forgiveness muscles," promotes self-examination, and encourages people to seek out role models.

One cannot read Drew's wonderful book without being impressed by the simplicity and clarity of her language, as well as her creative use of metaphor, stories, therapeutic activities, and games. We find this also in the next works reviewed. These techniques are readily embraced by clinicians working with children, but for some reason clinicians working with adults are often much more reticent to use them.

William Kreidler (1984, 1990, 1994) was a leader in the field of teaching nonviolent conflict resolution in what he called the "peaceable classroom." His books, written for teachers, counselors, and parents, present hundreds of interesting stories and activities designed to develop these skills in children and teenagers. Kreidler's key insight was to understand that these skills must be taught in a developmentally appropriate manner. Children learn through play, engaging activities, powerful stories, and, of course, through appropriate modeling by adults. Kathleen Hollenbeck (2001, 2003) followed his lead and presented additional "conflict resolution activities that work." She also presented "easy to read folk tale plays to teach conflict resolution," designed for students to perform in the classroom. To illustrate these techniques, I selected a few of Kreidler's activities from his 1984 work.

1. Students tell the story of a conflict using the "once upon a time" format, stop at the point of conflict, and ask the class for suggestions on how to resolve it.

2. Students are taught a method for "fair fighting" consisting of three steps and then helped to practice. The three steps are:
   - State the facts as calmly as possible. Refer only to the present situation, not the past or future.
   - Express how you feel without making negative remarks about the other person.
   - Find out what you can do about the situation. Try to think of a solution that will satisfy everyone.

3. Students role-play a conflict and then switch sides, role playing the adversary.

4. Students select cards with various problem behaviors and then discuss, in small groups, possible consequences. Note the use of "pick a card" as an engagement strategy.

5. Students put conflicts and successful resolution into comic strips that they draw.

6. In "superheroes for peace," students draw a superhero, give the hero a name, describe the power he or she has, and discuss how he or she solves conflicts. A related activity is "supervillains." Students draw supervillains and discuss how they start conflicts. They compare these with real-life conflicts and discuss what they would do if they met the supervillain.

7. To improve communication skills, students are shown a movie, but at an important moment the movie is stopped and students are asked to give an eyewitness account of what they saw. They can also be asked to give an account as a Martian would (that is, someone without any of the biases and frames of reference of human beings; a true neutral observer).

8. To help students handle anger, frustration, and avoid aggression, they are asked to list 10 things that "bug" them, rank-order them, compare all the level one items, and discuss ways to handle what "bugs" them. They are asked to list ways to express anger and then discuss how dangerous, hurtful, and effective each way is.

9. Students are given a difficult task like stacking up rows of 15 pennies or building a house of cards, and then discuss how they handle the frustration when the stacks or cards collapse.

10. Kreidler draws heavily on "cooperative games" where the group must work together to succeed. For instance, in a balloon freeze, students must keep a large number of balloons in the air at the same time. In

monster making, they must work together to design and construct a monster. In Aboard the Mayflower, a group must agree on what 10 items they can bring on board their boat to the new world. Additional cooperative games can be found in MacGregor (1998).

11. To teach tolerance, students are told stories about name-calling, scapegoating, and discrimination and assisted to analyze the stories and consider how they could behave differently.

Foundation Conflict Resolution Microskills

Based on the literature we reviewed, I present here a list of conflict resolution foundation microskills. This is not intended to be a finished list. One can always add more skills or break them down in a new way. Nor is it important what name we give to the skill with the caveat that we should use everyday language, not professional jargon. Most of these skills are presented in pictorial form on the CD-ROM accompanying this volume.

1. **Noticing and Naming the Conflict. Seeking Peaceful Ways to Solve It**
   - The ability to understand what a conflict is
   - The ability to notice that a conflict is happening
   - The ability to realize that the conflict provides an opportunity to use a skill
   - The ability to name what the conflict is about
   - The ability to see the value in solving a conflict peacefully

2. **Foundation Communication Skills**
   - Eye contact, leaning forward, paying attention
   - The ability to notice and name what you feel
   - The ability to notice and name what you want
   - Listening to the other person without interrupting
   - One person talking, then the other
   - Expressing feelings safely, without threats or assaults
   - Repeating back what the other person just said
   - Describing calmly what happened; no insults, threats, blaming, or criticizing
   - Making simple "I statements"
   - Trying to understand what the other person feels
   - Asking for help

3. **Foundation Negotiation Skills**
   - Discussing with an open mind. Trying to solve problems
   - Simple conflict resolution methods: flipping a coin, taking turns, voting, seeking assistance from an authority
   - Accepting when one loses

- Brainstorming, or the ability to consider many possible options for a solution
- Weighing pros and cons
- Compromising
- Asking for what you want. Not demanding
- Saying you are sorry
- Accepting an apology
- Showing a positive attitude (for example, We can solve the conflict)
- WIN–WIN

It is important to understand what more advanced conflict resolution skills look like so we know what we are aspiring to teach. These advanced skills include:

- Eliminating evaluative judgments from observations. A great deal of conflict resolution training focuses on this, especially in the NVC model.
- Reflective listening. This is sometimes accomplished first by asking each participant in a conflict to simply state back what he or she heard the other saying. A deeper layer of reflective listening, one which mental health counselors practice, is listening beneath the surface content for underlying feelings and beliefs.
- Being able to distinguish feelings from ideas and beliefs. The ability to describe what you think.
- Being able to distinguish feelings and wishes from needs.
- Being able to distinguish positions from interests (Fisher & Ury, 1981).
- Understanding the concept of point of view.
- Understanding one's own point of view and that of one's "conflict-partner."
- Self-analysis: understanding one's own feelings, wishes, beliefs, points of view, needs, and goals.
- The ability to understand what two people have in common or both need.
- More advanced "I statements." Not just "When you do X, I feel Y," but also, "When you do X, I feel Y, because my need for Z is or is not met."
- Attending for the feelings, wishes, beliefs, point of view, needs, and goals of one's conflict partner.
- Empathetically placing oneself in the shoes of one's opponent.
- More advanced than WIN–WIN is WIN–WIN–WIN. We both win and the relationship wins.

Conflict resolution skills deepen when participants learn to analyze their own positions and then that of their opponents. Initially, people argue simply that they want something, but they can be helped to discern the difference between a temporary desire and an underlying need. They can be helped to clarify their own values and goals. They can be helped to distinguish how they perceive a situation and other people from how others may perceive the same situation and how others perceive them. As people develop skills in self-analysis, understanding their underlying needs, goals, values, and perceptions, they become more psychologically sophisticated. They develop their internal resources for problem solving. But whatever skill level clients show, the task for their counselors is to recognize those skills and help advance them developmentally.

Prepared with this knowledge of the microskills of conflict resolution, with an appreciation of how advanced skills such as perspective taking develop out of simpler skills such as listening, we are prepared to help our LLC clients develop these skills. To do this, we use three strategies:

1. We help them identify the conflict resolution microskills they already have, no matter how "primitive" these skills might be.
2. We look at every crisis or conflict that occurs as an opportunity for collaborative problem solving and we develop client skills through these naturally occurring conflicts. As this occurs, we help clients recognize and take credit for their own abilities.
3. We do formal instruction in conflict resolution skills but we use innovative teaching methods like games, storytelling, and movies, which hold the interests of our clientele.

Discover the Conflict Resolution Microskills That Clients Already Have

A deaf mildly retarded man, admitted to the Unit because of aggressive behavior at his group home (he threatened a staff person when a reinforcer could not be given to him as quickly as he wanted), went through a few weeks without displaying any such threatening behaviors. He was praised for these safe behaviors. Staff drew out and labeled the skills he was already using (listening, cooperating, following rules, and so on). This proceeded well, but we expected that eventually we would see some of the same aggressive behaviors he had been showing in his program. He had not yet really been challenged to use the skills we were so busy identifying. One day, the dinner food arrived and was waiting outside the door to the Unit for staff to bring it in. Unfortunately, staff were preoccupied with another patient who needed help, and one staff person had to ask him to wait a few minutes. She asked him very respectfully. There was no provocation other than the fact that he had to wait. Suddenly, he waved his finger aggressively at her face, puffing up and posturing as if he was about to assault her, and signed to her angrily, "I-HATE-YOU" repeatedly. Two other staff redirected him, brought him to our "comfort room" to relax, and then talked him though the situation. When he seemed calm, we asked him to go back to the staff person he threatened and apologize to her. Perhaps this was the conflict resolution skill moment we were hoping for. He went back to her, immediately resumed arguing, and gave her the most hostile "SORRY" I have ever seen.

He eventually ate, calmed down some more, and a staff person was able to talk him through his feelings enough that he could give a more sincere apology. The next day, when we met again to discuss the incident, we had these positive skills to work with.

- He had enough control that he did not hit anyone.
- He did agree to go to the comfort room and to talk with staff.
- He did calm himself down somewhat in the comfort room.
- He did offer an apology to the staff person (the fact that he did this first in an angry way would take a lot more work to convey.)
- He remained calm the remainder of the evening.
- He talked with staff throughout the incident.

Our initial conversation was just this: noting and labeling these skills and offering praise. Starting in this positive way at least gets the conversation going and tends to increase the chance that the rest of the conversation will be positive also.

With the client's agreement, we folded the incident into the next day's conflict resolution group. There were two other members that day. I began by showing a series of conflict resolution cards and asking each person to pick one to explain. I had the other two clients, who were higher functioning, go first, and I encouraged them to pick a "harder" skill. Higher functioning clients sometimes say the cards are for children, but challenging them to pick from the more difficult cards may satisfy them. Sometimes I stack the cards so that clients are highly likely to pick cards that are relevant to them.* I directed one, who had difficulty arguing without insulting or threatening people, toward the card that calls for him to explain calmly what happened without threats, insults, and so forth. We practiced this on a topic relevant to him. I directed the second person, a man with difficulty asserting himself, to the WIN-WIN card. We role-played and discussed a conflict he was then having with staff. The skill he had to practice was to assert himself while still dealing with some hospital rules. Finally, we got to the client who threatened the staff the night before, and I directed him toward the ASK, DON'T DEMAND card. This was because in the previous night's conflict, while staff were preoccupied with helping another patient, he was demanding staff to get his dinner, and he blew up when he was asked to wait a few minutes.

The only way to have any chance of helping this patient understand the skills was to role-play them. He would not acquire the skills by talk alone or

---

* I am drawing here on skills I learned as a child magician. However, this "stacking" is as simple as only selecting for the deck those skills that are relevant to the people we are working with.

by reference to pictures. We put him in the staff role and had another client role-play a patient who needed help. That client dramatically fell over, feigning to be hurt, and calling out for help. We then directed our patient to help him, but at the same time a staff assistant, role-playing him, came up to him and demanded that he get his food right away. Both the patient role-playing being hurt and the staff assistant kept insisting he help them immediately. With his permission, they grabbed him by each arm and pulled him in different directions, giving him the felt experience of being torn between two people with conflicting needs. The patient giggled and laughed. He did not know what to do. From there it was relatively easy to help him understand why staff could not respond to him last night, and how he could have behaved more skillfully. He role-played the "right" and "wrong" way to behave, requesting versus demanding, waiting versus blowing up, and he seemed to be learning.

Once we have progress like this, our task is to cement it. We do this by praising, having the client practice some more, and them putting the client in the position of helping or teaching others the same skill (Meichenbaum & Biemiller, 1998). This strengthens not just his skill but also his story about his ability to use this skill.

A day later, we had a case conference on this patient. We reviewed the progress he had made, the specific skills he had used and practiced, but we also expressed our *shared worrying* about his continuing to threaten and hurt people. We asked him what he could do to make these skills stronger. We wanted him to say "practice," but he was not quite that insightful. So we asked, "What about practice?" and he nodded agreement.

As we usually find, this combination of praise for specific skills used followed by a one-down expression of concern and invitation for more skill practice, resulted in a treatment contract for just that. We ended that meeting with a transitional plan for the client to practice specific coping and conflict resolution skills both in the hospital and with the staff from his residential program. With his agreement to a concrete plan which he understood in place, arranging further practice sessions were not difficult. A new social worker had just been hired by his residential program, so we set up for this client to teach this social worker the specific skills he had been practicing with us.

This meeting provided this client with further opportunities to display skills, and it provided staff with more opportunities to notice and label the skills he was using. He was calm and safe throughout the meeting. He took turns appropriately in the conversation. He listened. He expressed his opinion. He even negotiated a plan for next steps. Of course, the client showed these skills because the staff managed the meeting skillfully. If we had collectively scolded him and then demanded that he practice more skills, it is very unlikely he would have shown the skills that he did. However, *no matter how skillfully staff behave, we must always make sure clients attribute progress to their own abilities* (Meichenbaum, 1996; Meichenbaum & Biemiller, 1998;

Meichenbaum & Turk, 1987). This is essential if we are to change the clients' story and thereby promote skill generalization.

The challenge for staff is to look at even the lowest functioning people as people with skills. We might be starting with "sitting in chair skills." We start by recognizing the skills the clients have, whatever their developmental level might be. Although it is sometimes a challenge, we have yet to find a person in whom we could not identify skills provided that *we have the skills to think developmentally.*

Collaborative Problem Solving

The second method for teaching conflict resolution skills is to seize on real-life conflicts and treat them as opportunities for collaborative problem solving.

In Chapter 5, we introduced Ross Greene's collaborative problem solving (CPS) model in the context of discussing problem solving as a means of coping (Greene, 1998; Greene & Ablon, 2006). Greene's approach teaches conflict resolution but not through formal skill training groups. Rather, he first helps parents, teachers, and counselors choose between three kinds of responses to their children, students, or clients. He then brings a simple conflict resolution formula to these interactions. The heart of his model is clarity about what he first called the "3 baskets" (Greene, 1998) but later reconceptualized as "3 plans" (Greene & Ablon, 2006).

Plan A refers to what we here call the "one-up" use of authority. Limits are set. The child or client is told no and may be sent to time out. Consequences are applied. Greene describes how traditional behavioral programs, in which clients are rewarded for compliance with behavioral expectations, work from this Plan A perspective. Level systems, which are ubiquitous in mental health settings that work with children and very low functioning adults, are examples of Plan A interventions. A common method of family therapy with parents of children with behavioral problems is to help the parents become more consistent with each other in their limit settings. They are helped to prevent the child from playing one off against the other. In psychiatric hospitals and residential treatment centers, the default response of untrained milieu staff is often limit-setting. Until taught to do otherwise, most of us seem to work from Plan A especially if that is what we learned from our parents, teachers, and other authorities.

Plan C occurs when the parents, teachers, or providers decide to back off from a demand, at least for the moment, because the child/client does not seem capable of complying and the struggle has become unproductive. Plan C is usually understood to be a temporary move. Counselors sometimes recommend Plan A interventions because they believe that too much Plan C has been going on. They believe that "this child/client has been allowed to get away with murder. He's spoiled. He needs limits." When we were working with Tim, many Deaf Unit staff believed I was using too much Plan C and not enough Plan A. What I really wanted to do, following Greene's model, was move us into the paradigm of Plan B.

In Plan B, we change the discussion from the question of whether or not to "give in" to the child or client to the more productive discussion of how we turn crises into opportunities for skill development. In the language of this book, our pretreatment goal is to bring all problems into Plan B, in which collaborative problem solving occurs. Greene describes the basic steps of Plan B as (a) empathy, (b) defining the problem, and (c) inviting the child/client to problem-solve. Empathy, as we have seen, is not only a key pretreatment strategy but is probably essential to all psychotherapy. Advising staff to empathize before doing any other intervention is a safe way to deescalate many brewing problems. For instance, when the client is rebelling against some rule, a good first step for staff is to try to understand his or her feelings and point of view. "So you think this rule is stupid and you are feeling frustrated and angry that you are asked to follow rules which you think are so dumb."

We know that defining the problem is a key conflict resolution skill. Greene and Ablon (2006) define a problem as "two concerns that have yet to be reconciled" (p. 57). He notes that even adults who empathize well may fail to define the problem appropriately because they never ask the client or child for their concern. They define the problem as *they* see it. A problem is not really defined unless all parties lay out their concerns.

A staff person tells me that two of the clients in his residential program were fighting over whether they should go to the movies or to the mall. The staff person, very proud of himself, suggested they go to the movies today and the mall tomorrow. The clients agreed to this and settled down. The staff person believed he had solved the problem by addressing both of their wishes. He did, but it was still a Plan A intervention because *he* solved the problem. Chances are excellent that with a little coaching the clients could have come to the same resolution. If that had happened, their skills would have been enhanced and, if the staff person had noted this success, their story about their own abilities would have been as well. Instead, a temporary peace was made, but clients remain dependent on staff for problem solving. No learning occurred except perhaps the lesson that one needs staff to solve one's problems.

Inviting the client to solve the problem involves taking a one-down stance and may involve asking permission for a conversation to occur. Greene says the key word in this third step is "let's" as in "let's think about how we can solve that problem" (p. 59). "Let's" is not the key word for users of ASL where the concept would be conveyed something like YOU ME PROBLEM SOLVE TOGETHER TRY, ALRIGHT? Efforts at brainstorming follow, with the idea that any solution must be (a) feasible and (b) mutually acceptable.

Greene and Ablon describe how many crucial psychosocial skills are trained through use of Plan B. They point out that "Plan B requires that participants have the capacity to identify and articulate their concerns so as *to identify the problem to be solved, consider possible solutions, and reflect on the feasibility and likely outcomes of solutions and the degree to which they are mutually satisfactory"* (emphasis in original, p. 121). They provide a simplification of the conflict resolution process, which is useful for LLC clients:

1. Ask for help.
2. Meet halfway/give a little.
3. Do it a different way. (p. 126)

An adolescent patient asked to meet me one day and presented me with a litany of complaints about our staff and program. Staff lied to her, she said, and were rude and mean to her. One group leader "kicked me out of a group for no reason." Another staff member "hid my mail from me." A third told her to "shut up and not talk about anything." As I listened to her, I could see why she was in so much conflict with people. Her listening skills were poor. She misunderstood what others said, jumped to conclusions about what they meant, and constructed damning evaluations of other people. I listened to her vent, asking myself how I could possibly get her to see these complaints as an opportunity to develop her skills. There is so much we could teach her, I am thinking, if only we can engage her in learning.

At this particular moment, the best I could do was listen and reflect her feelings empathically. Searching for skills and strengths, I commented on how she was handling these apparent provocations better than she used to. Even with all these stressors, she had not threatened or hit anyone. She was communicating her complaints to me verbally rather than acting out. I commended her on these gains and then wondered if she would be willing to use these provocations as opportunities to develop further her own skills and power. She told me, in no uncertain terms, that *no*, she was not. She did not want to talk to anyone else. She did not want to learn skills. She just wanted to vent. Fine, I said, as I thanked her for venting to me, commenting that even her venting was a skill. I lamented sadly to myself at the opportunities for growth that lay, untouched, in her path, but I resigned myself to the reality that this was all she could do, at least at this moment. Given how badly she has been beaten down, we might have to have this conversation dozens of times before she feels safe and powerful enough to take the next step into treatment. When she gets to the point of being willing to take that step, to actually agree to develop certain social skills, I felt confident that we could help her advance her skills, probably reasonably quickly.

The next day I found out that she actually did talk with one of the staff with whom she had been in conflict. Later in the day after she and I talked, she approached the staff person on her own and asked to talk. The staff person reported to me, in her presence, that the client listened to her. They clarified their misunderstandings and they came to a resolution. The client told me that she knows "I'm doing better than before but I could do better." She made a step forward in readiness to work on conflict resolution skills intentionally.

As it turns out, her saying "no" to me was not the end of the story. She said "no" at that moment, but then changed her mind and took steps on her own to solve the conflict. We had seen this happen before. When clients are shown a path, and given full permission to advance at their own pace, they often do so, *at their own pace*, which sometimes turns out to be quicker than their initial resistance suggested.

As new conflicts developed with this girl, we had new opportunities to practice skills. Her engagement in this process waxed and waned. As with Tim, we held certain bottom line expectations such as the ability to have a safe and reasonably respectful conversation about issues. As long as she could do that, our goal was to negotiate, and in that process point out to her skills she was using. When her ability to have respectful conversations collapsed and she became unsafe, we resorted to Plan A limit setting, but always with the expressed intention of resuming the Plan B problem-solving style as soon as the client allowed. Over time (sometimes a long, painful time), this strategy moves clients into a problem-solving, as opposed to an oppositional, frame of mind.

CPS is an important part of milieu treatment designed to teach skills. CPS efforts are enhanced in an environment dedicated totally to skill development, where skills are simplified, posted everywhere, taught in individual, group, and family treatment as well as in the moment of crisis, and everyone speaks the language of skills.

Formal Conflict Resolution Skills Training

Earlier in the development of the skill training program on the Deaf Unit, we put great faith in designated skill training groups. Three groups I developed and led were coping, conflict resolution, and relapse prevention skills. For years, these groups were cofacilitated by myself or another clinical staff person and rotating members of the direct care staff. Our goal was to familiarize the direct care staff with these skills so that when real-life opportunities for coping, conflict resolution, or relapse prevention occurred in the milieu, staff would seize the opportunities.

We used variations on a "simple" framework for conflict resolution. "Simple" is in quotes because the definition of simple depends on whom you are working with. We would list the skills on the board, review them, and then ask clients to volunteer examples of current conflicts for us to practice with. The steps were variations of the following:

1. Notice the conflict. What is the conflict about?
2. Agree to try to solve the conflict.
3. Each person talks. We take turns talking and listening.
4. Each person repeats back what the other person said.

5. We make a list of possible solutions.
6. We discuss each solution. What is good about it and bad about it?
7. We make a decision together. We negotiate.
8. Compromising. How can we both win?

On a good day, this approach worked fine. For many clients, however, this was too complex a task. They could not understand some of the steps. A concept like "compromising" could itself be the subject of many weeks of work. Often clients did not present conflicts they were having for discussion in the group. They were not able to step back from the conflicts they were having and see them as conflicts. Using the "red, yellow, green," metaphor, they were not able to "stop and notice." At other times, they lacked the interest or attention span to attend to even a 10-minute discussion of the steps. This led to my appreciation that formal conflict resolution skills training groups had to be complemented by the other two strategies cited. These skill training groups worked best when clients had moved from pretreatment to treatment. They saw a reason to attend. Even then, we needed a more compelling format than didactic instruction. We needed to make much more use of therapeutic games, activities, and stories. When clients agreed to process conflicts, we needed to act them out before we could possibly discuss them.*

Because we could not count on clients to raise a current conflict they were having for discussion, we needed a backup strategy for getting conflicts on the table. The backup plan we used most often was to rely on a set of conflict situation cards. These are pictures of people in conflicts (Figures 6.8 and 6.9), similar to the coping situation cards discussed in Chapter 5. Clients are asked to "pick a card," or the leader can preselect cards that are relevant. A set of conflict situation cards is included on the CD-ROM. Some of the conflict situations cards show:

- People fighting over the remote to the television.
- One person bumping into another.
- One person wanting the window open while the other person wants it closed.
- A child arguing with a parent over which ride to go on at a carnival.
- A couple arguing over what kind of house or car to buy.
- Someone cutting in line.
- A waiter bringing food that one did not order.
- Two people disagreeing on which movie to see.

We asked clients to role-play the conflicts. We asked them to make the conflicts worse and then better and identified the strategies they used that had each result. When they used a skill such as listening, we helped them identify

---

* In Chapter 9, I discuss how these changes reflected a move to a more "Deaf friendly" format.

Figure 6.8 A conflict resolution situation card.

Figure 6.9 A conflict resolution situation card.

it. We had pictures of many of the skills posted in the room, and we asked clients to point to the picture of the skill they just used. When the interest level was very low, we have clients earn points for skills used toward a prize awarded at the end of the session. Offering a prize can make the difference between a successful and unsuccessful group.

Sometimes conflicts broke out in the group itself. For instance, everyone in the group wanted the air conditioner turned on except for one member. Two people had had a conflict but only one was willing to discuss it. A group member was angry with the group leader because of something that happened earlier in the day. All of these, of course, presented opportunities for practicing conflict resolution that were more meaningful than hypothetical situations. The group leader has to see these conflicts not as barriers to treatment but as the very stuff of treatment.

The conflict resolution microskills are presented in pictorial form on the CD-ROM. It is helpful to have pictures of those skills available so one can point to them when they occur. It is generally more engaging to start with

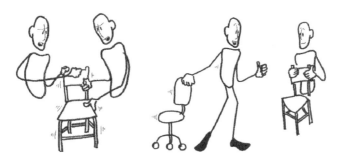

Figure 6.10 Conflict and resolution.

conflicts, real or hypothetical, and draw out the skills clients are using to solve them than it is to start with the skills, and ask clients to role-play these.

A conflict resolution group one day consisted of only mentally retarded, language dysfluent deaf clients. They were all very concrete thinkers who would not understand conflict resolution skills without doing them.

We began with a two sequence cartoon of two people fighting over a chair (Figure 6.10). The conflict is resolved when one person decides to pull over an additional chair. We showed the pictures to the group members and immediately started to act it out. The staff co-leader and I pretended to argue over a chair. I was sitting watching television, got up to go to the bathroom, and when I returned my colleague had taken my chair. I insisted it was my chair. I was sitting there. My colleague said that when I got up and walked away, I lost the chair. It was my fault. It was his chair now. We pretended to argue, and I pretended to be ready to hit him. The clients leaped up to stop me, telling me not to hit him, and then coached us in solving this conflict. As we argued, there was a free chair nearby, and we waited until one of the clients suggested bringing over that chair. This idea had been planted by the cartoon, but we wanted a client to suggest it. When he did, we commended him on how smart he was. We both sat down and watched television, and both said we were content. We shook hands, a concrete way our clients know to indicate that resolution has been achieved. In the course of a half hour, staff and clients role-played this same conflict over the chair, solving it in several different ways (for example, taking turns with the chair, flipping a coin, moving two chairs alongside each other, yielding the chair to the other person, and so forth). The clients' success in solving this problem was celebrated energetically with praise and applause.

About a year later, I found myself cofacilitating a skills training group with hearing adolescent psychiatric inpatients. These were ostensibly higher functioning people. All were fluent users of English and had intelligence in the average range. We were discussing "hassle logs" (Larson, 2005), and one client mentioned that he had been sitting in the day hall when another boy came over and demanded he get out of "his" chair. The boy had been sitting in the chair but he left a few minutes earlier without saying he was returning. In the eyes of his peer, he had given up the chair, and now he was demanding it back. The first boy refused to get out of the chair. The second boy became threatening and demanded he move. Staff came over and solved the problem by asking the first boy to move. They sided with the boy who had left. This was a lost opportunity for staff who decided the matter and deprived the students of the opportunity to do so themselves. However, we were able to discuss the conflict at a higher level now.

We talked about what made the chair hard to give up. What was at stake for each boy or, as one group member asked, "Why fight over a stupid chair?" What was at stake, of course, was honor and the fear of being disrespected. Each boy believed his honor was at stake and did not want to be seen as the loser in front of his peers. After we exposed this belief, we discussed how else one might view the matter. They could believe, as their peer said, that it was "just a stupid chair." They could also look at honor differently. Perhaps the person with the greatest honor was the person who was most generous. If they looked at it that way, would it help them solve the conflict? They could see it would. One of the boys then came up with another solution. He could have said, "I don't want to give up the chair, but here's another chair. Why don't you pull it over and sit next to me?" That might or might not have worked, but it was excellent example of several conflict resolution skills (empathy, problem solving, compromise, face saving). Thus the "simple" conflict over the chair can be processed differently, depending on the language and cognitive abilities of the clients.

Sometimes we use movie or television clips or made up stories to elicit a discussion or role play. For instance, we showed patients a clip from *Shark Tale* (Bergeron & Jenson, 2005) in which the father shark, played like a mafia godfather, scolds his timid and gentle shark son Lenny for not being a merciless killer. Lenny is making the family look bad, he says, leaving his legacy in doubt. In a desperate effort to force Lenny to prove he can be heartless, he grabs a defenseless shrimp and urges him to eat it immediately. The shrimp and his fellows all plead for its life, and Lenny, taking pity on them, grabs them all and helps them escape. The godfather shark, appalled by Lenny's timidity, urges his ruthless brother Frankie to teach Lenny how to be a real shark.

The 5-minute movie segment is poignant and funny and shows a very clear conflict between parent and child. A 5- or 6-year-old hearing child would have no difficulty understanding it. We can play it with the captions on, but that does not help clients with poor reading skills. We brought in interpreters, and after we played the segment we reviewed what happened and acted it out. Even still, one client did not understand that this episode showed a conflict. Asked what the father wanted, he replied that Lenny should eat the shrimp. Why should he eat the shrimp? Because he is hungry. What does Lenny do? He sends the shrimp away. Why? He does not know.

The story did, however, work well for other clients, and after a brief discussion of what was happening, we made a bridge to their parent–child conflicts. Some clients had parents they perceived to be mean and abusive, like the godfather shark. They told some stories of how this was so. Then we discussed how they would behave. Would they be like their parents? Would they be like the godfather shark? What advice would they give to Lenny?

The lowest functioning client grasped only some of this discussion but he attended, and we brought him into the discussion as best we could. He eventually opined that Lenny should ignore his father and not be mean. That led easily to a discussion and role play of how he could respond when other people, like the Godfather shark, are mean to him. The conflict only became real for him through the role play.

At the end of the discussion and role play, we identified the skills used. They included listening, turn taking, understanding how other people feel, and being nice. More sophisticated conflicts are well represented in segments of the film *Billy Elliot* (Brenman, Finn, & Daldry, 2001). This is the story of a boy growing up part of a family of coalminers in Britain during a very bitter miners' strike. Billy's macho father and brother are struggling to keep the family fed and housed during the strike. One of the brother's friends becomes a "strike breaker" and breaks the picket line. Meanwhile, the father spent precious funds to send Billy for training as a boxer, but Billy finds his way to the other side of the gymnasium and joins a ballet class. There is a powerful 10-minute segment showing a montage of conflicts: the strikers versus the police and strikebreakers, the father and brother versus their strikebreaking friend; Billy's father discovering his son in ballet class; a tense family meeting in which the ostensibly senile grandmother tries in her own meek way to defend Billy, and a physical altercation between Billy and his father. For clients who can grasp these conflicts, the film provides a wonderful segue into discussions of different kinds of conflicts and how one might try to solve them.

Thus, our formal conflict resolution groups have evolved away from abstract discussions of particular conflict resolution skills to viewing or enactments of particular conflicts, sometimes incorporated into a game, followed by discussion of the skills used in these particular conflicts to settle them. This structure of identifying the skills *after* examples are given, rather than at the start of the session, seems to work best.

Conclusions

The work done with Tim, presented at the start of this chapter, demonstrates how skill training can lead to a new narrative about developing abilities. We were not just interested in teaching Tim coping and conflict resolution skills.

We also wanted him to think of himself as a person who was developing those abilities. In all of this work, attitude is everything. When we can nurture in clients the attitude that welcomes treatment as opportunity to develop their skills further, the limits to what we can accomplish with them are boundless.

Skill building as a treatment model offers staff and clients a language for what they already know and have yet to learn. Clients are engaged by helping them discover skills they already have, and providing them real-life experiences in which they see how use of these skills pays off for them. Once Tim was willing to use his coping and conflict resolution skills to negotiate a behavioral plan with us, he got many immediate payoffs (praise, privileges, and a way out of the hospital). He also left with a framework of what can happen next: he can learn new skills. A path for meaningful, relevant psychotherapy was charted.

With higher functioning, more sophisticated clients, we could send them to skill training groups where it is reasonable to think any number of curricula would work. With these clients, individual psychotherapy might also be most of what they need. With our LLC clients, we are usually never very far from the pretreatment issues of eliciting informed understanding and willingness to engage in some treatment model. The most effective treatment programs will literally surround their clients in skill building and story construction opportunities. Staff will have moved away from limit setting as the default response to patient challenges and instead grasped the idea, said to be embedded in the Chinese character for the term, that *crisis equals opportunity*. Every problem that arises becomes a potential opportunity for skill development, and every venue of treatment (individual, group, milieu, family, community) becomes a place where skill development can occur.

To teach clients conflict resolution skills, staff have to know the foundational as well as more advanced microskills, and they need to adapt treatment to the cognitive developmental abilities of their clients. To pull clients into treatment, staff need to be skilled at discovering the conflict resolution microskills clients are already using and then inviting clients to develop their skills further. They also need to approach the daily behavioral challenges as opportunities for collaborative problem solving. This climate sets the stage for formal therapeutic groups where conflict resolution and other skills are taught and practiced. Individual psychotherapy also becomes a venue for skill development and story construction with more attention to the individual concerns of clients. The therapeutic alliance remains essential, but the creation of this alliance is facilitated when the counselor is involved in creating opportunities for clients to use skills successfully. Indeed, if in all venues of the treatment milieu, staff have learned to search tenaciously for client skills, a result will likely be more therapeutic relationships. This strength-based approach fosters relationship building and gives clients no escape from opportunities for growth.

7

Relapse Prevention and Crisis Management Skills

Introduction

Sheryl was a client with an overwhelming set of serious problems. Deaf, mildly mentally retarded, linguistically dysfluent in her best language of American Sign Language (ASL) and illiterate in English, she had life-threatening medical problems, a major psychotic disorder, and a long history of alcohol abuse. Although she was not normally violent, she would become so when intoxicated. For Sheryl, the consequence of continuing to abuse alcohol was death. Her parents and the agency service providers overseeing her care insisted that the group residential treatment program supervise her at all times. They also insisted that she be in counseling for all her problems. Because so much was at stake and people had so little faith in Sheryl's own motivation and skills for recovery, the system of people working with her collectively assumed a one-up stance with her of insisting on sobriety and full participation in her treatment. Family and agency staff took the same one-up posture with the community residential treatment program, insisting that they *make* Sheryl comply with these expectations. If this program could not keep Sheryl safe and engaged, they would pull the funding for her placement.

Everyone told Sheryl they wanted to help her, and everyone told her what she must do and not do. She must not drink. She must go to counseling. She must attend Alcoholics Anonymous (AA). She must take her medication. She must accept 24-hour supervision.

Of course, the only person not on board with this plan was Sheryl. What she wanted was independence. She wanted people to leave her alone and let her drink and do as she pleased. She did not want to go to therapy or to substance abuse groups, neither of which she understood or found meaningful. She responded to this authoritarian stance from all the people who wanted to help her by resisting and rebelling. She took off from her group home, became intoxicated, assaulted a staff person, and was rehospitalized on our Deaf psychiatric unit. A frantic set of providers now turned to us to "fix her."

Sheryl had relapsed. She resumed her long-standing problem of drinking, deteriorating cognitively, and becoming violent. In the process, she put her life at risk and hurt other people. The therapeutic challenge now was not just to stabilize her but to reengage her in the treatment process. Ideally, we would help her establish a relapse prevention plan. But how could we do this with someone who did not seem invested in her own sobriety?

Relapse prevention work requires even more of clients than does the use of coping and conflict resolution skills. It requires that clients be full agents in their own recovery. Relapse prevention is not something one does *to* another person. It is a set of skills that people use to manage *their own* recovery. Relapse prevention also requires a much higher level of language and cognitive ability than coping or conflict resolution skills. Relapse prevention requires the ability to anticipate problem symptoms or behaviors before they occur and proactively use skills to prevent their recurrence. Relapse prevention draws on coping and social skills but goes beyond them. Crisis intervention, by contrast, is a set of strategies that staff use to manage clients who may relapse and do something dangerous. When clients like Sheryl are in treatment programs, but are not able or willing to manage their own recovery, staff use crisis intervention skills to intervene to protect them. Staff doing crisis intervention struggle with the pretreatment problem discussed in Chapter 4. How do we help people with problem symptoms and behaviors when they are not willing or able to collaborate with us?

In this chapter, I review the major concepts and skills in relapse prevention. Because relapse prevention concepts pose particular problems of translation into ASL, the linguistic issues are explored. An important part of relapse prevention work is behavior analysis. This is the process of analysis of the factors leading to relapse. A good behavior analysis sets the stage for relapse prevention work because it highlights those factors that trigger a relapse. Armed with knowledge emerging from the behavior analysis, one can take actions to prevent the relapse. This chapter builds on the discussion in previous chapters to present creative means of engaging clients in relapse prevention treatment. Finally, I address how staff can use relapse prevention concepts in crisis management. The chapter ends with a discussion of the limitations of mental health care with clients who are unable and/or unwilling to make use of it, however skillfully presented.

What Is Relapse Prevention?

The originator of the relapse prevention treatment paradigm is G. Alan Marlatt (Marlatt & Gordon, 1985), who began his book on relapse prevention with a definition:

> Relapse prevention (RP) is a self-management program designed to enhance the maintenance stage of the habit-change process. The goal of RP is to teach individuals who are trying to change their behavior how to anticipate and cope with the problem of relapse.... Based on the principles of social-learning theory, RP is a self-control program that

combines behavioral skill training, cognitive interventions, and lifestyle change procedures.

Marlatt developed relapse prevention in explicit contrast to the then dominant treatment paradigm for substance abuse represented by AA and other 12-step programs. The medical model underlying AA presents addictions as medical illnesses. The first step of 12-step approaches involves recognition that one is powerless over problem behaviors unless, paradoxically, one relinquishes control to a "higher power." In relapse prevention, problem symptoms and behaviors are defined, not as illnesses, but as "acquired habit patterns." These habit patterns are learned and can be unlearned and new more adaptive behavior patterns can be learned. "Addictive behaviors are viewed as over-learned habits that can be analyzed and modified in the same manner as other habits" (p. 5). The learning of new behaviors, however, is an intentional act, requiring the subject to be an active agent of self-change. Marlatt commented:

> Self-control programs, even though they are often identified as a kind of behavioral "treatment" approach, differ from most externally-based treatment programs in that they teach the client to eventually become the agent of change. This distinction is crucial to the understanding of the RP model. Here one is reminded of the old adage attributed to Maimonides: "Give a man a fish and he eats for day; teach a man to fish and eats for a lifetime." Giving him a fish may provide a temporary solution to the problem, but teaching how to fish is clearly the best long-term solution. In self-control programs such as RP, the aim is to teach clients how to "do it" on their own. (p. 15)

Marlatt was initially concerned principally with substance abuse though he saw the possibilities for application to work with persons who were sexual offenders. Subsequently, relapse prevention has been applied to a broad range of clinical problems (Witkiewitz & Marlatt, 2007).

Marlatt's research focused on understanding the conditions that lead to relapse as well as the psychological processes that enable a relapse to occur. He found, for instance, that 35% of relapses in his sample were precipitated by negative emotional states, 16% by interpersonal conflict, and 20% by social pressure (Marlatt & Gordon, 1985). He discovered an important psychological process he called the *abstinence violation effect* (AVE). This refers to the process in which a person *lapses* or takes one drink, then concludes he has failed so that he might as well go "all the way." Marlatt developed treatment interventions designed to help clients anticipate the high-risk triggers and situations that provoke their own lapses, and then use coping and social skills, as well as treatment resources like AA meetings, to either avoid lapses (one time mistakes) or prevent them from becoming relapses (an ongoing pattern of worsening addictive behaviors).

The heart of RP consists of several concepts:

1. Lapses and relapses
2. Warning signs
3. Triggers
4. Risk factors
5. Seemingly unimportant decisions
6. Intentional use of coping skills to manage high-risk feelings, thoughts, behaviors, and situations
7. Intentional use of a recovery support system

Since Marlatt's pioneering work, many other people have written books using the relapse prevention approach for particular problems and client populations. Those books that are directed at youth are particularly relevant for us because they strive for simple, clear presentations. Even therapeutic books directed at children, however, require a higher level of English literacy than many of our clients have. In the next section, I summarize a few sample self-help books and then discuss how the ideas can be presented to our language and learning challenged (LLC) deaf clients.

Sample Relapse Prevention Books

Moving Beyond Sexually Abusive Behavior: A Relapse Prevention Curriculum, by Thomas Leversee (2002), provides a straightforward presentation of relapse prevention principles. This book "was written to provide a curriculum for treatment providers to facilitate sexually abusive youth in the completion of a written relapse prevention plan" (p. 4). The "relapse prevention curriculum" includes components designed to help youth:

- Identify the chain of situations, feelings, thoughts, beliefs, and behaviors that lead to relapse.
- Learn how to anticipate, avoid, or plan for high-risk situations and factors in the environment that increase the risk of relapse.
- Acquire new cognitive, social, and problem-solving skills in order to succeed in interrupting the chain that leads to relapse.
- Learn how to prevent and control abusive thoughts and fantasies.
- Identify an external supervisory situation.

The last item is designed to foster accountability in the youth. They are encouraged to work with people who are monitoring their adherence to their relapse prevention plan.

Leversee's curriculum emphasizes identification and anticipation of risk factors (risky thinking, beliefs fantasies, feelings behaviors, and places) and leaning new skills to manage these. Many of the skills involve new ways of talking to oneself. For instance, if one starts to have a sexual fantasy that involves abusive behavior, one is encouraged to think instead about the consequences of being caught in the act. Clients are also taught skills for dealing with feelings, managing aggression and stress, and creating a positive support network.

There are 10 criteria for enrollment in this program that are also used as measures of progress. This list of criteria is useful because it clarifies the cognitive and attitudinal demands required to do relapse prevention work. I have substituted the word "problem" for the word "abusive" so this list can apply to relapse prevention beyond sexual offending behaviors.

1. Acceptance of responsibility for the problem behavior.
2. Identification of the cycle of problem behavior.
3. Identification of high-risk thinking that supports or triggers problem behaviors.
4. Development of skills in order to interrupt the cycle before problem behaviors occur.
5. Development of victim awareness and empathy. (This is only relevant for behaviors that hurt other people.)
6. Development of a positive self-image.
7. Development of relapse prevention strategies and plan.
8. Development of a community-based support system.

Two additional items especially relevant where the relapse problem is sexually abusive behaviors are the following:

9. Understanding the role of sexual arousal in sexually abusive behaviors, reduction of deviant sexual arousal if applicable.
10. Addressing the cognitive, emotional, and behavioral outcomes of youth's own victimization, if present.

How can we adapt these important goals for our LLC clients? How will we explain concepts like "risk factors" to clients who cannot even give a linear description of events leading up to a relapse, and who may not understand the concept of relapse?

Daley and Marlatt (1997) developed substance abuse treatment materials, including both a therapist guide and a client manual, using a relapse prevention model. These two excellent books still assume client literacy as well as very sophisticated abstract thinking and self-analysis abilities. For example, here are some of the tasks clients are asked to complete using these materials:

1. Identify the short- and long-term pros and cons of staying sober and continuing drug use.
2. Identify therapy sabotaging behaviors.
3. Identify goals and steps toward change for physical, emotional, or psychological, family, social or interpersonal, spiritual, other (work economic, and so forth) aspects of one's life.
4. List triggers, rating the level of threat they pose and identifying relevant coping strategies.

5. Analyze cognitive distortions that lead to substance use.
6. Identify counter-thoughts to the thoughts that justify substance use.
7. Name and rate emotions and identify the relevant coping strategy.
8. Identify social pressures, the degree of difficulty they pose, and the relevant coping strategy.
9. Identify consequences of substance use on each member of one's family.
10. Identify problems caused by one's substance use and coming up with a way to improve the problem.
11. Identify one's own interpersonal style.
12. Identify the benefits associated with including particular people and organizations in one's recovery network

Each one of these tasks is relevant and important. The overall approach presents a framework for solid, evidence-based treatment of substance use. However, it also assumes a great deal about client abilities before they begin. Any one of these topics might be the subject of months of work with our clients and even then may represent wildly unrealistic objectives.

If half of relapse prevention is anticipating problems before they happen, the other half is carrying out a plan to *do something* when the antecedents of relapse occur. Commonly, what is called for is:

1. The client will use a coping skill (for example, distraction, self-talk, sensory modulation activities).
2. The client will draw on some kind of social support (for example, attend a 12-step meeting, call one's sponsor, talk to staff or a supervisor).

A book that focuses on the coping skills aspect of relapse prevention is *Treating Alcohol Dependence: A Coping Skills Training Guide* (Monti, Kadden, Rohsenow, Cooney, & Abrams, 2002). Most of this book is a manual for coping skills training. Coping skills as defined in this book includes both skills for dealing with internal distress (what we refer to in this book as coping skills) and skills for dealing with other people (which we refer to as social skills.). The skills for dealing with internal distress include managing urges to drink, problem solving, increasing pleasant activities, anger management, managing negative thoughts, identifying seemingly irrelevant decisions, and planning for emergencies. The skills for dealing with other people include many kinds of communication skills, drink refusal skills, and skills to develop social support networks and resolve relationship problems.

One issue in relapse prevention is how skills are acquired. Is it enough, for instance, that one have a relapse prevention plan that specifies what one will do when close to relapse or must there be active practice of skills? Suppose I develop a relapse prevention plan that specifies that whenever I feel an urge to drink I will recognize it as a warning sign and risk factor, and either call my sponsor or attend an AA meeting. Is that enough? Unfortunately, people develop wonderful plans only to ignore them when they need them. They have a plan, but faced with strong urges to drink, they disregard it and head for the nearest bar.

This may be partially because of something called "state dependent learning." Relapse prevention plans are usually developed when one is in a calm, rational state of mind. This is not the state of mind that one has when one actually needs the plan. At those moments, one may be experiencing physiological cravings or strong mood states like anger and depression. A plan developed when one is in a calm state will not necessarily be accessed when one is in a physiologically and emotionally aroused state. The plan is not really real until it is practiced in something approximating the mood state that it will actually be needed in.

The Monti et al. manual handles this by presenting a program for "cue exposure treatment with urge coping training."

> Alcoholics encounter a variety of alcohol-related cues, such as people, places, objects, time periods, and internal states that have been associated with past drinking. Cues can include the sight and smell of one's favorite alcoholic beverage; places such as bars, beaches, and homes where drinking occurred; mood states such as stress, anger, or wanting to celebrate; certain times, such as the end of work or Friday evening; and people who had been drinking companions. Because alcoholics are asked to avoid drinking cues while in treatment, our clients may first encounter these cues outside of the treatment setting unexpectedly, and with no one present to help them deal with their internal reactions, posing a risk for relapse. Cue exposure treatment (CET) was developed to help clients reduce the strength of the internal reactions and to provide an opportunity to practice use of coping skills while in the state of arousal that these cues generate. (Monti et al., 2002, p. 5)

An example of a cue exposure is to start a treatment session by exposing clients to the sight and smell of the clients' usual alcoholic drink. They are then asked to imagine being in various high-risk situations, using their coping skills and staying sober. This kind of treatment must be done very carefully even with high functioning clients because such cue exposure may do precisely what it usually does, trigger a relapse. This kind of treatment is recommended primarily for inpatient, day treatment, and residential settings where clients can be monitored and for highly engaged clients well along in their recovery. One's relapse prevention skills should be pretty solid before attempting such cue exposure.

Relapse prevention plans must, therefore, be practiced. Ironically, our LLC deaf clients may have one advantage in this effort. Higher functioning, highly verbal people expect to talk in therapy. They do not necessarily expect, and may actively resist, any kind of treatment that expects them to *do something*.

Our less verbal clients usually do not have the same expectations or interest in talk therapy and are more likely to value activity. This is one reason we emphasize skills rather than insight throughout their treatment. Counseling with LLC deaf clients, for instance, almost always involves role playing. Any strategy oriented toward practice is likely to make intuitive sense to them.

On the other hand, very concrete clients may have difficulty grasping the idea that we are practicing *not* relapsing. Before they are exposed to any kind of cue, they need to understand fully the reason for the exposure, and they must be on board with the goal of using the exposure as an opportunity to practice coping skills and *not relapse*. This is easier to do with certain problems, such as practicing not becoming aggressive in response to a provocation, than others, such as not drinking when exposed to alcohol.

What about materials developed for deaf individuals? The Minnesota Chemical Dependency Program for Deaf and Hard of Hearing Individuals developed a relapse prevention manual for deaf substance abusers (*Staying Sober: Relapse Prevention Guide*, 1993). This workbook was developed with an understanding of the need for simple English, but using it still requires English literacy at, I would estimate, a high school level, and it requires some capacity for self-analysis.

The first chapter defines and discusses warning signs and gives examples of *stinking thinking, euphoric recall, grandiosity, denial, and expectations*. It then asks people to write or draw an example of each. People are asked to list the positive and negative aspects of sobriety. They are asked to list things they are thankful for and to write about times when they had urges to use substances. Then they are asked to write new behaviors they could use when they have urges. Finally, they are asked to list their relapse warning signs, what happened when they relapsed, what they thought at that time, and what they did.

In the second chapter, readers are asked to list and discuss healthy and unhealthy ways of responding to anger and resentment. They are asked to list people who can help when they feel lonely as well as to discuss their fears and something they grieve. They are asked to discuss people or things that caused them shame, jealousy, and happiness and how they handle each.

The third chapter deals with beliefs and is designed to help people identify negative thoughts that may contribute to substance use. Chapter 4 helps people consider ways to have fun while staying sober. Chapter 5 considers the contribution of physical health and a healthy lifestyle to sobriety. The last chapter presents a template for a relapse prevention plan. The components of the plan are warning signs, people who can help me, things I can do if I have relapse signs, resources I can call for help, and a plan for what significant others can do if they see me showing warning signs.

We can see that even this manual requires English competency and pretty intact cognitive abilities. The manual is best used as part of a treatment program where signing clinicians can guide clients through it.

The purpose of this brief review of a few treatment manuals is to give us a blueprint for relapse prevention skills work. Next we face the challenge of adapting these concepts for LLC deaf clients. This will be tougher than teaching coping or conflict resolution skills because there are more abstract concepts to learn. Relapse prevention also cannot really be said to be occurring unless the client shows the fundamental skill of *directing one's own recovery.* This means it cannot be developed in clients who are still in a pretreatment frame of mind. However, as we will see, the basic concepts of relapse prevention are still relevant for staff working with these clients in hospital or residential treatment programs. In these instances, the concepts are used to inform a crisis intervention plan.

For counselors working with ASL using or LLC deaf clients, we also have to attend to problems associated with the different grammatical structures of ASL and English. Relapse prevention concepts are conveyed very differently in each language, and this requires a different approach to teaching and counseling.

Language and Translation Issues

Far more than with coping or conflict resolution skills, many concepts involved in relapse prevention do not lend themselves to easy translation into ASL. This is not because one cannot convey these concepts in ASL but because ASL and English differ on how the ideas are conceptualized. There are no exact semantic matches between English words and phrases like *relapse, lapse, warning sign, trigger, seemingly unimportant decisions, and risk factors* and corresponding signs. Signers who are English dominant and know these concepts can use signs that are approximations of the English words, but these signs will not be of use to ASL using or LLC deaf persons who do not know the concepts or English words. These concepts are very likely to be unfamiliar to LLC deaf clients and considerable attention must be paid to teaching these ideas. The common (hearing) teaching approach of providing definitions is not the best strategy. Rather, as we discuss below, giving multiple examples is more "Deaf friendly." ASL using clinicians almost certainly know this intuitively.

The semantic difficulty stems from the fact that each of these relapse prevention concepts refers to a superordinant category, and many superordinant categories are conveyed differently in ASL than in English. Superordinant categories are words like *furniture* and *fruit* which refer to a group of objects, actions, or ideas. Klima and Bellugi (1979) discuss this issue and present the following examples.*

---

* The dashes here indicate compound signs. These are not the only signs that can be used to convey these concepts and they do not have to occur in exactly this order. Crime could also be signed DO WRONG POLICE ARREST. The interpretation will depend on context. However, the main point is that ASL often establishes superordinant categories though listing specific instances whereas in English there are more often words for these superordinant categories. See Klima and Bellugi (1979) for a fuller discussion.

English	ASL
Tool	HAMMER-SAW-SCREWDRIVER
Weapon	GUN-KNIFE-BOMB
Musical instrument	CLARINET-PIANO-GUITAR
Crime	KILL-STAB-RAPE
Season	FALL, WINTER, SPRING, SUMMER

An example of how this difference in expression of superordinate categories effects basic conversation can be found in a question like "What is your race?" An appropriate ASL translation for this would be "YOU BLACK WHITE HISPANIC WHAT?" The question, "What is the season?" would be translated NOW FALL WINTER SPRING SUMMER WHAT? Conceptually they are the equivalent, but problems in understanding arise when people use English words for *race* and *season* as if there are clear signs with the same English meanings. This is especially confusing when people use signs that are conceptually inaccurate, for instance, the sign COMPETITION to mean race.

This difference in grammatical structure is notorious for creating problems in clinical and legal settings. For instance, clinicians doing mental status exams ask clients about their *mood*, and while there is a sign for mood, it is conceptually clearer to give examples of moods and sign WHAT? Clinicians may ask about *trauma* and *abuse* but for clients who do not know these concepts or the English words, specific examples must be given. Clinicians normally prefer to ask general questions so as to not lead the client, but the translation can interfere with that. Similarly, in legal situations, attorneys may ask about *crimes* and *weapons* and deliberately avoid being specific. The interpreter may have to list specifics, which can appear to suggest a particular response. If the interpreter is told to avoid listing specifics, he or she may have no way to convey the idea.

The concept of *relapse* means that a problem behavior (for example, drinking, drugging, sexual offending, aggression), problem symptom (for example, depression, mania, psychosis), or whatever else we choose to consider a target (for example, feelings, thoughts, attitudes, interactional patterns) has happened again. In many places, a sign that literally means FALL DOWN is used for relapse, but many deaf persons do not know this metaphorical extension of the sign. This became clear to me after many weeks of using the sign FALL DOWN with a patient while I mouthed *relapse*. It took these many weeks before the patient finally said to me, FALL DOWN, WHO? I realized then that he had been giving me the "empty nod," pretending to understand, and I allowed myself to believe I had been clear.

To convey the concept of *relapse* into ASL, one has to identify the particular problem behavior (for example, drinking), indicate that the person tried to or wanted to stop, but then began the problem behavior again. A close translation using drinking alcohol might be INDEX (for person) DRINK-ALCOHOL (sign modified to indicate repetition) STOP. SOBER ONE-YEAR., FINISH. DRINK-ALCOHOL AGAIN. Deaf people commonly introduce concepts in this manner and then, if they want to establish an English equivalent, agree on a sign. Besides FALL-DOWN, another sign commonly used more accurately means DETERIORATE. In our program, the Deaf staff and clients discussed the meaning of the concept (a therapeutic intervention in itself), and then collectively agreed on the sign that could be translated as CIRCLE or CYCLE. This was not ideal, because we also needed a way to convey *cycle* that distinguished the concept from *relapse*, but it is what we have used because the Deaf staff and clients decided on it. This sign needs to be retaught and reagreed on whenever there are new deaf persons involved. Of course, the need for a sign to correspond to the English word is mainly a problem for English dominant people who, even if they sign, cannot quite give up on English structure. With a higher level of ASL skill, one simply describes the process in which the problem recurs. The concept is there even if there is no one sign equivalent to *relapse*.

After establishing the concept of relapse, the next concept is "prevention." There is a sign PREVENT, a verb, and it is used like this. MY CAR, JOE STEAL TRY. ME PREVENT. (*Joe tried to steal my car. I prevented him.*) The sign is not equivalent to the English noun *prevention*. Therefore, using the sign that really means PREVENT after the concept RELAPSE can be confusing to someone without a knowledge of English. The concept of preventing relapse in alcohol use might be signed as follows: PAST, ME DRINK-ALCOHOL, DRINK-ALCOHOL, DRINK-ALCOHOL STOP. FUTURE DRINK-ALCOHOL AGAIN? PREVENT! (*I used to drink a lot of alcohol. I won't let myself drink again.*) Notice that PREVENT is used properly here as a verb (prevent), not a noun (prevention).

As an English native speaker and second language user of ASL, I proceeded merrily through weeks of work signing what I thought was *relapse* while my client kept seeing me talking about someone falling down. When I went on to sign FALL-DOWN PREVENT, I suppose he thought all those conversations where about how to avoid falling down. As a hearing signer, I do not think I am unique in making this kind of error.

In a Deaf treatment group, the vocabulary will usually be a focus of sustained attention, possibly for weeks. In a hearing treatment group, the vocabulary is usually assumed or just introduced quickly with an example or two. Hearing people outside of deafness almost never know this, and when they have these deaf patients referred for care, will use concepts like *relapse prevention* as if their meaning is readily understood by all, or they will assume the interpreter will "find the right signs."

Interpreters vary in their skill, and a hearing, nonsigning clinician will not know whether the interpreter is just using a sign to match an English word or taking the time to explain the concept appropriately in ASL. A linguistically unsophisticated interpreter, of which there are many, may indeed find some signs (for example, FALL-DOWN, DETERIORATE, PREVENT) that will work with English dominant deaf people, and use them even if the deaf consumer does not understand. A linguistically sophisticated interpreter will know better. She or he will hold the dilemma of being asked to bridge a cognitive, linguistic, and cultural gap that is so enormous that it cannot be done without time and energy specifically devoted to that purpose. The interpreter probably has to stop the clinician and let him or her know the problem. It will take special expertise to teach this concept. It cannot be done quickly. If the hearing clinician wants to proceed at his or her accustomed pace, the cost will be leaving the deaf consumer behind.

A *relapse* is not the same as a *lapse*. A *lapse* usually refers to either one recurrence of a problem behavior or a near recurrence of a problem behavior. A relapse refers to the full return of the pattern of worsening problem behaviors. The distinction is important because of the *abstinence violation effect* discussed above. We need to help clients understand that just because they *lapsed* does not mean they have to *relapse*. They can still stop themselves. One drink or one instance of a problem behavior does not mean they have failed and must therefore give up. This idea is best explained through stories and examples.

Joe tried to stop drinking. For one month, he did not go to the bar. He went to AA meetings every day. He did not see his drinking buddies. Then his wife yelled at him. He had a fight. He went to the bar and ordered one beer. After he drank one beer, he thought "well, I've failed. I can't stop drinking." So he drank more and more until he was completely drunk. Later on, he talked to his counselor. He told his counselor that he failed. He is drinking again. (Then show the sign established for relapse.) *The counselor commended him for coming to see him and for talking about the problem. The counselor said, "yes, you drank again, but you haven't failed. Put that aside. You just have to start again. You made a mistake but you don't have to continue with a full relapse. You just have to choose to practice your skills again. You made a mistake. Put it aside. A mistake and a relapse are different."* Here I'm using *mistake* to approximate the concept *lapse*.

Warning Signs and Triggers

Two of the key relapse prevention concepts are *warning signs* and *triggers*. In relapse prevention work, clients are asked to anticipate problem behaviors *before* they occur by looking for indications that they *might* occur. The key skills are being able to anticipate a problem and do something to prevent it from occurring. This skill presupposes some language and thinking abilities that our clients may not have. It presupposes an ability to sequence events in time and an understanding of cause and effect. It presupposes the ability to think conditionally (that is, if this happens, then that might happen). Because persons with normal intelligence and language skills almost always have these abilities, it is easy to assume our LLC clients do as well. We have learned, especially with

Figure 7.1 Warning sign.

deaf LLC clients, that it is dangerous to make this assumption.

In ASL, one can sign WARN or WARNING* but *warning sign* is less clear. *Signs* could be indicated with the sign To-SHOW but it is best to just omit it and sign WARNING. Teaching the concept of warning signs to unsophisticated deaf clients, we focus on the idea of *warning* and give numerous examples. We use pictures of a storm cloud forming over a person swimming (Figure 7.1). We ask what the danger is and how does the person know. What is the warning sign? (WARNING WHAT?) (Figure 7.2.) We show a picture of a person sneezing (Figure 7.3) and ask what

Warning, what?

Joe feels what?

What might Joe do?

What should Joe do?

Figure 7.2 Warning sign.

this warns of. This is followed by pictures of people thinking about drugs and alcohol or showing clenched body postures or thinking about death. Each picture leads to a discussion about warning signs. We build example after example until clients understand and can begin to apply this to themselves. What is their problem? What warns them that the problem may happen again? (PROBLEM APPEAR AGAIN, WARNING, WARNING WHAT?)

---

* This is an example of a "noun-verb pair." WARN and WARNING differ slightly. WARN, as a verb, can also be inflected to show who warns whom.

Warning, what maybe happen to Joe?

What should Joe do?

Figure 7.3 Warning sign.

One especially helpful picture is of a train going down a track past literal warning signs warning that the bridge ahead is broken (Figure 7.4). This picture has the advantage of making the concept of warning signs very concrete. Another set of pictures shows a mountain with tremors while a seismograph needle shakes violently (on CD-ROM under Metaphors, also cited in Glickman, 2003). This is a five-picture series, and clients can be asked to put them in order. The sequencing establishes time. What came before warns of what comes next.

The concept is also illustrated through stories, sometimes combined with games. For example, we developed a videotape of the following story, told in ASL. We show it and then discuss the warning signs of the "blow up" by Bob.

Bob lives in a group home. He stays awake until 4:00 A.M. watching TV. Staff person George encourages him to go to bed, but he refuses. He tells George, "I can watch TV if I want to. Stop bothering me." George reminds him he has to get up for work at 8:00 in the morning. "I'll be fine," he says. He goes to bed at 4:00. At 8:00, the morning staff Alan tries to wake him up for work. He refuses to get out of bed. Alan tells him, "you have to go to work. If you don't go to work, you will get less money. You can also lose your job. Remember, your boss gave you a warning already. You show up late too much." Bob gets up but he's in a very bad mood. He refuses breakfast. He asks for three cups of coffee. The house has a rule, only one cup of coffee. He argues with Alan. He says he's tired and wants two more cups. Alan says no, follow the rule. He says to Alan, "You are always bossing me around. You don't respect me. The rule is stupid. I don't like you." He glares at Alan in a mean way. Alan says, "Please stop glaring at me. You know the rules. George told you last night not to go to bed at 4:00. You wouldn't listen. Now let's go to work."

Figure 7.4 Warning sign.

Bob walks away. He slams the door to the kitchen. He refuses to take a shower. Alan notices that he smells. Alan goes up to him and says, "Please shower." Bob says, "I'll shower later." Alan says, "I don't want to embarrass you, but you smell. You can't go to work like that. You have to shower and be clean." Bob says, "I don't smell. You smell! You stink!" He gives him the finger. Alan says, "You can't go to work smelling and messy. You can't give me the finger. I don't accept it. Please go shower and change your clothes. If you don't, I won't drive you to work."

Bob gives him the finger again. He struts toward him in a menacing way. He pushes Alan down on the floor and walks out of the house.

This story, which represents a familiar scenario for many of our clients, may have to be told a few times. Sometimes we act it out. Sometimes we make this activity into a game by handing out small cardboard signs, which have the words *warning sign* printed on them. As the story is shown, clients are asked to raise their sign every time they see a warning sign. They get points for each correct answer, and the winner gets a prize.

We want clients to relate these concepts to themselves. What are *their* problem behaviors or symptoms and what are the warnings that *they* may act or show these behaviors again? Higher functioning people can often tell you these warning signs right away. For our clients, this may be a major learning objective. In a residential or hospital setting, when staff observe warning signs, they need to educate clients about what they see. Behaviors like pacing, glaring, arguing, swearing, and insulting may warn of upcoming assaults. Isolation, withdrawal, and refusing to communicate with staff may warn of impending self harm. When staff make these observations, they need to use the sign WARNING with clients to teach them the vocabulary.

The concept of trigger comes from a gun metaphor and refers to the process of provoking or setting in motion a process. It is similar to the concept of *cause,* for which there is a sign. Triggers are also defined as stimuli that elicit or cue memories or start a chain reaction. The smell of beer may trigger memories of being high and the urge to drink. The English word "trigger" is both a noun ("What are your triggers?) and a verb (What triggers you?). There is no one sign that represents either the noun or the verb exactly. The concept must be conveyed in a much more detailed way, described below.

English and ASL have different ways of structuring sentences that refer to how people or events influence each other. In English, I may embarrass you, but in ASL, I-TEASE-YOU, YOU FEEL-EMBARRASSED. In English, *I wake you up.* In ASL, I TAP-YOU. YOU WAKE-UP. In English, *my mother shames me by yelling at me.* In ASL, MOTHER BAWL-ME-OUT, I FEEL-SHAME. In ASL, I can watch people drink (PEOPLE DRINK-ALCOHOL, ME WATCH), and then I can have a reaction such as thinking about drinking or craving a drink. The concept is structured in ASL by showing something happen and then showing someone react. The trigger is not labeled as such but rather is implied.

In ASL, the concept of trigger may be conveyed through a story. The person has a problem behavior like drinking. He walked into a bar and saw people drinking. He smelled the alcohol. He remembered the feeling of being high. All of these things influenced or caused him to want to drink. The discussion is concrete and specific to the particular person and circumstances. By giving multiple examples like this, a concept like trigger can be established. Then some sign approximating the English idea, perhaps INFLUENCE or CAUSE combined with LIST-ON-FINGERS can be agreed on. This structure makes it difficult for non-English-speaking, ASL users to carry out such common relapse prevention activities as making a list of triggers. ASL structure does not predispose them to consider "triggers" as discrete events but rather to think about the story of how problems develop.

One highly visual way to teach the concept is by lining up a chain of dominoes at the same time one tells the events of a story. In the story about Bob above, each event can be represented by a domino as follows.

1. Bob stays awake until 4:00 watching TV.
2. Bob argues with George.
3. In the morning, Bob refuses to get up at first.
4. He finally gets up in a very bad mood.

And so on. Clients can be given a stack of dominoes and asked to lay them out as each event is mentioned. Handing them the dominoes to lay out involves them. At the end of the story (end of the row of dominoes), there is a blow up. That is easily represented by asking the client to knock down the first domino in the series and watch the rest fall. The tumbling of the dominoes demonstrates a causal chain and approximates the concept of trigger (Figure 7.5).

Another advantage of using dominoes is that they can also illustrate the process of relapse prevention. The "blow up" could have been avoided at any moment in this chain of events if Bob had realized what was happening and used a coping skill or behaved differently. Suppose Bob, at the start of the sequence, agreed to go to bed? Then he would get enough sleep and probably wake up in a better mood. The first domino is moved away from the others in the chain. When it is knocked over, it does not hit another domino and the row of dominoes stays erect. This is a simple, clear demonstration of the power of doing something to avoid an unwanted outcome.

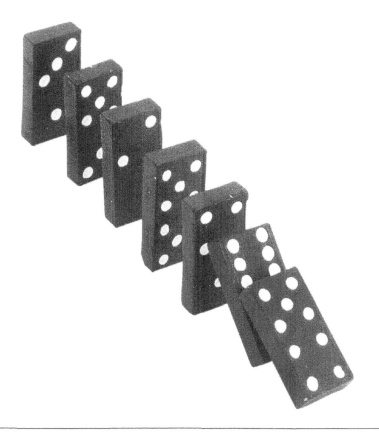

Figure 7.5 Dominoes falling representing triggers.

Risk Factors

Risk factors is another abstract concept that is essential in relapse prevention. By risk factors we mean places, situations, behaviors, feelings, and thoughts that increase the chances of relapse. *Risk factor* is also conceptualized in ASL differently from the way it is in English. There is a sign for DANGER that can also be translated as *risk*, but *factor* has no direct equivalent and is an English word that most of the clientele discussed here will not know. In ASL, it is better to start with specific instances or examples and move from there to general principles or larger categories. Therefore, we approach this concept by focusing on specific factors that are risky and then add an admonition like CAREFUL, DANGER, and then describe what might happen. For example, when talking about a person with an alcohol problem, we show a picture of the person walking into a bar to play pool. We then discuss what may happen and why playing pool in a bar is risky.

We usually introduce this topic by showing pictures of risky places, behaviors, feelings, and thoughts, in that order (that is, from most concrete to most abstract).* These pictures are on the CD-ROM. A playground is a risky place for a child molester (Figure 7.6). Partying with drinking buddies is a risky situation or risky behavior for someone trying to stay sober (Figure 7.7). Understanding how emotions can be risky is more challenging. In AA, the acronym HALT (hungry, angry, lonely, tired) is used to help members remember key emotions that make them vulnerable to drinking. For other people, different emotions or physical states like sadness or lust may be the main emotional risks.

Working with thoughts is an even more difficult skill. It sometimes works to explain that before one engages in any problem behavior, one *must* give oneself permission to do so. Before the alcoholic drinks, there will be an enabling thought like "I'll only have one" (Figure 7.8). Before an angry person assaults someone, there will be a thought about how I am a victim and the other person deserves to be hit. Before the child is molested, there will be a thought like "She really wants me." Clients are then encouraged to identify what they think before they relapse. Lots of examples help, but many clients cannot do this.

Exploring the relationship between thoughts, emotions, and behaviors is a hallmark of the school of cognitive therapy developed by Aaron Beck (A. Beck, 1976; A. Beck, Rush, Shaw, & Emery, 1979; A. Beck, Wright, Newman, & Liese, 1993; J. Beck, 1995), and a background in this is very helpful to understanding risky thinking. For instance, we know that the most common cognitive theme in suicidal people is hopelessness (Freeman & White, 1989). In chronically suicidal people, there is a very good chance that a key risk factor will be thoughts of how they have no hope. If people can recognize thoughts of

---

* A "risky situation" is also an abstraction so it is simpler and clearer to talk about risky behaviors.

A playground is a *risky place* for a child molester.

Figure 7.6 Risky place.

Partying with drinking buddies is a risky behavior.

Figure 7.7 Risky behavior.

hopelessness, they at least have the possibility of appreciating that they are in danger. If clinicians can recognize that clients are thinking they have no hope, they can help clients evaluate the reality of these ideas. Similarly, it helps clinicians to have grounding in the kind of beliefs typically associated with depression, anxiety, and anger disorders.

On the most concrete level, a relapse prevention plan may call for someone to avoid high-risk places like bars or behaviors like playing cards with one's drinking buddies. Other clients will be able to recognize and have plans for risky emotions and thoughts. Counselors should have this framework and determine what kinds of risk factors their clients are able to understand.

There is a wonderful movie called *The Woodsman* (Daniels & Kassell, 2005) that stars Kevin Bacon as a convicted pedophile recently released from prison. The movie follows him as he tries to establish a new life while fighting off urges

Figure 7.8 Risky thinking.

to reoffend. The suspense in the film comes from the question of whether or not he will relapse. He gets an apartment directly across the street from a school where he can watch children and also watch as another child molester grooms a child for molesting. He becomes preoccupied with a young girl, and he gets off the bus when she does and follows her into the park. She is bird watching, and he initiates a conversation with her about birds. Even though he is a child molester, he is portrayed in the film sympathetically, and watching him you worry, as he does, about whether he can keep from offending again. The film portrays risk factors, warning signs, and triggers, and can be a wonderful educational tool for those clients who can follow the story. This movie has been used with success in relapse prevention groups with severely psychiatrically impaired hearing sexual offenders. It may be a leap for some people to understand how it is relevant if their relapse issue is something other than sexual offending. Unfortunately, although this movie is available with captions, that only helps if one can read.

There is some overlap between the concepts of triggers, warning signs, and risk factors. The emotion of anger, for example, may be trigger, a warning sign, or a risk factor for aggression. The subtle distinctions are not so important as the understanding that the person must notice his or her own anger, realize that the problem behavior may follow, and *do something different* to prevent that from happening. People who are using relapse prevention plans think about where they can be, whom they can be with, and what emotions they have a hard time managing. Some will become aware of what people in AA call their "stinkin' thinking." The complexity and effectiveness of their relapse prevention plans depends in part on how many of these risk factors they can appreciate and the practicality of the plans they put in place for managing these issues. Even a simple, very concrete relapse prevention plan at least shows that people are agents in their own recovery, and that is our most important goal. If a client can show the skills of (a) noticing cravings to drink, (b) telling staff, and (c) engaging with staff in a distracting activity, they are doing relapse prevention. We want to recognize and label these skills appropriately and then invite the client to develop them further.

Seemingly Unimportant Decisions

Could there be a more awkward and difficult to translate English phrase that "seemingly unimportant decisions?" Could we possibly come up with an English phrase that is less "Deaf friendly?" To make matters worse, seemingly unimportant decisions are often called, simply, SUDS. If our deaf LLC clients know this word, they will likely be thinking of soap suds, which have nothing to do with it. Unfortunately, although the phrase "seemingly unimportant decisions" is cumbersome, the concept is very important.

The term seemingly unimportant decisions refers to choices of behaviors that seem innocent, or that one tells oneself are innocent, but that really correspond to early steps in the relapse process. For example, a client with a drug addiction problem wakes up in the morning, goes to his closet, and puts on his blue shirt. What could be more innocent? He goes downstairs and his partner notices the blue shirt and becomes concerned. The partner asks him, "Why are you wearing that shirt today?" He answers, "I like this shirt. It looks good on me." But his partner knows that his blue shirt is his party shirt. He saves this shirt for when he goes out drinking and drugging (Figure 7.9). Thus, the selection of this shirt only seems unimportant. By selecting this shirt, he has already put himself on the path toward drinking and drugging. He has already made the decision to do so even if only dimly aware of this.

A colleague tells this story about a series of seemingly unimportant decisions leading to his relapse. In this case, he is relapsing into eating habits that violate his diet.

I have a problem with dieting and ice cream is my weakest area. I just love ice cream, but I make sure to have no ice cream in my freezer. When I start craving ice cream, I have a coping skill plan. It involves going for a walk.

One hot day, when I was looking at the fridge a bit too long, I decided to go out for a walk. That would put some distance between me and the freezer.

When I left my house, I could have gone left or right. I happened to go left.

**JOE DECIDE WEAR BLUE SHIRT.
SEEM NOT IMPORTANT BUT...**

**JOE ALWAYS WEAR BLUE SHIRT AT PARTY.
PARTY HAVE DRINKS & DRUGS.**

Figure 7.9 Seemingly unimportant decisions.

As I was walking, I notice how hot it was and I noticed my sweating. In the distance I saw a group of stores. I thought, "they'll have air conditioning," and I headed toward them.

I randomly picked one of these stores to go into. It happened to be Ben and Jerry's ice cream parlor. I went in just to get out of the heat. I leaned against the wall and happened to notice that they were giving out free samples of Cherry Garcia, which is my favorite flavor. It has these huge cherries and chocolate bits. Anyway, I didn't want to offend the clerk. He looked like he was new at his job and was looking for business. He offered me a sample and, so as not to be rude, I accepted it.

Awhile later, as I was finishing off my Cherry Garcia sundae, I wondered how this happened.

When you tell a story like this, you can ask the client when the relapse began. You can give the client a set of dominoes and ask the client to use one domino to mark each step in the relapse. The idea is that the relapse is not the final moment of eating the ice cream. The relapse began when the person went for a walk in the direction of the ice cream store. Along the way, he made a series of decisions. They did not seem important, but they all led to, indeed were all part of, the relapse process.

Seemingly unimportant decisions refer to thinking errors, and it is a reach for many of our clients to understand their own thinking and relate it to their relapse process. If they grasp this, we would then have to help them understand how *thinking of which they are unaware* may be a factor. This challenge is like explaining the concept of the unconscious. It is a very abstract, counterintuitive idea. Nonetheless, with concrete stories such as these, clients may grasp the idea that they made a mistake or that they fooled themselves. Probably the concept of *fool self* is a good translation.

Using Coping Skills and Social Supports

After a person identifies the triggers, warning signs, and risk factors that precede a relapse, the task for them will be to *do something* to prevent the relapse. This usually means using some identified coping skill. Typically it also means drawing on some social support system.

People who anticipate the craving to drink, the impulse to hurt themselves or other people, or the thoughts that lead to sexual offending need a coping plan. If they anticipate that they will have trouble staying sober on New Year's Eve or at a planned family reunion, what will their strategy be? Will they go to an AA meeting, call their sponsor, ask a supportive friend to stay by their side, or let the party host know that they will not be drinking? Can and will they avoid risky places and people? Next time they are angry, sad, anxious, lonely, or sexually aroused, what will they do? Will they even remember at that time to use their plan?

For most individuals, recovery requires the help of other people. The 12-step meetings are based on a treatment philosophy different from relapse prevention but in practice they are often combined. In the 12-step philosophy, one realizes one's powerlessness and draws on a higher power. Addictions are referred to as diseases. In relapse prevention, addictions are understood as learned behaviors that people *can* learn to manage (even without a higher power). There is a theoretical difference between 12-step and relapse prevention models that does not seem to interfere in practice for most people. People may engage in relapse prevention and use a sponsor or their "Higher Power" as a coping strategy. This is all good.

After one develops a relapse prevention plan, the next step is practice. This may be done with the support of a counselor. A plan to use "time out" and to listen to music the next time one is angry may be good on paper, but it is not real unless it is practiced. This is where role playing becomes so important. In group or individual counseling sessions, one role plays the provocative situation and practices the coping skill. In a treatment environment such as a psychiatric hospital or residential treatment center, the skill may be learned in a counseling session and practiced in the milieu. Therefore, the milieu staff must know the client's coping skills and relapse plan so they can assist clients when they are in danger of relapsing. The first "real-life" practice the client is likely to experience will be in the treatment milieu.

A discussion of relapse prevention and crisis intervention is not complete without covering behavior analysis. Clinical staff working with clients need to have this skill, but with some simplification and practice it is also available to many paraprofessional staff and clients.

Behavior Analysis Made Relatively Simple

Relapse prevention work is based on the client having an understanding of the behaviors, feelings, thoughts, impulses, and environmental events that typically precede, as well as reinforce, a problem behavior or symptom. The process of determining what these factors are is generally called a behavior analysis.

Behavior analysis is a core problem-solving strategy in dialectical behavior therapy (DBT) (Linehan, 1993a) where the chronic self-harming behaviors of persons with borderline personality disorder are treated as *problems to be solved.* This is compatible with a relapse prevention framework in that the relapse problem is the self-harming behaviors. Linehan writes, "The purpose of a behavioral analysis is to figure out what the problem is, what is causing it, what is interfering with the resolution of the problem, and what aids are available to help solve the problem.... Behavioral analysis in DBT refers specifically to the in-depth analysis of one particular instance or set of instances of a problem or a targeted behavior. Thus it is a self-conscious and focused attempt on the part of the therapist (and, one hopes, the patient) to determine the factors leading up to, following, and 'controlling' or influencing the behavior" (pp. 254–255).

The approach to behavior analysis presented here is modeled on the approach in DBT although, like everything in this book, simplified perhaps beyond recognition for DBT purists. Our LLC clients are not going to do complex behavior analyses. We need a framework that can adapt to the cognitive framework of the clients, giving us a richer or sparser behavior analysis depending on their abilities.

When we strive to answer the question why a behavior occurred, it is natural to assume we are looking for a true explanation. However, in practice it is quite hard to determine what is true. Behaviors have many causes and influences, and truth, like beauty, can be in the eye of the beholder. Rather, the explanation or story must be *useful.* The story has to point to solutions that will really help the client avoid the problem behavior. As Linehan notes, "it is important to keep in mind ... that interpretations, like other theories, cannot be evaluated in terms of "truth," but only in terms of utility. They either help in the change process or do not help, and at times they can actually be detrimental" (p. 266).

The process of simple behavior analysis presented here will always lead to at least one of four explanations or theories about why a behavior occurred. Any and all of these may be part of the *truth,* but each of these is useful. We will always find that problem behaviors or symptoms occurred because:

1. The client could not tolerate an emotion, impulse, or bodily sensation.
2. The client did not respond skillfully to a problem.

3. The client made a thinking error and gave himself or herself permission to relapse.
4. Something in the environment reinforced the problem behavior.

We will "find" these explanations because that is the nature of the story we construct. We could find other explanations; for instance, that problem behaviors occur because of moral failings, the influence of ancestors, evil spirits, bad karma, unconscious motivation, economic and social forces, or interference by aliens, but these "truths" correspond to other narratives. More importantly, they are not useful.

To conduct a behavioral analysis with a client, these steps are followed:

1. Start with the problem behavior. The behavioral analysis is an analysis of *that* behavior, not of the problem in general. For instance, the relapse problem may be aggressive behaviors, but the behavior analysis is always of a particular instance of that behavior. Why did *that* behavior occur in *that* time and place? The particular incident needs to be described in, as we say, nauseating detail.
2. We then ask the client to *tell the story* of what happened. Depending on the client's abilities to construct a narrative, this may take quite some time. At the most concrete level, we just want to know what happened first, second, third, and so on. To flesh out the story, we help clients put events in sequential order (no small task with many clients) and we ask questions like, "What happened next?" With some of our LLC clients, most of the work of the behavior analysis consists of pulling out of them this story.
3. Depending on client abilities, we will also want to know what the client felt and thought at particular moments in the process. It is usually easier for clients to say what they felt than what they thought. We will probe for their thinking because if they can identify their thoughts and beliefs, we will have additional options for intervention.
4. We also want to know what happened after the problem behavior. Knowing the consequences of a behavior may clue us in to the client's motivation. For instance, if following an episode of cutting, the patient obtains an enormous amount of sympathy and support from staff, it is very likely that the staff response is reinforcing the behavior. It is possible the client's motivation is to elicit that support.

As the story is told, we look for the four themes listed above. The first theme is that the client felt an emotion or some other bodily sensation and could not tolerate it. This is the theme that DBT privileges. Linehan comments, "With respect to antecedent or eliciting variables, DBT focuses most closely on intense or aversive emotional states. Maladaptive behavior, to a large extent, is viewed as resulting from emotion dysregulation. The amelioration of unendurable emotional pain is always suspected as one of the primary motivational factors in borderline dysfunctional behavior" (p. 265).

Because, like DBT, our focus is primarily on skill development, we tend to also find that the reason the problem behavior occurred was that the client did not use a skill (explanations 1 and 2). If we see, for instance, that before an assault the client felt angry, then we know the client has a problem managing anger. We might represent this simply as:

Feel angry → blow-up

For some very limited patients, our finished behavioral analysis is no more complex than this. But even this simple analysis is useful. Fleshing it out a bit more with the client, we would conclude:

Feeling angry → don't use coping skill→ blow-up

In our cognitive behavioral framework, anger does not cause aggression. Rather, people become aggressive when they feel angry and lack skills to cope with the anger. Similarly, sadness or shame need not lead to cutting if the person has a coping strategy for sadness and shame. A drug or alcohol craving need not lead to substance abuse if the person recognizes the warning signs and seeks out assistance, like going to a 12-step meeting.

This simple behavior analysis points out one avenue of treatment. It leads the client to discover that what he or she lacks are skills to manage the high-risk emotions. If this is recognized, our treatment strategy is obvious. It is to help the client acquire the needed coping skills. To prevent relapse, this person needs to *stop and notice* the risky feeling and then use a coping skill. If the client engages in the behavior analysis meaningfully, the process can be another pretreatment intervention leading to a practical, relevant treatment plan.

The second theme a behavior analysis may show is a failure to use some other skill. For instance, if before an aggressive assault, the analysis shows that the client and a peer argued over a television program, the problem may be both failure to cope with anger and failure to use conflict resolution skills. If before a suicide attempt, the client and her spouse fought over money or sex or family responsibilities, and the client then blamed herself, she is showing both an inability to cope with the emotions as well as a lack of communication and conflict resolution skills. Our analysis could take us in either or both directions. The analysis could also reveal her dysfunctional thinking, discussed below.

Broadly speaking, all these skill deficits represent failures in problem solving. This is one of Linehan's major points. The client says "I'm suicidal" as if that were the problem. Becoming suicidal represents a failure in problem solving. This is highlighted in the phrase, often told to persons who are suicidal, that *suicide represents a permanent solution to a temporary problem.* What is the problem that the person tries to solve through suicide? Is it how to cope with painful emotion, how to repair damaged relationships, how to step away from the conclusion that one is a miserable failure, or something else? Our task is to develop clients' problem-solving skills so that they understand suicide to be one of many solutions, with the other solutions superior. If, in the process of conducting a behavior analysis, we can expose a moment when more skills would have led to a different outcome, we may reveal for clients a way out of the psychological impasse they experience.

The third theme a behavior analysis may show is what some cognitive therapists call a *thinking error*. The cognitive therapy approaches pioneered by Ellis (1962) and Beck (1976) are based on their understanding of how irrational or dysfunctional thinking patterns and beliefs contribute to psychopathology. Constructivist narrative cognitive behavioral therapy (CBT) (Meichenbaum, 1994, 2001) concerns itself with the impact of the story that clients tell themselves. In either case, there is a thinking pattern, belief, or story that contributes to the relapse. I think the simplest way to convey this idea is to explain that before people relapse they must say something to themselves to *give themselves permission to relapse*. They may not be aware of this because they are not attending to their thoughts and because they do not necessarily think in fully articulated sentences. But in some way they will think "Go ahead. It's ok to do it." If possible, we want to expose this for them.

All three of these themes are illustrated in the following story, an example of a behavior analysis with an LLC deaf client (Figure 7.10).

Figure 7.10 Use of a thought bubble in a behavior analysis.

Jim bumped into Emelio, and then Emelio punched Jim in the face. We are sitting with Emelio, doing a behavior analysis of his assault on Jim. We explain that we are meeting to understand better what led him to punch Jim and how he can avoid doing that in the future.

We ask Emelio to tell the story of what happened. Emelio's initial account, like most of our clients, is sparse. Jim bumped into him. Emelio punched him back. It's Jim's fault. We write these two events down.

"When Jim bumped into you, how did you feel?"

"Mad. He punched me. He did it on purpose. He's a jerk."

Emelio does not realize it, but he has just told us not only how he felt, but, just as importantly, what he thought Jim's behavior meant. People who are not aware of their thinking and beliefs will nonetheless tell you what they think. The counselor has to know the difference between a feeling (angry) and a thought (he did it on purpose; he's a jerk) so that the counselor can help the client recognize his own thinking. The counselor already knows that Emelio talked himself into feeling angry and gave himself permission to assault Jim. She is searching for a way to help Emelio discover this thinking.

"So he bumped into you. You felt mad. And then you thought, 'He's a jerk. He did it on purpose'."

"He is a jerk! He did do it on purpose." Emelio is repeating his interpretation of reality. His interpretation may or may not reflect Jim's intentions. The counselor is working on a different level. She's not arguing over what is "true." She is trying to show Emelio how he thinks.

To reveal Emilio's thinking, the counselor writes his thoughts down in a thought bubble. She adds some additional thoughts that she guesses may be there ("He always does that. I won't accept it. I'll show him I'm tough") but checks these out.*

"Is this what you thought? What else did you think?"

Emelio still does not quite get it. He continues to say what he thinks without recognizing that he is providing his beliefs. He thinks he is describing reality.

"Jim is an asshole. He pushes everyone around. He wants to beat me up."

The counselor just adds these new thoughts to the bubble.

"So all this is going on in your mind? Wow. No wonder you felt angry."

The counselor then makes an educated guess about what else Emelio probably thought. "Did you think that he deserved to get hit? That you'd teach him a lesson? That you'd show him you were tough?"

"Yeah."

The counselor adds this information to the behavior analysis without judging whether it was right or wrong. "Ok, so now we know what you were feeling, what you were thinking and what you did." She draws it on paper with arrows showing connections.

---

* Emelio can read simple words. The counselor signs to him what she wrote just in case.

Jim bumps into Emelio → Emelio thinks (shows the thought bubble) →
Emelio feels angry → Emelio punches Jim

Even this short discussion shows all three themes we have discussed so far. It shows what Emelio felt and thought. It also shows that he lacked both the coping skills to handle his own anger and the communication and problem-solving skills to respond to this perceived provocation from Jim in a nonviolent way. The treatment or relapse prevention plan we develop from this might focus on coping, conflict resolution, or problem-solving skills or helping Emelio change his thinking. In all likelihood, the cognitive avenue will not be available to Emelio immediately, but it is worth planting the seeds because sometimes clients surprise us.

The fourth theme that a behavior analysis might highlight is whether the consequences of the person's behavior in some way reinforced it. To find out if this is so in this case, we would need to ask Emelio what happened next. We want to know if his assault paid off for him in some way.

"After you hit Jim, what happened?"

"Jim yelled at me, but he didn't hit me. I think he was scared. Staff came over and separated us. Staff blamed me and I lost my privileges."

"Staff blamed you and you lost your privileges? Is that what you wanted?"

"No. It isn't fair."

"And how are you and Jim getting along? You used to be friends."

"He's not my friend."

"Is that what you want? I remember that you two used to hang out together a lot."

Jim is quiet for awhile and then answers. "I don't know. I don't care."

As best we can tell, Emelio did not want the outcome: staff being upset with him, loss of privileges, and at least temporary loss of his friendship with Jim. Therefore, it is unlikely that the consequences reinforced the behavior. We would have come to a different conclusion if the conversation went as follows:

"After you hit Jim, what happened?"

"Sue (staff) talked to me for a long time. We went for a walk. After I calmed down, we went for ice cream."

A fuller behavior analysis could reveal much more. What was Emelio's mood like before Jim bumped into him? Did he get enough sleep the night before? Was he hungry or stressed? Did he have a headache or was there some other physical or emotional stressor that set the stage for him coping badly? Has he been taking his medicine? What other stressors or perceived provocations were occurring in the environment? What do we know about Emelio and Jim's previous relationship that might bear on this encounter?

We have enough of a behavior analysis to reveal some of the factors that preceded Emelio's assault on Jim. The outline of a relapse prevention plan is implicit: helping Emelio recognize and name mood states, developing his repertoire of coping and conflict resolution skills, anticipating new situations where he will feel angry and think the same way, and developing and practicing a coping plan in advance. This is what we want to accomplish, but we will have to see how far along we can bring Emelio.

The counselor points toward the thought bubble with Emelio's thoughts. "So after Jim hit you, this is what you thought and you felt angry? I understand but I wonder if you had any other options?"

"What do you mean?"

"Well, you were angry. Do you have to hit someone because you are angry?"

"But if I don't hit him, he'll push me again."

"You *think* that if you don't hit him, he'll push you again. This is what you think. But is that true? Did you have another way to solve the problem?"

"I don't know." (He does know, but he is not quite ready to acknowledge it.)

"Well, if you bumped into me, what would I do?"

"But you're staff!"

"You mean staff don't get mad?"

"No, but staff can't hit patients."

"Why?"

"Cause you'd get fired."

"Right, exactly! We have to control our feelings. If you had controlled your feeling, if you'd used one of the coping skills, what would have been different?"

"I don't know."

"Sure you do. Would you have lost your privileges? Would you be in trouble? "

"No, but that's not fair. It's not my fault."

"Do you hear me blaming you? I'm only trying to help you see that you have other options. You could have used some skills. What could you have done?"

Emelio and the counselor discuss how both coping and conflict resolution skills could have been used. Then the counselor asks, "Do you think we can practice together some of those skills?"

"Ok."

"Where do you want to start? Should we think about how you and Jim could talk to each other?"

What about Emelio's thinking? Is he capable of understanding how his thinking led to his assault? It will certainly be difficult for Emelio to appreciate that his thinking reflects beliefs, not reality. He is unlikely to be able to analyze thinking errors or patterns. Expecting him to analyze his thinking is unlikely to be productive. A simpler cognitive skill, though still a reach for Emelio, is to change his self-talk.

The counselor reviews. "You see here what you tell yourself? You say, 'Jim's a jerk. He pushed me on purpose. He always does that. I won't accept this. I'll show him I'm tough.' You think that, and you feel what?" If Jim cannot come up with the answer on his own, the counselor assists by pointing to the words "Feel Angry" on the behavior analysis.

"Angry."

"Yes, and then what did you do?"

"I hit him."

"Suppose you said to yourself something different? Suppose you said, 'I feel like hitting Jim, but I won't because I don't want to get in trouble.' Or suppose you said, 'He pushed me, but if I blow up, he wins. If I stay calm, I win.' If you said that, would you still push him?"

"No."

"Would that be better?"

Emelio shrugs a tepid agreement.

"You're not sure. What if you told yourself something else? What if you told yourself, 'maybe that was an accident'?"

"It wasn't an accident!"

"You're sure of that, but I'm not. Because when I talked to Jim, he didn't know why you hit him. He says he did bump into you by accident."

"He's lying."

"When you tell yourself, 'He's lying. He did it on purpose to hurt me,' you feel angry and blow up. If you tell yourself, 'It's an accident,' what will you feel and what will you do?"

The counselor explores whether this line of questioning is productive. If Emelio can at least grasp the advantages to him of thinking differently, this can be practiced. He will have more skill resources available if he can. If this line of questioning does not work, the counselor falls back on more concrete coping strategies like "shield," "walking away," or the sensory modulation strategies described in Chapter 5.

The counselor should always remember that skills are being used in the current conversation. At *this* moment, Emelio is listening, taking turns talking, staying in control, and to some extent problem solving. If any skills like this are occurring, the counselor has evidence *in the present moment* of skills the client is capable of, and this can be pointed out and used as evidence of how the client can do better.

The counselor was aided in this behavior analysis by her knowledge of how angry people typically think. For example, when angry people show aggressive behaviors, the following thinking patterns are very likely (A. Beck, 1999; Larson, 2005; Meichenbaum, 2001):

1. The person is attending selectively to environmental cues, only seeing cues that reinforce his sense of being victimized. For instance,
   Emelio noticed Jim's bumping into him but did not notice Jim's apology, embarrassed look, or attempt to correct the situation.
2. Attributing hostile intent. Emelio was quick to conclude that Jim did
   it on purpose to hurt him. This may not have been Jim's motivation
   at all.
3. Thinking that the person should not behave that way and should
   know better.
4. Thinking that what the person did was awful and unbearable
   (A. Beck, 1976; A. Beck et al., 1979).
5. Thinking that the person *always* does that.
6. Applying a pejorative label such as "jerk" or "asshole."
7. Deciding that the person *deserves* to be hit.
8. Having a limited repertoire of problem-solving skills so that he actually knows how to handle the situation nonviolently.

Similarly, it helps to know how substance abusers talk themselves into
using substances (Beck et al., 1993), suicidal people convince themselves that
suicide is their only option (Freeman & White, 1989), child abusers or rapists
justify their behaviors to themselves (Marshall, Anderson, & Fernandez, 1999;
Schwartz & Canfield, 1996), people talk themselves into mood and anxiety
disorders (Beck, 1976; Beck et al., 1979), and so forth. The counselor armed
with knowledge of likely cognitive distortions associated with particular
problems is prepared to "discover" them in the behavior analysis.

Conducting behavior analysis with LLC clients involves adapting to their
cognitive and language abilities. I have a yoga teacher who guides a class of
students with widely differing abilities. Some can twist and contort themselves into pretzel like postures while others have difficulty holding their arms
erect over their heads. When this teacher introduces new postures, she always
asks students to notice whether this posture "is available to you." Many of the
postures she models are not "available" to me, but she always presents modifications and simplifications. Often these modifications are actually developmental precursors to the posture she is teaching. When we do the simpler
modifications with the right spirit, we are still doing yoga. We are doing the
yoga that is available to us.

If we are sitting with a client who is honestly interested in learning to control his or her behaviors, but whose capacity for analysis is very limited, we
may come up with a very simple behavior analysis. It may look like this:

Jim called me stupid → I got mad → I didn't use my shield → I hit him

This is just as much a behavior analysis as lying on one's back while observing one's breath is a yoga posture provided it is done with the right spirit.

Adapting the behavior analysis to fit the abilities of the client is like learning to modify yoga postures for the beginner. In both cases, the adaptations are relatively easy. It is engendering the right attitude and spirit that is the real clinical challenge.

Susan Salinas, a Deaf social worker on the Deaf Unit, developed a simple, pictorial way to conduct a behavior analysis with LLC deaf clients. She represents the different components of behavior analysis with construction paper cutouts. Thoughts are depicted with thought bubbles. Feelings are written inside cut-out hearts. The problem behaviors that are the focus of analysis are written inside a star. Other people's reactions are depicted with a circle, other events with squares. Sue cuts out sets of each of these and brings them with her to behavior analysis sessions. When the client identifies the problem behavior, she writes this in the starlike figure and puts it in the center of the table. As feelings became identified, they are written into the heart shapes. Thoughts were put into the thought bubbles, neutral events into the squares, other people's reactions into circles. The client tells her story, but so often it does not come out in a nice linear narrative. The linear narrative is actually "co-constructed" between the counselor and client as the client tells the story and Sue organizes it. Usually, they act out the story. Sue often has clients draw the moments of the story with faces expressing emotions and, where possible, thought bubbles with simple thoughts inside. Using these cutouts, pictures, and drawings, and sometimes giving hours to the task, she has engaged very language and cognitively impaired clients in behavior analysis. In her skillful work in this area, she is very much a yogi master.

Self-Monitoring and Relapse Prevention

In Chapter 4, I discussed how promoting client self-evaluation is a pre-treatment strategy. One means of self-evaluation is a self-monitoring form. These forms should be individually tailored to the needs of clients. On a self-monitoring form, clients may monitor:

- Moods and feelings
- Positive and negative behaviors
- Attitude
- Thoughts
- Symptoms
- Skills
- Activities

When clients understand the English relapse prevention terms, self-monitoring forms can also include:

- Warning signs
- Triggers

- Risky places, behaviors, emotions, and thoughts
- Seemingly unimportant decisions
- Coping skills
- Social supports

A self-monitoring form using these terms looks a lot like a written relapse prevention plan. Clients who do not understand these English words may be able to monitor specific components if these are identified or shown in pictures. The complexity of the forms, like the complexity of all our treatment interventions, is adjusted according to clients' abilities and needs. The CD-ROM accompanying this volume can assist in construction of pictorial self-monitoring forms for clients who do not read well. Clients may monitor these issues with or without understanding them as components of relapse prevention, but clients do need a rationale for the activity.

Very few of our LLC deaf clients develop detailed relapse prevention plans while they are in the hospital. This is as much because of the challenge of helping them assume full responsibility for their recovery as the challenge of presenting relapse information to them in a way they can use it. However, we can often conduct at least preliminary behavior analysis and gain some awareness of the factors contributing to their persisting problems. We can put what we learn into self-monitoring forms and crisis management plans. For instance, we had one assaultive client whose warning signs consisted of hostile glaring, refusing groups and other programming, "giving the finger," and making threats. This client was not motivated to monitor these things on her own but she did participate in the development of a self-monitoring form where pictures of these behaviors were presented. As part of our crisis management plan, when staff saw these warning signs they would take out the self-monitoring form and ask her to complete it at that moment. They would ask her, in particular, whether these behaviors indicated she was planning to assault someone. They would also invite her to use some of the coping skills that were in her skill repertoire. This strategy was sometimes successful in deescalating her behaviors.

Another deaf client used a self-monitoring form on his own as part of his relapse prevention plan. This client would hurt himself when he believed that various people were trying to poison him. He was intelligent and had good language skills and he was able to notice his thoughts, though he believed the conspiracy against him was real. He could also make the connection between his beliefs, accurate or not, and his self-harming behaviors. His relapse prevention plan called on him to monitor his mood, thoughts, and behaviors, including "obsessions with people poisoning me" that we identified as key risk factors. He had an identified coping strategy that was to communicate these thoughts to key people and allow them to reassure him that nobody was trying to poison him. This plan was very successful in helping him keep himself safe as well as reconnect with family members from whom he had distanced himself. However, this client had the resources to make use of a relapse prevention plan.

Using Relapse Prevention Games and Stories

One can pick up any workbook on relapse prevention and find exercises where people are asked to identify their warning signs, triggers, risk factors, and so on. With clients who can understand these concepts, we can also introduce them through a game. For example, a relapse prevention game can be made like the following:

Warning Signs	Triggers	Risks	Coping Skills	Supports
$25	$25	$25	$25	$25
$50	$50	$50	$50	$50
$75	$75	$75	$75	$75
$100	$100	$100	$100	$100

With each category, questions can be listed that get progressively more difficult. If a Jeopardy format (more complicated) is used, then the answers are listed and people are asked to give the questions. For instance, using a non-Jeopardy format, the questions for each category could be:

Warning Signs

$25 What are the warning signs of a cold?
$50 What are warning signs that a person may hit someone?
$75 What are warning signs that a person may use pot again?
$100 What are warning signs that a person may hurt himself?

Triggers

$25 What behavior could trigger someone to get sick?
$50 John sees his drinking friends go into his favorite bar. What might this trigger?
$75 Sam sees Susan spending time with Joe. Sam likes Susan and feels jealous. What might his jealousy trigger?
$100 How can a memory trigger a relapse?

Risks

$25 What is a risky place for an alcoholic?
$50 What is a risky emotion for someone who blows up?
$75 What is a risky emotion for someone who hurts themselves?
$100 It is New Year's Eve. Betty, an alcoholic, has some risky thoughts. What might they be?

Coping Skills

$25   What is a good way to cope with the flu?
$50   Describe a coping skill to help avoid blowing up.
$75   Name two coping skills to help someone not cut themselves.
$100   What can you do to cope with feeling lonely?

Supports

$25   Name one person you can talk to when you are angry.
$50   What is the name of a group that can help a drug addict?
$75   If you feel like hurting yourself, how can someone else help?
$100   What are the 12 steps and how can they help?

To spice a game like this up, one can add "daily double" or "bonus points" for certain questions. New questions can be developed to keep the game fresh.

A board game format can also be used in which people move through a path on a board, stopping at various points to address particular obstacles. One can land on spaces that require one to pick a card from categories like those given above. One can get points (or move forward on the board) for avoiding relapse and lose points (or move backward, or return to the hospital or jail) for relapsing. Some clients might enjoy constructing the board game with staff, an activity that would probably be more valuable than playing the game.

But a better means of teaching skills is through stories. A rather long story follows. We have videotaped this story using a native ASL user and shown it to clients, using it to create a discussion. It is too long and detailed for many clients, but people with better language skills and attention span, such as most staff learning the concepts, can make use of it. All the relapse prevention concepts are illustrated through the story.

George has a problem with drinking and aggression. When he gets drunk, he loses his temper easily and hits people. The last time he got drunk, he got into an argument with someone at a bar, broke a chair and threatened people, and the police came and arrested him. He stayed 2 days in jail, and then was sent to a hospital. In the hospital, the doctor told him he has bipolar disorder. That means sometimes he gets very depressed and sometimes he gets "manic." When he gets manic, he does not sleep well, stays out all night partying, drives fast, spends lots of money, picks up prostitutes, gambles and loses a lot of money, and drinks. That is usually when he gets in trouble.

George did not believe the doctor's diagnosis. He told the doctor that sometimes he likes to party but that's normal. He said he doesn't need any medicine. The doctor and the staff tried to convince him to take medicine but he refused. He said, "Medicine is for crazy people. I'm not crazy." He accepted that he has to stop drinking. He said, "I know I have a bad temper. I know I drink too much. I can stop drinking. I don't need any help." The staff tried to convince him to go to an AA meeting. George said "AA meetings are for losers! I don't fit in there." He insisted, "I can stop drinking on my own."

George is married and has two teenage kids. His wife Alice agrees he has a drinking problem. For years, she has told him to stop drinking. She is afraid of him when he gets drunk. Sometimes he breaks things and a few times he hit her. His kids do not like to be with him when he's drunk. Recently, his son, Ed, who is 15, started drinking beer.

When George was in the psychiatric hospital, he did not go to treatment groups. He refused to go to AA meetings and he did not want to develop a relapse prevention plan. He said, "My relapse prevention plan is my willpower. I refuse to drink again. Period." When George got out of the hospital, he promised his wife and kids he would not drink any more. At that time, he was serious. He meant it.

About a week later, George had a really bad day at work. He is a real estate salesman, and his boss has been bothering him about not selling enough houses. His boss told him that if he does not sell five more houses that month, he will lose his job. George does not like his boss. George is trying hard to sell houses but the economy is not good and people are not buying like they used to.

On Friday, George was very close to selling one big house. The person agreed to buy the house and the seller and buyer agreed on a price. George had spent 3 days helping them negotiate a deal. They went to the final meeting to sign the house contract. At the last meeting, the seller changed his mind. He said he decided not to sell the house. George had wasted 3 days of work and gotten no money. He told his boss that the deal did not go through. His boss said, "You don't seem to know how to sell a house. I'll give you one more week to make a deal or you are fired."

George thought about going for a drink, but he remembered that he promised not to drink. He checked his wallet and saw he had $10. He thought about picking up few beers on the way home. He took the $10 out of his wallet and put it in a separate envelope so he would have it "just in case." "I won't drink," he said "unless things get really, really bad."

George was not taking any medication. He was feeling tired and depressed about his job. He did not know how he could sell a house in the next week. He would talk to Alice about it but she never seemed to understand him. She just argued. He felt like he just wanted to go hide.

When he got home that day, Alice told him that the school had called about Ed. The principal said Ed has skipped school the last 3 days and today he showed up smelling of alcohol. When the principal confronted Ed about it, Ed denied drinking and told the principal to "go to hell." Then the principal suspended Ed for a week.

When George got home, Alice told him right away about Ed. He was tired and worried about work. He told Alice, "You go talk to Ed." Alice said, "You are *his father. He will listen to you more. Besides, he just drinks because he sees you drinking. He copies you. If you tell him to stop, he will."*

George got mad at Alice. "You are blaming me for Ed's drinking? Maybe he drinks because his mother ignores him. At least I play basketball with him. What do you do? You never do anything fun with him. Maybe if you were a better mother, he wouldn't be in trouble now."

Alice said to him, "Don't blame me! I'm not the one who drinks and gambles and wastes all our money. This is your fault and you have to fix it." Then she walked away.

George was really angry and started thinking mean things about his wife. He thought about hitting her, but he stopped himself. He went to talk to Ed who was in his room.

He said to Ed, "I heard you got suspended for skipping school and drinking. What's the matter with you? Do you want to grow up to be a bum? You are grounded for the whole week, and if you skip school again, you'll be grounded for the year."

Ed said, "It's not fair! You didn't even ask my opinion. Besides, you drink all the time. Why can't I drink a few beers if you drink all the time?"

"I'm an adult and you're a kid," said George. "And I've stopped drinking."

"I'm not a kid. I'm 15. I can do what I want."

"You are grounded!" said George. "Your attitude stinks."

George walked out and Ed slammed the door. George almost went back in to yell at him, but then he had another idea. He thought about the $10 he had put away in the envelope.

George thought about all his problems. He thought about losing his job. He thought about his fights with his wife and son. He and Alice had not been getting along for months. She refused to have sex with him. He felt like a failure. He was mad at everyone. He thought, "What's the point of trying to be sober when nothing I do works anyway. I might as well have a drink so I can feel better. I'll just have one. Then I'll stop. Alice won't know."

George left the house and went down to the bar. He went in and ordered a beer. That cost $4.00. After he drank one, he felt a little better, so he ordered a second. "Two is no big deal. After the hard day I've had, I deserve it," he thought. After he had the second, he wanted to order a third, but he realized he did not have enough money. He went up to someone he knew and asked to borrow a few dollars. The man's name was Bill. "No way," said Bill. "The way you drink and gamble, I wouldn't lend you a penny."

This really got George mad. "Go to hell!" he said to Bill. Then he shoved him. Bill was surprised at the shove, and he turned around and punched George in the face. Then they started fighting. George grabbed a beer bottle and tried to hit Bill in the head with it. He missed but broke the bottle on the table and damaged the table. The bouncer threw them both out and the bartender called the police. When the police came, they arrested both George and Bill.

Some of the questions that can be used with this story include:

1. How did this relapse happen?
2. What stressors did George face?
3. What were his triggers and warning signs?
4. Did George make a "seemingly unimportant decision" that led to his relapse?
5. What were high-risk places, behaviors, thoughts, and feelings for George?
6. What role did George's mental illness have in his relapse?
7. What skills did George not use?
8. What skills could he have used to avoid this relapse?

Again, this story is far too complex for many LLC clients. Stories should be constructed to fit the cognitive and language capacities of clients. Another potential weakness of this story, and the shorter one about Bob given earlier in the chapter, is that the characters relapse and there is no positive ending. Shapiro (1993; Shapiro & Shore, 1993), in his book on stories and storytelling techniques with children, stresses the importance of stories providing positive modeling. The hero of the story should in the end demonstrate the skills and behaviors that are desired. I am not sure this is always needed in storytelling with adults, but certainly we want to discuss how the hero could have behaved differently, how the relapse could have been avoided. An option is to ask the group to devise a new ending in which the client, using relapse prevention skills, avoids the problem behavior.

Another narrative technique that often engages people is the shared storytelling technique developed by Gardner (1986). In this technique, a story is collaboratively developed between counselor and clients. Because the story is ostensibly about someone else, it is not likely to elicit the defensiveness that direct questions to clients may elicit. The counselor can still shape the story so that the issues addressed are similar to those that clients struggle with. One can also teach relapse prevention concepts through the story. In one group we held, the counselor began by listing these concepts on the board and asking the clients to make up some examples. The "template" for the story then looked like this:

Client: *Tom, age 23, alcoholic, lives in a halfway house*
Relapse problem: *Drinking*
Warning signs: *He disappears without telling staff, lies to people, shows a negative attitude*
Triggers: *Seeing his friend Joe drinking; feeling sad and angry*
Risky places: *Bars, liquor stores, parties where people are drinking*
Risky emotions: *Depression, anger*

Risky thoughts: *"I'll just have one drink," "I worked hard all day and I deserve a drink"*
Support system: *AA, sponsor, counselor, family, group home staff*
Coping skills: *Go to work, focus on his health, go to AA every day*

With this template on the board, staff and clients proceeded in a round, developing and embellishing the story. The counselor started the story, describing how Tom became a problem drinker and how he got to live in the halfway house. The clients picked up the story, and though it was a bit disjointed they nonetheless produced a generally coherent narrative (a feat in itself) reflecting relevant themes. One of the clients involved in the group was someone who minimized the obstacles to recovery, telling staff repeatedly that he had decided to become sober and did not need a relapse prevention plan. By asking him to develop the story about Tom's struggle to recover, the counselor was able to lessen his resistance to discussing his own path toward relapse. We also had the group fashion alternative endings to the story, one of relapse and one of continued sobriety.

What Use Are Relapse Prevention Skills With Very Low Functioning Clients?

We have seen that relapse prevention work requires a much higher level of responsibility taking, cognitive functioning, and psychosocial skill than either coping or conflict resolution skills. Is there any point in doing this work with clients with severe language and learning challenges? Throughout this book, I have emphasized that all this work must be approached developmentally. That is, we move from pretreatment to treatment, from simple to more complex skills, and we bring our clients as far as they can go. Thus the issue is not whether someone can acquire relapse prevention skills, yes or no, but rather what aspects of relapse prevention work they can do. In the following two cases, clients could do very little formal relapse prevention, but the framework was useful for helping staff explore what they were capable of. The relapse prevention skills framework also provided the template for treatment and crisis intervention plans.

Dave is Deaf, mildly retarded, and severely language dysfluent. He has a problem of sexually assaulting women by grabbing their breasts and buttocks. He was hospitalized after new incidents of this. He is a client of the Department of Mental Health, and he carries a diagnosis of a major psychotic disorder. This is the main reason he was hospitalized rather than arrested. After a few days on our Unit, he grabbed the breasts of a female peer. They were separated and counseled, and the peer was moved to another unit for safety. Soon after, I attempted to engage him in a behavior analysis. I wanted to explore what he could understand. I was looking to see if he could narrate to me the story of the series of events leading up to his assault. Could he say what happened first, second, and third? Can he describe his feelings and thoughts at that time? Because I do not have the native ASL skills that are required to work effectively with him, I worked alongside our lead interpreter, a native signer.

Dave remembered the assault. He described what happened that morning. He remembered the layout of the room and where everyone was standing. He remembered going up to his female peer and grabbing her breasts from behind. But what was he feeling right before he grabbed her? Dave could only answer by repeating a sign that might mean STRESS or PRESSURE but was not clear in this context. He also signed (two hands, five fingers extended and moving toward him repeatedly) something that could be translated roughly as COMING-AT-ME. He did not say what was coming at him. He described some of his thinking (something was coming at him) but he could not identify it as thinking. As best we could tell, he was saying that staff were pressuring him to touch the girl. It was the staff pressure that was coming at him. That was our best guess. Failing to get him to be clearer on his own, we asked him, "Did you think staff were telling you to touch her?" He answered yes, and continued to answer yes when we asked him differently. But is that what he really thought or was he just agreeing with our suggestions?

We went on to ask an even more difficult question. Is he sure staff told him to touch her or might he have imagined it? He answered predictably that staff told him. He may not have understood the sign for IMAGINE or MAKE-UP. We replied that if staff told him that they should all be fired. Grabbing her breasts was wrong and staff would not suggest that. Did staff not grab him to pull him away afterward? We knew that Dave had stopped taking his medication and that these kinds of behaviors occurred before when he was off his medication. We knew he was very confused at the time. We reminded him that when he stops his medicine, his mind "goes down." Maybe that happened here. Maybe he thought staff told him that but they did not. We then put a series of dominoes out in a row and pointed to each one as we described what may have happened.

1. He stopped taking his medicine.
2. His mind became more confused.
3. The girl was here in a group.
4. He felt "pressure" to grab her.
5. He thought staff were telling him to go ahead.
6. He forgot about the consequences.
7. He grabbed her breasts.

Dave agreed with this story, but both the interpreter and I felt unsure it represented his account. My doubt was partly due to his poor language skills and my need to impose some kind of linguistic structure on his vagueness. Maybe we pulled the story from him but maybe he was just agreeing with whatever we came up with. Part of my doubt was wondering whether, language issues aside, he might be showing run-of-the-mill blaming, denial, and evasiveness. LLC clients are also capable of lying but because of their communication problems we tend to give them the benefit of the doubt. We have even known LLC clients who are smart enough to pretend to understand less than they do.

This account represents the best behavioral analysis that we could construct collaboratively with Dave. Its accuracy is highly questionable but the exercise of doing this analysis served a therapeutic purpose. In the course of constructing this story, Dave was helped to understand that he needed his medication to avoid new sexual assaults. Later that day, he approached his psychiatrist unprompted and explained to him that he wanted more medication so he would not touch any woman again. The only insight he may have derived from this discussion was that he needed to stay on his medication, but as anyone working with severely mentally ill people knows, that was itself a major accomplishment.

What can we say about Dave and relapse prevention skills?

1. Dave does not seem able to recognize his own feelings, impulses, and thoughts and to relate them to his sexual assaults.
2. Dave does not seem capable of managing his own impulses without supervision.
3. Dave verbalizes understanding and agreement with the plan to take medication.
4. Dave accepts that grabbing women's breasts is wrong and that he can get in a lot of trouble for it.
5. Dave is probably not competent at this moment to make decisions regarding sexual activity with other people. He appears to lack the skills to solicit consenting partners. He does not appear to consider consent in his search for a partner. At the very least, he is in need of a great deal of sex education; and that might well be the focus of much treatment.
6. Dave does not understand the concepts involved in relapse prevention. He may also not have a strong grounding in the grammatical construction of conditional sentences, "if x, then y." Conditional thinking is crucial for relapse prevention.
7. Dave can learn some coping skills but it is not yet clear whether he will use these in an intentional self-directed way. He is, however, likely to accept prompts from staff if *they* know his coping skills.
8. Dave has a limited support system through the Department of Mental Health. However, Dave is not likely to seek out assistance on his own. He does not see how he can use a support system. He sees his supports as people who supervise and control him, not as allies in a shared desire to keep everyone safe.

This assessment yields the following treatment goals:

1. Dave will understand why grabbing a woman's breasts or buttocks is wrong, and he will verbalize a continuing intention to not do it.
2. Dave will willingly accept medication as a means of self-control. He will see the connection between his medication refusal, cognitive decline, and behavioral aggression.
3. Dave will learn simple coping skills.
4. Dave will receive basic sex education.
5. Dave will accept supervision and a crisis intervention plan designed to help him stay safe.

Let's return to Sheryl, the client discussed at the beginning of this chapter. Can she make use of relapse prevention skills? Sheryl, it may be remembered, is mildly retarded, a lifelong alcoholic, with multiple serious health problems and a major psychotic disorder. She is linguistically dysfluent in her best language, ASL, and she has a history of becoming violent when intoxicated.

Sheryl has positive qualities as well. She can be friendly, engaging, funny, and sociable. She develops friendships and relationships with professionals and paraprofessionals in which she shows empathy, caring, and concern. Whenever she is violent, she shows genuine remorse afterward and indicates her intention to be safe and sober from that point on.

Sheryl was hospitalized with us a number of times, and she developed strong relationships with many Unit staff. This certainly helped, but the most engaged she ever became in treatment was when we asked her to help other people. For instance, she was not at all interested in learning about relapse prevention until we asked her to help teach it to other clients. We explained to her that she had an important story to tell like the other people she has seen tell their stories at 12-step meetings. She agreed to make a videotape to tell her story, and discuss the benefits of sobriety and the dangers of alcohol. These were benefits and dangers she never acknowledged until she was placed in the role of helping others. Staff worked with her over several sessions to prepare her presentation. This was the exact same work we would hope to do in therapy except we called it "practicing for the videotape." During these sessions, staff discussed most of the relapse prevention concepts. She did not develop a reliable understanding of these concepts, but she was able to make a coherent presentation about her own story and about why alcohol was bad for her.

At the end of her hospitalization, Sheryl could demonstrate a number of skills. She could describe reasons to stay clean and sober. She could tell a reasonably coherent story about her own substance use and anger problems. She could name and demonstrate some coping skills. Like many of our clients, the coping skill she relied on the most was "red, yellow, green," discussed in Chapter 5. She brought a copy of it home and hung it up in her room as a reminder.

Sheryl could sometimes notice when she was being provoked and walk away. She could sometimes notice when she was feeling stressed and overwhelmed and ask for a break. She came to see her staff as a resource and would seek them out when she needed help. She attended some AA meetings that were sign interpreted although she did not appear to understand most of what was discussed at those meetings.

The treatment work with her continued for years after her hospitalization. She is not expected to ever become someone who can self-manage, independently using a relapse prevention plan, but she is generally in agreement with staff efforts to keep her sober and healthy. She lapsed in her sobriety on a few occasions, but she recovered quickly and reengaged with her treatment program. Given her skill deficits and life challenges, this has to be considered a great success for her and the staff who work with her.

Crisis Intervention Work With Incompetent, Noncompliant, and Antisocial Clients

As we have seen, the most important thing about relapse prevention is that it is a strategy for self-management. Relapse prevention requires that one become a full agent in one's own recovery, *self-directing* the recovery process. More than any particular skill, this pretreatment goal is the greatest challenge.

When clients cannot or will not engage in relapse prevention, the responsibility falls on other people to intervene for them. Both relapse prevention and crisis management depend on good behavior analyses. Both are concerned with warning signs, risk factors, triggers, cycles, and seemingly unimportant decisions. Both involve developing plans for what to do when these precursors to relapse occur. The main difference between relapse prevention and crisis intervention is in who are the agents of change. In relapse prevention, the client self-manages. The client intentionally uses some planned coping skill to prevent the problem from happening. For instance, an alcoholic decides to spend New Year's Eve, a high-risk time for drinking, at an AA meeting. In crisis intervention, other people develop a plan to manage the client. *They* plan for New Year's Eve, for instance, by supervising the client more intensely, distracting him, giving him more medicine, or bringing him to an AA meeting. They will do their best to elicit cooperation, but when push comes to shove, they may initiate some action, like a call to the police, that the client does not want.

Crisis intervention plans are inherently weaker than relapse prevention plans because we never have the kind of control over other people that we have over ourselves. The key skill in crisis intervention is the ability to maintain an alliance while preventing someone from doing something. This is the same difficult challenge that mental health programs have when they seek to develop relationships with people with whom they are simultaneously setting limits. Crisis intervention takes us into the role of being agents of social control, responsible to manage someone else's behavior. Many mental health and rehabilitation people are uncomfortable in this role. The times we assume the role of agent of social control are also when we are clinically weakest.

These challenges were present in the work with Dave and Sheryl. Both Dave and Sheryl came to understand that drinking was dangerous for them. Both understood that physical or sexual assaults on other people are bad. Both told staff they will not do it again, but neither had the ability to understand and use a relapse prevention plan. Neither one really understood why other people insisted on supervising them. They thought that their stated intentions to *not do it again* were enough.

The counseling strategies used with both involved empathizing with their desires for independence and frustration with the supervision being imposed on them. Staff also empathized with their fear of incarceration and justified the counseling and supervision as efforts to help them stay out of jail.

In fact, the justice system was not going to put either Dave or Sheryl in jail. This is because both were determined to be legally incompetent to stand trial. Once this determination was made, the legal system deferred to the mental health system to manage them. Police or judges at times threatened to incarcerate them, but they had no intention to follow through. Their problems were considered mental health problems, no matter what they did. This really makes the mental health system into the de facto social control agents for these clients even though the mental health system cannot incarcerate or punish. Indeed, sometimes even minor limit setting with clients like these hurts a therapeutic alliance, pulls people out of a treatment mind-set, and fosters greater oppositionality.

The behavioral management of such clients, without the backing of the true agents of social control in the justice system, constitutes an enormous problem for mental health and rehabilitation programs. Staff in such programs may have to fall back on the threat of their going to jail, even while knowing this threat is empty, because Dave and Sheryl do not understand the implications of being legally incompetent. Because the mental health system really has very limited ability to forcefully prevent clients from displaying bad behaviors, and because the justice system is shirking its responsibility to set limits and administer consequences, a strategy like this is necessary and justified even if it involves some deception.

The staff involved with Sheryl and Dave conducted behavior analyses and set up crisis plans. Although both clients could not identify their own warning signs, the staff who worked with them could, and they guided them through coping strategies at those times. In Sheryl's case, staff in her *Deaf* community program created as many opportunities for her to do the things that she enjoyed as resources allowed. They reinforced desired behaviors from her and, with some training, came to adopt a one-down stance with her that usually worked. For instance, they would ask her help and set up opportunities for her to help her peers. They went out of their way to treat her with respect.

When they had to set limits, they reminded her of the court and sometimes even apologized for having to supervise her. This stance was generally effective. Sheryl did not do relapse prevention, but she became compliant with her program's expectations *for the most part.*

After about a year in which Sheryl maintained complete sobriety and had no serious behavioral incidents, she did take off from her program and do some drinking. Fortunately, this one incident did not set back her health. Her parents and the state agency case management staff, however, became furious with the vendor company that was paid to care for her. They accused the agency staff of being negligent and incompetent. I heard about this afterward and it struck me as very unfair. The fact that Sheryl, with so few resources and such enormous obstacles, could maintain safe and sober behavior for a year, and that her program staff could guide her through this, was a remarkable achievement. Sheryl quickly resumed her sobriety. Her program staff were able to process the incident with her and get her back on track largely thanks to the relationships they had established with her and the positive approach they had taken.

Sheryl's parents and case managers appeared to hold the expectation for the vendor agency that Sheryl never elope and relapse. They held this expectation even though the justice system had no intention of enforcing these expectations. This is an unrealistic expectation for any program. *Unless we want to lock people up for life, we simply do not have that kind of power, and the pressure on staff to control the client at all costs creates authoritarian relationships which provoke resistance, rebellion, and relapse.*

Sheryl was fortunate to be discharged into a Deaf transitional program where staff could communicate effectively with her. Her direct care staff needed a great deal of training to work with her, but they could learn with the right supervisory structure.

Dave was discharged into a hearing program with no staff who could communicate with him. The plan was for an interpreter to come by a few hours a week. He was set up with a counselor who would also work with an interpreter. Because of a lack of understanding in local area administrators of the importance of funding an out-of-area Deaf placement, and a scarcity of other resources, it took us months to get even this inaccessible program for him. Dave was adamant he did not want to stay longer in the hospital waiting for a Deaf program. Unfortunately, this plan had relapse written all over it. Program staff had a basic crisis plan, but as no one in the program could communicate with Dave without an interpreter, we wondered how they would implement it. We also pitied the counselor who had agreed to work with Dave through an interpreter. Because Dave's program was so poorly equipped to help him, everyone would look to the counselor to address all Dave's problems. Without a background in working with LLC deaf clients, the counselor was almost guaranteed to proceed as if she were working with more verbal, motivated clients. We expected that within a short time, Dave would refuse to attend and the counselor would tell agency staff that Dave was a poor candidate for counseling. Soon after that, a relapse of his problem behaviors could be expected to occur. A few months later, this is, in fact, what happened.

Sometimes area administrators need to see this happen several times before they grasp the importance of developing *Deaf* community treatment resources.

The skills and stories treatment program described in this book is based on the assumption that mental health care is collaborative. Therefore, we make soliciting meaningful client engagement a primary goal, and as part of that pretreatment effort we avoid the one-up stance associated with being a social control agent as best we can. We do not succeed in that completely as there are many instances when we must act unilaterally, with authority, without client consent. The most obvious cause for acting one-up, setting limits, is when clients are not collaborating and they are doing something very unsafe. Because such limit setting can have the effect of provoking greater resistance and rebellion, or at least damaging therapeutic relationships, the message conveyed to clients at this time is very important. The message we try to convey is the following:

We will do everything in our power to work with you in a collaborative way. If you can have reasonable discussions with us, without violence, solving problems and conflicts together with us, and if you can stay safe, our intent is to support you and help you reach your goals. We also have some responsibility for your safety, but if we are working together well, communicating well, we can trust you more and take more risks. If you cannot or will not have those conversations with us, and if you continue to do things to hurt yourself or other people, then we will make decisions that affect you without your consent. In the hospital, this can mean restricting you to the Unit, and in the really dangerous situations it may mean physically restraining you. In the community, it may mean calling the police. When we do this, we feel very sad. This is not what we want. We want to work with you, as a team. If we cannot do that today, we promise we will try again tomorrow.

For most of our clients, this therapeutic stance, conveyed as best we can so they can understand, provides the best way to reconcile our dual responsibilities to treat and to assure safety. There are two kinds of clients with whom this kind of stance has not worked, and with whom we have found we must be much more authoritative in the treatment process. The first kind of client comprises persons whose language skills and cognitive functioning are so impaired that they are really not capable of collaborative problem solving. This might be people who are very psychotic though with medication and structure these people usually get better. When they are thinking more clearly, we can become more collaborative. This might also be people with moderate or greater mental retardation or other forms of severe brain pathology.

Juanita, the very language dysfluent, mentally retarded client presented in Chapter 2, was one example. Juanita had a very limited set of things that she was concerned about. One was food. She wanted to eat the same food every day, and she was completely inflexible about this. Unfortunately, she also had diabetes, and the diet she prescribed for herself would kill her. The staff in our program tried in every way we could think to explain this to her. We used excellent signers and visual-gestural communicators. We used pictorial skill cards. We role-played and told stories. Sometimes an hour or two of work would deescalate a crisis around food only to have the same issues rise again a few hours later. Juanita could not, for instance, agree to have her desired food at lunch and a different food at dinner. She would say yes in the moment, only to become assaultive when she could not get her preferred food later in the day. After many months of trying, we came to understand that our attempts at negotiation with her were making things worse. She could not handle the ambiguity involved in negotiation. Finally, we put a structure in place for when she could have her preferred food, and we never varied from that structure. When she was discharged, we recommended to her community providers that they do the same. Juanita functioned much better in this environment of benevolent control by staff. A consistent staff structure designed with staff knowledge of her preferences was what she needed.

The other kind of clients with whom this treatment method may not work consists of those people who do have the skills to control their behavior but lack the motivation to do so. There are people who take pleasure in bullying and frightening other people. Even if these behaviors are rooted in their own victimization, these people are not helped, in my experience, by being excused from accountability.

If one wanted to parody the strength-based treatment approach presented in this book, one would cite an example of a client who murdered someone on Monday. To engage him, staff commended him for *not* murdering anyone on Tuesday and then asked him how he could do better. Or one could note staff commending an ax murderer because he *also* used his ax to chop wood. This parody makes our pretreatment strategies seem ridiculous, yet there is something to be said for *not* minimizing serious crimes in the interests of establishing treatment engagement. People who commit serious crimes need to face appropriate consequences, sometimes even more so when they are language and learning challenged, because their fear of punishment may be what motivates them to engage in treatment. The people administering the consequences, however, cannot be the same people performing these pretreatment strategies to solicit their engagement.

There are court-ordered treatment programs in which a client is accountable to a judge or probation officer, and regular open communication between counselor and justice department official is a condition of treatment. In these cases, clients can choose whether to participate or not, and the justice system has the responsibilities of addressing treatment noncompliance. With LLC clients, deaf or hearing, whom the justice system avoids holding accountable, the mental health system is tasked with the impossible: to elicit their engagement in treatment efforts, teach them the skills they need to function safely, and at the same time control them and prevent any mishaps. The treatment approach described here, with its emphasis on pretreatment engagement strategies, presents the most effective techniques available to engage clients; but this approach does not support excusing bad behavior. Rather, we advocate continuously for the justice system to do its job so that we can do ours.

Happily, most of the LLC deaf clients we have served have thrived in treatment environments dedicated to drawing out and developing their skills. The strength-based approach of noticing skills they already use, working one down, inviting their participation, placing them in helper roles, and so on, brings them into a meaningful treatment process. But sometimes this work will not succeed in the absence of real limit setting and accountability. For this small group of antisocial clients, effective treatment will require a better collaboration between mental health and justice departments than we have so far been able to create.

8

Staff and Program Development

Introduction: The Program Director's Role

In the summer of 1986, my colleague Sherry Zitter and I were hired to establish a psychiatric inpatient unit for deaf persons at Westborough State Hospital in Massachusetts. At that time, I had a master's in "Counseling of the Hearing Impaired" and 3 years post-master's experience as a vocational rehabilitation counselor with deaf persons. Sherry was a licensed social worker specializing in working with deaf people. We are both hearing. We are also friends. When we found out that we were the two finalists for the job, we faced a dilemma. As friends, we did not want to compete against each other. We both placed the survival of our friendship higher than getting the job. We both also had a fair amount of *chutzpa*, so the weekend before the final interviews, we got together and redesigned the job. We turned it into two jobs, one that she could do and one that I could do, and we proposed that they hire us both as codirectors. To our astonishment, the interviewing team bought the idea, and we both began the exciting project of creating this new specialty Deaf mental health program (Glickman, 2003; Glickman & Zitter, 1989).

The first 6 months of planning this program were among the most exciting in my professional career. We were guided by an idealistic vision of culturally affirmative treatment in which Deaf and hearing people would work together collaboratively to create a humane, effective treatment milieu noteworthy for its communication excellence and support for Deaf culture. Although Sherry had much more clinical experience than I, neither of us was even remotely prepared for the challenges that lay ahead. In terms of the realities of psychiatric inpatient care, we were "green," and we hired staff who were equally enthusiastic, idealistic, and unprepared. When it came to hiring a psychiatrist, we found a progressive man who shared our idealistic vision. He did not sign, but he grasped easily the importance of affirming American Sign Language (ASL) and Deaf culture. Most of our hiring interview with him was spent discussing the nature of psychiatry in Cuba. We wanted to hire Deaf and hearing staff with signing competencies and a similar vision. We knew that recruiting existing state hospital employees who were all hearing and did not sign would be the kiss of death to our effort to create an environment affirming for Deaf people. An especially progressive union steward supported us, and we were able to staff the program almost entirely with Deaf and hearing persons new to the state hospital system. With one or two exceptions, these were all persons with excellent signing abilities and really positive attitudes but little or no psychiatric inpatient experience.

With our new staff, we organized a month of creative team-building activities. Then we admitted our first patient, a 25-year-old brain-damaged, language dysfluent, severely traumatized, and chronically assaultive Deaf man who had been languishing on a back ward of one of our state hospitals. The Unit was established with the expectation that we would serve people like him. We brought him into our signing treatment environment, and he immediately began to assault the staff. On our very first day of operation, he chased our newly hired social worker into her office. She closed the door to keep him out, and he stood outside it banging, screaming, and posturing like he was going to kill her. Our newly hired, enthusiastic, culturally competent staff had no idea how to intervene. The social worker, terrified, quit on the spot. After we opened for business, she lasted 1 day.

Our second patient was a deaf-blind autistic man who would go into fits of rages without any warning. When he raged, he destroyed everything he could get his hands on. It literally took eight men to restrain him. Our third patient was a huge man from a third-world country who had no education and virtually no language. Because of his size and the difficulty communicating with him, he has lived most of his life with no rules or expectations placed on him. When he became angry he was extremely scary. Staff lived in terror of him becoming assaultive.

Our precious sign communication skills did not seem to be helping us with these patients. I remember a moment when our first patient shoved one of our best Deaf communicators under a table and started pounding her. After we pulled him off of her, she got up and announced confidently, "The problem is communication!" That was a moment of insight for me. It was the moment I realized that the problem *was not* communication.

After a few weeks of experiencing nearly constant assaults and threats of assaults, staff began to talk about the Unit as a war zone. Morale dropped dramatically. Some staff quit, and other staff started arguing with each other. To make matters worse, in our hiring process, by rejecting the applications of the internal candidates who were actually experienced in inpatient care, we had alienated most of the hospital community. We strongly suspected that the rest of the hospital staff were quite content to see how we were floundering. We read "I told you so," and "So much for your great vision. Welcome to *our* world," in every interaction with people outside our unit. At that point, Sherry and I thanked God that neither of us had been hired alone. At least we could close our office door and cry on each other's shoulder.

Somewhere in our first year, I had another moment of insight. It was at one of those times when Sherry and I were complaining to each other behind the closed door of our office. We were complaining about how the staff did not get along. Our patients were tough enough, but why were the clinical and nursing staff arguing over treatment approaches? Why could the different nursing shifts not agree on one plan of nursing care? Why had the Deaf and hearing staff not come together in our shared vision? Surely, we did not need Deaf staff accusing the hearing staff of "oppressing" them while the hearing staff complained about the Deaf staff's lack of clinical competence. It seemed to us that everyone was fighting everyone, and almost no one had a clue about how to work with these clients. Of course, embedded in our distress was the unspoken assumption that all these people *should* get along just because we wanted them to. They *should* know what to do because we wanted them to know what to do. They *should* be able to see the value of both communication and clinical competence without pitting one against the other. The insight moment came when I suddenly realized that none of this would happen without good management. *This was our job.* As managers, we had to create the conditions that fostered good, collaborative, culturally affirmative, and clinically sound treatment.

As soon as I realized that my *shoulds* were not helping, and that my job was to figure out how to fashion the right treatment milieu, my stress decreased. Well, this was my job. Conflict would happen in our setting whether we liked it or not, so what kind of environment could we create to promote healthy conflict resolution? I began then my search for the perspective that combined cultural and clinical competence, the perspective presented in this book, written 20 years later.

There are some wonderful books available to guide managers in creating the kind of organizational cultures that they believe in (Kotter, 1996; Schein, 2004). Neither Sherry nor I had any administrative experience at that time. Though we had a vision of culturally affirmative care for Deaf people, we had no model for what an appropriate treatment program would look like for persons with severe language, learning, and behavioral challenges. We had no model of pretreatment. We had some awareness of the limitations of traditional psychodynamic therapy for our population but only a vague, sketchy idea of how to make psychotherapy more relevant for them. We both grossly overestimated the value that would come from signing staff. We never wavered in our belief that having Deaf, signing staff was essential, but we became increasingly clear about how this was not sufficient. We would have to train staff according to a treatment model which we as yet did not have.

Fortunately, we had two staff persons who had some idea about what our treatment program should look like. The first was our expressive therapist, a wonderfully talented clinician who used art and movement as her therapeutic media. She was the first clinician to show me how psychotherapy could be done with minimal reliance on language. The second was our occupational therapist. She had not been confused by psychodynamic training into imagining that we had to help our patients develop insight into their unconscious motivation. Unlike trained psychotherapists, she was not stymied by the challenge of getting our language, learning, and behaviorally disordered clients to talk meaningfully about their lives. Occupational therapists are more practical. Their primary focus is on helping clients develop skills.

When we began designing our treatment groups, we found that most of our clients did better in the task-oriented occupational therapy groups than insight-oriented therapy groups. The success of our occupational therapist in engaging difficult patients in the process of learning skills prepared me to embrace cognitive-behavioral therapy (CBT) when I discovered it years later. After 3 years, I left the Deaf Unit to pursue my doctorate, and I worked for a year in the day treatment program of a psychiatric hospital with hearing patients. There too I saw how much more effective occupational therapists were in engaging severely disturbed clients in treatment than were clinicians working from insight-oriented therapy models. I returned to the Deaf Unit in 1996, and once again was blessed to observe the work of talented occupational therapists, helping clients develop skills. When we eventually moved to incorporate sensory modulation into our repertoire of coping skills, it was our occupational therapists that again led the way (Trikakis, Curci, & Strom, 2003). I have occupational therapists to thank for first showing me how much more effective we would be when we based our treatment not around insight, but around skills.

Five Great Challenges

Communication

Deaf mental health and rehabilitation programs have five great challenges. The most commonly cited challenge is the need to assure genuine communication inclusion. The primary obstacle to accomplishing this goal is that so many people with no experience of working with Deaf people hold a grossly simplistic understanding of what is required to provide this communication inclusion. Commonly, they assume that it is accomplished either through the provision of a sign language interpreter or the hiring/development of one staff person designated as the "deafness expert"(Glickman, 2003).

High functioning Deaf people with fluent language skills can gain *some* access to services when qualified interpreters are provided. These same high functioning people may work well with a clinician who signs and is sensitive to the experience of Deaf people. Higher functioning Deaf people, however, are not the typical clients of mental health and rehabilitation programs; and even when they are, interpreters and "deafness experts" are only available for limited hours. The inclusion these programs claim to provide is often an illusion (DeVinney, 2003). If the deaf consumer requires more than an hour per week of treatment in a clinician's office, then a day or residential program needs to be accessed. Generally, people with more entrenched problems and fewer resources, such as the language and learning challenged (LLC) clients discussed in this book, require more extensive therapeutic programming. They require programs where there are similar peers and signing staff who can communicate with them 24 hours a day.

The main reason that hearing administrators outside the deafness field often do not "get it" when Deaf advocates push for specialized Deaf treatment programs is that they have no frame of reference for understanding language dysfluency related to language deprivation. They have never met an adult who did not know a language fluently, and the only model they have to understand this would be severe brain pathology. They will not understand how common this problem is for deaf people raised without adequate exposure to natural sign languages.

The high number of deaf persons who are language dysfluent due to language deprivation, and who commonly have associated neurological, emotional, and behavioral difficulties, means that the cultural model alone cannot address all the pertinent treatment issues. These language dysfluent persons are very handicapped, and for them at least the medical–pathological and disability models are relevant. These persons, for both cultural and disability reasons, require programs and treatment approaches tailored specifically for them. *To be clear, the disability in question is not deafness. It is language dysfluency related to language deprivation. This language dysfluency is a result of educational and social policy and practices. It is largely preventable.*

When we advocate for Deaf services purely on the basis of the cultural model of deafness, we teach a number of important things. We teach about the importance of sign language and why speech reading is inadequate for communication. We teach that the Deaf Community has its own culture and that ASL is a central part of this culture. Having taught administrators this, however, we should not then be surprised when they seek to create access for our Deaf clients in the same way they handle other linguistic minorities. This is almost always through interpreters and clinicians who speak the language. It is not by providing specialized treatment programs.

The real reason we need specialized Deaf services is because of the combination of cultural and disability issues that raise such unique assessment and treatment barriers that these persons cannot be integrated into general treatment settings. They cannot be integrated even when interpreting services are provided around the clock; something that virtually never happens. One can appreciate that ASL is a real language and that Deaf members of the Deaf Community are cultural minorities while still recognizing that language deprivation results in profound handicaps that cannot be accommodated in nonspecialized settings. In Chapter 2, for instance, I showed how without a great deal of specialized expertise, clinicians assessing deaf persons with language dysfluency are highly likely to misconstrue this problem to be a form of psychosis.

Although advocates for Deaf people commonly argue that the major communication issue between Deaf and hearing people is that some Deaf people use ASL, that is in fact the "easy" problem. The more difficult problem is language deprivation. We need treatment settings that go well beyond providing ASL access. They need to provide genuine inclusion for the significant portion of our treatment population who are language dysfluent. That just does not happen unless the program is actually designed for the varying communication needs of deaf consumers.

Cross-Cultural Dynamics

When we are able to persuade the powers that be of the need for specialized Deaf treatment programs, we face challenge number two. This is to create a climate where Deaf and hearing colleagues work together productively, skillfully managing the cross-cultural and power dynamics. Anyone who has tried to administer such programs will tell you this is much easier said than done. This challenge is very analogous to that which presents itself in other mental health programs that treat minorities (Andrade, 1978; Glickman, 1996).

It is exceptionally easy for unhealthy dynamics between majority and minority staff to reemerge in the treatment setting, and exceptionally difficult to separate these dynamics from more prosaic work performance issues. For instance, consider the issues involved in hiring, supervising, and, when necessary, terminating minority staff. The Deaf programs I know have wanted very badly to hire qualified Deaf staff. They value the communication expertise Deaf people bring to a program, and they realize the program will lack "cross-cultural legitimacy" without strong representation from the minority community in the staff (Glickman, 2003). Program administrators sometimes want and need to hire Deaf or signing staff so badly that they hire otherwise unqualified people or people with serious problems of their own. They may also hire these persons without an adequate plan for staff development.

Residential and hospital programs depend heavily on a large group of paraprofessional staff who provide most of the direct service to clients. Because such positions do not require college degrees, there is generally a larger pool of Deaf applicants than for the professional positions. We know that most deaf people are raised in hearing families where there is inadequate sign communication. We know that the absence of good communication in the family predisposes hearing parents to do more authoritarian limit setting and interferes with their ability to teach their children to solve problems through dialogue. We also know that poor parent–child communication can interfere with attachment and the development of social and relationship skills (Mindel and Vernon, 1971; Schlesinger, 1972). As most deaf children are now mainstreamed, it is likely that they continued to receive inadequate communication in school. Deaf children educated in programs with inadequate communication will likely experience more behavioral limit setting than problem solving through dialogue. After they survive their childhood, it is the products of these terrible child rearing and educational practices that we hire. To hire them without an appreciation of what they have likely experienced, and without a solid plan for staff development, may be a set up for failure.

Without adequate guidance, it will be natural for the staff to replicate the same authoritarian stances and behaviors that were modeled for them as children. If they work in programs operating from traditional behavioral approaches, where level systems, time outs, and the administration of consequences are the principal means of intervention, their authoritarian tendencies are easily reinforced. In these contexts, and without adequate training, direct care staff may make serious errors. Although most are not abusive, their authoritarian limit settings trigger clients who, generally speaking, are there because they lack skills in coping, problem solving, and conflict resolution. Thus our programs for persons with behavioral difficulties become settings where clients are triggered by authoritarian staff, arbitrary rules, and unnecessary limit setting.

Hearing staff can also work in an arbitrary, authoritarian manner. After all, deaf people usually learn this behavior from hearing parents, teachers, and others in authority. But people raised in linguistically rich environments have a huge advantage over those who are linguistically deprived when it comes to appreciating how we use language for problem solving. In my experience, hospital, residential, and rehabilitation programs where there are large numbers of paraprofessional staff typically grossly underestimate the amount of training and supervision these staff require if the intent is for them to contribute meaningfully to treatment goals. If these programs want their paraprofessional staff to help their clients use language rather than behaviors to solve problems, they may well have to teach the staff these same skills. Supervisors certainly have to model such skills and not resort to the same arbitrary limit setting with staff that so frequently triggers clients.

When the direct care staff make serious errors, disciplinary procedures may follow, including termination. The stage is then set for the sorts of highly emotional confrontations that are common in Deaf schools and psychiatric and rehabilitation programs. Is the problem that the staff were incompetent or that the administrators failed to train them? Was too much faith placed, as it was by Sherry and me when we opened the Westborough Deaf Unit, on the power of excellent sign communication alone, as if good communication were all that was needed? Did the administrators, deaf or hearing, fail to adequately address some crucial aspects of Deaf culture, leading to the perception that the program failed because it was too "hearing"? Were employees terminated because they did bad work or because the hearing administrators, unable to sign well and unappreciative of the talents of the Deaf staff, were unable to see the contributions their Deaf staff were actually making? Does the program need to be more clinically sound or more culturally aligned? What happens when these two values appear to conflict?*

Because these labor problems occur in the context of hearing-Deaf, majority-minority dynamics, each side will inevitably construct a different story to account for what occurred. The Deaf staff usually construct a story centered on poor communication, unexamined hearing biases, and prejudice toward Deaf people, what Lane (1992) calls *audism*. Hearing staff usually construct a story centered on what they perceive to be poor skills or work attitudes in the Deaf employees and colleagues. In Deaf programs that fail, the two stories do not reconcile, and these completely predictable forms of cross-cultural conflict foster animosity, low morale, and poor clinical work with clients. In Deaf programs that succeed, the cross-cultural dynamics are worked with mindfully and skillfully. The Deaf–hearing issues are on the table, the subject of respectful dialogue. Skill training of all staff, with a special priority given to the mentorship and development of Deaf employees, will be the mantra of the administration.

Violence

The third challenge faced by these programs is violence. The major reason that deaf persons are referred to the Deaf Unit at Westborough is, by far, aggression. The review of the Deafness mental health literature in Chapter 1 suggests this is true wherever Deaf programs have been established. The high incidence of "challenging behavior" in deaf people is discussed in a recent volume devoted exclusively to this topic (Austen & Jeffery, 2007) and in work discussing forensic psychiatry and deaf people (Hindley, Kitson, & Leach, 2000). The behavioral problems, as we have seen, often accompany the language problems and are a natural consequence of growing up without adequate language exposure and without the daily practice of using language to solve problems. The behavioral problems may also be an implication of neurological disorders and insults that cause the deafness, and they may be a by-product of authoritarian parenting and educational practices. Where deaf children are physically or sexually abused, especially when they lack the language skills needed to understand their experience, this trauma may strengthen and deepen patterns of self-harm and aggression. The treatment environment, where it replicates patterns of abuse and communication isolation, may then trigger new incidents of aggression. Deaf persons treated in such settings are at high risk for facing further potentially traumatizing experiences like mechanical restraint and seclusion (National Association of State Mental Health Program

---

* A really fascinating example of these cross-cultural dynamics at play in the development of a new mental health program is provided in Andrade (1978). This study concerns itself with the establishment of culturally affirmative mental health services for Chicano residents of southern Texas. The parallels with the experience of setting up culturally affirmative Deaf programs are striking. Elsewhere (Glickman, 1996), I discuss this program in relation to culturally affirmative programming for Deaf people.

Directors Medical Directors Council, 2002). However, as Sherry and I discovered when we opened our program, the presence of culturally affirmative treatment environments does not guarantee that violent behavior will cease or even that mechanical restraint of patients will not be resorted to.

On the Deaf Unit at Westborough, the greatest obstacle to creating a culturally affirmative treatment program has not been the communication and cross-cultural issues but rather the challenge of recruiting, developing, and retaining staff to work with a small number of highly aggressive persons. It should be said that most Deaf Unit patients, and certainly most Deaf people, are not violent, but challenging behaviors in this clientele are common enough that one must develop programming specifically targeting these problems. If one is to have any chance of reducing aggression from these persons, the presence of native signers is essential, but even these Deaf signers can be battered by violent patients. When this happens, they may resign and cause others to resign, which compromises the communication and cultural competence of the program, in turn creating treatment environments more likely to trigger new aggression. Thus, effective communication is necessary but insufficient as a means of addressing these behavioral problems.

Creating treatment environments that do not repeat subtle as well as gross patterns of abuse is very difficult. The failure to adequately train staff, as well as the failure to work constructively with the Deaf–hearing conflicts that *always* occur, creates treatment environments that trigger clients to new incidents of aggression and self-harm. We then find the cycle of arbitrary limit setting and behavioral acting out, low staff morale, and patient failure to improve. This is a systemic problem, but the players in the system will pin the blame differently. It is a truism to assert that when a treatment system is in disarray, the clients will act out the problems of the staff.

Adapting Treatment

One has to program for clients with challenging behaviors, and one has to make this programming a central focus. The fourth great challenge faced by mental health and rehabilitation programs serving deaf persons is to adapt established best practices so that they match the language and conceptual abilities of LLC clients. The skills and stories approach presented here is an adaptation of best practices taken primarily from the CBT domain. The simplification of psychosocial skills, their presentation in pictures, and the use of Deaf-friendly teaching methods are examples of specialized programming that must occur to reach these clients.

It is impossible to adapt treatment if one's notion of access is that it is accomplished through interpreters or an isolated deafness expert. LLC deaf clients placed in nonspecialized treatment programs receive "business as usual," with or without a few hours of interpreting, and this rarely meets their needs. Treatment needs to be refashioned for LLC deaf clientele, and for many hearing LLC clients as well. The great tragedy for hearing persons and programs faced with serving this clientele is not only that they are unable to adapt treatment for this population, *but that usually they are not even aware of the need to do so.*

Pretreatment

The fifth great challenge is the one referred to in this book as *pretreatment*. Even with such noteworthy contributions as motivational interviewing (Miller & Rollnick, 2002), the pretreatment challenge has not been given anywhere near the attention it deserves in the mental health literature. With LLC clients, the pretreatment efforts to solicit meaningful treatment engagement are often much more difficult than the treatment itself. As I described in Chapter 4, much of what is done in traditional psychotherapy presumes cognitive and language skills as well as motivation. This is especially true for psychodynamic psychotherapies, but it can also be true for some variations of CBT. Without the framework and strategies of pretreatment, clinicians working with this population face enormous frustration and the risk of burnout. The pretreatment framework names the problem, and the pretreatment strategies give program staff tools for this necessary but infrequently discussed crucial first step of work.

Meichenbaum, Linehan, and Greene on the Role of Direct Care Staff

Because our mental health and rehabilitation programs are so heavily dependent on paraprofessional staff, special attention must be devoted to developing their skills. We must also consider their roles. The three counseling theorists we have relied on most heavily throughout this book all have considered the role of direct care staff.

In 1985, Meichenbaum first suggested using direct care staff as skill coaches (Meichenbaum, 1985). Meichenbaum trained direct care staff so they could help clients use coping skills in naturally occurring stressful situations in the treatment milieu.

> Joint stress management sessions were conducted with both client and counselors. Both in sessions and on the ward, counselors modeled how they used the coping skills to control their own stress, and they could prompt and guide clients in the use of the coping procedures. In fact, clients would remind counselors when they should use coping strategies such as relaxation and problem solving. Counselors and clients had rap sessions at the end of the day to review how they used their coping skills and to consider when they could use such skills the next day (that is, identification of high-risk situations). The basic idea was to build generalization into the day-to-day transactions. (Meichenbaum, 1985, p. 82)

Linehan and Greene developed this idea further. Behavioral Tech, LLC, the group associated with Linehan that trains clinicians in dialectical behavioral therapy (DBT), now also conducts workshops for the clinical support staff in mental health programs. In these workshops, the fundamentals of DBT are reviewed, and there is a focus on teaching direct care staff the same psychosocial skills taught to clients in DBT. These are skills in mindfulness, distress tolerance, emotion regulation, and interpersonal effectiveness. In outpatient therapy, the psychotherapist has the role of coaching clients in their use of these skills. In hospital and other residential settings, the direct care staff are given the role of coaching clients in their skills at those moments of emotional dysregulation (Swenson, Witterholt, & Bohus, 2007). It is imperative, therefore, that the staff know the skills and that they model and use them themselves. In DBT programs, great attention must be focused on teaching all staff DBT skills.

Another helpful component of DBT is that staff involved in the clients' treatment belong to a team that receives regular consultation. Team members are helped to use the same set of skills to manage their own emotional responses to clients and each other. Staff are taught these skills to help their clients but also to help themselves stay engaged and effective. Staff also teach the skills by modeling them. An emotionally disregulated staff person will not be a credible skills coach; and a team of staff in constant conflict with each other will not be capable of teaching interpersonal effectiveness. Thus, regular consultation/supervision for all staff is built into DBT.

In DBT, the focus is on coaching clients to respond skillfully to their environments. Besides training staff, DBT practitioners do not normally intervene in the environment per se. This contrasts significantly with the collaborative problem-solving (CPS) approach of Greene, which attends to both client skill development and the fashioning of flexible treatment environments.

Ross Greene's work on CPS was reviewed in Chapter 4 (problem solving with clients as a means of pretreatment engagement), Chapter 5 (problem solving as a means of coping), and Chapter 6 (problem solving as a means of conflict resolution). One great advantage of this approach is that it teaches psychosocial skills in the moment when they are actually needed. This makes the skills more likely to generalize to new situations. CPS elevates the role of the milieu staff so that entire treatment programs, not just psychotherapy sessions, are the venue of treatment. Compared with DBT, CPS has a far less sophisticated skills training program. CPS emphasizes skill training in the moments it is needed rather than in formal treatment groups.

Another difference is that CPS includes more shaping of responses of parents, teachers, and counselors. In DBT, one focuses on helping clients accept or cope with reality. In CPS, one also works to change that reality. Greene argues that parents, teachers, or providers who are themselves rigid actually promote explosions in clients. He offers this wonderfully insightful account of how rigid and authoritarian responses from staff make client behaviors worse:

> ... Explosive episodes frequently follow a common pattern: (1) a staff member observes a resident exhibiting an inappropriate behavior ("I'm not eating this crap for breakfast!"); (2) the staff member issues a command in an effort to stop the inappropriate behavior or to remind the resident of the rules ("Number one, that's inappropriate language and, number two, that's what's for breakfast."); (3) the resident becomes more agitated ("It sucks—I'm not eating it!"); (4) the staff member reminds the resident of the consequences of noncompliance, that is, a reduction in level and corresponding loss of privileges ("If you don't stop swearing, you're going to lose your points"); (5) the resident becomes more agitated and his or her behavior worsens or intensifies (throwing the food tray on the floor and stating, "I don't give a damn what you do to me. I'm not eating that crap!"); (6) the staff member confirms the promised loss of points ("You just lost 2 points—now go to your room!) as other staff, having heard the commotion arrive on the scene; (7) the resident, now both far more aroused and far less capable of rational thought, does something irrational (tipping over a chair or table); and (8) the staff, now both far more aroused and far less capable of rational thought, restrains the resident (or worse). (Greene & Ablon, 2006, p. 190)

Greene goes on to describe how the explosion could have been avoided if the staff person responded first with empathy and an invitation to problem solve ("You don't like French toast ... and that's what they brought for breakfast ... let's think of what we can do about that"). The client is given the opportunity to practice a skill even without knowing he or she is doing so.

Needless to say, most of us were not raised in environments where conflicts were viewed as opportunities to develop skills. This is especially true for deaf persons raised in inadequately signing environments. We therefore have to learn these skills as adults in order to model and teach them to our clients. One Deaf colleague, commenting on how controlling his parents were with him, tells the story of how, when he was 14, his parents would not let him walk down the street unless his 10-year-old hearing brother supervised him. Another Deaf staff person said to me, "My father never discussed anything with me. He could barely sign. We could hardly communicate. All I ever got was 'no,'" I asked him whether he wanted to treat his clients the way his father raised him. His response was immediate. "No!" He had no difficulty seeing how the rigid way he was raised was hurtful, and he was eager to learn skills so he could treat his own clients and children differently.

From Meichenbaum, Linehan, and Greene, we get the model of using direct care staff as skill coaches. We teach skills in every forum: in individual and group psychotherapy, in family meetings, and in the milieu. All staff in the program work on skill development in their respective venues. I believe that Greene's CPS is an advance over DBT in the awareness it brings to the importance not merely of teaching clients to cope but also of shaping the responses of parents, teachers, and treatment providers. I believe his analysis of how *we* trigger our clients through arbitrary, one-up interventions is right on target. Therefore, we must concern ourselves not merely with putting our staff in the role of skill coaches but with teaching them to model the same skills we want clients to show. That means teaching staff to see every conflict or problem that arises as an opportunity to practice skills. Staff who come to appreciate this have developed the ability to think *clinically*.

The Parallel Process Between Staff and Clients

There is a period of work with staff analogous to the pretreatment work with clients. This is the period before there is staff buy-in to a treatment approach, and the work of clinical leadership is essentially educational and motivational. There are good reasons staff may resist implementing this treatment approach just as there are good reasons clients resist our treatment efforts. For instance, clinical staff may have been trained in some other treatment model. They may continue to see insight-oriented psychotherapy as the gold standard of mental health care and see the skill-oriented CBT work as an inferior substitute. Direct care staff may object to the extra work and enhanced clinical role this approach gives them, to the deemphasis on traditional limit setting, to the expectation they find skills in clients who are behaving very badly, and to the use of one-down clinical stances. Regan's (2006) efforts to implement CPS on an adolescent inpatient unit shows the kind of resistance that is likely, and the long, painstaking efforts it takes to work through this resistance.

There are also powerful reasons staff may embrace these efforts. They already know how difficult this work is. It is very likely that they have experienced threats and assaults from clients and they are looking for solutions that will make their work environments safer. If current treatment efforts are working beautifully, there is, in fact, no reason to change. There is no reason, for instance, to downplay insight-oriented psychotherapy when it works. Pretreatment strategies were developed because of the difficulty we have engaging our clientele in treatment, and in my experience this difficulty is readily apparent to our staff. Generalizations always fail to apply in some instances, and there is no reason for arguing in those instances in which other approaches are successful.

The skills and stories approach presented here strives for clarity, simplicity, and practicality. This generally makes it more appealing to direct care staff than more complex approaches utilizing very sophisticated clinical theories. Psychodynamic approaches, as we have seen, are based on very abstract concepts (unconscious, defenses, transference, countertransference, object relations, and so forth) that require more education, are counterintuitive, and do not translate easily into practical strategies. Even DBT, while it has many practical treatment strategies, has a theory whose complexity rivals any in the psychodynamic camp. Theoretical complexity is not a bad thing, but it is not an advantage when trying to organize a cohesive treatment program staffed largely by persons without college degrees or formal psychotherapy training.

There is also great utility to being able to use exactly the same concepts with staff as with clients. Whatever the problem that arises, with clients or with staff, we look for solutions through the use of skills. Staff and clients all need coping skills to manage strong emotions. They all need nonviolent conflict resolution skills. More often than we like to acknowledge, staff have many of the same clinical problems as clients. They have difficulty managing their emotions. They have terrible interpersonal conflicts. They have their own psychiatric symptoms and problem behaviors. For instance, an enormous number of our staff have their own trauma histories, mood, and substance abuse problems. The difference between "us" staff and "them" clients is that we usually have more resources with which to work, are getting paid, and have more authority.

If we use the same concepts with staff as with clients, then every time we address a staff issue we are also providing clinical mentoring. For instance, we approach staff who are emotionally dysregulated by helping them draw on their own coping skills. We approach staff conflicts as an opportunity to develop our own conflict resolution skills. The rationale is that this helps us function as staff and it also helps us develop the skills we need to model and teach to clients. Fundamentally, we want to teach everyone to approach all the obstacles in life as opportunities for CPS.

The pretreatment strategies used to engage clients in treatment are also useful to bring staff on board with the treatment approach. Specifically:

1. Leadership uses the language of skills to describe staff work.
2. Leadership starts by noticing, labeling, and praising skills that staff are already using.
3. Leadership sometimes uses a one-down style.
4. Leadership asks questions that guide staff to evaluate the effectiveness of their own efforts.
5. Leadership uses empathy and validation.
6. Leadership engages staff in a process of CPS.
7. Leadership looks for opportunities to promote the professional development of staff by, for instance, having them present, teach, or write about their work.
8. Leadership helps staff construct a story in which their own abilities and strengths are highlighted.

This parallel between work with staff and work with clients is not perfect. One difference is that we must also hold staff, and ourselves, accountable for outcomes. Another difference is that we require our staff to go through a training and credentialing process before they are allowed to have certain roles. This means that program administration and leadership calls for more use of authority and power than does mental health treatment. Nonetheless, program leaders cannot teach staff to work collaboratively with clients if they only work in an authoritarian manner. They cannot teach skillful communication by communicating badly. They cannot teach staff to show coping skills if they model emotional dysregulation. In Ross Greene's language, they cannot teach Plan B behaviors by modeling Plan A behaviors. More colloquially, administrators need not just to "talk the talk" but to "walk the walk."

For example, when a staff person shows skills such as those involved in deescalating a crisis, does the leadership notice? Or do leaders just notice when staff make mistakes?

On a hearing adolescent unit, two groups of adolescent patients are in the day hall. One group is watching TV, and the other group is at the opposite end of the room, the members talking loudly with one another. A patient in the group watching TV calls over to a staff person, loud enough so all the patients in the room can hear, "Yo! Bitch! Can't you get them to quiet down so we can hear the TV?"

The staff person who was just insulted walks over to the patient who insulted her and, to the astonishment and delight of the clinical supervisor who was nearby, begins with empathy, rather than limit setting. "Are you feeling particularly angry or annoyed with me right now?"

The patient replies, "What? No, I just want them to pipe down."

"I see, and you want me to help with that? So you call over to me and you call me a 'bitch.' What do you think my response to that is likely to be?"

"What? I don't know. I just want you to tell them to quiet down."

"Yes, I get that. Do you think that calling me a bitch will motivate me to want to help you?"

"Ok. Ok. I'm sorry."

"Well, I appreciate you saying you are sorry. I'm wondering if you can think of a more skillful way to ask for help?"

"Yeah, I know. Alright. Sorry."

After the staff person walks away, the supervisor comments to her on how she (a) responded with empathy, (b) worked one down, (c) helped the client evaluate himself, and (4) used skill language. She points out that if she had just reflexively set a limit, that probably would have provoked a confrontation, and they might well now be dealing with a restraint.

An 18-year-old patient is arguing with a 13-year-old peer. The 13-year-old provokes the 18-year-old by calling him an "asshole." The 18-year-old shoves the 13-year-old backward and then walks away angrily. He goes to sit down in a corner of the day hall. He's angry with his peer, but the look on his face suggests he's angry with himself. He mutters to himself, "I'm 18, he's 13. I'm 18, he's 13." A staff person approaches him. The interaction between the two adolescents just got physical, and an intervention is called for.

The staff person begins, "What's going on?"

"John bugs the shit out of me! He pisses me off! I lost it again."

"I saw you push him. I also saw you walk away. He really gets to you, huh?"

"I know I shouldn't of pushed him. I'm 5 years older than he is."

"You feel bad that you weren't able to stay in control. What really impresses me, though, is how hard you are trying to stay in control. You didn't want to push him, and now you feel bad about it. What does that say about you?"

The staff person stays empathic with him until he settles down, and then asks him how he wishes he had handled it. The staff person brings this up later in supervision, which gives the supervisor the opportunity to notice his amazing skill at empathy, his ability to notice the patient's strengths (he walked away, he felt badly about his behavior, he wanted to stay in control), as well as how skillfully he guided the patient to evaluate his own behavior.

Sometimes staff intervene in different or contradictory ways, raising good material for discussion in supervision. This happens frequently when not everyone is on board with a treatment approach. A deaf patient is pacing the halls and banging against the walls. A counselor becomes concerned and approaches her to talk, but the patient will not engage. She goes to her room. The nurse approaches the counselor to ask what is happening. He gives her a summary and advises that they let the patient calm down in her room. The nurse approaches the patient anyway, insisting that he take some medicine to calm down. The patient punches the nurse in the face.

On another day, a hearing patient approaches staff and demands to use the "fuckin' phone." A first staff person responds with empathy. "You seem angry. Sure you can use the phone, but can you settle down first? What's going on?"

The patient calms down a little and begins to talk about how mad he is with staff because of various restrictions and rules. The staff continues to show empathy. "So you feel like you have no power around here and everyone is your boss?" The patient is calming down, and the staff person is ready to give him the phone. At this point, a second staff person comes over, sees the first staff person about to hand over the phone, and announces, "He can't use the phone any more. He's been hogging the phone for hours. Someone else needs a chance." That intervention instantly undoes the skillful intervention of the previous staff person. The patient escalates and a dangerous shouting match follows. Staff manage to direct him to his room without restraining him.

Later, the first staff person is talking with him in his room. It is bedtime, and the Unit expectation is for him to stay in his room and go to sleep. The patient complains that he cannot settle down right now and he wants to sit outside in the hall. They negotiate for the patient to sit on a chair outside his room quietly. They are about to implement this when another staff person comes along and announces, "He can't be sitting in the hall. He's got to be in his room right now." Once again, the patient is triggered by an unnecessary and arbitrary limit, and good skill development of both staff and patient is undermined. The patient starts destroying property and banging his head until he is restrained.

These last three incidents are wonderful fodder for group supervision. They demonstrate one-up and one-down stances, arbitrary limit setting, and CPS. The task for the supervisor is to help staff see the impact of each style of intervention.

Two deaf patients who are roommates are arguing about whether the light in the room should be left on. A staff person walking by doing patient checks notices them arguing and enters the room. "You two ok?" he signs. The patient starts to argue, and then one of them signs, "Leave the light on for half an hour, then turn it off. Ok?" The other patient stops arguing and agrees. The staff person says, "Nice job," smiles, and walks away. Later in supervision, the staff person brings up the issue. He points out that he gave positive feedback to the clients.

The supervisor agrees. "Yes, you gave positive feedback. That was good. But could you have shown even more skill?"

"What do you mean?"

"You told them 'good job,' giving positive feedback. How could you have shown even more skill?"

The staff person thinks for a moment and then says, "Well, I could have told them what they did well."

"Exactly, and what would you have said?"

"Well, good job solving this conflict. You made an agreement with each other."

"Do you see how that would have been more skillful? Being specific. Labeling the skill?"

"Yeah."

"So let me challenge you one more time. What could you have done that would have shown even greater skill than that?"

"I don't know."

"You gave them specific feedback, but you did it in the form of a statement. Instead of telling them what they did well, could you have pulled this out of them? How could you get them to identify their own skills?"

"Well, I could say, "You two solved the conflict. Wow. How did you do it?"

"Right. Maybe they could answer that or maybe not. But if they could identify their own skill use, do you see how that would be more powerful for them than you giving the answer? And by the way, the first thing you did when you checked in on them was very skillful. It was one of our pretreatment strategies. Do you know what it was?"

"I asked them how they were doing."

"Well, that's not what I was thinking of. When they solved the problem on their own, what did you do?"

"I said 'good job.'"

"Yes, and what pretreatment skill was that?"

The staff person looks puzzled. The supervisor continues using a leading question. "You noticed the two of them...?"

"Oh, I noticed they solved the conflict themselves."

"Exactly! You noticed skills clients were already using. That was an important moment and you caught it and praised them for it."

Here the supervisor is trying to model the same skills she is teaching. She catches staff using skills and helps them evaluate themselves and label their own skills. She uses leading questions more than declarative statements. She gives specific feedback.

The most useful way I have found to implement this approach is to model it in regular meetings with staff. Because the supervisor begins in a positive way, identifying skills that staff already show, this helps overcome resistance and pull staff into the treatment approach. The other pretreatment skills apply as well. The supervisor avoids being heavy-handed and overly directive. Once there is some staff buy in, formal instruction in the model is more accepted. In addition, it is very useful to have direct care staff serve as cotherapists in skill-building groups. They learn the skills by observing the clinician and helping teach clients. More accomplished staff can also serve as mentors for new staff or staff having difficulty. They may have more credibility with their peers, and they can help sell the model.

If one wants to develop a unified, seamless approach to treatment, with a strong therapeutic milieu, there is no way around this process of continuous supervision and training. Of course, seamlessness is not a steady state. Even the best of teams will relapse into less skillful behaviors. An appreciation that strong emotions and interpersonal conflict are normal, that all teams struggle in the face of such enormous clinical challenges, and that we have no recourse but to redouble our efforts to respond more skillfully, creates a climate where crisis equals opportunity.

Cross-Cultural Conflict Resolution Skills

This chapter addresses the development of an appropriate clinical program for deaf LLC clients. I do not address here the nature of culturally affirmative treatment environments for Deaf people. Principles of such environments, which I have discussed elsewhere (Glickman, 2003), include the following:

1. Culturally affirmative programs serve only deaf people, usually from a large geographic area.
2. Culturally affirmative programs strive to hire large numbers of competent Deaf staff at all levels of the organization.
3. Culturally affirmative programs need genuine communication excellence.

4. Culturally affirmative programs create an affirmative physical environment.
5. Culturally affirmative programs have Deaf people manage the communication dynamics.
6. Culturally affirmative programs work mindfully with Deaf–hearing cross-cultural transference, countertransference, as well as cultural biases.
7. Culturally affirmative programs approach psychotherapy differently.

I am aware that in most of the United States, and certainly the world, no such programs exist. Deaf consumers may not even have a counselor with specialized training and communication skills, much less a program. This means that designated "deafness mental health experts," where they exist, face impossible demands to be all things to all deaf people, and to make up for the lack of a continuum of mental health services. It means that when deaf consumers are in hearing treatment programs, the expectation falls on the signing therapist (or worse, nonsigning therapist with an interpreter) to make up for the fact that the entire treatment milieu is inaccessible. This would be a tall enough order were our clients all sophisticated, engaged consumers of psychotherapy. As we have seen, most are not.

Where there are specialized Deaf treatment programs and schools, there is much greater likelihood, but no guarantee, that communication at least will be appropriate. The programs I have seen have been staffed by Deaf and hearing persons with varying communication abilities, cultural orientations, and sensitivity to the Deaf experience. To my knowledge, cross-cultural conflicts between Deaf and hearing persons occur in all of these settings, although they are usually understood in personal rather than cross-cultural terms. That is to say, people take things personally. Both Deaf and hearing people complain about being oppressed, and take great offense at what others are doing. In the absence of a constructive framework for conflict resolution, these painful conflicts can destroy programs and cause burnout of dedicated, talented people.

In the interests of demonstrating how easy it is for staff to fall into these conflicts, I want to share some examples of conflicts that have occurred on the Westborough Deaf Unit. This complements an earlier discussion of this dynamic I presented elsewhere (Glickman, 2003).

1. One morning, the direct care staff consists of the lead mental health worker, who is Deaf, two Deaf Unit hearing mental health workers who sign, and a "float" staff from another unit who does not sign. A phone call comes in and the hearing float staff person answers. The caller is looking for one of the patients who failed to show up for the shuttle bus to the day program. The hearing staff overhear the conversation and realize that this patient is unaccounted for. The

float staff person reports it to the nurse who initiates a search for the patient. By the time the search has commenced, everyone working is aware of the missing patient except the Deaf mental health worker. He is the lead mental health worker and should have been the first to learn about the missing patient. He did not overhear this crucial piece of information, and in the panic of the moment the hearing staff had not bothered to tell him. He was left out of the communication flow, compromising his authority and ability to do his job, and no doubt triggering many painful associations.

After the patient is located and the crisis passes, a heated argument develops, taking a familiar Deaf versus hearing dynamic. The Deaf staff and their allies accuse the hearing staff of oppressing them by not telling the lead mental health worker what had happened. The hearing staff bristle at being accused of oppression. They insist they did not intend to exclude him. They apologize, but insist it was an innocent mistake and the Deaf staff are making too much of it. This seems to enrage the Deaf staff further, and they start raising other examples of alleged insensitivity to Deaf people. The hearing float staff person, who was assigned to work on the unit that day and knows nothing about Deaf people, thinks the lead Deaf mental health worker has a bad attitude. He complains about having been assigned to the Unit and accuses the Deaf staff of oppressing him because they sign without talking.

2. A newly hired ASL-using Deaf employee is talking with a patient. A hearing staff person who has worked on the Unit for several years approaches her to discuss a crucial safety concern that requires immediate attention. She is concerned that the Deaf employee is not attending to something very important. The Deaf employee is focused on the patient and signs to the hearing employee HOLD without making eye contact. That is, of course, a Deaf culturally appropriate way of acknowledging someone who is waiting and saying "I'll be right with you." The hearing employee, however, reads this from a hearing perspective. She is put off by the lack of eye contact and being told to wait by an employee barely finished with orientation. She interprets the Deaf employee's behavior as reflecting a lack of respect for her. She would not be interrupting if she did not have something important to say. There was another patient that needed immediate attention, and this new employee's refusal to attend to that reflected, in the senior staff person's eyes, poor judgment that put patient safety at risk.

This cross-cultural misunderstanding escalates into an argument. The Deaf employee turns her attention to her hearing colleague, but says she does not understand her English-based signing and asks for an interpreter. The hearing staff person takes this as evidence of further disrespect and tells her that "we don't need an interpreter. You understand me fine." This enrages the Deaf employee who begins to "shout" in sign at her colleague. From her perspective, the hearing staff person misunderstood her cultural signals, decided for her whether or not an interpreter was needed, and told her what she did and did not understand. To her, this was classic oppression. The hearing staff person saw a new employee not attending to a crucial safety matter, acting disrespectfully to a senior colleague, not following directions, and then losing her temper inappropriately. She also reacted to what she saw as an arrogant, know-it-all attitude from someone barely off orientation. She believes her signing is fine, and that the Deaf employee is complaining just to invalidate her abilities. The argument gets personal as each starts name calling toward the other, and soon others take sides.

3. A new hearing nurse who does not sign has a conflict with the Unit's sign language interpreter. The nurse complains that the interpreter is signing with deaf clients without voicing, leaving him out. He does not understand the linguistic reasons the interpreter is not voicing and interprets her behavior as an attempt to disempower him, to keep him from having the information he needs to manage the Unit. Feeling uncomfortable with the interpreter, he asks a hearing signer to interpret for him. The hearing signer, not appreciating the limits of his own communication abilities, agrees to help. The interpreter sees the nurse calling on unqualified staff to interpret when she is available and sees this as the nurse not respecting her role and abilities. They argue, and the nurse calls his supervisor to complain about the interpreter. The nursing supervisor then comes to the Unit director, demanding he "do something" about the interpreter, whom he supervises. When he speaks with the interpreter, she complains about the cultural insensitivity of the new nurse, how he does not draw on her expertise, and how his nonverbal behaviors are so "hearing" that deaf patients and staff are misunderstanding him.

4. After many years of requesting it, the Deaf Unit finally obtained new videophone (VP) technology, which allows Deaf people to communicate using sign language over a computer with a video camera. Unfortunately, the only room we could place it in was our group treatment room. This room is normally kept locked because there are items in it that people can use to hurt themselves. As this is a psychiatric hospital and we have many patients who harm themselves, we consider carefully patient access to any area where there are potentially dangerous items.

Patients in the hospital have what are considered fundamental rights, and chief among these is access to the phone. Since opening, we have had 24-hour-a-day text telephone (tty) access in a public area of the unit. Tty use, of course, depends on the ability to have a conversation in written English, and many of our LLC clients could not use the tty unassisted. It is also old technology, no longer in favor. Thus, we were delighted when the VP technology seemed to provide a way for nonliterate patients to use the phone. Deaf patients could sign directly to an interpreter or to a signing person on the other end of the line. The problem is that this task also requires linguistic competence. It requires enough sign competency that one can have a reasonable conversation, and it requires some ability to work with a sign interpreter. The question arose for us of how to determine whether the deaf patient could use the VP unassisted and unsupervised in a room where there are objects that can be used to harm oneself.

The Unit agreed pretty easily on a protocol for assessing safety to be in the group room unsupervised. As long as patients were not considered by the psychiatrist to be an imminent risk of hurting themselves, they would be given reasonable access to this room to make calls. Our cross-cultural conflict occurred when we had to decide what to do with a very linguistically dysfluent client who was perfectly safe to be in the room but incompetent to make the phone calls. Should we require that she be supervised? If so, would this violate her fundamental right to privacy when using the phone?

This patient asked regularly to have access to use the VP technology she had never seen before. To assess her competence, the communication specialist observed her making a call. The call began when the VP interpreter signed hello and asked for a phone number. The patient gave a phone number with the wrong number of digits. When the interpreter asked for a correct number, the patient did not understand what she was being asked for and started signing as if she was talking to her mother, whom she wanted to call. Staff assisted her in getting the right number to the interpreter. The interpreter then signed that "the phone is ringing." The patient did not understand that and proceeded to try to communicate with her mother, signing repeatedly "CLOTHING, MONEY" with a lot of irrelevant, nonsensical, and incomprehensible signs and gestures. The interpreter tried to convey that the phone was still ringing. Then the interpreter tried to convey that an answering machine had picked up. The patient did not understand this at all, and continued to repeat CLOTHING, MONEY and her other tangential comments. Eventually, the interpreter became so frustrated that she hung up on the client. The communication specialist met with the patient trying to explain to her what happened and what an answering machine was but was not able to successfully convey the idea.

At this point, a variety of other staff on the Unit weighed in on the question of what the patient could understand. These were staff at varying levels of communication skills but nothing approaching the communication skills of the staff in the communication department. Several hearing staff disagreed vigorously with the communication specialist. They insisted that when they helped the client, she had no trouble with the VP procedure. A nurse complained that she was being put in the position of denying to a patient her legal right to access to the phone. This brought in the human rights officer, a legal advocate for the patient, and the hospital administration.

A struggle followed over whether the patient should have unsupervised access to the VP in the group room. Most of the nursing staff did not want to be in the position of denying to this patient one of her fundamental rights. They were backed in this by the human rights officer, legal advocate, and hospital administration. On the other side were some of the Deaf staff, and the communication department, who argued that the patient was not linguistically competent to use the VP unassisted, that she was completely misunderstanding what was occurring over the VP, that she was becoming frustrated because she thought she had communicated something to her family when really she had not. They argued also that it was not fair to subject the relay interpreter to a client we knew could not use the technology appropriately. This conflict tapped into a deeper reservoir of cross-cultural tension and emotions flared.

To the Deaf staff and their allies, this incident provided yet another example of hearing people not appreciating the special communication needs of Deaf persons, assuming people understand when they do not, and applying procedures designed for hearing people. One Deaf staff person even argued that the legal rights should not apply in this instance because they were developed and implemented by hearing people. Those on the other side argued that this was a legal matter, that Deaf people could not make up their own legal rules, and that denying the patient access to the VP was causing unnecessary friction with her, possibly triggering her to become aggressive. Behind their arguments were feelings of annoyance and a strong belief that just because someone is deaf, this does not trump all the usual standards of clinical practice.

Ultimately, this matter was resolved after we got an opinion from the legal advocate for our deaf patients, a lawyer who signs and specializes in work with deaf people who had credibility with all parties. Her job was also to advocate for the legal rights of deaf patients. She advised us that the deaf patient had a legal right to use the VP even if she were incompetent to do so. She also agreed with the assessment that the patient was incompetent to use the equipment and supported the idea that she be directed to make these calls only when the appropriate staff were there to assist her. Bottom line, however, was that she could have reasonable access to the VP at other times as well, as long as she was safe and her clinical condition did not deteriorate as a result of the misunderstandings that were occurring. As for the relay interpreter, she was not our client and we had no obligation to protect her from an incompetent consumer.

This last conflict developed 11 years into my tenure as Unit Director at a time when I had a well-established orientation to conflict resolution. I frequently told staff that conflict was normal, especially in cross-cultural context, and that we were responsible to handle these conflicts skillfully. I saw this conflict as a product of a social process (the conflicts of groups of people with different life experiences, roles, and perceptions) rather than as a result of good or bad staff. Thus, it was particularly disheartening to me to see staff resorting to unskilled means of conflict resolution. Staff resorted to personal attacks, refused to talk to each other, filed complaints, and everyone expected me, as Unit Director, to "fix" the other parties. The familiar and ugly specter of "Deaf versus hearing" crept into this. This monster keeps rearing its head every so often. It does get tiring.

The legal advocate's assistance helped resolve the immediate crisis of what to do when the patient requested VP access. The larger issue of how we functioned as a staff remained. This episode was frustrating for me, but fortunately I held certain beliefs that facilitated my own coping. I expect conflict, and while I am frustrated when staff are not more skillful, I understand that it is my job to manage this. I did not believe, as I did when I began this job, that conflicts like this *should not happen*, and if they do that means something is wrong with the people involved and with me. I understood they *will* happen, in spite of my best efforts, and that the framework of helping staff develop the same set of nonviolent conflict resolution skills that we wish our clients to have is the best help that any manager can offer.

Although staff in these situations do demonstrate different degrees of sensitivity and skills, there are, I have come to realize, no heroes and no villains. There are just people who, because of very different life experiences, see and interpret the world differently. Cross-cultural dynamics adds a layer of complexity to conflict resolution in that one needs to develop skill in understanding cultural as well as individual perspectives. In almost all these cross-cultural conflicts, Deaf people, who are exquisitely attuned to the issue of communication inclusion, bristle when they perceive hearing people not delivering access to the same information, not appreciating their special communication skills and needs, and deciding important matters for them. Hearing people do vary enormously in how much they appreciate these concerns. Because communication comes naturally to them, hearing people, as a group, tend to believe that Deaf people make too much of communication matters. Hearing people object when they perceive Deaf people arguing that they know better just because they are Deaf or that because someone is Deaf means they should not be held to the same standards as hearing people. In other words, hearing people are quick to see Deaf advocates as *entitled*, and they can even see themselves as the victims when faced with Deaf people who appear hostile and confrontational. Hearing people who only know one language, who do not understand the grammatical differences between English and ASL, and why Deaf people sign without speaking, usually do not see how signed English is not clear, or understand why voicing interferes with good signing. They can be quick to conclude that Deaf advocates are being unreasonable, provocative, and even belligerent.

There is nothing particularly odd about any of these beliefs. They flow naturally from very different life experiences and are predictable expressions of those experiences. As an analogy, consider what happens when a large group of people is trying to get on to a long, crowded trolley car. People board from the back, and at this end of the trolley, people are crowded, pushing each other and stepping on each other's toes. At the other end of the large trolley car, however, there is plenty of space, and no one feels any urgency to move. The people in the back of the trolley shout for people to "move down," and think that those people in the front are inconsiderate and self-centered. At the front of the trolley, there is enough room and people may not even be aware of the crowd at the back. If they hear a commotion, they may think, "What's wrong with the people back there? Why are they so loud and rude?" The people pushing and shoving at the back of the trolley are not better or worse people than those blissfully ignorant of their plight in the front. Each perceives the world and each other differently based on circumstance. Chances are good that if the people in the back moved to the front, and vice versa, they would each adopt the belief system and behaviors of their respective groups. To get beyond this is going to require some new skills, especially in empathy and perspective taking.

If our goal is for one side to defeat the other, there will be no outcome from this but bitter conflict and burnout. The only framework I knew that takes us out of this oppressor/victim mentality is to focus on skills. If we do this work, we will encounter these conflicts. What skills do we need to succeed? While all the communication and conflict resolution skills discussed in Chapter 5 apply, fundamentally we need the skill of *listening to each other with empathy*. This is also the fundamental skill we need when working with clients. Thus, the work of using skills to solve our own conflicts is also good clinical training. If necessary, we can draw on the same conflict resolution microskill cards we use with clients to remind us, for instance, to communicate *cleanly*, without insults, criticism, or disrespect. Our goal with each other, as with our clients, must always be WIN, WIN, WIN.

If the Problem Is Not Communication, What Is the Problem?

More than 20 years ago in our brand new Deaf inpatient unit, I witnessed a very disturbed deaf patient knock over a Deaf, native signing staff person. When the Deaf staff person got up, she announced that "the problem is communication," and at that moment I realized that the problem *was not* communication. But if the problem was not communication, what then was the problem?

The issue of communication is so prominent in work with deaf people that it is sometimes hard to see beyond it. Deaf children and adults so rarely receive treatment in environments that are accessible, much less culturally affirmative, and so much effort is directed to procuring appropriate communication that the treatment issues sometimes may languish in the background. The issue of communication is so salient for Deaf people that it often becomes the guiding lens through which they see the world. Communication is almost always first in their list of concerns, and how could it not be? Yet there are culturally affirmative schools and mental health and rehabilitation programs, and in these programs deaf students and clients still show enormous problems. It is not that the culturally affirmative environments make the problems go away but that they allow them, perhaps for the first time, to be seen. Only in a communication-rich environment will it become apparent that the problem is not communication. Only when the communication needs are well addressed can one see beyond communication to the underlying clinical problems.

The young deaf man referred to earlier who assaulted so many of our deaf and hearing staff was raised without adequate ASL exposure, so certainly for him lack of communication skills as part of the problem. From our current perspective, I would broaden this to say that he lacked many other skills crucial for living: skills for managing his inner experience, for establishing and maintaining relationships with other people, for taking care of his body and his environment, for managing problem symptoms, for reading, learning, working, and problem solving. In fairness to him, I would also say that the problem was that those of us assigned to help him also lacked skills. We were completely unprepared for the behavioral challenges he presented. We had only a vague sense of the tools needed to engage and treat him. So to reduce a complex problem down to its essentials, I would say that the problem was lack of skills, in him and in us.

When the staff of the Deaf Unit greeted our first patients in 1987, we were idealistic and naïve but we were not wrong about the importance of a culturally affirmative treatment milieu. With the LLC deaf clients we would come to serve, people with such enormous challenges and so few resources, we would never have reached first base without the right cultural and language environment. To get to second base, however, we needed more than that. We needed the appropriate clinical model.

We know much more now about what such an appropriate clinical model looks like. Based on best practices in the CBT field, approaches like the constructivist narrative CBT of Meichenbaum, DBT from Linehan, and CPS from Greene, we know we need to focus on the development of psychosocial skills. We know we have to adapt these approaches. We have to simplify them; select those elements that our clientele can use, and rely heavily on visual aids. We know also we should bring a developmental framework to our work. That is, our LLC clients are not usually in rehabilitation. They are in *habilitation*. They are learning these skills for the first time. The skills need to be presented in a developmentally appropriate way: simpler skills first and use of engaging treatment methods like games, activities, and stories. We also know that one of our biggest clinical challenges is the pretreatment issue of soliciting meaningful treatment engagement. Ignoring pretreatment issues and applying psychotherapeutic techniques and thinking that were designed for verbally and intellectually competent people put one on the royal road to failure and burnout.

The challenges of this work are so formidable that it takes a team to do it. The norm may be to imagine that a "super-deafness therapist" will fix everything, but there are few super-deafness therapists among us who can be all things to all deaf people. Although there are many talented and dedicated clinicians working with this population, it is extremely difficult for them to be effective working alone. Perhaps it helps to think about the work of psychotherapy as being that of marshalling resources to promote psychological development in people. Usually, psychotherapists focus on internal resources: finding skills, strengths, insights, and resiliency and bringing these to the forefront. We also draw on external resources, members of clients' family and network that can contribute to clients' development. The fewer the internal resources that clients are able to bring to their development, the more we need to draw on resources from their external world. I learned that lesson from a supervisor who once told me that when you are stuck with a client, bring in more people. Because these clients are so challenging, we need to serve them through trained, effective therapy teams in specialty programs. In the "real world" this may not be available, but it nonetheless is what is needed.

If I were to start a new treatment or rehabilitation program for deaf persons, I would still do everything in my power to prioritize communication access in setting up staffing. I would do this even if it meant, as it did at Westborough State Hospital in 1987, that we alienated a good number of the existing hospital employees. I would do this because I know, as all of us in the deafness field know, that we cannot provide effective treatment without good communication. What I would do differently is focus immediately on these skill-building best practices. Because I know this work requires a team, I would devote most of my energy to staff development, especially of the direct care staff who have the majority of interactions with clients. Many Deaf schools and programs today get the communication right but the treatment wrong. They work from insight-oriented models that are a poor match for this clientele and leave paraprofessional staff with little guidance on what they should do. Or they use traditional behavioral modification (that is, limits, token plans, management of reinforcers, time outs, level systems) that reinforces authoritarian tendencies in staff and often provokes clients who lack the skills to comply with rigid expectations. They also rely too heavily on the magic they hope will occur in an isolated psychotherapy hour and not enough on shaping treatment milieu so that they surround our clients with opportunities for skill development.

Does this mean there is no role for insight in our work? Of course not. The capacity for insight is a resource, and our work will be much easier when that resource is available. Motivation to use the counseling process to make some change in oneself is another huge resource. I think all counselors want clients to have that resource. It is just that when they do not, this does not mean they are "inappropriate for psychotherapy." Instead, it means we have to bring the psychotherapy to them, to use models of treatment that match their capacities and frames of reference.

It is sometimes said that insight is the ability to come to see things the same way as one's therapist. Similarly, resistance can be viewed as the stubborn refusal to agree with one's therapist. More fairly, insight can be viewed as the ability to make a new connection between, for instance, a feeling and a thought, or a past incident and a current behavior. Some people think insight is the sudden awareness of the Truth. These people usually also think that Truth is self-evident and clear (and coincidentally consistent with how they view the world). I think it is more helpful to conceptualize truth as a more helpful story. Insight, then, would refer to any time one constructs a story that more helpfully addresses life challenges.

We can help our LLC clients develop insight by helping them construct a new story about themselves. This is the story of their abilities, skills, and resiliency in spite of all the obstacles they have faced. Clients who have mastered "shield" or "red, yellow, green" have insight into a new story about themselves. The staff person who catches two clients solving a conflict by flipping a coin and points this out to them is doing cognitive therapy, fostering insight, and creating a new story. The new story has the theme, *I can do this*. When staff apply these skills to help clients and also discover the relevancy of the skills for themselves, their self stories also change. Their stories then also have the theme, *I can do this*. Skill building and story construction reinforce each other, in both clients and staff. Skill-building work, then, is as profound as any other kind of treatment, especially when we reflect on the skills to change the story. Skill building takes us to our deepest resources. When skill development is noticed, talked about, and affirmed, insight happens. This process can be summarized in one sentence: *skills, linked by a story, create identity*.

9
Summary and Conclusions

In this final chapter, I summarize in list form the main ideas expressed in this book. I then conclude with three brief discussions. First, I will name and propose diagnostic criteria for the syndrome or disorder in deaf people associated with severe language deprivation. Second, I will shift focus to consider the nature of psychotherapy with higher functioning Deaf people, those who are fluent users of American Sign Language (ASL), and without cognitive impairments interfering with learning. I will argue that teaching and psychotherapy for these persons also requires adaptations, and to that end I will consider some innovative recent work that sheds light on the nature of such "Deaf friendly" treatment. Finally, I will offer some broad observations on what it takes to provide appropriate mental health care for Deaf persons.

Summary of Main Points

1. The population of "low functioning" deaf people is well recognized in the deafness mental health literature and among service providers who work with deaf people. It is also well recognized among deaf people themselves. Currently, the preferred term to describe this group of people is "traditionally underserved deaf." The chief characteristic of this group is language dysfluency, and this is understood to contribute significantly to an array of psychosocial, developmental, and behavioral problems.

2. Evidence from the Westborough State Hospital Deaf Unit, viewed in light of previous studies, suggests that the majority of deaf persons referred to psychiatric inpatient programs are not suffering from major mental illnesses such as schizophrenia. Most do have emotional, personality, and behavioral problems of a nonpsychotic nature. Many are from this traditionally underserved group.

3. This group of traditionally underserved deaf persons is notoriously vulnerable to misdiagnosis and inappropriate treatment interventions. It is exceptionally easy for clinicians who do not specialize in work with deaf people to wrongly attribute their language dysfluency, and array of other problems, to major mental illnesses.

4. There are many cautions in the deafness mental health literature against misdiagnosing deaf people as psychotic or mentally retarded.

These cautions are important, yet the data from Westborough and other facilities suggest that deaf persons with mental retardation are indeed more likely to be referred to designated treatment programs, and that they are well represented in the traditionally underserved group.

5. Deaf psychiatric patients have some notable differences from hearing psychiatric patients beyond the obvious: hearing loss and possible use of sign. One difference is the presence of this traditionally underserved group in whom one is more likely to see deficits in developmental skills than severe mental illness. Another difference is the prevalence of language dysfluency that is related mainly to language deprivation, not mental illness. This language dysfluency has long been noted in spoken language skills, but I am referring here to language dysfluency in the person's best language or communication modality. Other deaf clients, of course, are fluent, even articulate users of ASL and/or spoken languages. Yet another difference is that they are likely to have a much more limited fund of information about their social world (Pollard, 1998).

6. The data from Westborough indicates a high incidence of known traumatic experiences in the deaf inpatient population. The real incidence is suspected to be higher but is often unknown because so many clients have poor abilities to provide their own history. The nature of trauma in deaf persons is also presumed to be more complex because it often occurs in persons without the language skills to talk about it and certainly to make sense of it. Indeed, the prolonged experience of language deprivation is itself a form of trauma quite apart from experiences of physical or sexual abuse. These factors taken together would be expected to contribute to attachment difficulties and behavioral disorders. In adulthood, these may become diagnosed as personality disorders. Thirty-seven percent of deaf patients at Westborough State Hospital were diagnosed as having a personality disorder or personality disorder trait as compared to 22% of hearing patients. Again, this does not mean there is a higher incidence of deaf persons with personality disorders in the general population, but it does suggest that the kinds of traumatic experiences deaf persons are exposed to can manifest in some significant psychopathology, *not* of a psychotic nature.

7. The presence of a large cohort of language and learning challenged deaf persons (i.e., the traditionally underserved group) is a key difference between mental health care of deaf and hearing persons. The complexity of the problems of such persons, especially their language dysfluency, means that nonspecialized treatment programs are completely unprepared for them. Illusions that staff in such programs may hold about the efficacy of using interpreters compounds the problem

of serving them. Specialized Deaf mental health and rehabilitation programs are needed not just because of the presence of ASL using members of the Deaf Community (the language and cultural reason) but even more so because of profound and unique forms of psychopathology found in this LLC group. In nonspecialized settings, these problems are very likely to be mischaracterized. Inappropriate, ineffective, and even harmful treatment interventions are easily applied by persons who are ignorant about how to serve this population.

8. I have chosen to use the term "language and learning challenged" (LLC) because it is more descriptive, less pejorative than "low functioning," and applicable to use with hearing persons as well. In both hearing and deaf populations, we find people with language and learning challenges such as poor vocabulary, visual-spatial abilities, attention span, memory, ability to process information quickly, problem-solving skills, and academic abilities. These deficits may be measured and categorized as indicating specific brain problems like aphasias, learning disabilities, or low levels of intelligence. These deficits occur without the presence of severe mental illness although such illnesses may contribute to worsening of language and learning challenges.

9. The language and learning challenges of traditionally underserved deaf people stem primarily from severe language deprivation associated with inadequate exposure to ASL or other sign languages. Neurological problems may also contribute. This experience of language deprivation creates language and learning challenges that are a different order of magnitude of seriousness from those found more commonly in the population of troubled hearing children and adolescents, such as those described in Chapter 3. Apart from neuropathology or psychosis, there is simply no reason that hearing children would display the kind of language deficits that deaf children, raised without exposure to sign language, commonly develop.

10. Some of the specific language deficits observed in deaf psychiatric patients at Westborough State Hospital *that are not assumed to be related to mental illness* include:

   a. Limited vocabulary with many signs incorrectly formed or used inappropriately.
   b. Limited ability to use tense or time referents. Difficulty conveying the linear narrative of a story.
   c. Poor use of the signing space to establish pronouns and relationships resulting in confusion over who did what to whom.
   d. Confused and incorrect syntax (sign order).
   e. Difficulty conveying plurality.

326 • CBT for Deaf and Hearing Persons With LLC

    f. Use of idiosyncratic "home signs" familiar to only a small group of people.

    g. Mixture of formal sign with gesture and pantomime.

11. Some clues that a deaf person with language dysfluency is suffering from a thought disorder include:

    a. Inappropriate (for Deaf culture) facial and emotional expression.

    b. Language content that is bizarre.

    c. Nonverbal behaviors suggesting hallucinations.

    d. Guardedness, suspiciousness, and volatility.

    e. Language skills that have deteriorated recently and dramatically.

    f. Personal appearance and behavior that is strikingly unusual and culturally inappropriate.

    g. Language skills that improve when antipsychotic medicine is administered.

12. Some of the reasons that many deaf persons with language and learning challenges appear unmotivated for mental health treatment include:

    a. They do not understand or embrace insight-oriented therapy models.

    b. Their language and cognitive impairments make verbal counseling strategies difficult.

    c. They resist the disempowered client role and story.

13. Pretreatment refers to strategies designed to educate clients about the mental health treatment process and engage them in it. At Westborough, we have found that the "thought worlds" of many deaf clients are so different from those of mental health professionals that enormous effort must be devoted to this pretreatment process. We have found it useful to distinguish pretreatment from treatment. It forces us to consider constantly client readiness for treatment interventions, and to avoid staff generated treatment plans (e.g., patient will attend 12 step meetings and practice relapse prevention; patient will explore in therapy the reasons for his aggressive behaviors), which have no relationship to our clients' frame of reference.

14. A core pretreatment strategy is the way we conceptualize treatment itself. We need to literally give our clients a language or map for mental health treatment, and this language needs to be as simple, clear, and compelling as possible. The only treatment paradigm that offers such clear language is cognitive behavioral therapy (CBT), though even this must be adapted and simplified. From CBT, particularly the work of Meichenbaum, we understand treatment to consist primarily of developing skills. We build our treatment approach primarily around this idea of skills. We use this language with staff and clients. We build skill-centered environments.

15. A second core pretreatment strategy is learning how to be strength-based. This is crucial because LLC clients usually lead "problem-saturated lives," and they are often unmotivated to continue discussions of their problems with us. A strength-based focus means learning to notice and label skills that clients already have, to engage them first through discussions of these abilities, and to set up opportunities for them to develop these skills further.

16. Often the skills and strengths of LLC clients are not readily apparent. To see these skills, we have to learn to think developmentally. We have to see coping skills when a person does *not* become aggressive by, for instance, rocking in a chair. We have to see conflict resolution skills whenever a person engages in a reasonable conversation; listening, taking turns, staying in control, using appropriate nonverbal attending skills. The ability to approach skills developmentally, as one would with children, is the key to doing such strength based work.

17. Another crucial pretreatment strategy has to do with the "stance" we take with our clients. Essentially, we learn ways to *invite* them to participate, and we avoid heavy-handed use of authority and power. This means learning to work from a "one-down" stance. This is a primary reason why this pretreatment work is incompatible with the role of agent of social control that mental health and rehabilitation people are expected to assume when the police and courts defer to us to manage antisocial behaviors. We need to insist that our job is to engage our clients in the process of developing psychosocial skills and that we cannot do this while we are simultaneously expected to control and even punish them.

18. Besides skills, another, perhaps "deeper" treatment strategy is to change the stories that clients tell themselves. In essence, we want to help them develop a story about their abilities. We can do this by noticing instances of skill use and "connecting the dots" to construct a story about the client's abilities. We comment, "You used coping skills five times today. What does this say about you?"

19. Fortunately, this focus on the development of psychosocial skills is a hallmark of contemporary best practice as found in the CBT literature. The three approaches referenced most heavily in this book are all forms of best practice. They are Meichenbaum's constructivist narrative cognitive behavioral therapy, Linehan's dialectical behavior therapy (DBT), and Greene's collaborative problem solving. All three contribute useful treatment strategies for developing such skills, but Meichenbaum's work presents the best overall framework suitable to this population.

20. Treatment strategies derived from Meichenbaum's work but adapted for LLC deaf clients include:
  a. The emphasis on helping clients develop coping skills.
  b. The use of stress inoculation procedures, rather than a specific coping skill curriculum, as the framework for skill training.
  c. The importance of the conceptualization phase, which we call pretreatment, in which client engagement and collaboration are obtained.
  d. The importance of working one-down, "Columbo" style.
  e. The importance of fostering clients self-appraisal though use of self-monitoring.
  f. The importance of developing a menu of coping skills that are clear and compelling for the clients served. With the assistance of a talented artist, Michael Krajnak, we created a visual representations of these skills (that is, skill cards) to help concretize them.
  g. The importance of active practice of skills with increasingly more difficult challenges and in diverse situations.
  h. The use of self-instructional training as a cognitive therapy strategy to help clients change thoughts.
  i. The concern with skill generalization, including the need to anticipate and prepare for relapses in client problems.
  j. The use of skillful questioning, usually from a one-down stance, to guide clients to drawing new conclusions.
  k. The use of simple metaphors, spoken and visual, to conceptualize treatment concepts and as means of engagement of clients. We also look for opportunities to "pluck" metaphors from clients when they offer them.
  l. The use of stories, including those shown in television and movie segments, to engage and teach.
  m. Attention to helping clients construct new stories about their own abilities. This is done by helping them notice when they are using skillful behaviors and connecting these examples for them into a pattern. *Skills connected by a story create identity.*
  n. Setting up opportunities for clients to demonstrate skill use, for example, by helping and teaching others, and using these successes as evidence of their capabilities.
21. An additional important set of coping skills for LLC deaf clients are those that draw primarily on physical, sensory-based activities. In this regard, the work by occupational therapists such as Tina Champagne (2006) and Karen Moore (2005) is relevant, practical, and powerful.
22. Coping skills are defined in this work as skills designed to help people manage their "inner life," such as feelings, thoughts, physical sensations,

and memories. This is contrasted with social skills, designed to help people manage other people and the world around them. The social skill emphasized here is that of nonviolent conflict resolution, key components of which are effective communication and problem solving.

23. Both coping and conflict resolution skills need to be taught in a clear and compelling manner, appropriate for the particular clients. Three treatment strategies are emphasized for both:

   a. Noticing and labeling the skills that clients already use no matter how developmentally simple these may be.

   b. Approaching every crisis or conflict that occurs as an opportunity for collaborative problem solving. Developing client skills in the midst of naturally occurring conflicts or problems. This is the approach emphasized by Greene and Ablon (2006).

   c. Formal skill training groups using innovative teaching methods like games, storytelling, and movies that capture the interest of clients.

24. By reviewing a number of important works on conflict resolution, including works on this subject developed for children, I developed a menu of conflict resolution skills. As with the coping skills, these are illustrated with pictorial "skill cards" that can be downloaded from the enclosed CD-ROM. Many of these "microskills" represent developmental antecedents of more advanced conflict resolution skills. These conflict resolution microskills are presented on page 230.

25. Relapse prevention refers to the set of skills that people use to manage their own recovery. Relapse prevention skills are more difficult than coping or conflict resolution because they build on these and they assume a commitment to self-management. They also assume the linguistic and cognitive capacity to anticipate problems before they occur and do something proactively to prevent these problems from occurring.

26. Key relapse prevention concepts are relapse, lapse, warning sign, trigger, risk factors, and seemingly unimportant decisions. These abstract ideas are conceptualized differently in ASL than in English; and these linguistic differences imply the need to teach the concepts differently. When working with deaf LLC clients, it is especially important to draw on examples and stories as teaching/counseling methods. Visual aids, such as relapse prevention skill cards, also help. Another useful technique is that of putting clients in the helper or teacher role.

27. Crisis management draws on the same relapse prevention concepts, but in crisis management one person or group manages the crises of someone else, usually a client. Because it is much harder to manage another person than to manage oneself, crisis management plans are

inherently weaker than relapse prevention plans. Crisis management is one example of how mental health and rehabilitation personnel are called on to act in the role of agents of social control. Because mental health work is by its nature collaborative, this social control function can interfere with therapeutic relationships and plans. It is much clearer and cleaner to have social control functions exerted by the police and legal system.

28. Many deaf clients with language and learning challenges are not legally competent to stand trial. They are not competent for cognitive and linguistic reasons, not the usual reasons of mental illness (Vernon & Miller, 2001, 2005). Effective collaboration between the legal and mental health system in their management and treatment is, in most locales, still to be developed.

29. Deaf mental health and rehabilitation programs generally face five great challenges:
    a. The linguistic challenge of working with clients who use ASL as their primary or exclusive language and the challenge of working with language dysfluent clients.
    b. The cross-cultural challenge of creating programs in which Deaf and hearing people work together productively, skillfully managing minority–majority dynamics characteristic of Deaf/hearing interactions.
    c. The challenge of violence, associated with work with many clients who are language dysfluent and behaviorally disturbed, sometimes severely.
    d. The challenge of adapting best practices in mental health and rehabilitation so that they are "culturally affirmative" or "Deaf friendly."
    e. The pretreatment challenge of engaging LLC clients in meaningful, relevant treatment programs.

30. Deaf clients with language and learning challenges are served best in specialized programs where they have peers and staff who can communicate with them easily. However, hiring signing staff is the beginning of creating appropriate programs, not the end. Treatment still has to be adapted. Because these programs rely so heavily on paraprofessional direct care staff, a heavy investment in staff development is essential.

31. There is a parallel process between how supervisors and management respond to direct care staff and how these staff respond to clients. The skill-building framework needs to be embraced at all levels of the organization. Staff also need to develop and demonstrate coping and conflict resolution skills. The same skill-based language can be used for both staff and client problems.

32. Deaf and hearing persons working in the same settings often have cross-cultural conflicts. These conflicts are normal, but staff need to understand them as cross-cultural (rather than personal) conflicts and develop the specific cross-cultural conflict resolution skills to manage them. Chief among these skills are empathic listening and perspective taking, the ability to communicate "cleanly" (that is, without evaluative judgments and provocative language), and stay in a problem-solving frame of mind.

Conclusions

A Unique Clinical Syndrome

Is there enough of a similarity between the characteristics and problems of many deaf persons with language and learning challenges to hypothesize about a unique clinical syndrome? As discussed in Chapter 1, this has already been done frequently. It is seen in the proposed diagnosis of surdophrenia (Basilier, 1964), primitive personality disorder (Rainer and Altshuler, 1966), borderline syndrome (Grinker et al., 1969), minimal brain injury, nonclassified psychosis, and problems related to deafness (Denmark 1994), the diagnostic tags of *atypical* and *not otherwise specified* that one encounters frequently in assessments of deaf people, or just in the large number of patients that clinicians felt they could not diagnose (Daigle, 1994; Pollard, 1994). It is also reflected in various criteria that have been given for *traditionally underserved deaf* (Dew, 1999; Long, Long, & Ouellette 1993). Vernon and Raifman (1997) offered the following criteria for the proposed disorder of primitive personality disorder, which they also called surdophrenia:

1. A meager or total absence of knowledge of sign language, English, or a foreign language.
2. Corollary to the above, those with primitive personality are functionally illiterate, that is, they read at grade level 2.9 or below as measured by a standardized educational achievement test, preferably the appropriate battery of the Stanford Achievement Test.
3. A history of little or no formal education.
4. A pervasive cognitive deprivation involving little or no knowledge of such basics as what the U.S. Constitution is, Social Security, how to make change, pay taxes, follow recipes, plan a budget, how to function on a job, and so on.
5. A performance IQ score of 70 or above.

The term *surdophrenia* is objectionable to many because it sounds like schizophrenia and implies that people with this problem have a brain disorder. Some may have a brain disorder, if we consider the deafness etiologies that have neurological comorbidity (Vernon & Andrews, 1990), but for the most

part we are discussing a condition that accompanies severe language deprivation. This language deprivation is primarily a result of social and educational
policy and practice. It occurs when medical and educational professionals, as
well as family members, prevent deaf children from having sufficient exposure
to sign language. It is true that some deaf children raised orally do not develop
these emotional and behavioral problems. These "oral successes" are exceptions, as it is much more common for deaf children raised without adequate
exposure to sign language to develop language and behavioral problems
(Paijmans, 2007; Schlesinger & Meadow, 1972). Deafness mental health specialists commonly recognize this disorder or syndrome even while lacking a
name for it. Probably the most common term used is "low functioning deaf."

Use of the term *primitive personality disorder* seems even more pejorative
than the term *low functioning*. It would further stigmatize this group of people
and obscure again the social origins of this condition. A diagnostic category
with that title would also interfere with our pretreatment efforts to engage such
persons. On the other hand, use of a term like *primitive personality disorder*
does not sugarcoat the seriousness of the pathology that commonly stems from
severe language deprivation. If we are trying to get special educational, habilitation, and mental health services for these persons, it helps to have a diagnosis
that captures the severity of the problems associated with this syndrome.

The criteria proposed by Vernon and Raifman for primitive personality
disorder/surdophrenia also do not reflect the contemporary reality, at least
for American citizens, that deaf children do receive education services, however linguistically inappropriate, and usually develop some language skills. As
discussed in Chapter 1, on the Deaf Unit at Westborough State Hospital the
only patients we have seen with virtually no functional language were raised
in third-world settings and immigrated to this country. This fact also under-
scores the social origins of this condition.

Throughout this book, I have argued that a unique feature of mental health
and rehabilitation work with deaf people is the presence of this subgroup of
persons with significant language and learning challenges. Our lack of an
appropriate term for these deaf clients who appear to have a unique clinical
syndrome increases the risk of confusing it with severe conditions like schizophrenia. Ironically, our lack of a term for this disorder also results in these
people being denied important social services when they are presumed not to
have a severe psychiatric disorder.

For instance, on the Westborough Deaf Unit, where we are very careful
to *not* jump to conclusions that our patients have major mental illnesses, our
conservative and cautious approach has sometimes meant that persons who
were functioning very poorly in society were found ineligible for Department
of Mental Health services. On a practical level, *not* being diagnosed with a
major mental illness may mean loss of housing services that are still badly

needed. When they are referred to us, many of these persons have already demonstrated their inability to live independently, and they are desperately in need of help. We need to be able to diagnose them correctly, as having this developmental disorder, and still have them qualify for the support services they need.

Thus, diagnostic imprecision is not a mere academic problem. It had resulted in catastrophic mistakes: unnecessary and prolonged hospitalizations, placing patients on powerful psychotropic medications, and the failure to develop appropriate treatment programs or provide needed services. One of the pioneering psychologists and educators in the deafness field, McCay Vernon, has been warning about this problem, and advocating for the establishment of such a diagnosis, for years (Vernon & Andrews, 1990; Vernon & Daigle-King, 1999; Vernon & Miller, 2001, 2005; Vernon & Raifman, 1997). He has been particularly eloquent in describing the tragedies that have befallen deaf persons with this syndrome unlucky enough to find themselves charged and convicted of crimes (Vernon & Miller, 2001, 2005; Vernon & Raifman, 1997). Therefore, there is a pressing urgency to correctly name this syndrome but to do so in a way that (1) does not further stigmatize and (2) does capture the severity of problems that follow severe language deprivation.

In this book, I have used the term *language and learning challenged*. This term, as we have seen, is broad enough to include hearing persons. It lacks the specificity needed to define a clinical syndrome. Rather than create a new term like *surdophrenia*, a better label would be descriptive. The syndrome name I propose is *language deprivation with deficiencies in behavioral, emotional, and social adjustment*.

The first essential feature of this syndrome is severe language deprivation associated with early childhood deafness and inadequate exposure to sign language. *It must be continuously stressed that this language deprivation is not an inevitable by-product of deafness but it is an inevitable by-product of social and educational policy and practice that prevents deaf children from being exposed to sign language rich environments.* The second essential feature of this disorder is that these persons have global deficiencies in behavioral, emotional, and social adjustment as well as huge deficits in fund of information about the world (Pollard, 1998a). Third, these deficiencies are developmental problems, starting in early childhood and persisting into adulthood. Persons with this disorder are vulnerable to developing the other established psychiatric and substance abuse disorders because language deprivation has such an enormous impact on psychological development. These problems can be worsened by developmental disabilities such as mental retardation and autism spectrum disorders, with which they may co-occur, and of course by major mental illnesses, but they occur in the absence of any of these conditions.

The proposed diagnostic criteria for this disorder are:

a. The person is born with a hearing loss severe enough so as to preclude the ability to comprehend oral language or the child loses that ability before the acquisition of oral language.

b. The hearing loss can not be remediated, or is not remediated, sufficiently for the person to be able to acquire and comprehend oral language effectively.

c. The child is not exposed to American Sign Language (or other sign languages) sufficiently so as to acquire it as a native user.

d. The person is severely dysfluent in his or her best language or communication modality, either receptively, expressively, or both, as measured by objective tests or determined by expert evaluators of that language. The person is functionally illiterate in the spoken/written language of the larger community. If the primary communication modality is sign language, one sees deficits such as these:

    i. Severely impoverished vocabulary as well as signs used with the incorrect meaning.

    ii. Absence or minimal use of grammatical features and vocabulary for tense and time resulting in the inability to give an historical, linear account of events.

    iii. The person communicates mostly in signs or phrases rather than full sentences. Sentence structure, where it exists, is simple.

    iv. The person frequently omits subjects and/or objects, or conveys these haphazardly, so as to convey poorly *who* did what to *whom* or *what* happened.

    v. In sign language, spatial location and movement are used haphazardly resulting in a visual message that is disorganized and unclear.

e. From early childhood, the child displays a global pattern of behavioral, social, and emotional disturbances such as aggression, self-harm, a gross lack of social skills, and poor school performance. These problems occur at home, school, and all other settings.

f. The person demonstrates an enormous deficit in fund of information about the world (e.g., social norms, knowledge of history, government, current events, rights and responsibilities of being a citizen).

g. As an adult, the person experiences great difficulties developing work skills, in particular in the interpersonal and attitudinal aspects of work, and learning to live independently.

h. The person is at least 14 years of age.

i. The person does not have mental retardation, schizophrenia, or another psychotic disorder. If adolescent, they do not have a conduct disorder; and if adult, they do not have antisocial personality disorder.

One objection that can be raised to this proposed diagnostic criteria is the absence of a validated, generally accepted, and easily utilized measure of linguistic competency in ASL. That same objection can and should be raised to the entire discussion of ASL language dysfluency throughout this book, but it is an objection which I hope future linguistic research will remedy. Unfortunately, it would require great linguistic competence in ASL, and not merely clinical competence, to make this assessment; and diagnostic assessments made by nondeafness specialists would have to be considered suspect. In most circumstances it would probably require a team of, at least, a clinician with enough special training to understand the issue and an ASL communication specialist to make this assessment.

Because this proposed syndrome is a developmental disorder, like mental retardation, and because these persons may be functionally retarded, the decision might be made to code it, using the *Diagnostic and Statistical Manual's* multiaxial diagnostic system, on Axis II. I believe this syndrome can co-occur with these other developmental disorders, as well as with Axis I disorders, but for research purposes, the rule-out of these other disorders are necessary. Researchers wishing to test out the validity of this syndrome on another population of deaf patients might inquire about how many "pure" cases they have and how many patients fit the criteria if one also considers comorbid disorders. For instance, some of the persons fitting the criteria treated at Westborough have had tested intelligence in the mildly mentally retarded range, but the diagnosis of mild mental retardation does not account for the language and behavioral problems they display.

The rule out of conduct disorder and antisocial disorder is crucial so this diagnosis does not become a backdoor means for characterizing patterns of criminal behaviors as a new form of psychopathology. As characterized here, persons with this syndrome are thought to suffer, essentially, from deficits in language and the development of psychosocial skills. The treatment recommended is psychosocial skills training, appropriately adapted for language and cognition, as described in this book. However, persons with this syndrome may engage in a pattern of antisocial and criminal behavior consistent with conduct disorder in adolescents and antisocial personality disorder in adults. They may also be persons without any other diagnosable disorder who engage in criminal behaviors. There are reasons apart from skill deficits that can account for their behaviors. While some of these persons will do better given treatment environments designed to meet their needs, others are more appropriately managed by the police and legal system. The depiction of this syndrome is not meant to excuse criminal behaviors or to imply that persons with this syndrome should not be held accountable for their behaviors.

Those deaf persons who are incompetent to stand trial due to linguistic reasons, who may also have conduct disorder or antisocial personality disorder, can pose enormous challenges to the mental health system, even when such linguistically and clinically appropriate treatment is available. This is because mental health practitioners have difficulty setting limits, imposing consequences, and simultaneously soliciting treatment engagement. We are not the police or the courts, and we should not have to act as substitutes for them. It is also because deaf persons who have experienced severe language deprivation are not easily made competent, and they therefore may languish in mental health facilities for years. Imagine the case, for instance, of a deaf person arrested for stealing and found incompetent to stand trial. He might be released without trial, but he might also be hospitalized on the presumption that he has a mental illness which, if treated, would result in him becoming competent. In reality, he does not have a mental illness, and the hospital is not able to help him overcome a lifetime of language deprivation and become competent. He therefore remains stuck in an inpatient unit whereas if he were just able to go to trial, he would have paid a fine or some other penalty and been released.

The issue of deaf persons found incompetent for linguistic reasons, who may or may not be violent, who may have committed a minor or a serious crime, is badly in need of a serious discussion between professionals in the deafness mental health and legal professions. LaVigne and Vernon's (2003) work is probably the best overview of this problem currently available. Parcing out the difference between persons with this syndrome who have not yet received a fair chance at help and those who have already hardened into criminals, albeit low functioning criminals, is another major challenge our field must confront.

The development of diagnostic clarity regarding this syndrome and official recognition would therefore accomplish much for deaf people interacting with the mental health and legal systems. It would help avoid the confusion between this syndrome and major mental illnesses that has so confounded the psychiatric and psychological assessment of deaf people. It would allow clinicians to say that these persons have developmental disorders which can make them functionally retarded and then to advocate that programs such as Medicaid and Medicare support their treatment. It would remove from clinicians the ethical dilemmas that arise when the only way to get someone services is to misdiagnose them as severely mentally ill. It would foster awareness in the legal system about how language skill bears on the competence to stand trial. It would help avoid those tragic circumstances in which deaf people are hospitalized in psychiatric facilities when the underlying problem is language deprivation, not the major mental illness that such facilities treat. It would clarify one of the key reasons why providing mental health services through a sign language interpreter is often unsuccessful. It would explain and justify the need for clinical specialists and specialized programs for deaf persons with language and learning challenges and would prompt the training of specialists in this field. Perhaps most importantly, it would highlight for medical and educational specialists, and for parents, the potentially catastrophic consequences of depriving deaf children access to linguistically rich signing environments.

"Deaf-Friendly" Teaching and Counseling

This book is devoted to the question of how to adapt mental health care for persons with language and learning challenges, especially those deaf people who have experienced language deprivation. However, there are also good reasons to say that mental health care of higher functioning deaf people, those who are fluent users of ASL and without cognitive impairments to learning, also requires adaptations from standard practice. They also require services that are "culturally affirmative" (Glickman and Gulati, 2003; Glickman and Harvey, 1996) or, to use a term currently popular, "Deaf friendly." But what exactly does this mean? What would be different about counseling or teaching for linguistically competent, signing Deaf people that would make it Deaf friendly?

To answer this question, one has to first clear the room of the false answer that hearing people unfamiliar with deaf people commonly offer: provide an interpreter.

Dean and Pollard (2005) provide a superb discussion of why interpreters do not magically overcome the huge communication, cognitive, and cultural barriers that often exist between deaf and hearing people. As they explain, there are many variables that influence the ability of interpreters to bridge the gap in *thought worlds* between people who use different languages. One key variable is whether interpreters are considered partners in the communication process; able to comment on how ideas are conceptualized differently in different languages, or whether they are treated as machines, assumed to be able to "just sign what I say" even when there is no exact equivalent of the English words in sign. They give this example, very familiar to any interpreter working in a medical or legal context:

> An interpreter working with a deaf psychiatric patient with limited sign language proficiency was asked to interpret for an attorney who was required to inform the patient of his legal rights pertaining to involuntary commitment to the hospital. The attorney read to the patient from a prepared text containing complex legal concepts and instructions on how to assert his rights if he felt they were being violated. It was obvious to the interpreter that she could not effectively convey this information to the patient, not only because of his limited sign language skills but also his impaired mental status. The interpreter properly chose to

inform the attorney about this difficulty and the apparent impossibility of accomplishing the desired task in the brief time allotted. The attorney said, "Just interpret what I say the best you can" and after one more reading of the document, the attorney prepared to leave. The interpreter again expressed her opinion that the patient did not comprehend the information. The attorney said, "The main thing is that he knows he has rights and can contact me if needed." He then wrote a brief note in the patient's chart, asking the interpreter for the spelling of her name. The interpreter was concerned that the treatment team might not be informed of her view that the communication had been ineffective and thereby presume, from the attorney's visit and chart note, that it had been. (p. 272)

I have heard may deaf people complain that they feel excluded from lectures or trainings that occur even with interpreters present. This can be difficult for them to acknowledge publicly because they may share the belief that if an interpreter is provided, they should understand. When they do not understand, it is difficult for them to know why. Is the problem due to their own limitations? Are they just not smart enough? Is the problem that the interpreter is not skilled enough? It is easy and common to blame interpreters for not overcoming impossible communication challenges. Or is there something about the communication dynamics of the situation that precludes genuine inclusion? Because I have witnessed this happen repeatedly with bright, linguistically competent deaf people working with qualified, skilled interpreters, I have come to increasingly appreciate how the problem is in the communication dynamics of the situation. For example, consider the common experience of deaf employees undergoing new staff orientation, done with interpreters. They hear numerous speakers and confront an intimidating array of policies and procedures, sometimes at a hurried pace. Common dynamics are as follows:

1. The speakers lecture and there is little opportunity for dialogue or questions. The speakers assume their material is presented adequately. They do not check this out. They do not give time to assessing comprehension, answering questions, and clarifying confusions.
2. There is heavy use of written English material that uses jargon, difficult to translate idioms and metaphors, or just vocabulary and sentence structure that assumes college level literacy. English dense Power Point slides are flashed onto a screen while the speaker speaks, not pausing to let the viewers read the slides if they can. Packets of policies and procedures, written in college level *bureaucratese*, are passed out for quick review, and participants are asked to sign that they have read and understood them. This is done even in settings where a large part of the workforce consists of noncollege-educated recent immigrants and second language users of English.

3. The presentation of information is auditory, not visual. Few or no visual aids, apart from Power Point slides, are used. No consideration is given to the different experience of participants who take in information through their eyes rather than their ears. For instance, visual learners probably need more breaks and may be more dependent on information being clearly organized and presented.

4. Abstract, highly theoretical information is given with few practical examples or, even better, stories to anchor the theory.

5. The speaker does not manage the communication dynamics so that all participants have equal access. The interpreter and deaf participants are ignored. Participants in a group meeting are allowed to all talk at once. Members make side comments that are highly distracting. Environmental noises like the overhead paging system, loud laughter from the neighboring room, or carpenters drilling and hammering in a nearby hallway, interfere with the interpreter's concentration. The speaker is not aware that participants depending on the interpreter are always a number of seconds behind so they are never first to raise their hands when questioning opportunities arise. O'Hearn and Pollard (in press) comment:

Further, group dynamics are difficult for a deaf person to manage in a hearing group environment. The time lag necessary for an interpreter to process English information and make appropriate ASL translations means that hearing people in the group always get the information before the deaf individual does. Joining a fast-paced group discussion among hearing people, which often includes simultaneous spoken comments that are impossible for the interpreter to translate in real time (or in their entirety), effectively precludes active and full participation by a deaf individual. These challenges result in deaf clients frequently feeling lost, not knowing who is talking, and missing opportunities to join in the discussion in interpreted meetings.

These hearing communication dynamics are one reason even linguistically competent deaf people can struggle in a discussion or therapy group accessed through the provision of an interpreter. It is a key reason even these linguistically competent deaf persons may be better served in Deaf-only, or Deaf-majority groups.

I attended a lecture once by a group of architects designing a new hospital. This hospital would have a deaf mental health program so deaf consumers and staff were invited. The lectures were detailed, technical discussions of the proposed building design in which the speakers repeatedly referred to the "DNA of the building." Not being an architect, I had no idea what that meant, but I assumed it was architect jargon. I also was pretty confident that most of the hearing people in the audience who were not architects did not know the term either. So while I was annoyed at the speakers' use of jargon, I never thought that I was stupid for not understanding. The interpreters also did not appear to know what to do with that phrase so they just signed BUILDING D-N-A. As the phrase kept reappearing, I wondered what the deaf participants were making of it; that is, those who were still paying attention. Did they think that the hearing people present understood this term? Did they think the interpreters were doing a bad job? Did they think that if they were smarter or had better English, that they would understand? This was just one problem in a series of lectures that were filled with technical information and jargon that were very difficult to interpret. It is fair to say that the speakers, who had included interpreters, assumed the presentation was accessible to deaf people. Through observation and inquiry, I learned that most of the deaf participants just tuned out. When follow-up sessions were held, again with interpreters, most of the deaf participants did not return.

I am not saying that interpreters should not be provided as one means of fostering inclusion of deaf people. Of course they should. But genuine inclusion of deaf people, that which really takes into account their learning styles and communication needs, requires much more. To begin with, it requires that the communication dynamics be managed so that interpreters can do their job (Dean & Pollard, 2001, 2005). It also requires attention to the issue of how information is presented. Deaf people and their advocates struggle so much over the issue of obtaining interpreters that they rarely get to the more profound, interesting, and relevant issue of how to organize and present information so that deaf consumers are most able to receive it.

To illustrate what it really takes to make a treatment program Deaf friendly, we can examine the work of clinician/researchers at the Deaf Wellness Center at the University of Rochester (New York) Medical Center. In this book, I have borrowed ideas and techniques from DBT even while arguing that the framework as a whole is not suitable for LLC clients. Robert Pollard, Amanda O'Hearn, and colleagues at the Deaf Wellness Center, working closely with staff from the Behavioral Tech, LLC group that teaches and disseminates DBT, demonstrate that it is indeed possible to fashion a Deaf-friendly DBT, loyal to the original but suitable for, at least, linguistically competent deaf people. Examining their work illustrates beautifully many of the ways that mental health care must be adapted in order for it to work for deaf people (O'Hearn & Pollard, in press).

O'Hearn and Pollard recognize the potential value of DBT to deaf people. They describe how common it is for deaf people to experience "invalidating environments" growing up, and how, in DBT, people are taught psychosocial skills they never learned in these environments. They also lament, as I have in Chapter 5, many of the ways in which standard DBT is Deaf unfriendly. These include the heavy reliance on written English materials, the use of culturally inappropriate metaphor, the use of mnemonics, and most especially the didactic format through which DBT skills are taught. Much of DBT is taught through lecture, and the very detailed skill-training modules were not developed with deaf people, or a Deaf learning style, in mind.

From O'Hearn and Pollard's adaptation of DBT, we can discern some of the elements of Deaf-friendly counseling and teaching:

1. The use of a dialogic as opposed to a didactic teaching style.
2. Close attention to whether or not participants are understanding.
3. Reliance on stories to illustrate points.
4. Reliance on practical examples and building definitions, abstractions, and theory from these examples.
5. Simplification of English language–based material and inclusion of more visual aids.

O'Hearn and Pollard argue that adapting DBT for deaf people requires movement from a didactic to a dialogic teaching style. They describe their adaptation of two DBT training films:

> We utilized a dialogic teaching style that mirrors Deaf cultural communication patterns. For most deaf people, watching a lecture (the format used in the source films) presented in spoken English, even with captions (subtitles) present, is a much less accessible method of learning than watching deaf people having an ASL conversation about the topic.

O'Hearn and Pollard note that between English-speaking hearing people and ASL-using Deaf people, there is a difference in *discourse style* that is directly pertinent to how people learn and need to be taught (Metzger & Bahan, 2005). A Deaf-friendly training is one in which a culturally Deaf discourse style is used. This issue of discourse style is particularly difficult to explain simply and clearly to people who use only one language. Monolingual people do not readily appreciate how languages organize information, and how differently people can think about themselves and the world based on the language they use.

Differences in English versus ASL discourse style also impede learning in an interpreted DBT group. In hearing DBT groups, there is less time for storytelling, dialogic communication, and introduction of specific Deaf-relevant metaphors and life experiences. Because of time and role constraints, interpreters are not able to create a bicultural environment, invent Deaf-relevant metaphors or fully rectify the fund of information gaps.

A dialogic teaching style means that information is taught more through dialogue than lecture. O'Hearn and Pollard give an excellent example of this. In one of the Deaf DBT DVDs (Pollard & Dimeff, 2007), a therapist and her supervisor are shown discussing the concept of "radical acceptance." The therapist discusses her difficultly understanding and applying the concept and the supervisor offers clarification. This is followed by a series of other Deaf persons telling stories about their own difficulties applying radical acceptance to their own lives.

Implicit in this dialogic style is a second element of Deaf-friendly discourse. This is the close attention to whether or not the "audience" understands.

Deaf people can never assume they will receive and understand the information they need. Hearing people, of course, do not understand everything they hear, but they know that information is there, readily available, and they can select what they want to attend to and learn. Deaf people have to fight for much less information access, and in educational or counseling contexts, even when information is signed, they are at a huge disadvantage. It follows naturally that a Deaf teaching style pays much more attention to whether or not the students are learning. There is more frequent check in, sometimes by asking whether or not one is "clear" (the culturally appropriate alternative to asking whether they understand), but usually just through the process of dialogue. A key reason monologues and lectures do not work as well is that they do not involve this check-in process. They do not bring the student along with the teacher.

A third element of a Deaf-friendly discourse is the use of stories, especially those relevant to the Deaf experience. O'Hearn and Pollard (2007) added a section to one of their DVDs on "Deaf stories." The Deaf actors in this section tell personal life stories that illustrate the main teaching points. I have shown this DVD to deaf staff and patients in my program and watched as they perked up as soon as the Deaf stories section began. It worked. It opened up the world of DBT to deaf people in a way that a straightforward lecture never could.

The use of storytelling techniques is emphasized throughout this book as a key strategy for mental health work with deaf LLC clients. This technique works because ASL discourse has a dialogic style and because a storytelling tradition is well established within Deaf culture (Freedman, 1994; Haggerty, 2007; Isenberg, 2006; Metzger & Bahan, 2005; Padden & Humphries, 1988).

Related to the use of stories is a fourth element, the reliance on practical examples and the building of definitions, abstractions, theories, and discussions of meaning and implications from these examples. At the risk of over-simplification, we could say that in a Deaf-friendly discourse, examples come first, theory later. This is the reverse of the more typical style of academic discourse where people begin with definitions and abstract principles.

Examples are important because deaf people do not have access to the same fund of information as hearing people (Pollard, 1998a). As O'Hearn and Pollard note, they might not have prior familiarity with such crucial DBT concepts as "mindfulness;" and they will learn this best through examples and direct experience, not definitions and a theoretical discussion.

In Chapter 7, while discussing the difficulties in translating abstract relapse prevention concepts like *triggers, warning signs, seemingly unimportant decisions,* and *risk factors* into ASL, I noted that in ASL, abstract categories are often built on lists of particular instances. There is a way in which ASL discourse builds from specific to general (Klima & Bellugi, 1979). For example, the concept of "abuse" or "trauma" is taught by giving examples of particular kinds of abuse and trauma.

Recognition of this point has influenced how the psychosocial skill training described in this book, the teaching of coping, conflict resolution, and relapse prevention, is done. Earlier in our work, we used a less successful "hearing" style of beginning with definitions. For instance, we would begin a group on coping skills by defining coping skills as "skills people use to manage emotions like anger, sadness, and anxiety." We would begin conflict resolution skills by discussing the nature of conflict or reviewing a list of steps toward solving a conflict. It took a while for us to appreciate that we would be more successful if we reversed the order of presentation. We learned to begin our groups with examples of skills or conflicts, illustrated with our skill cards or through stories, act these out, and then elicit a broader discussion based on what the members have just experienced. This style of work also underlies the pretreatment strategy, discussed in Chapter 4, of noting skills that clients already use. This is a Deaf-friendly clinical strategy because it begins with the specific (the skills used) and moves to the general (a contract for treatment to accomplish a goal).

O'Hearn and Pollard also review efforts to simplify tools written in English. They developed new materials using some of the pictures drawn by Michael Krajnak and contained on the CD-ROM accompanying this book and its predecessor (Glickman & Gulati, 2003). Of course, with deaf clients with language and learning challenges, English literacy cannot be assumed at all. Some tools need to be entirely, or nearly entirely, pictorial.

Defining further the characteristics of Deaf-friendly discourse and drawing out the implications for teaching and counseling deaf people is a badly needed area of research. Needless to say, such research will depend on the existence of designated Deaf educational, rehabilitation, and mental health settings. The relevant questions are never asked in contexts where deaf people have to fight for an interpreter to be present and where the provision of an interpreter is considered full inclusion. In those hearing contexts, there is no power base from which deaf people can challenge hearing assumptions about communication. The wrong questions are asked, and wrong questions always lead to wrong answers.

What Does It Take to Provide Appropriate Mental Health Care to Deaf People?

In 1996, Robert Pollard wrote about the "emergence of a discipline" of professional psychology and deaf people (Pollard, 1996). He wrote:

> The need for specialized training programs in deafness and psychology has been recognized for decades (Elliott, Glass, & Evans, 1988; Knell,

1983; Levine, 1977; Pollard, Gutman, DeMatteo, & Stewart, 1991; Sussman, 1989). Experts agree that competence in this field implies sign language fluency; knowledge about deafness from audiological, developmental, educational, vocational, legal, social, and cultural perspectives; and of course, a solid background in mental health. One particularly needs a thorough understanding of the implications of deafness and the use of sign language for making diagnoses and conducting treatment with persons who are deaf or hard of hearing. Few clinicians have these skills, and the presence of a sign language interpreter does not substitute for them, because interpreters' professional education does not involve such mental health training. (p. 392)

Pollard described in his article the resources for training mental health professionals to work with deaf people, the professional organizations, national and international conferences, and professional journals devoted to this field, and the dramatic impact that the growing number of deaf professionals is having. More than 10 years later, these trends have continued. There is a growing body of literature that specialists in deafness mental health need to master. Sophistication about the impact of cultural variables on mental health treatment continues to grow (Glickman, 1996, 2003; Lane, 1996). The array of specialized skills required to do this work goes well beyond fluency in ASL (itself a competency very difficult to obtain) to detailed knowledge of how to adapt mental health interventions so that they match the skills, deficits, and perspectives of deaf people.

In an earlier work (Glickman, 1996), I described how culturally affirmative psychotherapy consists of three dimensions: cultural self-awareness, knowledge of the community and culture, and culture-specific skills. One of the culture-specific skills I discussed then is the ability to adapt psychotherapy so that it fits with culturally influenced attitudes, beliefs, and behaviors. The work of the Deaf Wellness Center, describe above, is an excellent example of this. I hope this book also contributes to the knowledge and skills pertaining to adapting psychotherapy for work with LLC clients, deaf and hearing.

The knowledge and skills dimensions of culturally affirmative work are challenging enough. They require special training, as Pollard noted. The cultural self-awareness dimension is just as important but it is more difficult to teach. It requires the ability to see oneself, and one's group, from the point of view of people in another group, a skill we know is also crucial to nonviolent conflict resolution. It requires the ability to appreciate that being hearing is just as relevant to forming our attitudes and belief systems as race, class, religion, sexual orientation, and other dimensions of social stratification. Hearing people, as such, have socially constructed attitudes toward deaf people; that they are disabled, that they *miss* something crucial to being human, that they communicate in an inferior way, that it is tragic and awful to be deaf, that deaf people need their help. Hearing people also have the corresponding attitudes about themselves; that *they* are fully human, that they communicate in the optimal way, that they are always objective and well intentioned with regard to deaf people, that it is their place to offer help, to bestow it, to be generous. These unexamined hearing assumptions and beliefs provide the framework from which clinical mistakes, such as quickness to find entitlement, hostility, paranoia, and other forms of psychopathology in deaf people, are made (Lane, 1992, 2003).

As soon as hearing people are asked to do more than provide a sign language interpreter, these assumptions and beliefs, really prejudices, are exposed. It is normally very difficult for people to perceive their own personal biases, much less racial, gender, and other cultural biases. The ideas that they also have biases as hearing people, and that nonspecialized programs are systematically biased against genuine inclusion of deaf people, will strike them as bizarre or perhaps as coming from an angry political agenda. Yet these biases, as absurd as they can seem to hearing people, are patently obvious to astute deaf people. The experience of even high functioning deaf people in nonspecialized hearing mental health programs can be a series of emotional insults, often creating new trauma (DeVinney, 2003). Hearing clinicians who resist the idea of cultural deafness, who fail to see that Deaf people have a unique and valid vantage point, themselves have an ideological bias. They just do not know that they do, and in a clinical context this unconscious bias predisposes them to make dangerous errors.

There is a famous passage in Freud's *Introductory Lectures on Psychoanalysis* where he describes why he believes people resist the insights of psychoanalysis (1966, pp. 284–285). He says that people resisted the insights of Copernicus because he demonstrated that the Earth was not the center of the solar system. This threatened their sense of self-importance. Later, they resisted the insights of Darwin because he demonstrated that humans evolved from lower forms of animal life. This threatened their belief that they should have dominion over the animal kingdom and that they are special in God's eyes. Finally, he says, they resist his own work because he demonstrated how "man" is not even master of his own mind. He was referring to what he saw as the role of unconscious thoughts and motivation. This idea also challenged beliefs people like to have about their mastery of their own behavior.

Cross-cultural work can have a similar impact on consciousness and may be resisted for similar reasons. Opening oneself, fully and deeply, to the experience of another, is a sure path toward personal growth; and opening oneself, fully and deeply, to the experience of another group, is the surest path toward conflict resolution and peace. On a personal and social level, we grow and we act as positive forces in the world when we give up some of our beliefs in our own uniqueness and superiority and empathically tune in to the experiences and perspectives of others, especially with regard to how *they* perceive *us*. But to do this we have to give up these narcissistic beliefs.

Does opening oneself to the Deaf perspective lead to personal growth in hearing people? I cannot cite research on this, but my own observations suggest that many hearing people who work with deaf people in a respectful, culturally affirmative manner, experience often the following personal changes:

They become more emotionally and physically expressive.
They learn to give examples and tell stories.
They become more comfortable in role play.
They pay attention more to whether their clients understand.
They strive to be clearer and more organized.
They simplify written materials and get rid of professional jargon.
They become more interactive in their teaching style.
They come to appreciate differing worldviews and cultural perspectives.
They become less arrogant and more respectful of diversity.

Research to investigate whether these observations are true would be very informative.

Deaf people are best served in specialized mental health and rehabilitation programs designed for them to be "culturally affirmative" (Glickman & Gulati, 2003). It is only in such specialized programs that deaf people such as those described in this book can get the help they need. We know such programs benefit deaf people, but is there a way that they benefit hearing people as well?

At Westborough State Hospital, the attention we gave to adapting treatment for LLC deaf clients was recognized by the hearing adolescent programs as relevant to them because their clients also were LLC. They also needed greatly simplified CBT strategies. They needed pictorial aids. They needed strategies for the pretreatment challenge of engaging and motivating clients. They needed a simpler, clearer, more "user friendly" model of treatment than DBT. Many of the strategies we have developed to make treatment work for LLC deaf clients, and also to make treatment Deaf friendly, appear to be useful for hearing clients, and not just "lower functioning" ones.

Each time we develop the competencies to expand mental health services to a new group, we deepen our understanding of what it means to help in the human community. Paradoxically, work with deaf people can open our eyes to how belief systems and cultural frameworks coalesce also around the social experience of hearing. Learning sign languages can open up understanding of the nature of spoken languages. Struggling to adapt mental health care so that it works for people with language and learning challenges, be they deaf or hearing, forces us to become better counselors and teachers. Our skills develop too. As we let our clients influence us, it can become difficult to discern who is helping whom.

APPENDIX I
How to Use the CD-ROM

The picture aids, which as a group we call *skill cards,* on this CD-ROM were developed by Michael Krajnak. Several hundred of his skill cards were presented on the CD-ROM accompanying *Mental Health Care of Deaf Persons* (Glickman & Gulati, 2003). In the 5 years since publication of that book, he has drawn well over 1,000 more skill cards. He has redrawn many, improving their quality, and organized them more clearly. As the popularity of these cards has spread, we have also discovered more ways to use them. We find that educators and counselors are always looking for ways to make complex ideas simpler and clearer, and not just for persons with language and learning challenges. The folders of psychoeducational pictorial tools, for instance, are suitable for people learning about symptoms of mental illness or side effects of medication and could easily be used to accompany graduate school lectures on the subject. There is some overlap between this CD-ROM and what we are now calling Version 1, but I believe people comparing the two will agree this version presents a huge qualitative advance.

The categories of pictures can be organized as follows:

1. Cards that represent concrete skills (the more narrow definition of skill cards)
2. Cards that present pictures of behaviors
3. Cards depicting feelings and thoughts
4. Situation cards that depict situations that elicit use of skills
5. Cards depicting substance abuse and treatment concepts
6. Sample rating scales, self-monitoring forms, and behavioral plans
7. Psychoeducational materials including cards depicting medical and psychiatric symptoms, medication benefits and side effects, and medical procedures
8. Cards presenting legal matters such as patient rights, health proxies, HIPAA regulations, and insurance issues
9. Useful metaphors
10. Miscellaneous cards

The cards are best used as tools by linguistically competent staff. They are not designed to be substitutes for such staff; and do not, in and of themselves, provide "effective communication" with deaf persons, as mandated by the Americans with Disabilities Act. The tools are also used on the Westborough Deaf Unit by nonsigners or beginning signers as communication aids, but this is a context in which a communication specialist can oversee their use and other communication resources, like staff with competent signing skills and interpreters, which are available. Nonsigners working in non-Deaf contexts should be cautioned against assuming that use of pictures like these is always appropriate with deaf persons and that the pictures are clear enough to substitute for language. Neither assumption is true. The pictures are tools designed to support teaching and counseling efforts, not substitutes for them.

Clients vary in whether or not they "relate" to pictures. Some clients are insulted by the use of pictures. A hearing nonsigner who attempts to communicate with a literate Deaf person through pictures had better be prepared for a strong negative response. Others clients, especially many deaf persons with language and learning challenges, embrace them. The best approach is simply to ask clients how they feel about use of pictures and honor their wishes.

It is not always completely clear what a picture depicts, so simple captions are usually helpful, if not for the clients then for the staff assisting them. There is also the question of what English words to use to caption the pictures. Some of the pictures on the CD-ROM have captions. Others do not. We tend to use English words that we are fairly sure our deaf clients know. We also sometimes use ASL syntax (for instance, "blame stop"). We have not found a solution that works for everyone as some clients (and staff) prefer "normal English" and others do not. Users are encouraged to change or develop captions as they see fit.

We have found it useful to get an inexpensive lamination machine so we can laminate some of the most commonly used cards. This facilitates use of the cards in group activities. The invitation to "pick a card," discussed in several chapters in this book, has gotten us through many groups where participation was otherwise lagging.

There is a directory to the folders and files on the CD-ROM in the folder titled Skill Cards Menu. I suggest starting by downloading and printing this as a reference aid. The pictures used to illustrate chapters of the text are contained in one folder labeled PICTURES IN TEXT. There are numerous ways to download pictures. For people using Microsoft Word, the easiest way is just to use the INSERT-PICTURE-FROM-FILE function. That also enables one to scan the pictures in particular folders before selecting any. Upon scanning, one will notice that some of the pictures are in landscape layout. On the preview, these files will appear to be perpendicular. When inserted, they will also be perpendicular to the desired view. To rotate them, go to the View function and select Toolbars. Under Toolbars, select the Picture toolbar. On this Toolbar, you will find functions for rotating as well as cropping. If you cannot immediately rotate the picture, it is probably because it is too big. In that case, left-click on the picture to make the border appear. Place the cursor on a corner until you get the double-sided arrow. Holding down the cursor, shrink the size of the box until it is small enough to rotate and fit the width of the page. You can then type a caption under the picture if you wish.

Pictures can also be downloaded into Excel spreadsheets using the same INSERT-PICTURE-FROM-FILE function. If you want to download numerous pictures onto one page, such as when one is designing self-monitoring forms, Excel is actually preferable to Word. In an Excel spreadsheet file, you can use the grid lines to align and lay out pictures. It is much harder to do this in Word. Shrink the size of the pictures to fit the desired number onto one page and add captions, if desired, using gridlines to locate the center. The Print-Preview function allows you to test out what the printed page will look like before printing and to make necessary adjustments.

Cards Depicting Concrete Skills

Included here are pictures of concrete "microskills" that are used for coping, conflict resolution, social interactions, and activities of daily living. We post many of these pictures in rooms throughout the milieu as visual reminders of the skills. In morning community meetings, we ask clients to select what skills they will use that day. We direct clients to the skill cards posted at the front of the room. We have pictures of grooming activities (proper tooth brushing, showering, bodily cleaning) posted in the bathrooms. We have poster boards or charts with groups of skills (for example, coping, conflict resolution, or relapse prevention) organized together. When a client's treatment plan emphasizes particular skills, we may post these in that client's bedroom (with permission, of course.)

There are also a great number of cards depicting sensory modulation skills. These are activities that involve the senses that can be used either to alert or calm a person. With clients who have very poor language skills or very significant cognitive limitations, we rely heavily on sensory modulation interventions (as discussed in Chapter 5). We use these cards primarily as examples of coping skills. For instance, a treatment goal might be for a client to "stop and notice" when he or she is upset (the red light in the traffic light coping skill) and then use a sensory modulation activity like rocking in a chair with a heavy blanket or going for a walk.

I discuss throughout this book the benefits of depicting simple, concrete activities that people do to feel good, to help themselves, or to help others as skills. A key treatment goal is usually to help our clients become mindful and intentional in managing their own behaviors. To do this, we need to have a simple, clear language for growth and health. The skill framework provides this. When we use the pretreatment strategy of turning clients into helpers and teachers, the skill pictures help orient them to what they are teaching. For instance, we had a group of Deaf clients present a workshop on coping skills at a consumer-oriented rehabilitation conference. In this workshop, they used a Power Point presentation that staff created for them. The slides of the presentation consisted mainly of pictures of various skills. Clients described sensory modulation skills by going through many pictures of these skills and talking about how these activities helped them feel good.

These pictures are easily brought into Power Point, Word, or Excel documents. For instance, nursing and occupational therapy staff from the Adolescent Units at Westborough borrowed many of the pictures in designing posters of skills they are teaching and promoting. The hospital pharmacist borrowed pictures of medication benefits and side effects (see below) to create teaching tools for pharmacy students.

Cards Presenting Pictures of Behaviors

There are many cards showing examples of good and bad behaviors. These cards are appropriate for many children or older persons with cognitive and behavioral problems. They are used mainly in the development of visual self-monitoring forms and behavior and treatment plans. The goal might be for a client to demonstrate particular good behaviors and avoid particular bad behaviors. Pictures depicting these behaviors could be placed on a self-monitoring form followed by a box where the clients check off "yes" or "no" to indicate whether or not they did them that day.

Also present are cards showing problem sexual behaviors (in the Sexuality folder). Some of these cards are, of course, fairly graphic. This is sometimes a problem for staff but rarely a problem for clients. We would not use such pictures with clients if we could adequately address the issue using language. These pictures especially have to be used tactfully. For instance, it may be appropriate to develop a self-monitoring form that includes pictures of sexual behaviors or uses words like "shit." The use of graphic sexual pictures or street language on forms with clients obviously needs to be done with sensitivity and tact.*

---

* At one point, we had a deaf mentally retarded LLC patient on the unit who had problems with inappropriate sexual behaviors. Our treatment consisted of providing him a lot of sex education, and we used these pictures to illustrate different behaviors. We also designed for him a self-monitoring form where he was asked to check off which sexual behaviors he had displayed. This was done tactfully and privately and the client benefited. However, one day a new nurse was assigned to the unit and, upon discovering the pictorial self-monitoring form, complained to my supervisor that we were using "pornography" with patients. The hospital human rights officer also learned of this complaint and reviewed our work. With some education, they both relaxed. The human rights officer initially had more difficulty understanding why on some of these forms we used the English word "shit" rather than "defecate" or "bowel movement." The idea that we are being unnecessarily crude reflects a cultural misunderstanding.

Cards Depicting Feelings and Thoughts

Part of mental health treatment is teaching people to identify and label their feelings and moods. Virtually every self-monitoring form we develop starts with a rating of current moods, most commonly represented as ratings of happiness, sadness, anger, and anxiety. We begin community meetings and many groups with a check-in, in which clients rate their emotions at that moment. We sometimes do this before and after an activity as a way of demonstrating to clients that what they do affects what they feel. The pictures of emotions are usually copied into self-monitoring forms. When it is relevant, depictions of feelings can include cravings, for instance, to use a drug or to cut oneself. Helping clients develop awareness of their cravings (i.e., stopping and noticing) is the first step toward helping them develop skills in responding to these cravings differently.

Recognizing thoughts is a more advanced skill than recognizing feelings. People commonly confuse feelings and thoughts. For English users, this confusion is compounded by our tendency to make sentences like, "I feel that ... you are wrong."* The most common way we represent a thought is by putting it in a thought bubble. While some thought bubbles are included for illustration, these are easily constructed using common word processing software such as Microsoft Word. To use the thought bubbles presented on the CD-ROM, the words will have to be written into the bubble. It is easier to do this using the "callouts" feature under Autoshapes in Word.

Situation Cards Depicting Situations That Elicit Use of Skills

Situation cards present pictures of situations that call for coping and conflict resolution skills. The cards are often used in group treatment, frequently as part of a game format as discussed in Chapters 5 and 6. For instance, clients are asked to "pick a card" depicting a particular provocative situation and the group then role-plays the use of various skills in response. The folder on provocations/triggers presents more situation cards that can be used in teaching relapse prevention skills and concepts such as "trigger." Behaviors depicted in the Good and Bad Behaviors folders may provide additional provocations and triggers. Other resources are in the substance abuse folder.

Cards Depicting Substance Abuse Concepts and Treatment Concepts

The substance abuse folder has three subfolders. The first one, indicators of drug use, contains a large number of pictures depicting signs and symptoms of drug use. These are organized under personality (for example, mood

---

* A rule of thumb is that if the word "that" follows the word "feel" then what follows is a thought, not a feeling. If we are describing a feeling, we would simply say "I feel ... happy." In ASL, the sign FEEL is not necessary. One signs I HAPPY. Feeling is implied.

swings, secretive, stealing), physical appearance (for example, poor grooming, not sleeping), school and social activities (for example, low grades, loss of
interest in friends), and by specific drugs. In this third folder, common signs
and symptoms are organized by the class of drugs. These pictures are easily
incorporated into substance abuse education. They can be placed on posters
and other educational tools such as Power Point slides. They can also be used
as part of self-monitoring forms (that is, download the picture and place it
alongside some kind of rating such as "yes or no").

The relapse prevention folder contains pictures that can be used in psychoeducation about relapse as well as in treatment sessions. It includes folders
with pictures for cravings, cycles, lapses and relapses, recovery skills, risk
factors and triggers, and warning signs. As discussed in Chapter 7, relapse
prevention skills have broader applicability than just substance abuse treatment. Concepts like relapse, trigger, warning sign, and seemingly unimportant decisions are not easily translated for LLC signing deaf clients, and many
of these pictures can help. Some of the cycle pictures were developed for actual
clients. They would not be appropriate for other persons, and are presented as
examples of pictorial representations of relapse cycles.

The recovery skills folder contains a wealth of pictures of specific skills
essential to treatment. There are cards depicting concepts like "admit problem," "blame stop," "honest," and "notice cravings drink." We would conceptualize and teach these as skills.

Sample Rating Scales, Self-Monitoring Forms, and Behavioral Plans

Cards can be used as pictorial self-monitoring forms or to create them. The
pictures are placed on a page alongside some rating scale, most commonly
0 to 10 or yes/no. Other rating scales are faces with different emotions and
thumbs up, thumbs middle, and thumbs down. Forms can be developed with
or without words. Our experience has been that it usually helps to add simple
words beneath pictures because clients may be able to read the words and it
also helps orient staff. A few sample self-monitoring plans are included but
these need to be individualized for each client. Besides considering whether or
not to use pictures, and what kind of rating scale, clinicians also consider what
they are asking clients to monitor. Options include: good and bad behaviors;
feelings and moods; thoughts, symptoms, attitudes, activities engaged in, and
skills used. People who can write may prefer a more open ended self-monitoring system in which they describe what they were thinking, feeling, or doing.

The card for daily activities of daily living (ADLs) is a simple check-off of
care of one's body and environment. The safety tool is a pictorial version of one
of our restraint reduction tools in which clients are helped to identify strategies for coping. The concept of a diary card comes from dialectical behavior
therapy and is just another name for a self-monitoring form.

Construction of pictorial behavior and relapse prevention plans is similar to that of self-monitoring forms. For instance, if the plan calls for someone to use a particular skill or demonstrate a particular positive behavior (as in a traditional reinforcement plan), pictures of that skill or behaviors can be used. In a self-monitoring plan, the client (possibly with staff) checks off whether or not he or she displayed that skill or behavior. In a relapse prevention plan, the clients monitor themselves for warning signs, triggers, risk factors, and so on (see Chapter 7). This can be done in the form of a pictorial version of the relapse cycle (see cycle folder under substance abuse/relapse prevention). In a behavioral plan, a picture of the desired behavior or skill is used along with a picture of the planned reinforcer. They can be connected by arrows. Some pictures that can be used as reinforcers are found in the money and work folders, but as almost anything could be a reinforcer, users may need to turn to additional clip art programs.

Psychoeducational Materials

Psychoeducation is one of the main uses for skill cards. Although psychoeducation is a commonly recognized treatment intervention, I do not recommend providing this until a therapeutic relationship is established and someone is willing to receive the information. If, for instance, one seeks to teach clients about the symptoms of their mental illness, doing this during the pretreatment phase of work may actually increase their resistance (see Chapter 4). However, when patients are ready, these cards are very helpful.

Some of the most useful cards here include:

- Pictures of common allergies.
- Procedures during a medical checkup.
- Pain scales.
- Pictures of behaviors that worsen health ("poor health behaviors").
- Rating scales for particular classifications of medications (see rating scales side effects). Physicians should look at these cards before they are used because they may disagree with our selection and organization of side effects. In these cases, new cards with pictures of many side effects can be created.

There are also a wealth of cards depicting symptoms of mental illness, organized roughly by syndrome. Cards depict symptoms associated with mood, anxiety, psychotic, and behavioral disorders. Personality disorders are trickier to convey in pictorial form, and pictures do tend to simplify and exaggerate. This is one reason the pictures are designed to supplement therapeutic dialogue, not substitute for it. Nonetheless, the pictures here help illustrate antisocial, borderline, histrionic, narcissistic, schizoid, and schizotypal personality disorders.

Cards Presenting Legal Matters Such as Patient Rights, Health Proxies, HIPAA Regulations, and Insurance Issues

We are constantly faced with the challenge of explaining abstract and complex legal matters to persons with language and learning challenges. Where they have very limited capacity to understand these matters, we consider the need for a guardian. However, staff are often too quick to assume that clients cannot understand these matters when they (staff) lack the language skills and appropriate tools to explain them. The deficit is also with staff, yet it is the client who may suffer when a guardian is appointed to represent the client.

Cards found here help explain the concept of healthy proxy, the elements of the HIPAA law as it pertains to patient records, and common patient rights. The picture of the "3-day letter" depicts the steps that patients in Massachusetts must go through to petition to be discharged from a psychiatric hospital.

Useful Metaphors

Included here are some of the metaphors we have found useful in treatment:

- *Bait fish*: Suggests temptation, deception, or possibility of making an important mistake
- *Detective*: Metaphor for stopping and noticing, searching, exploring
- *Dialectic*: Illustrated with a Slinky
- *Dominoes*: Used to illustrate triggers and the relapse process
- *Fire hazards, lifeboat, mountain volcano, runaway train, swim clouds*: Depict warnings signs and risk factors
- *Climbing out of a pit, climbing over walls, choosing a path, climbing a ladder*: Depict the process of treatment, striving for goals, making decisions
- *Traffic light, shield* (see Chapter 5)
- *Psychic*: Making predictions, anticipation, as in relapse prevention work

Miscellaneous Cards

Included here are cards depicting aspects of religious practice, people and animals, time, community, and the treatment team.

Final Note

Both the author and illustrator are interested in learning about more possible uses of these cards as well as suggestions for new cards for future upgrades of this CD-ROM. The author is especially interested in learning about therapeutic metaphors or stories that others have found useful in working with this population. Both can be reached through the publisher. E-mail addresses at the time of publication are Neil.Glickman@dmh.state.ma.us; Neilglickman@rcn.com; Mkraj@mac.com.

APPENDIX II
Skill Card Menu

Activities of Daily Living (ADLs)

Clothing

Armpits
Attire Loose
Attire Tight
Clean Bra
Clean Socks
Clean Underwear
Clean Underwear Daily
Dirty Pants
Undress

Female Hygiene

Butt Wipe Right
Butt Wipe Wrong
Female Genitals
Tissue Hands
Wash Right
Wash Wrong

Hair

Comb Hair
Hair After
Hair Before
Hair Before and After
Work Bad Hair

Laundry

Dirty Laundry Dark
Dirty Laundry Light
Dirty Laundry White
Full Wash
Right Wash

Washer Dryer
Washing Machine

Room

Clean Linens
Drooling
Make Bed
Room Clean
Room Messy
Sleep, No Shoes

Shower

01 Take off Dirty Clothes
02 Shower
03 Shampoo
04 Shampoo 2
05 Rinse Hair
06 Soap Hand
07 Whole Face
08 Wash Chest
09 Armpit
10 Female Dirty
10 Male Dirty
11 Female Wash
11 Male Wash
11a Wash Vagina
12 Wash Feet
13 Rinse All
14 Towel Dry
15 Brush Teeth
16 Shave
17 Deodorant 1
17 Deodorant 2

18 Hands Wash
19 Dress Clean Clothes
20 Feel Clean

Bath

Dirty Towels
Get in Shower
Hamper
Shower
Showering
Shower, 10 Minutes
Sweaty
Wash Hair
Wash Hands

Toilet Issues

Butt Wipe, Female
Butt Wipe, Male
Soiled Tissues
Tissue Hand
Toilet
Toilet Soiled
Urinate Right
Urinate Wrong
Use Toilet
Wash Hands
Wipe Right

Behaviors, Thoughts, and Feelings

Behaviors

Bad Behaviors

1 finger
2 Fingers
911
Agitation
Aloof
Ambulatory
Argue
Argue Down
Ashamed
Avoid Eye Contact
Back Off

Bad Attitude
Big Head
Block TV
Blocking
Blow Up
Bottled Anger
Boundaries Step Over
Break Furniture
Bump
Calling Out Wrong
Complain
Closed Mind
Cocky
Defecate
Demanding
Fire Alarm
Force to Talk
Gamey
Gawking
Getting Spit
Give Finger Subtly
Giving Fingers
Glare 1
Glare 2
Glare Point Finger
Go Every Room
Go in Team Room
Hand in Your Face
Hit Easy
Hit Hard
Hit Window
Hurt Animals
Imitate
Induce Vomit
Intend to Hurt Self
Kick
Kick Wall
Lie
Lose Temper
Mad Inside
Needy
Nosy
Obsessed Favorite

Obsessing
Overexcited
Peek in Bedroom
Peekaboo
Pissed
Posturing
Provoke 1
Provoke 2
Provoke 3
Puffy
Punch Wall
Push
Pushing Buttons
Racism
Refuse
Refuse Clean Up
Refuse Comfort Room
Refuse Coping Skills
Refuse Help
Refuse Look
Refuse Meeting
Refuse Talk
Rip Paper Wrong
Run Away
Shadow Boxing
Sitting Not Proper
Slam Door
Snap
Sneaking
Spit
Spit in Trash
Spitter
Spitting at Staff
Stab
Stalk
Stand Chair
Steal Consequences
Steal Temptation
Stealing
Stop It
Scratch
Stuff Toilet
Talk All Over

Talk Negative
Talk Nonsense
Talk Nonstop
Talk Too Much
Thought Bad Attitude
Threat 1
Threat 2
Threat Talk
Threat With Scissors
Throw Things
Too Close
Touch
Urinate
Walk With Anger
We Can't
Yell

Good Behavior
Accept
Accept No
Ask for Help Yes
Calling Out
Calm Down
Cooperate 1
Cooperate 2
Discussing
Express Self
Feel Good
Focus
Good Mad
Greeter
Have Money
Idea
Improving
Join Class
Join Group 1
Join Group 2
Meeting
Not Mad
Open Mind
Please
Practice
Practice Traffic

Put Food in Trash
Quiet Calendar
Relieved
Safe
Safe Cooperate
Sleep Group
Speak to Group
Understands
Use Coping Skills
With Group

Sexuality
Grab
Intercourse
Look 1
Look 2
Masturbate Male Private
Masturbation Female
Masturbation Male
Molest
Molest Thoughts
Naked Female
Naked Female 1
Naked Male
Naked Male 1
Naked Male 2
Penis
Playground
Sex-No
Sex-Yes
Touch
Touch Breasts
Touch Butts
Vagina

Feelings

Faces—Negative
Angry
Annoyed
Despair
Desperate
Discouraged

Fearful
Furious
Glaring
Gross
Irritated
Pissed
Shocked
Tearful
Whiny

Faces—Positive
Contented
Fake Smile
Grin
Grin Wide
Laughing Too Hard
Mischievous
Oomph
Open Smile
Smirk
Smug
Tired Laugh
Whistling

Faces—Ranges
01 Angry
02 Angrier
03 Angriest
Anger 0
Anger 10
Angry
Anxious
Anxious 0
Anxious 10
Emotion Fill in the Blank
Emotion Other
Happy
Happy 0
Happy 10
Sad
Sad 0
Sad 10

Other Feelings

Blecch
Blow Up
Bored
Calm Down
Calming Down
Defend Self
Disappointed
Explain
Explain Feel
Feel Angry
Feel Anxious
Feel Calm
Feel Despair
Feel Down
Feel Ecstatic
Feel Fine
Feel Good
Feel Overwhelmed
Feel Scared
Feel Sick
Feel Sleepy
Feel Stressed
Like Not
Like
Listen Not
Okay
Overwhelmed
Satisfied
Shocked
Talk About How Feel
TV Feel 1
Undecided
Worried
Yawning

Thoughts

Bright Idea 1
Bright Idea 2
Dream Beach
Drug Thoughts

Explain Happen
Finger Bubble
Forget
No Idea 1
No Idea 2
Remember
Talk Bubble 01
Talk Bubble 02
Talk Bubble 03
Talk Bubble 04
Talk Bubble 05
Talk Bubble 06
Talk Bubble 07
Talk Bubble 08
Think Blow Up
Think Confusing
Think Drunk
Think Junk Food
Think New Sneakers
Think Touch
Thinking
Thought Bubble 01
Thought Bubble 02
Thought Bubble 03
Thought Lose Temper
Thoughts Aggression
Thoughts of Dying
Thoughts Use Coping Skills
TV Metaphor 1
TV Metaphor 2

Conflict Resolution Skills

Accept Apology
Accept Lose
Ask for Help
Ask Please
Brainstorm
Brainstorming
Compromise
Deep Thinking
Defend Self
Describe Problem

Discussing
Don't Demand
Express Self
I Can 1
I Can 2
I Feel Statements
I Statements
Listen
Name Conflict
Notice Conflict
One Person Talk at a Time
Open Mind
Pay Attention
Positive
Problem Solving 1
Problem Solving 2
Pros and Cons
Repeat Back
Say Sorry
Self Thumb Up
Suggesting 1
Suggesting 2
Thumbs Up
Toss Coin
Try Understand
Understanding 1
Understanding 2
Use Skills
Visit Friends
We Can
We Can't
Win, Win
Writing
You're Right 1
You're Right 2

Coping Skills

Art
Ask for Forgiveness
Basketball
Board Games
Brainstorming
Breathing

Card Game 1
Card Game 2
Chi Kung
Deep Breaths
Deep Thinking
Distraction
Empathy
Forgive
Jigsaw
Laughter 1
Laughter 2
Laughter 3
Letting Go
Lock up Problems
Meditate
Open and Close Mind
Positive Self Talk
Practice
Pray 1
Pray 2
Putting on Makeup
Red Yellow Green
Rip Paper
Self Accept
Sensory
Shield
Sleeping
Spiritual Skills
Stop and Notice
Stop Notice Feel
Think Success
Thinking 1
Thinking 2
Thinking Skills
Time Out
Time Out Bedroom
Time Out Comfort Room
Videogames
Waiting
Watch TV
Woodwork
Writing Journal
Yoga

Legal

Courtroom

Court
Court Setting
Courtroom
Handcuffed
Hospital Why
Jail
Jailbird
Policeman
Probation Officer

Health Proxy

Health Proxy 1
Health Proxy 2
Health Proxy 3
Turn off Machine

HIPAA

HIPAA 1
HIPAA 2
HIPAA 3
HIPAA 4
HIPAA 5
HIPAA 6

Insurance

Insurance Card

Interpreters

Interpreter

Patient Rights

3 Day Letter
Confidential
Right to Lawyer
Right to Mail
Right to Personal Stuff
Right to Phone
Right to Phone TTY
Right to Refuse Treatment

Right to Treatment
Right to Visitors

Medicine and Physical Health

Allergies

Causes
Bee
Eggs
Peanuts
Seafood
Strawberries

Rate Allergies

Rate—Allergies Bees
Rate—Allergies Berries
Rate—Allergies Eggs
Rate—Allergies Meds
Rate—Allergies Nuts
Rate—Allergies Pain
Rate—Allergies Seafood

Checkup

Exam Table
Take Blood
Check Blood Sugar
Check Bp 1
Check Bp 2
Check Ear
Check Eye
Check Genital 1
Check Genital 2
Check Leg 1
Check Leg 2
Check Nose
Check Pulse
Check Stomach 1
Check Stomach 2
Check Temp
Check Weight
Checking Pulse
Doctor 1
Doctor 2
High Blood Sugar

Listen Stomach
Mouth Light
Nurse
Put on Gown
Say Ahh
Self Breast Exam
Self Testicles Exam 1
Self Testicles Exam 2
Stethoscope
Stirrups 1
Stirrups 2
Sugar Level
Urine Cup
Urine Cup—Female
Urine Cup—Male
Urine Male

Dentistry

Bad Breath
Brush Teeth 1
Brush Teeth 2
Brush Teeth 3
Brush Teeth 4
Brush Teeth 5
Brush Teeth 6
Brush Teeth 7
Brush Teeth 8
Floss
Floss Close Up
Teeth
Teeth Bad
Teeth Good
Three Times a Day
Toothbrush 1
Toothbrush 2
Upclose of Teeth

Medication Cards

Meds Card 1
Meds Card 2
Meds List
Meds List 1

Meds List 2
Meds List 3
Meds List 4

Medicine Side Effects

Blurry Vision
Bp Low
Bp Normal
Breasts Leak
Breasts Leak Male
Breathe Hard
Constipation
Cramps
Diarrhea
Diet 1
Diet 2
Dizzy
Dry Mouth
Enlarged Breasts
Enlarged Breasts—Female
Enlarged Breasts—Male
Erection Painful
Fever
Hard Swallow
Hard to Pee
Head Cold
Headache
High Blood Sugar
Hives
Impotence
Irregular Heartbeats
Liver Disease
Low White Blood Cells
Menstruation Schedule Good
Menstruation Schedule Wrong
Mood Stable
Nausea
Nervous
NMS (Neuroleptic Malignant
    Syndrome)
Orgasm Delay

Rash Itchy
Rash Spots
Restless
Runny Nose
Seizure
Snail Move Slow
Stiff
Sun Sensitive
Sweating 1
Sweating 2
Swollen
Td (Tardive Dyskinesia)
Tired
Too Much Saliva
Tremors
Vomit
Weight Gain
Weight Loss

Nutrition

Chinese
Don't Want Eat
Eat Healthy
Eating
Meals
Rice Bowl
Snacks

Pain

Pain 1/8
Pain 2/8
Pain 3/8
Pain 4/8
Pain 5/8
Pain 6/8
Pain 7/8
Pain 8/8
Rate—Pain

Poor Health Behavior

Picking Ear
Picking Nose

Poor ADLs 1
Poor ADLs 2
Refuse Meds

Rate Side Effects

Rate—Manage Side Effects
Rate—SE Anti-Psy NMS
Rate—SE Antianxiety
Rate—SE Anticonvulsant
Rate—SE Antidepressants
Rate—SE Anti-Psy
Rate—Side Effects 01
Rate—Side Effects 02
Rate—Side Effects 03
Rate—Side Effects 04

Symptoms

White Kills Red
Chest Pains
Cough 1
Cough 2
Cover Face
Dying Angel
Dying
Face Hurt
Feel Better
Frostbite
Hospital 1
Hospital 2
Injured
Petit Mal
Red Fights White
Sick
Sick Hospital
Sneeze
Sneeze Sick
TB
Thyroid

Take Medicine

Alka Seltzer
Cough Drops

Cough Syrup
Different Rx
Doctor Give Meds
Doctor Rx
Drugstore
Ear Drops
Eye Drops
Give Meds
Inhaler
Jacket
Medicine Cabinet
Nose Spray
Ointment
Pill
Pillbox
Purse
Refuse Meds
Rx Description
Rx From Doctor
Syringe Meds 1
Syringe Meds 2
Take Meds 1
Take Meds 2
Take Meds 3
Take Meds Drink
Vitamins

The Body

Arm Left
Arm Right
Face
Feel Strong
Feel Weak
Foot Left
Foot Right
Hand Left
Hand Right
Muscles
Pregnant
The Body
The Body—Neutral

Mental Illness Symptoms

Mood and Psychosis

Anxiety, Fear, Panic

Breathing Hard
Breathing Fast
Can't Sleep
Chest Pains
Chills
Choking
Difficult Breathing
Difficult Swallowing
Dizzy
Dry Mouth
Embarrassed
Fear Being Stared At
Fear Bridge
Fear Crazy
Fear Death
Fear Go Outside
Fear Long Lines
Fear of Dying
Fear of Going Crazy
Fear of Objects
Fear Public Speaking
Feel Not Real
Feel Stupid
Flashback
Forgetful
Heart Racing
Heartbeats
Nausea
Nervous
Numb Hands On! Panicked
Sweating
Tingling Fingers
Tremors
Worry

Depression

Can't Concentrate
Can't Sleep

Depression
Depression—Thoughts
Feel Worthless
Hopelessness
Left Out
Loss of Appetite
Loss of Interest
No Energy
Sleep All Day
Snail Move Slow
Thoughts of Death
Too Much Appetite
Withdrawn 1
Withdrawn 2

Grief

Broken Heart
Crash
Dan's Grief Timeline
Deaf School
Deaf Sick
Divorce
Dog Died
Grief Timeline
Hospital
Jail
Kick Out
Moved
Pop Died
Tow

Manic

Awake All Time
Distractible
Fast Movement
Grandiose
Hyper
Irritated
King Attitude
Lots of Energy
Mood Up and Down
Racing Thoughts

Sleeping Around Bi Female
Sleeping Around Bi Male
Sleeping Around Gay
Sleeping Around Lesbian
Sleeping Around Straight
    Female
Sleeping Around Straight Male
Spend Money Foolishly
Very Talkative

Obsessive-Compulsive Disorder (OCD)

Clean Floor
Counting
Counting Cracks
Door Locked
Lock Door
OCD Time
Turn off Stove
Wash Hands

Psychotic Thinking

Anger Control
Confused
Confused Thoughts
Feel Things
Hopelessness
No Trust
One Person
Paranoid 1
Paranoid 2
Racing Thoughts
See Things
Sleep Can't
Think God
Try to Apology
TV Talk Back
Two People
Voices

Posttraumatic Stress Disorder (PTSD)

Abuse
Bad Dreams—Abuse

Bad Dreams—Monster
Can't Concentrate
Flashback 1
Flashback 2
Flashback 3
Hypervigilance
Irritated
PTSD—Thoughts
Startled Response

Self-Injury
Cutting Self
Hurt Self
Intend to Overdose
Overdose
Self Bang Head
Self Bite
Self Scratch
Suicide Avoid

Personality Disorders

Antisocial
Drive Fast
Fight
Hit
Impulsive
Liar
Mugshot
No Feelings
Too Many Bills

Borderline
Anger Control
Anger out of Control
Binge Eating
Cling Arm
Cling Leg
Dissociation
Empty
Fast Driving
Identity 1
Identity 2
Identity 3

Identity 4
Identity 5
Identity 6
Identity 7
Mood Changes
Self Harm
Sleeping Around Bi Female
Sleeping Around Bi Male
Sleeping Around Gay
Sleeping Around Lesbian
Sleeping Around Straight
    Female
Sleeping Around Straight Male
Unstable Relationship 1
Unstable Relationship 2
Unstable Relationship 3
Unstable Relationship 4

Histrionic
Dramatic
Dramatic Appearance
Flirt
Hates Alone
Mixed Messages
Say No
Say Yes
Sexy
Theatricality 1
Theatricality 2
Wedding—Overdoing It

Narcissistic
All About Me
Apathy to Suffering
Applause for Me
Entitled
For My Gain
I Me Myself
Status

Schizoid
Alone
Face Blank

Not Caring
Not Interested
Not Involved
Room Alone

Schizotypal

Afraid of People
Alone
Don't Want People Help You
Folks Not Understand
Paranoid
Sad Laughter
Shadow at Door
Superstitious
Suspicious
Talk
Talking About You
They Don't Understand You
Think Their Body Deform

Rate Symptoms

Rate—Depression
Rate—Fear
Rate—Manic
Rate—Pain
Rate—Psychotic Thinking

Metaphors

Bait Fish
Climbing Ladder
Detective
Dialectic
Dominoes 1
Dominoes 2
Dominoes 3
Dominoes 4
Fire Hazard—High
Fire Hazard—Low
Fire Hazard—Normal
Lifeboat
Mountain 1
Mountain 2
Mountain 3

Mountain 4
Mountain 5
Pit
Psychic
Runaway Train
Shield
Swim Clouds
What Wall Climb Over?
Which Way Choose?

Miscellaneous

Community

Beach
Commuting
Deaf School
Deaf Service
Door to Outside
Eating
Hammock
House
Look for House
Nervous Discharge
Support System
Working

Money

Ask for Bank Slip
Borrow $10 A
Borrow $10 B
Borrow $100 A
Borrow $100 B
Budgeting Skills
Dollar Bill
Dollar Bills
Have Money
One Dollar
Plan Budget
Prioritize Money
Prioritizing

People and Animals

Artist
Baby

Bird
Black Person 01
Black Person 02
Cat
Chunky
Couple
Dog
Female Teen
Fishbowl
Hearing Aid
Helper
Helpers
Lady
Lovers—Gay
Lovers—Lesbian
Lovers—Straight
Loving Duo
Nerd—Female
Nerd—Male
Old Female
Old Lady
Old Male
Parents
Teen Boy
Teen Girl
Thin
Wheelchair
Young Lady
Young Man

Religion

Angel
Devil
God
Jesus
Meditate
Pray 1
Pray 2
Spiritual Skills

Time

10 Min
Clock

Month
Morning
Night
Time of Day
Time Flies
Year

Treatment Team

Doctor Team
Doctors
Join Treatment Team
Review Plan
Tx Team 1
Tx Team 2
Tx Team Color 1
Tx Team Color 2

Work

Cash Register
Chips
Chop Veggies
Clean Cabinets
Clean Counter
Clean Microwave
Clean Table
Coffee
Coffee Pot
Condiments
Cup With Cover
Dish Put Away
Dishwash
Egg Salad
Order Slip
Pile Up Chairs
Salad
Soda
Soup Bowls
Straws Napkins Sugar
Sweep
Take out Trash
Tuna Salad
Vacuum
Wash Floor

Pictures in Text

Chapter 4

Figure 4.1
Figure 4.2
Figure 4.3

Chapter 5

Figure 5.1
Figure 5.2
Figure 5.3
Figure 5.4
Figure 5.5
Figure 5.6
Figure 5.7
Figure 5.8
Figure 5.9

Chapter 6

Figure 6.1
Figure 6.2
Figure 6.3
Figure 6.4
Figure 6.5
Figure 6.6
Figure 6.7
Figure 6.8
Figure 6.9
Figure 6.10

Chapter 7

Figure 7.1
Figure 7.2
Figure 7.3
Figure 7.4
Figure 7.5
Figure 7.6
Figure 7.7
Figure 7.8
Figure 7.9
Figure 7.10

Self-Monitoring

Diary Card
Everyday ADLs
Good Behaviors

Rating Scales

Five Emotions
Scale Angry
Scale Anxious
Scale Happy
Scale Sad
Thermometer—Anger
Thermometer—Worry
Thumb DOWN
Thumb MIDDLE
Thumb UP
You Feel What
Safety Tool page 1
Safety Tool page 2
Self-Monitoring 1 A
Self-Monitoring 1 B
Self-Monitoring 2
Self-Monitoring 3
Self-Monitoring 4 A
Self-Monitoring 4 B
Self-Monitoring 5
Self-Monitoring 6

Sensory Modulation Skills

Auditory

Chirping Birds
Fan
Fountain
Humming
Listen Radio
Listening
Music Box
Ocean
Orchestra
People Talking
Quiet Music Headphones
Rainy Window

Singer
Theater Show
Ticking Clock
Whistling
White Noise
Wind Chime

General

Moodmeter
Sensory Meter
Sensory Skills

Movement

Beanbag
Bike
Building
Cartwheel
Chewing Gum
Chewing Straw
Chopping Wood
Dance
Doodling
Driving
Food Shopping
Foxtail
Garden
Guitar
Heavy Blanket
Heavy Teddybear
High Low
Ice Cubes
Iceskating
Jogging
Jumping Ropes
Knuckles
Kooshbasket
Ladybug
Loud Music
Medicine Ball
Music Vibration
Parachute
Pillow Hug
Pound Clay

Pound Pillow
Push-Ups
Raking
Rearranging
Rocking Chair
Roller-Coaster 1
Roller-Coaster 2
Rubber Band Wrist
Shake Hands
Shake Feet
Sit-ups
Slinky
Squeeze
Stamping
Steps
Stressball
Stretching
Swimming
Theraband
Trampoline 1
Trampoline 2
Venting Safely
Walk 1
Walk Friend
Walk Outside Friend
Walk Outside Staff
Walk Staff
Walk Unit Friend
Walk Unit Staff
Walking
Walking Outside
Walking—On Unit
Wash Hands
Washing Car
Weightlifting
Yard Work
Yawn
Yoga

Smelling

Baked Cookies
Chopped Wood
Cologne

Deep Breaths 1
Deep Breaths 2
Essential Oils
Flowers
Fruits
Hanging Linen
Herbal Tea
Incense
Mowed Grass
Perfume
Scented Candle
Smell Coffee
Smell Rose
Smell Scented Candle
Smell Trash
Spices

Taste

Basket
Bite Lemon
Carrot Sticks
Chewing Gum
Chewing Straw
Chocolate Bar
Crunchy Food
Fire Breath
Hot Ball
Hot Coffee
Hot Tea
Lollipop
Milkshake
Mint Candy
Mint Strips
Popsicle
Soda
Sourball
Spicy Food
Strong Mints

Touch and Temperature

Baking
Barefooted
Basking Sun

Bath
Blanket
Bottlecaps
Brush
Cat Hold
Chew Ice
Cold Cloth—Head
Cold Cloth—Neck
Eye Pillow
Feel Fabric
Fidgeting
Get Massage
Hair Cut
Hair Wash
Hand Lotion
Knitting
Massage Seat
Pedicure Manicure
Petting
Pottery
Putting on Makeup
Sewing
Stressball
Teddybear Hug
Twisting Hair
Washing Dishes

Visual

Autumn
Baseball
Cloud Formations
Colored Glasses 1
Colored Glasses 2
Computer
Fireplace
Fishbowl
Goldfish
Kids Playing
Lava Lamp
Mobile
Movies
Photo Album
Photography

Picture Book
Reading
Snowing
Starry Night
Starry Night 1
Starry Night 2
Sunrise
Waterfall
Window Shopping
Zoo

Situation Cards

Conflict Resolution

Backstabbing
Bossy Staff
Breaking Your Locker
Bumped Into
Chair 1
Chair 2
Decide Car
Decide Commit
Decide House
Decide One Item
Decide Rides
Decide Which Movie
Dilemma Trip
Dilemma TV
Dilemma Work
Fight Candy
Fight Laundry
Fight Phone
Fight Remote
Fight TV
Force Oral
Gang Up
Getting Interrupted
Give Finger 1
Give Finger 2
Hot or Cold
Mad at Parents
More Work
Movies Dilemma

Needs Not Meet
Now Now
Parents Can't
Patronizing
Pizza or Chinese Food
Room Clean Messy
Saving Seats
Share Attention
Siblings Upset
Snap at Person
Speak Different Language
Staff Forgot
Stop Provoking
Store Closed
Talk Inappropriate
Tattletale
Telling What to Do
Two Cigarettes
Two O'clock

Coping

Bad Traffic
Bed All Day
Bored
Car Won't Start
Computer Down
Cutting in Line
Delay
Elevator Scenario 1
Elevator Scenario 2
Fast Food Complaint
I Am Busy
Job Rejection
Late to Work
Laughing at You
Laundry Wait
Locker Wait
Long Line
More Wait Angry
More Work
Needs Not Met
No Privacy
No Privileges

Noisy Night
Pager Down
Report Card Scenario 1
Report Card Scenario 2
Report Card Scenario 3
Rushed During Meal
Spilled Water Scenario 1
Spilled Water Scenario 2
Spilled Water Scenario 3
Staff Busy You Mad
Store Closed
Swim Clouds
Think Success
Trip Left Behind
Vending Machine Problems
Wait a Minute
Wrong Order

Provocation and Triggers

Artist Disappointed
Bait—Drinking
Being Yelled At
Car Accident
Criticize
Door Open Bedroom
Forced to Talk
Giving Bad Review
Harts His Art
Loud
Making Fun of Black
Making Fun of Deaf
Making Fun of Hc
Making Fun of Hearing
Making Fun of Obesity
Mocking
Mocking—Deaf
Mocking—Hc (Handicapped)
Mocking—Hearing
Mocking—Obesity
Offended—Deaf
Offended—Hc
Offended—Hearing
Offended—Obesity

Overcrowded
Sad Memory
Shot Dead
Smell Pot
Staff Not Listen
Stressed
Stressed Thoughts
Thoughts of Drugs and
    Alcohol
Uniform

Skill Card Menu

Skill Card Menu (document)

Social Skills

Affection

Affection Mother Child
Affection No Boundary
Affection Two Friends

Asking Skills

Ask for Help 1
Ask for Help 2
Asking

Assertive Skills

Assert Opinion
Assert—Talk
Assert—That
Assertive

Attention Getters

2 Hand Wave
Attention 1
Attention 2
Attention—Floor
Attention—Table
Attention—Yelling
Switch Lights

Conversation Interruptions

Conversation Interrupt 1

Conversation Interrupt 2
Conversation Interrupt 3

Game Manners

01 Winning
02 Winning Bragging
02 You'll Win
03 Say Good Job

Good Manners

Leave Alone
Say Please
Say Thank You
Want Help

Greeting Skills

Rush to Staff
Waving to Staff

Honesty

Honest Accept
Honest Talk

Ignoring Skills

Ignore—Read
Ignore—TV
Inform Provoking
Inform Staff
Provoking
Reaction 01
Reaction 02
Reaction 03
Reaction 04
Reaction 05
Reaction 06

Listening Skills

Affirm
Listen Appropriately
Listen Not
Listen Right
Listening
Listening, Think
Understand

Miscellaneous Social Skills

Apologizing
Borrow 1
Borrow 2
Boundaries
Change Beliefs
Compromising Skills
Decision Making
Discuss Group
Explain 1
Explain 2
Good Job
Help Others
Help Yes
I Have a Problem
Interrupt Right
Self-Coaching

Negotiating Skills

01 Disagree
02 Agree

Privacy

No Privacy
Privacy

Shaking Hands

Shake Hands Clean
Shake Hands Dirty
Shake Hands
Shaking Hands

Table Manners

Eating
Napkin Hands Lap
Say Please for Milk
Talk Appropriate

Taking Turns

Fidgeting
Take Turns
Talk Turns

Talking

    Chatting With Buddy
    Chatting With Staff
    Communicate
    Explain
    Explain in Order
    Frustrated 1
    Frustrated 2
    I Have a Problem
    Organized Thoughts
    Swearing
    Talk About Sex
    Talk Pros and Cons 1
    Talk Pros and Cons 2
    Talk Right
    Talk Wrong
    We Can
    You're Right
    Your Fault

Teasing

    Tease—Blow Up
    Tease—Cry
    Tease—Finger
    Tease—I Feel
    Tease—No Affect
    Tease—Right Approach
    Tease—Stop
    Tease—Use Shield
    Teasing

Try Explain

    Explain
    Explain Try
    Staff Not Listen
    Think Hard
    Try Explaining
    Understand Finally

Waiting Skills

    Wait—No Patience
    Wait—Sitting
    Wait—Stand

Substance Abuse

Indicators of Drug Use

Personality

    Extreme Mood Swings
    Have Lot of Money
    Less Outgoing
    Need More Money
    Not Interested in Valuable
    Secretive
    Stealing
    Verbally Abusive
    Withdrawal From Family

Physical Appearance

    Hyperactive
    Loss of Appetite
    Not Sleeping
    Poor Grooming
    Sleeping Too Much
    Too Little Energy
    Weight Gain
    Weight Loss

Social & School Activities

    Getting Low Grades
    Lose Concentration
    Lose Interest Friends
    Skip School
    Sleep in Class

Specific Drugs

Alcohol

    Agitation
    Confused
    Depressed
    Drinking
    Drinks
    Drowsiness
    Drunk
    Drunk—Bother
    Impaired Judgment
    Incoordination
    Nauseated

Respiratory Ailments
Slurred Speech
Tremors
Vomit

Cocaine and Crack Cocaine
Agitation
Anxiety 1
Anxiety 2
Choices
Crack, Moods Swings
Dilated Pupils
Emotions Crash
Euphoria
Excitability
Feel Strong
Hallucinations
High
High Energy
Increased Pulse Rate
Loss of Appetite
Moods Drop
Nosebleed
Paranoid
Snorting 1
Snorting 2
Very Talkative

Depressants
Confused
Dilated Pupils
Drowsiness
Hard Breathing
Incoordination
Slurred Speech
Snail Move Slow
Tremors

Hallucinogens
Euphoria
Excitation
Hallucinations
Increased Pulse Rate

Insomnia
Trance Like

Inhalants
Hard Breathing
Incoordination
Nauseated
Slurred Speech
Vomit

Marijuana
Delusions 1
Delusions 2
Dilated Pupils
Dry Mouth
Euphoria
Increased Appetite
Increased Pulse Rate
Mood Swings
Snail Move Slow

Narcotics
Constipation
Constricted Pupils
Drowsiness
Euphoria
Hard Breathing
Lethargic
Nauseated

Stimulants
Bad Breath
Dilated Pupils
Dry Mouth
Excitability
Hallucinations
Insomnia
Paranoid
Sweating
Tremors
Weight Loss

Tobacco
Asthma Attack

Chewing Tobacco
Coughing
Mouth Problems
Out of Shape
Shortness of Breath
Smelly Breath
Smelly Clothes
Smelly Hair
Yellow Teeth

Relapse Prevention

Cravings
Cigarettes
Cravings 1
Cravings 2
Cravings Drug–Alcohol 1
Cravings Drug–Alcohol 2
Drugs
Drugs Alcohol
Excuses
Family High
Feel High
Feel Pain
Feel Sexy
Feel Sick
Feel Tired
Feelings
Fight High
Friends Get High
Gum
I Feel
Patch
Smoking Ratings
Stoned
Thoughts
Want
Want Sober

Cycles
Blank Cycle
Cycle Example
Cycle Safety
Cycle Spending Money

Cycle Thought
Cycle—Money
Demanding 1
Demanding 2
Explain Cycle
Have Money
Junk Food
Obsessing
Panicked
Relapse
Spend Money Foolishly
Talk Cycle
Talk All Over
Worried

Lapses and Relapses
Halt
Leave Drink
One Drink
Relapse 1 of 4
Relapse 2 of 4
Relapse 3 of 4
Relapse 4 of 4
Relapse A
Relapse B
Relapse Bar
Relapse Coffee
Relapse Drugs
Risky Thinking
Safer Thinking
Saw Drug Friends
Sick and Tempted
Trigger 1
Trigger 2
Trigger 3

Recovery Skills
Admit
Admit Problem
Ask for Help
Avoid
Avoid Drug Using People
Avoid Place

Blame
Blame Others
Blame Stop
Busy
Cover Up
Cover Up Stop
Deny
Deny Admit
Deny Problems Top
Drink
Excuses
Explain Happen
Explain How Stay Sober
Explain Why Cover Up
Explain Why Drugs Bad
Feelings
Group High
Help
History
Honest
Honest Talk
Keep Busy
Mind Open—Close
Minimize
Mock Explain
Notice Cravings and Desires
Notice Cravings Drink
Notice Cravings Drugs
Powerlessness
Practice Avoid
Recovery Yes 1
Recovery Yes 2
Resist
Say No
Sherlock
Story
Talk Bad Drugs
Talk Cravings
Talk Good Sober
Talk Negative

Talk Sober
Tell Your Story 1
Tell Your Story 2
Think Success
Thoughts
Thoughts Want
Unmanageable

Risk Factors and Triggers
Bad Judgment
Bar
Boss Yell at You
Concert
Depressed at Bar
Drinking Buddies
Drunk Talk
Few Beers Thought
Fireman
Gun
High Ladder
Making Fun of You
Not Enough Staff
One Beer
Party Shirt
Pot Party
Rocket
Scary Movie PTSD
Sick and Tempted

Warning Signs
Fire Hazard—High
Fire Hazard—Low
Fire Hazard—Normal
Mountain 1
Mountain 2
Mountain 3
Mountain 4
Mountain 5
Runaway Train
Swim Clouds

References

Acosta, F., Yamamoto, J., & Evans, L. (1892). *Effective psychotherapy for low-income and minority patients.* New York: Plenum.

Affleck, G., & Tennen, H. (1996). Construing benefits from adversity: Adaptational significance and dispositional underpinnings. *Journal of Personality, 64,* 899–922.

Allen, C. K., Blue, T., & Earhart, C. (1995). *Understanding cognitive performance modes.* Ormond, FL: Allen Conferences.

Allen, C. K., Earhart, C. K., & Blue, T. (1992). *Occupational therapy treatment goals for the physically and cognitively disabled.* Rockville, MD: AOTA.

Anderson, H., & Goolishian, H. (1992). The client is the expert: A not-knowing approach to therapy. In S. McNamee & K. J. Gergen (Eds.), *Therapy as social construction* (pp. 25–39). Newbury Park, CA: Sage.

Andrade, S. J. (1978). *Chicano mental health: The case of Cristal.* Austin, TX: Hogg Foundation for Mental Health.

Altshuler, K. (1971). Studies of the deaf: Relevance to psychiatric theory. *American Journal of Psychiatry, 127,* 1521–1526.

Altshuler, K. Z., & Rainer, J. D. (Eds.). (1968). *Mental health and the deaf: Approaches and prospects.* Washington, DC: U.S. Department of Health, Education, and Welfare.

American Psychiatric Association. (1994). *Diagnostic and statistical manual of mental disorders* (4th ed.). Washington, DC: Author.

American Psychiatric Association. (2000). Diagnostic and Statistical Manual of Mental Disorders (DSM-IV-TR), Fourth Edition. Washington, D.C: American Psychiatric Association.

American Psychological Association. (2002). *Ethical principles of psychologists and code of conduct.* Washington, DC: Author [On-line]. Available http://www.apa.org/ethics/code2002.pdf.

Atkinson, J. R., Gleeson, K., Cromwell, J., & O'Rourke, S. (2007). Exploring the perceptual characteristics of voice-hallucinations in deaf people. *Cognitive Neuropsychiatry, 12*(4), 339–361.

Austen, S., & Jeffery, D. (Eds.). (2007). *Deafness and challenging behavior.* West Sussex, UK: John Wiley & Sons.

Ayres, J. A. (1979). *Sensory integration and the child.* Los Angeles, CA: Western Psychological Services.

Barry, J. R. (2002). *Investigation of reliability and validity of the Current Evaluation of Risk and Functioning Scale–Revised, an assessment tool for use with adults with serious and persistent mental illness.* Unpublished doctoral dissertation, Northeastern University, Boston, MA.

Barry, J., Lambert, D. R., Vinter, P., & Fenby, B. L. (2007). Evaluating risk and functioning in persons with serious and persistent mental illness. *Psychological Services, 4*(3), 181–192.

Basilier, T. (1964). Surdophrenia: The psychic consequences of congenital or early acquired deafness. *Acta Psychiatrica Scandinavica, 40,* 362–372.

Beam, A. (2001). *Gracefully insane: The rise and fall of America's premier mental hospital.* New York: Public Affairs.

Beck, A. (1976). *Cognitive therapy and emotional disorders.* New York: International Universities Press.

Beck, A. (1999). Prisoners of hate: *The cognitive basis of anger, hostility, and violence.* New York: HarperCollins.

Beck, A. T., Rush, A., Shaw, B., & Emery, G. (1979). *Cognitive therapy of depression.* New York: Guilford Press.

Beck, A., Wright, F., Newman, C., & Liese, B. (1993). *Cognitive therapy of substance abuse.* New York: Guilford Press.

Beck, J. (1995). *Cognitive-therapy: Basics and beyond.* New York: Guilford Press.

Bedell, J. R., & Lennox, S. (1997). *Handbook for communication and problem solving skills training: A cognitive-behavioral approach.* New York: John Wiley & Sons.

Bellach, A. S., Mueser, K. T., Gingerich, S., & Agresta, J. (2004). *Social skills training for schizophrenia* (2nd ed.). New York: Guilford Press.

Berg, I. K. (1994). *Family based services: A solution-focused approach.* New York: W. W. Norton.

Bergeron, B., & Jenson, V. (Producers). (2005). *Shark tale* [Film]. DreamWorks Animated.

Black, P. (2005). *Language dysfluency in the deaf inpatient population.* Unpublished doctoral dissertation, Fielding University, Santa Barbara, CA.

Black, P., & Glickman, N. (2005). Language dysfluency in the deaf inpatient population. *JADARA, 39*(1), 1–28.

Black, P., & Glickman, N. (2006). Demographics, psychiatric diagnoses, and other characteristics of North American deaf and hard-of-hearing inpatients. *Journal of Deaf Studies and Deaf Education, 11*(3), 303–321.

Bowe, F. G. (2004). Economics and adults identified as low-functioning Deaf. *Journal of Disability Policy Studies, 15*(1), 43–49.

Bradshaw, J. (Producer) & Zemeckis, R. (Director) (2002). *Cast away.* [Film]. Twentieth Century Fox and DreamWorks.

Brenman, G & Finn, J. (Producers), & Daldry, S. (Director). (2001). *Billy Elliot.* [Motion Picture]. Hollywood, CA: Universal Studios.

Burns, D. (1999). *The feeling good handbook.* New York: Plume.

Burns, G. W. (2001). *101 Healing stories: Using metaphors in therapy.* New York: John Wiley & Sons.

Burns, G. W. (2005). *101 Healing stories for kids and teens: Using metaphors in therapy.* Hoboken, NJ: John Wiley & Sons.

Champagne, T. (2006). *Sensory modulation and environment: Essential elements of occupation* (2nd ed.). Southampton, MA: Champagne Conferences and Consultation.

Champagne, T., & Stromberg, N. (2004). Sensory approaches in inpatient psychiatric settings: Innovative alternatives to seclusion and restraint. *Journal of Psychosocial Nursing, 42*(9), 35–44.

Corey, G. (2005). *Theory and practice of counseling and psychotherapy* (7th ed.). Belmont, CA: Brooks/Cole.

Crick, N. R., & Dodge, K. A. (1994). A review and reformulation of social information-processing mechanisms in children's social adjustment. *Psychological Bulletin, 115,* 74–101.

Critchley, E. M. R., Denmark, J., Warren, F., & Wilson, K. (1981). Hallucinatory experiences of prelingually profoundly deaf schizophrenics. *British Journal of Psychiatry, 138,* 30–32.

Daigle, B. V. (1994). *An analysis of a deaf psychotic inpatient population.* Unpublished master's thesis, Western Maryland College, Westminister.

Daley, D. C., & Marlatt, G. A. (1997). *Managing your drug or alcohol problem: Therapist guide.* USA: TherapyWorks.

Daniels, L. (Producer) & Kassell, N. (Director) (2005). *The woodsman.* [Film]. Newmarket Films.

Daprati, E., Nico, D., Saimpont, A., Franck, N., & Sirigu, A. (2005). Memory and action: An experimental study on normal subjects and schizophrenic patients. *Neuropsychologia, 43*(2), 281–293.

Dean, R. K. & Pollard, R. Q. (2001). Application of demand-control theory to sign language interpreting: Implications for stress and interpreter training. *Journal of Deaf Studies and Deaf Education, 6*(1), 10–12.

Dean, R. K. & Pollard, R. Q. (2005). Consumers and service effectiveness in interpreting work: A practice profession perspective. In M. Marschark, R. Peterson, & E. Winston (Eds.) *Interpreting and interpreter education: Directions for research and practice* (pp. 259–282). New York: Oxford University Press.

Denmark, J. (1994). *Deafness and mental health.* London: Jessica Kingsley Publishers.

de Shazer, S. (1985). *Keys to solution in brief therapy.* New York: W. W. Norton.

de Shazer, S. (1988). *Clues: Investigating solutions in brief therapy.* New York: W. W. Norton.

DeVinney, J. (2003). My story. In N. Glickman & S. Gulati (Eds.). *Mental health care of deaf people: A culturally affirmative model.* Mahwah, NJ: Lawrence Erlbaum Associates.

Dew, D. W. (Ed.). (1999). Serving individuals who are low-functioning deaf. Washington, DC: George Washington University Regional Rehabilitation Continuing Education Program.

Dolgin, D., Salazar, A., & Cruz, S. (1987). The Hispanic treatment program: Principles of effective psychotherapy. *Journal of Contemporary Psychotherapy, 17*(4), 285–289.

Drew, N. (2004). *The kids' guide to working out conflicts.* Minneapolis, MN: Free Spirit Publishing.

Duffy, K. (1999). Clinical case management with traditionally underserved deaf adults. In I. W. Leigh (Ed.). *Psychotherapy with deaf clients from diverse groups.* Washington, DC: Gallaudet University Press.

Elliott, H., Glass, L., & Evans, J.W. (Eds.). (1988). *Mental health assessment of deaf clients: A practical manual.* Boston, MA: Little Brown.

Ellis, A. (1962). *Reason and emotion in psychotherapy.* New York: Lyle Stuart.

Evans, J. W., & Elliott, H. (1981). Screening criteria for the diagnosis of schizophrenia in deaf patients. *Archives of General Psychiatry, 38,* 787–790.

Evans, J. W., & Elliott, H. (1987). The mental status examination. In H. Elliott & L. Glass & J. W. Evans (Eds.). *Mental health assessment of deaf clients: A practical manual* (pp. 83–92). Boston: College Hill Press.

Feu, M. D., & McKenna, P. J. (1996). Auditory hallucinations in profoundly deaf schizophrenic patients: A phenomenological analysis. *European Psychiatry, 11*(Suppl. 4), 296–297.

Feu, M. D, & McKenna, P. J. (1999). Prelingually profoundly deaf schizophrenic patients who hear voices: A phenomenological analysis. *Acta Psychiatrica Scandinavica, 6,* 453–459.

Finkelman, P. (2003). *Defending slavery: Proslavery thought in the old South.* Bedford: St. Martin's.

Fisher, R., & Ury, W. (1981). *Getting to yes.* New York: Penguin.

Forman, M. (Director). (1975). *One flew over the cuckoo's nest.* In S. Zalentz & M. Douglas (Producers): Fantasy Films.

Forrest, B.J. (2004). The utility of math difficulties, internalized psychopathology, and visual-spatial deficits to identify children with the nonverbal learning disability syndrome: Evidence for a visual-spatial disability. *Child Neuropsychology, 10*(2), 129–146.

Freedman, P. (1994). Counseling with deaf clients: The need for culturally and linguistically sensitive interventions. *Journal of the American Deafness and Rehabilitation Association, 27*(4), 16–28.

Freedman, J., & Combs, G. (1996). *Narrative therapy: The social construction of preferred realities.* New York: W. W. Norton.

Freeman, A., & White, D. M. (1989). The treatment of suicidal behavior. In A. Freeman, K. M. Simon, L. E. Beutler, & H. Arkowitz (Eds.). *Comprehensive handbook of cognitive therapy.* New York: Plenum Press.

Freud. S. (1966). *Introductory lectures on psychoanalysis.* New York: W. W. Norton.

Gardner, R. (1986). *The psychotherapeutic techniques of Richard Gardner.* Cresskill, NJ: Creative Therapeutics.

Gazzaniga, M.S. (2000). Regional differences in cortical organization. *Science, 289*(5486), 187–188.

Gladding, W. T. (1992). *Counseling: A comprehensive profession* (4th ed.). Upper Saddle River, NJ: Merrill.

Glasser, W. (2000). *Counseling with choice theory: The new reality therapy.* New York: HarperCollins.

Glickman, N. (1996). What is culturally affirmative psychotherapy? In N. Glickman & M. Harvey (Eds.). *Culturally affirmative psychotherapy with deaf persons.* Mahwah, NJ: Lawrence Erlbaum Associates.

Glickman, N. (2003). Culturally affirmative inpatient treatment with psychologically unsophisticated deaf people. In N. Glickman & S. Gulati (Eds.). *Mental health care of deaf people: A culturally affirmative approach.* Mahwah, NJ: Lawrence Erlbaum Associates.

Glickman, N. (2007). Do you hear voices? Problems in assessment of mental status in deaf persons with severe language deprivation. *Journal of Deaf Studies and Deaf Education. 12*(2), 127–147.

Glickman, N., & Gulati, S. (Eds.). (2003). *Mental health care of deaf people: A culturally affirmative approach.* Mahwah, NJ: Lawrence Erlbaum Associates.

Glickman, N., & Harvey, M. (Eds.). (1996). *Culturally affirmative psychotherapy with deaf persons.* Mahwah, NJ: Lawrence Erlbaum Associates.

Glickman, N., & Zitter, S. (1989). On establishing a culturally affirmative psychiatric unit for deaf people. *Journal of the American Deafness and Rehabilitation Association, 23*(2), 46–59.

Goleman, D. (1996). *Emotional intelligence.* London: Bloomsbury Publishing.

Greene, R. (1998). *The explosive child.* New York: HarperCollins.

Greene, R. W., & Ablon, J. S. (2006). *Treating explosive kids: The collaborative problem-solving approach*. London: Guilford Press.

Grinker, R., Vernon, M., Mindel, E., Rothstein, D. A., Easton, H., Koh, S. A., & Collums, L. (1969). *Psychiatric diagnosis, therapy and research on the psychotic deaf* (Research Grant RD-2407-S). Washington, DC: U.S. Department of Health, Education and Welfare.

Gulati, S. (2003). Psychiatric care of culturally deaf people. In N. Glickman & S. Gulati (Eds.). *Mental health care of deaf people: A culturally affirmative approach* (pp. 33–107). Mahwah, NJ: Lawrence Erlbaum Associates.

Gutman, V. (2002). *Ethics in mental health and deafness* (2nd ed.). Washington, DC: Gallaudet University Press.

Haggerty, L. D. (2007). Storytelling and leadership in the Deaf community. *JADARA, 41*(1), 39–64.

Harmon, M., Carr, N., & Johnson, T. (1998). Services to low functioning deaf and hard of hearing persons. In M. Kolvitz (Ed.). *Empowerment through partnerships: PEPNET '98* (pp. 290–300). Knoxville, TN: University of Tennessee, PEPNET.

Herman, J. (1992). *Trauma and recovery*. New York: Basic Books.

Hindley, P., Kitson, N., & Leach, V. (2000). Forensic psychiatry and deaf people. In P. Hindley & N. Kitson (Eds.). *Mental health and deafness*. London: Whurr Publishers.

Hoffmeister, R., & Harvey, M. (1996). Is there a psychology of the hearing? In N. Glickman & M. Harvey (Eds.). *Culturally affirmative psychotherapy with deaf persons*. Mahwah, NJ: Lawrence Erlbaum Associates.

Hollenbeck, K. (2003). *Easy-to-read folktale plays to teach conflict resolution*. New York: Scholastic.

Hollenbeck, K. M. (2001). *Conflict resolution activities that work*. New York: Scholastic Professional Books.

Hughes, J. (Producer) & Columbus, C. (Director). (1990). *Home alone*. [Film]. Hughes Entertainment.

Isenberg, G. (1993). Storytelling and the use of culturally appropriate metaphors in psychotherapy with deaf people. In N. Glickman & M. Harvey (Eds.). *Culturally affirmative psychotherapy with deaf persons*. Mahwah, NJ: Lawrence Erlbaum Associates.

Iverson, G. L., Lange, R. T., Viljoen, H., & Brink, J. (2006). WAIS-III general ability index in neuropsychiatric and forensic psychiatry inpatient samples. *Archives of Clinical Neuropsychology, 21*(1), 77–82.

Ivey, A. (1971). *Microcounseling: Innovations in interviewing training*. Springfield, IL: Charles C Thomas.

Ivey, A. (1986). *Developmental therapy*. San Francisco, CA: Jossey-Bass.

Ivey, A. (1991). *Developmental strategies for helpers: Individual, family and network interventions*. Pacific Grove, CA: Brooks/Cole.

Ivey, A. E., & Ivey, M. B. (2003). *Intentional interviewing and counseling: Facilitating client development in a multicultural society* (5th ed.). Pacific Grove, CA: Brooks/Cole.

Ivey, A., D'Andrea, M., Ivey, M. B., & Simek-Morgan, L. (2002). *Theories of counseling and psychotherapy: A multicultural perspective*. Boston: Allyn & Bacon.

Jacobs, E. (1992). *Creative counseling techniques: An illustrated guide*. Odessa, FL: Psychological Assessment Resources.

Jacobs, E. (1994). *Impact therapy*. Odessa, FL: Psychological Assessment Resources.

Jaeger, J., Burns, S., Tigner, A., & Douglas, E. (1992). Remediation of neuropsychological deficits in psychiatric populations: Rationale and methodological considerations. *Psychopharmacology Bulletin, 28*(4), 367–390.

Kabat-Zinn, J. (1990). *Full catastrophe living.* New York: Dell.

Karlin, T. (2003). "Umm, the interpreter didn't understand." Interpreting for individuals with though disorder. *Views, 20*(4).

Kato, K., Galynker, I. I., Miner, C. R., & Rosenblum, J. L. (1995). Cognitive impairment in psychiatric patients and length of hospital stay. *Comprehensive Psychiatry, 36*(3), 213–217.

Kitson, N., & Thacker, A. (2000). Adult psychiatry. In P. Hindley & N. Kitson (Eds.). *Mental health and deafness.* London: Whurr Publishers.

Klima, E., & Bellugi, U. (1979). *The signs of language.* Cambridge, MA: Harvard University Press.

Knell, S. (1983). Training mental health professionals in deafness: Current programs and future prospects. In B. Heller & D. Watson (Eds.). *Mental health and deafness: Strategic perspectives* (pp. 302–311). Silver Spring, MD: American Deafness and Rehabilitation Association.

Koerner, K & Dimeff, L. (2007). Overview of dialectical behavior therapy. In Demeff, L. & Koerner, K. (Eds.). *Dialectical behavior therapy in clinical practice.* New York: Guilford Press.

Kohut, H. (1984). How does analysis cure? Chicago: University of Chicago Press.

Kotter, J. P. (1996). *Leading change.* Boston: Harvard Business School Press.

Kreidler, W. (1984). *Creative conflict resolution.* Glenview, IL: Scott Foresman.

Kreidler, W. (1990). *Elementary perspectives 1: Teaching concepts of peace and conflict.* Cambridge, MA: Educators for Social Responsibility.

Kreidler, W. J. (1994). *Teaching conflict resolution through children's literature.* New York: Scholastic Professional Books.

Kronenberger, W. G., & Dunn, D. W. (2003). Learning disorders. *Neurologic Clinics, 21*(4), 941–952.

Kuhn, C., Langer, J., Kohlberg, L., & Haan, N. S. (1977). The development of formal operations in logical and moral judgment. *Genetic Psychology Monographs, 95,* 97–188.

Lambert, D. R., Fenby, B. L., Foti, M. E., McCorkle, B. H., Patel, J., & Rubano, M. (1996). Clinical evaluation of risk and functioning (CERF). Westborough, MA: Metrowest Area Office, Department of Mental Health, Commonwealth of Massachusetts.

Lambert, D. R., McCorkle, B. H., Fenby, B. L., Patel, J. N., Rubano, M., & Vinter, P. G. (1999). Clinical evaluation of risk and functioning scale–revised (CERF-R). Westborough, MA: Metrowest Area Office, Department of Mental Health, Commonwealth of Massachusetts.

Lane, H. (1992). *The mask of benevolence.* New York: Knoff.

Lane, H. (1996). Cultural self-awareness in hearing people. In N. Glickman & M. Harvey (Eds.). *Culturally affirmative psychotherapy with deaf persons.* Mahwah, NJ: Lawrence Erlbaum Associates.

Larson, J. (2005). *Think first: Addressing aggressive behavior in secondary schools.* New York: Guilford Press.

LaVigne, M., & Vernon, M. (2003). An interpreter isn't enough: Deafness, language, and due process. *Wisconsin Law Review, 5,* 844–936.

Laurance, J. (2003). *Pure madness: How fear drives the mental health system.* London: Routledge.

LeBel, J., Stromberg, N., Duckworth, K., Kerzer, J., Goldstein, R., & Weeks, M. (2004). Child and adolescent inpatient restraint reduction: A state initiative to promote strength-based care. *Journal of the American Academy of Child and Adolescent Psychiatry, 43,* 37–45.

Leroy, M. (Producer) & Fleming, V. (Director) (1939). *The Wizard of Oz.* [Film]. Warner Brothers Family Entertainment.

Leu, L. (2003). *Nonviolent communication companion workbook.* Encinitas, CA: Puddle Dancer Press.

Leversee, T. (2002). *Moving beyond sexually abusive behavior: A relapse prevention curriculum.* Holyoke, MA: NEARI Press.

Levine, E. (1960). *The psychology of deafness.* New York: Columbia University Press.

Levine, E. (1977). The preparation of psychological service providers to the deaf: A report of the Spartanburg conference on the functions, competencies and training of psychological service providers to the deaf: PRWAD Monograph No. 4.

Linehan, M. (1993a). *Cognitive behavioral treatment of borderline personality disorder.* New York: Guilford Press.

Linehan, M. (1993b). *Skills training manual for treating borderline personality disorder.* New York: Guilford Press.

Loera, P. A., & Meichenbaum, D. (1993). The "potential" contributions of cognitive behavior modification to literacy training for deaf students. *American Annals of the Deaf, 138*(2), 87–95.

Long, G., Long, N., & Ouellette, S. E. (1993). Service provision issues with traditionally underserved persons who are deaf. In O. M. Welch (Ed.). *Research and practice in deafness: Issues and questions in education, psychology and vocational service provision.* Springfield, IL: Charles C Thomas.

Long, N. (1993). Historical overview of services to traditionally underserved persons who are deaf. *American Rehabilitation* (Winter).

MacGregor, C. (1998). *Everyone wins: 150 non-competitive games for kids.* Holbrook, MA: Adams Media Corporation.

Marlatt, G. A., & Gordon, J. (Eds.). (1985). *Relapse prevention.* New York: Guilford Press.

Marshall, W., Anderson, D., & Fernandez, Y. (1999). *Cognitive behavioral treatment of sexual offenders.* West Sussex, UK: John Wiley & Sons.

Masson, J. M. (1988). *Against therapy: Emotional tyranny and the myth of psychological healing.* New York: Atheneum.

Mathay, G., & LaFayette, R. H. (1990). Low achieving deaf adults: an interview survey of service providers. *Journal of the American Deafness and Rehabilitation Association, 24*(1), 23–32.

Mayer, B. (2000). *The dynamics of conflict resolution: A practitioner's guide.* San Francisco: Jossey-Bass.

McKay, M., Fanning, P., & Paleg, K. (1994). *Couple skills: Making your relationship work.* Oakland, CA: New Harbinger.

Meichenbaum, D. (1977a). *Cognitive-behavioral modification: An integrative approach.* New York: Plenum Press.

Meichenbaum, D. (1977b). Stress-inoculation training. In D. Meichenbaum. *Cognitive-behavior modification.* New York: Plenum Press.

Meichenbaum, D. (1985). *Stress inoculation training.* Elmsford, NY: Pergamon Press.

Meichenbaum, D. (1994). *A clinical handbook/practical therapist manual for assessing and treating adults with post-traumatic stress disorder.* Waterloo, Canada: Institute Press.

Meichenbaum, D. (1996). *Mixed anxiety and depression: A cognitive-behavioral approach.* New York: Newbridge Communications.

Meichenbaum, D. (2001). *Treatment of individuals with anger-control problems and aggressive behaviors: A clinical handbook.* Clearwater, FL: Institute Press.

Meichenbaum, D. (2007). Stress inoculation training: A preventative and treatment approach. In P. M. Lehrer, R. L. Woolfolk, & W. S. Sime (Eds.). *Principles and practice of stress management* (3rd ed.). New York: Guilford Press.

Meichenbaum, D., & Biemiller, A. (1998). *Nurturing independent learners: Helping students take charge of their learning.* Newton, MA: Brookline Books.

Meichenbaum, D., & Goodman, J. (1971). Training impulsive children to talk to themselves: A means of developing self-control. *Journal of Abnormal Psychology, 77,* 115–126.

Meichenbaum, D., & Turk, D. (1987). *Facilitating treatment adherence: A practitioner's guide.* New York: Plenum Press.

Metzger, M., & Bahan, B. (2005). Discourse analysis. In C. Valli, C. Lucas, & K. Mulrooney (Eds.). *Linguistics of American Sign Language* (4th ed., pp. 490–515). Washington, DC: Gallaudet University Press.

Miller, W. R., & Rollnick, S. (2002). *Motivational interviewing: Preparing people for change* (2nd ed.). New York: Guilford Press.

Mindel, E. D., & Vernon, M. (1971). *They grow in silence.* Silver Spring, MD: National Association for the Deaf Press.

Monti, P. M., Kadden, R. M., Rohsenow, D. J., Cooney, N. L., & Abrams, D. B. (2002). *Treating alcohol dependence: A coping skills training guide* (2nd ed.). New York: Guilford Press.

Moore, K. M. (2005). *The sensory connection program.* Framingham, MA: Therapro.

Morgan, A. (2000). *What is narrative therapy?* Adelaide, South Australia: Dulwich Centre Publications.

Myklebust, H. (1964). *The psychology of deafness.* New York: Grune & Stratton.

National Association of State Mental Health Program Directors Medical Directors Council. (2002). *Reducing the use of seclusion and restraint, Part III: Lessons from the deaf and hard of hearing communities.* Alexandria, VA: National Technical Assistance Center or State Mental Health Planning (NTAC).

O'Hanlon, W. (1994). The third wave: The promise of narrative. *The Family Therapy Networker, 18*(6), 19–26, 28–29.

Padden, C., & Humphries, T. (1988). *Deaf in America: Voices from a culture.* Cambridge, MA: Harvard University Press.

Paijmans, R. (2007). Neuropsychological, behavioral and linguistic factors in challenge behavior in deaf people. In S. Austen. & D. Jeffery (Eds.). *Deafness and challenging behavior.* West Sussex, UK: John Wiley & Sons.

Paijmans, R., Cromwell, J., & Austen, S. (2006). Do profoundly prelingually deaf patients with psychosis really hear voices? *American Annals of the Deaf, 151*(1), 42–48.

Paul, P. V., & Jackson, D. W. (1993). *Toward a psychology of deafness: Theoretical and empirical perspectives.* Boston: Allyn & Bacon.

Pelak, V. B., & Liu, G. T. (2004). Visual hallucinations. *Current Treatment Options in Neurology, 6,* 75–83.

Piaget, J. (1963). *The origins of intelligence in children.* New York: W. W. Norton.

Poizner, H., Klima, E. S., & Bellugi, U. (1987). What the hands reveal about the brain. Cambridge, MA: MIT Press.

Pollard, R. (1994). Public mental health service and diagnostic trends regarding individuals who are deaf or hard of hearing. *Rehabilitation Psychology, 39*(3), 147–160.

Pollard, R. Q. (1996). Professional psychology and deaf people: The emergence of a discipline. *American Psychologist, 51*(4), 389–396.

Pollard, R. (1998a). Psychopathology. In M. Marschark & M. D. Clark (Eds.). *Psychological perspectives on deafness* (Vols. 171–197) (pp. 171–197). Mahwah, NJ: Lawrence Erlbaum Associates.

Pollard, R. (Ed.). (1998b). Mental health interpreting: A mentored curriculum. Rochester, NY: University of Rochester School of Medicine.

Pollard, R. Q. & Dimeff, L. (Executive producers). (2007). *Practicing radical acceptance: An adaptation from the Deaf perspective* [Film]. (Available from Behavioral Tech, LLC, 2133 Third Avenue, Suite 205, Seattle, WA 98101.)

Pollard, R., Gutman, V., DeMatteo, A., & Stewart, L. (1991). Training in deafness and mental health: Status and issues. Paper presented at the A 99th annual meeting of the American Psychological Association, San Francisco, CA.

Rainer, J. D., & Altshuler, K. Z. (1966). *Comprehensive mental health services for the deaf.* New York: New York Psychiatric Institute, Department of Medical Genetics, Columbia University.

Rainer, J. D., Altshuler, K. Z., & Kallman, F. J. (Eds.). (1963). *Family and mental health problems in the deaf population.* New York: New York Psychiatric Institute, Department of Medical Genetics, Columbia University.

Regan, K. (2006). *Opening our arms: Helping troubled kids do well.* Boulder, CO: Bull.

Robinson, L. D. (1978). *Sound minds in a soundless world.* Washington, DC: U.S. Government Printing Office.

Rogers, C. (1951). *Client-centered therapy.* Boston: Houghton Mifflin.

Rosenberg, M. (2003). *Nonviolent communication: A language of life.* Encinitas, CA: Puddle Dancer Press.

Rosenberg, M. B. (2005). *Speak peace in a world of conflict.* Encinitas, CA: Puddle Dancer Press.

Schein, E. H. (2004). *Organizational culture and leadership* (3rd ed.). San Francisco: Jossey-Bass.

Schlesinger, H. S. & Meadow, K. P. (1972). *Sound and sign: Childhood deafness and mental health.* Berkeley, CA: California University Press.

Schwartz, B. K., & Canfield, G. M. S. (1996). *Facing the shadow: A guided workbook for understanding and controlling sexual deviance.* Kingston, NJ: Civic Research Institute.

Segal, Z. V., Williams, J. M. G., & Teasdale, J. D. (2002). *Mindfulness-based cognitive therapy for depression.* New York: Guilford Press.

Shapiro, L. (1993). *55 Favorite stories and storytelling techniques that teach the importance of good behavior.* Norwalk, CT: Play2grow, LLC.

Shapiro, L., & Shore, H. (1993). *The book of psychotherapy games: A review of the most popular games used in psychotherapy.* Plainview, NY: Childsworld/Childsplay.

Shenal, B. V., Harrison, D. W., & Demaree, H. A. (2003). The neuropsychology of depression: A literature review and preliminary model. *Neuropsychology Review, 13*(1), 33–42.

Snyder, C. R., & Dinoff, B. L. (1999). Coping: Where have you been? In C. R. Snyder (Ed.), *Coping: The psychology of what works*. New York: Oxford University Press.

Stansfield, M. (1981). Psychological issues in mental health interpreting. *RID Journal, 1,* 18–31.

Staying sober: Relapse prevention guide. (1993). Minneapolis, MN: Minnesota Chemical Dependency Program for Deaf and Hard of Hearing People, Fairview Riverside Medical Center.

Steven, M. (1998). *Simon Birch*. [Film]. L. Mark & R. Birnbaum (Producer). Caravan Pictures.

Sue, S., & Morishima, J. (1982). *The mental health of Asian-Americans*. San Francisco: Jossey-Bass.

Sussman, A. (1989). Training in mental health services. In R. G. Brill (Ed.), *Proceedings of the national conference on deaf and hard of hearing people* (pp. 31–32). Silver Spring, MD: T.J. Publishers.

Swenson, C., Sanderson, C., Dulit, R., & Linehan, M. (2001). The application of dialectical behavior therapy for patients with borderline personality disorder on inpatient units. *Psychiatric Quarterly, 53*(4), 307–325.

Swenson, C. R., Witterholt, S., & Bohus, M. (2007). Dialectical behavior therapy on inpatient units. In L. A. Dimeff & K. Koerner (Eds.). *Dialectical behavior therapy in clinical practice*. New York: Guilford Press.

Tennen, H., & Affleck, G. (1999). Finding benefits in adversity. In C. R. Snyder (Ed.). *Coping: The psychology of what works*. New York: Oxford University Press.

Thacker, A. (1994). Formal communication disorder: Sign language in deaf people with schizophrenia. *British Journal of Psychiatry, 165,* 818–823.

Thacker, A. (1998). *The manifestation of schizophrenic formal communication disorder in sign language*. Unpublished doctoral dissertation, St. George Hospital Medical School, London.

Torrey, E. F. (2001). *Surviving schizophrenia*. New York: Quill.

Trikakis, D., Curci, N., & Strom, H. (2003). Sensory strategies for self-regulation: Nonlinguistic body-based treatment for deaf psychiatric patients. In N. Glickman & S. Gulati (Eds.). *Mental health care of deaf people: A culturally affirmative approach*. Mahwah, NJ: Lawrence Erlbaum Associates

Trybus, R. J. (1983). Hearing-impaired patients in public psychiatric hospitals throughout the United States. In D. Watson & B. Heller (Eds.). *Mental health and deafness: Strategic perspectives* (pp. 1–19). Silver Spring, MD: American Deafness and Rehabilitation Association.

Veltri, D., & Stansfield, M. (1986). Assessment from the perspective of the sign language interpreter. In H. Elliott & L. Glass & J. W. Evans (Eds.). *Mental health assessment of deaf clients: A practical manual*. Boston: Little, Brown.

Vernon, M., & Andrews, J. F. (1990). *The psychology of deafness*. New York: Longman.

Vernon, M., & Daigle-King, B. (1999). Historical overview of inpatient care of mental patients who are deaf. *American Annals of the Deaf, 144*(1), 51–60.

Vernon, M., & Miller, K. (2001). Linguistic incompetence to stand trial: A unique condition in some deaf defendants. *Journal of Interpretation,* 99–120.

Vernon, M., & Miller, K. (2005). Obstacles faced by deaf people in the criminal justice system. *American Annals of the Deaf, 150*(3).

Vernon, M., & Raifman, L. J. (1997). Recognizing and handling problems of incompetent deaf defendants charged with serious offenses. *International Journal of Law and Psychiatry, 20*(3), 373–387.

Vitiello, B., & Stoff, D. M. (1997). Subtypes of aggression and their relevance to child psychiatry. *Journal of the American Academy of Child and Adolescent Psychiatry, 36,* 307–318.

Wampold, B. E. (2001). The great psychotherapy debate: Models, methods, findings. Mahwah, NJ: Lawrence Erlbaum Associates.

Watson, J. C. (2002). Re-visioning empathy. In D. J. Cain & J. Seeman (Eds.). *Humanistic psychotherapies: Handbook of research and practice* (pp. 445–471). Washington, DC: American Psychological Association.

Weeks, D. (1992). *The eight essential steps to conflict resolution.* New York: Jeremy P. Tarcher/Putnam.

Whitaker, R. (2002). *Mad in America: Bad science, bad medicine, and the enduring mistreatment of the mentally ill.* Cambridge, MA: Perseus.

White, M. (1995). *Reauthoring lives: Interviews and essays.* Adelaide, South Australia: Dulwich Centre Publications.

White, M. (2007). *Maps of narrative practice.* New York: W. W. Norton.

White, M., & Epston, D. (1990). *Narrative means to therapeutic ends.* New York: W. W. Norton.

Witkiewitz, K., & Marlatt, G. A. (Eds.). (2007). *Therapist guide to evidence based relapse prevention.* Burlington, MA: Academic Press.

Wubbolding, R. (2000). *Reality therapy for the 21st century.* Bridgeport, NJ: Brunner-Routledge.

Zaentz, S. & Douglas, M. (Producers) & Forman, M. (Director) (1975). *One flew over the cuckoo's nest.* [Film]. Fantasy Films.

Zitter, S. (1996). Report from the front lines: Balancing multiple roles of a deafness therapist. In N. S. Glickman & M. Harvey (Eds.). *Culturally affirmative psychotherapy with deaf persons.* Mahwah, NJ: Lawrence Erlbaum Associates.

Index

An environmentally friendly book printed and bound in England by www.printondemand-worldwide.com

PEFC Certified

This product is
from sustainably
managed forests
and controlled
sources

www.pefc.org

PEFC/16-33-415

This book is made of chain-of-custody materials; FSC materials for the cover and PEFC materials for the text pages.

#0156 - 020216 - C0 - 234/156/26 - PB - 9780805863994